Collins
Spanish
Verbs & Practice

HarperCollins Publishers
Westerhill Road
Bishopbriggs
Glasgow
G64 2QT
Great Britain

First Edition 2012

Reprint 12 11 10 9 8 7 6 5 4 3 2 1 0

ISBN 978-0-00-745009-1

Collins® is a registered trademark of HarperCollins Publishers Limited

www.collinslanguage.com

A catalogue record for this book is available from the British Library

HarperCollins Publishers
10 East 53rd Street
New York, NY 10022

COLLINS BEGINNER'S SPANISH VERBS AND PRACTICE.
First US Edition 2012

ISBN 978-0-06-219173-1

www.harpercollins.com

HarperCollins books may be purchased for educational, business, or sales promotional use. For information, please write to:
Special Markets Department,
HarperCollins Publishers,
10 East 53rd Street,
New York, NY 10022

Typeset by Davidson Publishing Solutions, Glasgow

Printed in Italy by LEGO Spa, Lavis (Trento)

Acknowledgements
We would like to thank those authors and publishers who kindly gave permission for copyright material to be used in the Collins Word Web. We would also like to thank Times Newspapers Ltd for providing valuable data.

SERIES EDITOR
Rob Scriven

PROJECT MANAGEMENT
Patrick Gillard
Susanne Reichert

CONTRIBUTORS
Ana Cristina Llompart

FOR THE PUBLISHER
Gaëlle Amiot-Cadey
Lucy Cooper
Elaine Higgleton
Lisa Sutherland

Contents

Note on trademarks

Foreword for language teachers

The ***Easy Learning Spanish Verbs & Practice*** is designed to be used with both young and adult learners, as a group revision and practice book to complement your course book during classes, or as a recommended text for self-study and homework/coursework.

The text specifically targets learners from *ab initio* to intermediate or GCSE level, and therefore its structural content and vocabulary have been matched to the relevant specifications up to and including Higher GCSE.

The approach aims to develop knowledge and understanding of verbs and to improve the ability of learners to apply it by:

- minimizing the use of grammar terminology and providing clear explanations of terms both within the text and in the **Glossary**

- illustrating points with examples (and their translations) based on topics and contexts which are relevant to beginner and intermediate course content

The text helps you develop positive attitudes to grammar learning in your classes by:

- giving clear, easy-to-follow explanations

- prioritizing content according to relevant specifications for the levels

- highlighting useful **Tips** to deal with common difficulties

- summarizing **Key points** at the end of sections to consolidate learning

In addition to fostering success and building a thorough foundation in Spanish grammar and verbs, the optional **Grammar Extra** sections will encourage and challenge your learners to further their studies to higher and advanced levels.

Introduction for students

Whether you are starting to learn Spanish for the very first time or revising for your GCSE exams, the ***Easy Learning Spanish Verbs & Practice*** is here to help. This easy-to-use guide takes you through all the basics you will need to use Spanish verbs correctly and understand modern, everyday Spanish.

Newcomers can sometimes struggle with the technical terms they come across when they start to explore the grammar of a new language. The ***Easy Learning Spanish Verbs & Practice*** explains how to get to grips with all the verb tenses you will need to know, using simple language and cutting out jargon.

The text is divided into sections, each dealing with a particular area of verbs. Each section can be studied individually, as numerous cross-references in the text guide you to relevant points in other sections of the book for further information.

Every major section begins with an explanation of the area of grammar covered on the following pages. For quick reference, these definitions are also collected together on pages viii–xii in a glossary of essential grammar terms.

What is a verb?

A **verb** is a 'doing' word which describes what someone or something does, what someone or something is, or what happens to them, for example, *be, sing, live*.

Each point in the text is followed by simple examples of real Spanish, complete with English translations, helping you understand the rules. Underlining has been used in examples throughout the text to highlight the point being explained.

➤ When telling someone TO DO something, you join the reflexive pronoun onto the end of the verb.

¡Siénten<u>se</u>!	Sit down!
¡Cálla<u>te</u>!	Be quiet!

In Spanish, as with any foreign language, there are certain pitfalls which have to be avoided. **Tips** and **Information** notes throughout the text are useful reminders of the things that often trip learners up.

Tip

he/has/ha and so on must NEVER be separated from the past participle. Any object pronouns go before the form of **haber** being used, and NOT between the form of **haber** and the past participle.

No <u>lo</u> he visto.	I haven't seen it.
¿<u>Lo</u> has hecho ya?	Have you done it yet?

Key points sum up all the important facts about a particular area of grammar, to save you time when you are revising and help you focus on the main grammatical points.

> **KEY POINTS**
> ✔ Only use the present continuous in Spanish for actions that are happening right now.
> ✔ To form the present continuous tense in Spanish, take the present tense of **estar** and add the gerund of the main verb.

After each Key point you can find a number of exercises to help you practise all the important points. You can find the answers to each exercise on pages 163-176.

If you think you would like to continue with your Spanish studies to a higher level, check out the **Grammar Extra** sections. These are intended for advanced students who are interested in knowing a little more about the structures they will come across beyond GCSE.

Grammar Extra!
Some verbs mean ALMOST the same in the reflexive as when they are used on their own.

Duermo.	I sleep.
Me duermo.	I go to sleep.
¿Quieres ir al cine?	Do you want to go to the cinema?
Acaba de irse.	He has just left.

Finally, the supplement at the end of the book contains **Verb Tables**, where 120 important Spanish verbs (both regular and irregular) are conjugated in full. Examples show you how to use these verbs in your own work. If you are unsure how a verb is conjugated in Spanish, you can look up the **Verb Index** on pages 122-127 to find a cross-reference to a model verb.

We hope that you will enjoy using the ***Easy Learning Spanish Verbs & Practice*** and find it useful in the course of your studies.

Glossary of Grammar Terms

ACTIVE a form of the verb that is used when the subject of the verb is the person or thing doing the action, for example, I wrote a letter. Compare with **passive**.

AFFIRMATIVE an affirmative sentence or instruction is one that does not contain a negative word such as not. Compare with **negative**.

AGREE (to) in the case of verbs, to have the form which goes with the person or thing carrying out the action.

AUXILIARY VERB a verb such as be, have or do used with a main verb to form tenses.

BASE FORM the form of the verb without any endings added to it, for example, walk, have, be, go.

CLAUSE a group of words containing a verb.

CONDITIONAL a verb form used to talk about things that would happen or would be true under certain conditions, for example, I would help you if I could. It is also used to say what you would like or need, for example, Could you give me the bill?

CONJUGATE (to) to give a verb different endings according to whether you are referring to I, you, they and so on, and according to whether you are referring to the present, past or future, for example, I have, she had, they will have.

CONJUGATION a group of verbs which have the same endings as each other or change according to the same pattern.

CONTINUOUS TENSE a verb tense formed using to be and the -ing form of the main verb, for example, They're swimming (present continuous); He was eating (past continuous).

DIRECT OBJECT a noun or pronoun used with verbs to show who or what is acted on by the verb. For example, in He wrote a letter and He wrote me a letter, letter is the direct object. Compare **indirect object**.

DIRECT OBJECT PRONOUN a word such as me, him, us and them which is used instead of a noun to stand in for the person or thing most directly affected by the action expressed by the verb. Compare with **indirect object pronoun**.

ENDING a form added to something such as a verb, for example, go > goes.

FUTURE a verb tense used to talk about something that will happen or will be true.

GERUND a verb form in English ending in -ing, for example, eating, sleeping.

IMPERATIVE the form of a verb used when giving orders and instructions, for example, Shut the door!; Sit down!; Don't go!; Let's eat.

IMPERFECT one of the verb tenses used to talk about the past in Spanish, especially in descriptions, and to say what was happening or used to happen, for example, It was sunny at the weekend; We were living in Spain at the time; I used to walk to school. Compare with **preterite**.

IMPERSONAL VERB a verb whose subject is it, but where the it does not refer to any specific thing, for example, It's raining; It's 10 o'clock.

INDICATIVE ordinary verb forms that aren't subjunctive, such as the present, preterite or future. Compare with **subjunctive**.

INDIRECT OBJECT a noun or pronoun used with verbs to show who benefits or is harmed by an action. For example, in I gave the carrot to the rabbit, the rabbit is the indirect object and the carrot is the direct object. Compare with **direct object**.

INDIRECT OBJECT PRONOUN a pronoun used with verbs to show who benefits or is harmed by an action. For example, in I gave him the carrot and I gave it to him, him is the indirect object and the carrot and it are the direct objects. Compare with **direct object pronoun**.

INDIRECT SPEECH the words you use to report what someone has said when you aren't using their actual words, for example, He said that he was going out. Also called **reported speech**.

INFINITIVE a form of the verb that hasn't any endings added to it and doesn't relate to any particular tense. In English the infinitive is usually shown with to, as in to speak, to eat.

INTransitive verb a type of verb that does not take a direct object, for example, to sleep, to rise, to laugh. Compare with **transitive verb**.

IRREGULAR VERB a verb whose forms do not follow a general pattern. Compare with **regular verb**.

NEGATIVE a question or statement which contains a word such as not, never or nothing, and is used to say that something is not happening, is not true or is absent, for example, I never eat meat; Don't you love me? Compare with **positive**.

OBJECT a noun or pronoun which refers to a person or thing that is affected by the action described by the verb. Compare with **direct object**, **indirect object** and **subject**.

OBJECT PRONOUN one of the set of pronouns including me, him and them, which are used instead of the noun as the object of a verb or preposition. Compare with **subject pronoun**.

PASSIVE a form of the verb that is used when the subject of the verb is the person or thing that is affected by the action, for example, We were told or It was sold.

PAST PARTICIPLE a verb form which is used to form perfect and pluperfect tenses and passives, for example, watched, swum. Some past participles are also used as adjectives, for example, a broken watch.

PAST PERFECT see **pluperfect**.

PERFECT a verb form used to talk about what has or hasn't happened, for example, I've broken my glasses; We haven't eaten yet.

PERSON one of three classes: the first person (I, we), the second person (you singular and you plural), and the third person (he, she, it and they).

PERSONAL PRONOUN one of the group of words including I, you and they which are used to refer to you, the people you are talking to, or the people or things you are talking about.

PLUPERFECT one of the verb tenses used to describe something that had happened or had been true at a point in the past, for example, I'd forgotten to finish my homework. Also called **past perfect**.

PLURAL the form of a word which is used to refer to more than one person or thing. Compare with **singular**.

POSITIVE a positive sentence or instruction is one that does not contain a negative word such as not. Compare with **negative**.

PREPOSITION is a word such as at, for, with, into or from, which is usually followed by a noun, pronoun or, in English, a word ending in -ing. Prepositions show how people and things relate to the rest of the sentence, for example, She's at home; a tool for cutting grass; It's from David.

PRESENT a verb form used to talk about what is true at the moment, what happens regularly, and what is happening now, for example, I'm a student; I travel to college by train; I'm studying languages.

PRESENT CONTINUOUS see **continuous tense**.

PRESENT PARTICIPLE a verb form in English ending in -ing, for example, eating, sleeping.

PRESENT SIMPLE see **simple tense**.

PRETERITE a verb form used to talk about actions that were completed in the past in Spanish. It often corresponds to the ordinary past tense in English, for example, I bought a new bike; Mary went to the shops; I typed two reports yesterday.

PRONOUN a word which you use instead of a noun, when you do not need or want to name someone or something directly, for example, it, you, none.

PROPER NOUN the name of a person, place, organization or thing. Proper nouns are always written with a capital letter, for example, Kevin, Glasgow, Europe.

RADICAL-CHANGING VERBS in Spanish, verbs which change their stem or root in certain tenses and in certain persons.

REFLEXIVE PRONOUN a word ending in -self or -selves, such as myself or themselves, which refers back to the subject, for example, He hurt himself; Take care of yourself.

REFLEXIVE VERB a verb where the subject and object are the same, and where the action 'reflects back' on the subject. A reflexive verb is used with a reflexive pronoun such as myself, yourself, herself, for example, I washed myself; He shaved himself.

REGULAR VERB a verb whose forms follow a general pattern or the normal rules. Compare with **irregular verb**.

SIMPLE TENSE a verb tense in which the verb form is made up of one word, rather than being formed from to have and a past participle or to be and an -ing form; for example, She plays tennis; He wrote a book.

SINGULAR the form of a word which is used to refer to one person or thing. Compare with **plural**.

STEM the main part of a verb to which endings are added.

SUBJECT a noun or pronoun that refers to the person or thing doing the action or being in the state described by the verb, for example, My cat doesn't drink milk. Compare with **object**.

SUBJECT PRONOUN a word such as I, he, she and they which carries out the action described by the verb. Pronouns stand in for nouns when it is clear who is being talked about, for example, My brother isn't here at the moment. He'll be back in an hour. Compare with **object pronoun**.

SUBJUNCTIVE a verb form used in certain circumstances to indicate some sort of feeling, or to show doubt about whether something will happen or whether something is true. It is only used occasionally in modern English, for example, If I were you, I wouldn't bother; So be it.

TENSE the form of a verb which shows whether you are referring to the past, present or future.

TRANSITIVE VERB a type of verb that takes a direct object, for example, to spend, to raise, to waste. Compare with **intransitive verb**.

VERB a 'doing' word which describes what someone or something does, is, or what happens to them, for example, be, sing, live.

verb reference & exercises

Verbs

What is a verb?
A **verb** is a 'doing' word which describes what someone or something does, what someone or something is, or what happens to them, for example, *be*, *sing*, *live*.

Overview of verbs

➤ Verbs are frequently used with a noun, with somebody's name or, particularly in English, with a pronoun such as *I*, *you* or *she*. They can relate to the present, the past and the future; this is called their tense.

➤ Verbs are either:

- **regular**; their forms follow the normal rules
- **irregular**; their forms do not follow normal rules

➤ Almost all verbs have a form called the infinitive. This is a base form of the verb (for example, *walk*, *see*, *hear*) that hasn't had any endings added to it and doesn't relate to any particular tense. In English, the infinitive is usually shown with *to*, as in *to speak*, *to eat*, *to live*.

➤ In Spanish, the infinitive is always made up of just one word (never two as in *to speak* in English) and ends in **-ar, -er** or **-ir**: for example, **hablar** (meaning *to speak*), **comer** (meaning *to eat*) and **vivir** (meaning *to live*). All Spanish verbs belong to one of these three types, which are called conjugations. We will look at each of these three conjugations in turn on the next few pages.

➤ Regular English verbs have other forms apart from the infinitive: a form ending in *-s* (*walks*), a form ending in *-ing* (*walking*), and a form ending in *-ed* (*walked*).

➤ Spanish verbs have many more forms than this, which are made up of endings added to a stem. The stem of a verb can usually be worked out from the infinitive.

➤ Spanish verb endings change depending on who or what is doing the action and on when the action takes place. In fact, the ending is very often the only thing that shows you who is doing the action, as the Spanish equivalents of *I*, *you*, *he* and so on (**yo, tú, él** and so on) are not used very much. So, both **hablo** on its own and **yo hablo** mean *I speak*. Sometimes there is a name or a noun in the sentence to make it clear who is doing the action.

José habla español.	José speaks Spanish.
El profesor habla español.	The teacher speaks Spanish.

➤ Spanish verb forms also change depending on whether you are talking about the present, past or future, so **(yo) hablaré** means *I will speak* while **(yo) hablé** means *I spoke*.

➤ Some verbs in Spanish do not follow the usual patterns. These irregular verbs include some very common and important verbs like **ir** (meaning *to go*), **ser** and **estar** (meaning *to be*) and **hacer** (meaning *to do* or *to make*). Other verbs are only slightly irregular, changing their stems in certain tenses.

➪ *For **Verb Tables**, see supplement.*

KEY POINTS

- ✔ Spanish verbs have different forms depending on who or what is doing the action and on the tense.
- ✔ Spanish verb forms are made up of a stem and an ending. The stem is usually based on the infinitive of the verb. The ending depends on who or what is doing the action and on when the action takes place.
- ✔ Regular verbs follow the standard patterns for **-ar**, **-er** and **-ir** verbs. Irregular verbs do not.

Test yourself

1 **Write the stem of these verbs by taking away the ending *-ar*, *-er* or *-ir*.**

a entrar ....

b decidir ....

c escribir ....

d comer ....

e escuchar ....

f obrar ....

g celebrar ....

h beber ....

i ayudar ....

j romper ....

2 **Write the infinitive of the following irregular verbs. Use a dictionary and the verb tables in this book to help you.**

a salían

b fueran ....

c habían ....

d conduzco ....

e puesto ....

f caí ....

g soy ....

h van ....

i viniendo ....

j dé ....

Test yourself

3 Say whether the following verbs belong to the *-ar*, *-er* or *-ir* type. Use a dictionary and the verb tables in this book to help you.

a **pescaban**......................................

b **comían**.......................................

c **gustan**..

d **recibimos**....................................

e **limpiábamos**..............................

f **repasaron**....................................

g **dividimos**....................................

h **resolvemos**.................................

i **consultamos**...............................

j **gruñía**...

4 Translate the following into Spanish.

a What's your name? ....

b I work in a school. ....

c He lives in Barcelona. ....

d Her name is Clara. ....

e Do you speak English? ....

f My house is not far. ....

g Ana is fifteen. ....

h It's sunny. ....

i I live with some friends. ....

j He is really tall. ....

5 Match the two parts of the sentence, making sure the subject matches the form of the verb in the present.

a **Ana**	no entiendo nada.
b **Sus padres**	tiene un perro.
c **Yo**	vamos en autobús.
d **Nosotros**	termináis en diez minutos.
e **Vosotros**	llegan por la tarde.

The present tenses

> **What are the present tenses?**
> The **present tenses** are the verb forms that are used to talk about what is true at the moment, what happens regularly and what is happening now; for example, *I'm a student; I travel to college by train; I'm studying languages.*

➤ In English, there are two tenses you can use to talk about the present:

- the present simple tense
  I live here. — They get up early.

- the present continuous tense
  He is eating an apple. — You aren't working very hard.

➤ In Spanish, there is also a present simple and a present continuous tense. As in English, the present simple in Spanish is used to talk about:

- things that are generally true
  En invierno hace frío. — It's cold in winter.

- things that are true at the moment
  Carlos no come carne. — Carlos doesn't eat meat.

- things that happen at intervals
  A menudo vamos al cine. — We often go to the cinema.

➤ The present continuous tense in Spanish is used to talk about things that are happening right now or at the time of writing:
  Marta está viendo la televisión. — Marta is watching television.

➤ However, there are times where the use of the present tenses in the two languages is not exactly the same.

⇨ *For more information on the use of the* ***Present tenses****, see pages 2 and 34.*

The present simple tense

Forming the present simple tense of regular -ar verbs

➤ If the infinitive of the Spanish verb ends in **-ar**, it means that the verb belongs to the first conjugation, for example, **hablar**, **lavar**, **llamar**.

➤ To know which form of the verb to use in Spanish, you need to work out what the stem of the verb is and then add the correct ending. The stem of regular **-ar** verbs in the present simple tense is formed by taking the infinitive and chopping off **-ar**.

Infinitive	**Stem** (without **-ar**)
hablar (*to speak*)	**habl-**
lavar (*to wash*)	**lav-**

➤ Now you know how to find the stem of a verb you can add the correct ending. The one you choose will depend on who or what is doing the action.

ℹ Note that as the ending generally makes it clear who is doing the action, you usually don't need to add a subject pronoun such as **yo** (meaning *I*), **tú** (meaning *you*) as well.

➤ Here are the present simple endings for regular **-ar** verbs:

Present simple endings	Present simple of hablar	Meaning: *to speak*
-o	(yo) habl<u>o</u>	I speak
-as	(tú) habl<u>as</u>	you speak
-a	(él/ella) habl<u>a</u> (usted) habl<u>a</u>	he/she/it speaks you speak
-amos	(nosotros/nosotras) habl<u>amos</u>	we speak
-áis	(vosotros/vosotras) habl<u>áis</u>	you speak
-an	(ellos/ellas) habl<u>an</u> (ustedes) habl<u>an</u>	they speak you speak

➤ You use the **él/ella** (*third person singular*) form of the verb with nouns and with people's names when you are just talking about one person, animal or thing.

Lydia habl<u>a</u> inglés. Lydia speaks English.
Mi profesor me ayud<u>a</u> mucho. My teacher helps me a lot.

➤ You use the **ellos/ellas** (*third person plural*) form of the verb with nouns and with people's names when you are talking about more than one person, animal or thing.

Lydia y Carlos habl<u>an</u> inglés. Lydia and Carlos speak English.
Mis profesores me ayud<u>an</u> mucho. My teachers help me a lot.

ℹ Note that even though you use the **él/ella** and **ellos/ellas** <u>forms</u> of the verb to talk about things in Spanish, you should <u>never</u> include the pronouns **él**, **ella**, **ellos** or **ellas** themselves in the sentence when referring to things.

Funciona bien. It works well. **Funcionan bien.** They work well.

Key points

✔ Verbs ending in **-ar** belong to the first conjugation. Regular **-ar** verbs form their present tense stem by losing the **-ar**.
✔ The present tense endings for regular **-ar** verbs are: **-o, -as, -a, -amos, -áis, -an.**
✔ You usually don't need to give a pronoun in Spanish as the ending of the verb makes it clear who or what is doing the action.

Test yourself

6 Match the two columns.

a Los alumnos trabaja por las noches.
b Mi amiga dura dos horas.
c La película estudias?
d Salimos repasan la lección.
e ¿Cuándo los dos a la vez.

7 Complete the following sentences with the correct form of the present tense. Remember that, in Spanish, the subject of a verb is included in the verb form, so it is not necessary to state it. Where it is not obvious, the subject of the verb is shown in square brackets.

a …… todos los inviernos. **(nevar)**
b Ana …… sobre todo paisajes. **(pintar)**
c ¿Cómo …… este problema? **(solucionar [tú])**
d …… mucho con sus hijos. **(hablar [él])**
e …… en Londres. **(estudiar [ellos])**
f Los miembros del grupo …… sus intrumentos. **(dominar)**
g Yo …… de este lado. **(estirar)**
h Vosotros dos …… la fruta y yo las patatas. **(pelar)**
i …… demasiado. **(gastar [él])**
j Iván y Paxi …… un viaje. **(planear)**

8 Translate the following sentences into Spanish.

a Do you study French? ……
b She speaks with Laura every week. ……
c The film starts at nine. ……
d She always travels by car. ……
e I clean the house on Fridays. ……
f She hates pop music. ……
g I sing in a choir. ……
h They arrive in the morning. ……

i What's your name? ....

j Do you all have breakfast in the kitchen?

....

9 **Create a sentence using the elements given. Remember that, in Spanish, the subject of a verb is included in the verb form, so it is not necessary to state it. Where it is not obvious, the subject of the verb is shown in square brackets. Remember also that when the object of the verb is a pronoun, it usually comes before the verb.**

a exagerar/mucho /[tú] ....

b Alicia/esperar/a ella/en la parada del autobús

....

c los dos/pintar/muebles ....

d muchos jóvenes/emigrar/pronto/al extranjero

....

e ¿dónde/filmar/película/[ellos]? ....

f ¿por dónde/entrar/a la casa[vosotros]? ....

g sólo/cocinar/fines de semana/[nosotros]

....

h los domingos/mirar/la televisión/[nosotros] ....

i por la noche/siempre/arropar/a ellos/[yo] ....

j Aitana/siempre/repasar/lección/antes del examen

....

10 **Cross out the nouns that do not go with the verb.**

a escaparon	los prisioneros/los rehenes/el secuestrador/los leones
b descansan	el perro/mis padres/yo/Luis
c calienta	el sol/las estufas/el fuego
d llora	el bebé/tú/mi amiga/María y tú
e exploráis	los turistas/vosotros dos/tú y Marta/el guía
f patinan	los alumnos/mis abuelos/el deportista
g limpiamos	la señora de la limpieza/mi padre/nosotros/Yolanda y yo
h adelantan	los camiones/el coche/Andrés/los periodistas

i **consulto** un amigo/las dudas/yo/muchas personas

j **ordena** el librero/la normativa/los jefes/los conferenciantes

11 Complete the following sentences with the correct form of the present tense. Remember that, in Spanish, the subject of a verb is included in the verb form, so it is not necessary to state it. Where it is not obvious, the subject of the verb is shown in square brackets.

a Mi madre .... verduras en el huerto. **(cultivar)**

b Los organismos .... en el tiempo. **(evolucionar)**

c ¿No .... la respuesta? **(adivinar [tú])**

d .... mucho a tu padre. **(admirar [yo])**

e Todos los veranos .... en el mar. **(bucear [ellos])**

f A veces .... demasiado las cosas. **(complicar [vosotros])**

g Nosotros .... la dirección. **(copiar)**

h .... con la calculadora. **(sumar [ellos])**

i No .... mucho dinero. **(ganar [ellos])**

j La ley .... pagar una multa. **(ordenar)**

12 Complete the following set of instructions in the present using the correct *nosotros* form of the following verbs: *pegar, cortar, rellenar, dibujar, doblar*.

a Primero .... la cartulina por la mitad.

b Luego .... una figura en la cartulina con el lápiz.

c Después .... papeles de colores con las tijeras.

d .... totalmente la figura con los papeles.

e Finalmente .... los papeles en el dibujo.

13 Complete the following sentences in the present tense, using the correct form of the following verbs: *dibujar, lavar, gastar, fumar, nadar, cavar, cortar, escapar, mirar, cultivar*.

a .... los platos [vosotros]

b .... con las tijeras [ellos]

c .... con una pala [yo]

d .... un cigarrillo [nosotros]

e .... verduras [ellos]

Test yourself

f .... de la cárcel [ella]

g .... la tele [vosotros]

h .... dinero en las tiendas [tú]

i .... en el mar [yo]

j .... con el lápiz [usted]

14 Complete the following sentences using the third person singular of the present tense. Remember that the pronouns *él/ella* should not be included when they refer to things.

a .... el papel automáticamente. **(cortar)**

b .... demasiado. **(brillar)**

c .... un poco. **(quemar)**

d .... a 90°. **(lavar)**

e Es falso, pero .... mucho el salón. **(adornar)**

f .... perfectamente. **(funcionar)**

g .... con electricidad y tiene también horno. **(cocinar)**

h .... toda la calle. **(iluminar)**

i .... mucha energía. **(ahorrar)**

j No .... bien el sonido. **(grabar)**

Forming the present simple tense of regular -er verbs

➤ If the infinitive of the Spanish verb ends in **-er**, it means that the verb belongs to the second conjugation, for example, **comer**, **depender**.

➤ The stem of regular **-er** verbs in the present simple tense is formed by taking the infinitive and chopping off **-er**.

Infinitive	**Stem** (without **-er**)
comer (*to eat*)	**com-**
depender (*to depend*)	**depend-**

➤ Now add the correct ending, depending on who or what is doing the action.

ℹ Note that as the ending generally makes it clear who is doing the action, you usually don't need to add a subject pronoun such as **yo** (meaning *I*) or **tú** (meaning *you*) as well.

➤ Here are the present simple endings for regular **-er** verbs:

Present simple endings	**Present simple of comer**	**Meaning:** ***to eat***
-o	**(yo) como**	I eat
-es	**(tú) comes**	you eat
-e	**(él/ella) come** **(usted) come**	he/she/it eats you eat
-emos	**(nosotros/nosotras) comemos**	we eat
-éis	**(vosotros/vosotras) coméis**	you eat
-en	**(ellos/ellas) comen** **(ustedes) comen**	they eat you eat

➤ You use the **él/ella** (*third person singular*) form of the verb with nouns and with people's names when you are just talking about one person, animal or thing.

Juan come demasiado. — Juan eats too much.
Mi padre me debe 15 euros. — My father owes me 15 euros.

➤ You use the **ellos/ellas** (*third person plural*) form of the verb with nouns and with people's names when you are talking about more than one person, animal or thing.

Juan y Pedro comen demasiado. — Juan and Pedro eat too much.
Mis padres me deben 15 euros. — My parents owe me 15 euros.

ℹ Note that even though you use the **él/ella** and **ellos/ellas** forms of the verb to talk about things in Spanish, you should never include the pronouns **él**, **ella**, **ellos** or **ellas** themselves in the sentence when referring to things.

Depende. — It depends.

Key points

- ✔ Verbs ending in **-er** belong to the second conjugation. Regular **-er** verbs form their present tense stem by losing the **-er**.
- ✔ The present tense endings for regular **-er** verbs are: **-o, -es, -e, -emos, -éis, -en.**
- ✔ You usually don't need to give a pronoun in Spanish as the ending of the verb makes it clear who or what is doing the action.

Test yourself

15 Match the two columns.

a Estas flores	recorre toda la costa.
b El autobús	tose un poco.
c El niño	los dos juntos.
d Comemos	veo más tarde.
e Te	crecen en el campo.

16 Complete the following sentences with the correct form of the present tense. Remember that, in Spanish, the subject of a verb is included in the verb form, so it is not necessary to state it. Where it is not obvious, the subject of the verb is shown in square brackets to show you which verb form to use.

a No .... el problema. **(comprender [yo])**

b .... demasiados dulces. **(comer [ellos])**

c Los jefes .... mucho dinero. **(deber)**

d ¿Qué .... hoy? **(beber [tú])**

e José sólo .... libros de ciencia ficción. **(leer)**

f Se .... con facilidad. **(ofender [él])**

g .... la mejor tecnología. **(vender [nosotros])**

h No .... de tí. **(depender)**

i ¿........................ lo que digo? **(entender [vosotros])**

j ¿Cómo .... al programa? **(acceder [tú])**

17 Create a sentence in the present tense using the elements given. Remember that, in Spanish, the subject of a verb is included in the verb form so it is not necessary to state it. Where it is not obvious, the subject of the verb is shown in square brackets to show you which verb form to use.

a ¿dónde/meter/cajas/[nosotros]? ....

b no/comprender/ejercicios/[yo] ....

c alumnos/leer/cada día/en clase

....

d la raíces/absorber/el agua ....

e ¿a cuánto/vender/los tomates/[vosotros] ....

f Lucía/ver/películas/en el ordenador

....

Test yourself

g así/no/ofender/a nadie [yo] ....

h no/entender/a Susana [él] ....

i primero/responder/a tus preguntas [nosotros]

....

j mi madre/meterse/en la cama/a las diez ....

18 **Complete the following text using the correct form of the present tense of the following verbs: *deber, aprender, comer, responder, coger, beber, hacer*.**

a Alicia .... inglés en una academia.

b .... el autobús cerca de su casa.

c La clase dura dos horas. Alicia .... un bocadillo y .... un refresco en el descanso.

d Alicia .... estudiar mucho por las tardes.

e .... los ejercicios y .... a las preguntas del libro.

19 **Complete the following sentences using the present tense. Use the following verbs: *entender, meter, beber, recorrer, coser, tejer, deber, saber, aprender, comer*.**

a .... ciruelas [tú]

b .... agua [nosotros]

c .... con aguja e hilo [ellos]

d .... ropa en una tienda [ella]

e .... música en el colegio [usted]

f .... dinero en el banco [tú]

g .... un jersey [vosotros]

h .... la zona [ellos]

i .... de ordenadores [nosotros]

j .... dinero [nosotros]

20 **Complete the following sentences with the correct form of the present tense. Remember that, in Spanish, the subject of a verb is included in the verb form, so it is not necessary to state it. Where it is not obvious, the subject of the verb is shown in square brackets to show you which form to use.**

a .... más que ayer. **(toser [tú])**

b Te .... no llegar tarde. **(prometer [yo])**

c No .... carne. **(comer [él])**

d A lo mejor .... el coche. **(vender [nosotros])**

e Si .... este botón queda bien. **(coser [tú])**

f .... tu nerviosismo. **(comprender [yo])**

g ¿........................ su respuesta? **(temer [vosotros])**

h Siempre nos .... **sorprender [ellos]**

i ¿Por dónde .... la llave? **(meter [vosotros])**

j ¿Y si .... el examen? **(suspender [nosotros])**

21 Translate the following sentences into English. Use a dictionary and the verb tables in this book.

a Do they sell batteries for mobile phones here?

....

b I sweep the kitchen every day. ....

c I don't drink alcohol. ....

d Pablo learns Chinese at school. ....

e I don't put the jam in the fridge. ....

f She reads books in the library. ....

g Do you all owe him money? ....

h I see Ana at college. ....

i Do you know him? ....

j They watch very little TV. ....

22 Match the two columns.

a Crecimos	que no es cierto.
b Creo	los dos en el mismo pueblo.
c ¿Vosotros	temen a su padre.
d Los niños	venden ropa?
e ¿En el supermercado	bebéis leche en el desayuno?

Test yourself

23 Complete the following sentences using the third person singular of the present tense. Remember that the pronouns *él/ella/ellos/ellas* should not be included when they refer to things. Refer to the verb tables in this book.

a Sonia y Nuria .... a tocar el clarinete después del colegio. **(aprender)**

b .... ser cierto. **(deber)**

c .... bien. **(arder)**

d Te lo .... **(prometer)**

e .... la humedad. **(absorber)**

f .... grandes distancias con poca gasolina. **(recorrer)**

g .... un jersey en pocas horas. **(tejer)**

h ¿Cómo .... al archivo? **(acceder)**

i .... baterías de móvil. **(vender)**

j Casi todos .... el examen. **(suspender)**

24 Create a sentence in the present tense using the elements given. Remember that, in Spanish, the subject of a verb is included in the verb form so it is not necessary to state it. Where it is not obvious, the subject of the verb is shown in square brackets to show you which verb form to use. Remember also that when the object of the verb is a pronoun it comes before the verb.

a ¿cómo/conocer/a ellas/[tú]? ....

b Luis/ver/a ella/todas las semanas.

....

c no/comprender/ello/[yo] ....

d prometer/lo/a vosotros/[nosotros] ....

e mi madre/meter/ellos/antes/en agua

....

f ver/ello/en la pantalla [tú] ....

g siempre/sorprender/a ella [nosotros] ....

h ¿a cuánto/vender/ello/[nosotros]? ....

i entender/a ella [yo] ....

j ¿por qué/no/comer/ello [vosotros]? ....

Forming the present simple tense of regular -ir verbs

➤ If the infinitive of the Spanish verb ends in **-ir**, it means that the verb belongs to the third conjugation, for example, **vivir**, **recibir**.

➤ The stem of regular **-ir** verbs in the present simple tense is formed by taking the infinitive and chopping off **-ir**.

Infinitive	**Stem** (without **-ir**)
vivir (*to live*)	**viv-**
recibir (*to receive, to get*)	**recib-**

➤ Now add the correct ending depending on who or what is doing the action.

ℹ Note that as the ending generally makes it clear who is doing the action, you usually don't need to add a subject pronoun such as **yo** (meaning *I*) or **tú** (meaning *you*) as well.

➤ Here are the present simple endings for regular **-ir** verbs:

Present simple endings	**Present simple of vivir**	**Meaning:** ***to live***
-o	**(yo) vivo**	I live
-es	**(tú) vives**	you live
-e	**(él/ella) vive** **(usted) vive**	he/she/it lives you live
-imos	**(nosotros/nosotras) vivimos**	we live
-ís	**(vosotros/vosotras) vivís**	you live
-en	**(ellos/ellas) viven** **(ustedes) viven**	they live you live

➤ You use the **él/ella** (*third person singular*) form of the verb with nouns and with people's names when you are just talking about one person, animal or thing.

Javier vive aquí. — Javier lives here.
Mi padre recibe muchas cartas. — My father gets a lot of letters.

➤ You use the **ellos/ellas** (*third person plural*) form of the verb with nouns and with people's names, when you are talking about more than one person, animal or thing.

Javier y Antonia viven aquí. — Javier and Antonia live here.
Mis padres reciben muchas cartas. — My parents get a lot of letters.

ℹ Note that even though you use the **él/ella** and **ellos/ellas** forms of the verb to talk about things in Spanish, you should never include the pronouns **él**, **ella**, **ellos** or **ellas** themselves in the sentence when referring to things.

Ocurrió ayer. — It happened yesterday.

Key points

- ✔ Verbs ending in **-ir** belong to the third conjugation. Regular **-ir** verbs form their present tense stem by losing the **-ir**.
- ✔ The present tense endings for regular **-ir** verbs are: - **o, -es, -e, -imos, -ís, -en.**
- ✔ You usually don't need to give a pronoun in Spanish as the ending of the verb makes it clear who or what is doing the action.

Test yourself

25 Complete the following sentences with the correct form of the present tense. Remember that, in Spanish, the subject of a verb is included in the verb form, so it is not necessary to state it. Where it is not obvious, the subject of the verb is shown in square brackets to show you which verb form to use

a Miriam y yo .... un piso. **(compartir)**

b Su novia .... en Sevilla. **(vivir)**

c Me .... todas las semanas. **(escribir [ellos])**

d ¿Por dónde .... a la casa? **(subir [vosotros])**

e Las reglas no lo .... **(permitir)**

f Siempre .... cuando hablo. **(interrumpir [tú])**

g ¿Cómo .... el archivo? **(abrir [nosotros])**

h Ahora .... el pan **(partir [yo])**

i Apenas .... mensajes. **(recibir [nosotros])**

j ¿En qué papel .... el documento? **(imprimir [yo])**

26 Translate the following sentences into Spanish. Use a dictionary and the verb tables in this books to help you.

a I always insist on it. ....

b They live together. ....

c I receive pictures on my mobile. ....

d They divide the tasks among the three of them.

....

e How do you write your name? ....

f Do they live near? ....

g They don't permit it. ....

h I cover it with a cloth. ....

i Why do you insist? ....

j These plants survive very extreme conditions.

....

Test yourself

27 Create a sentence in the present tense using the elements given. Remember that, in Spanish, the subject of a verb is included in the verb form so it is not necessary to state it. Where it is not obvious, the subject of the verb is shown in square brackets to show you which verb form to use. Remember also that object pronouns usually go before the verb.

a Alicia/no/subir/nunca/en ascensor

....

b mis padres/no permitir fumar/a mí/en casa

....

c ¿subir/ellos/por la escalera [tú]?. ....

d todas las mañanas/vestir/a ellos/[yo]

....

e los profesores/no permitir/móviles/en clase/a nosotros

....

f siempre/recibir/muchos regalos/[ellos] ....

g nunca/interrumpir/a la profesora/[nosotros]

....

h cuándo/recibir/la paga/[vosotros] ....

i ¿por qué/interrumpir/a mí[tú]? ....

28 Complete the following sentences using the correct form of the present tense of the *'yo'* form. Use the following verbs: *escribir, vivir, imprimir, recibir, compartir.*

a Yo .... en Manchester.

b .... piso con unas amigas

c Trabajo en una oficina. Hago y .... muchos mensajes del extranjero.

d .... los mensajes en el ordenador y los .... en la impresora.

e Todos los meses .... mi sueldo en el banco.

29 Complete the following sentences using the correct form of the present tense. Use the verbs: *subir, unir, recibir, partir, sobrevivir, escribir, aplaudir, abrir, imprimir, interrumpir.*

a .... las escaleras [nosotros]

b .... una puerta/una caja/una maleta [ellos]

c .... con un lápiz [vosotros]

d .... una guerra/una sequía [nosotros]

e .... un documento en la impresora [ella]

f .... el pan con un cuchillo [yo]

g .... una obra en el teatro [tú]

h .... una llamada/un mensaje [vosotros]

i .... dos partes [nosotros]

j .... una conversación [tú]

30 Complete the following sentences using the third person singular of the present tense. Remember that the pronouns *él/ella/ellos/ellas* should not be included when they refer to things.

a Los profesores no lo .... **(permitir)**

b .... a color y a blanco y negro. **(imprimir)**

c Juan......................... una llamada importante. **(recibir)**

d .... las piezas automáticamente. **(partir)**

e Todos............................. con ganas al grupo. **(aplaudir)**

f ¿Por qué no lo .... a la cuenta? **(añadir)**

g Las hojas .... con el viento. **(crujir)**

h .... la puerta cuando aprietas este botón. **(abrir)**

i Mis padres .... a veces. **(discutir)**

j Mis hermanas .... una habitación. **(compartir)**

31 Complete the following sentences with the correct form of the present tense. Remember that, in Spanish, the subject of a verb is included in the verb form, so it is not necessary to state it. Where it is not obvious, the subject of the verb is shown in square brackets to show you which verb form to use.

a Estas plantas .... bajo el agua. **(vivir)**

b .... todos los veranos. **(ocurrir)**

c En el trabajo .... muchas llamadas. **(recibir [él])**

d ¿............................. aquí tu dirección, por favor? **(escribir [tú])**

e .... a verme los domingos. **(subir [ellos])**

f ¿Cómo .... la masa? **(divides [tú])**

g Nosotros dos .... muchas cosas. **(compartir)**

h Mi perro .... a los desconocidos. **(gruñir)**

Test yourself

32 Cross out the nouns that verb cannot refer to.

a impedimos	la profesora/Carla y yo/la policía
b ocurren	una historia/un accidente/los sucesos
c suben	los vendedores/el portero/Ana y José
d une	el trabajador/tú/mi hermana
e gruñen	los perros/el león/los niños
f compartimos	mis padres y yo/mis amigos/los de nuestro grupo
g viven	mi primo/mi novia/Isabel y Pedro
h partes	Ana/tú/el médico
i imprimen	los profesores/Pedro y Tomás/mi profesor
j unís	tú y tus padres/Pedro y tú/el obrero

33 Match the two columns.

a Ocurre	aplaudo mucho.
b Los problemas	vivimos en el campo.
c Si me gusta el espectáculo,	no recibe mensajes.
d Mi novia y yo	en las mejores familias.
e Mi móvil	unen a los amigos.

34 Translate the following sentences into Spanish. Use a dictionary and the verb tables in this book.

a She does not live with her parents. ....

b I never open your mail. ....

c Where do your parents live? ....

d You join the two parts with this. ....

e The sports teacher always divides the class into three groups.

....

f This animal survives with little water.

....

g They often come up to see me. ....

h I don't receive calls here. ....

i I climb three floors every day. ....

j He never argues with her. ....

Forming the present simple tense of less regular verbs

➤ Many Spanish verbs do not follow the regular patterns shown previously. There are lots of verbs that change their stem in the present tense when the stress is on the stem. This means that all forms are affected in the present simple APART FROM the **nosotros** and **vosotros** forms. Such verbs are often called radical-changing verbs, meaning root-changing verbs.

➤ For example, some verbs containing an **-o** in the stem change it to **-ue** in the present simple for all forms APART FROM the **nosotros/nosotras** and **vosotros/vosotras** forms.

	encontrar *to find*	**recordar** *to remember*	**poder** *to be able*	**dormir** *to sleep*
(yo)	**encuentro**	**recuerdo**	**puedo**	**duermo**
(tú)	**encuentras**	**recuerdas**	**puedes**	**duermes**
(él/ella/ usted)	**encuentra**	**recuerda**	**puede**	**duerme**
(nosotros/as)	**encontramos**	**recordamos**	**podemos**	**dormimos**
(vosotros/as)	**encontráis**	**recordáis**	**podéis**	**dormís**
(ellos/ellas/ ustedes)	**encuentran**	**recuerdan**	**pueden**	**duermen**

➤ Other verbs containing an **-e** in the stem change it to **-ie** for all forms APART FROM the **nosotros/nosotras** and **vosotros/vosotras** forms.

	cerrar *to close*	**pensar** *to think*	**entender** *to understand*	**perder** *to lose*	**preferir** *to prefer*
(yo)	**cierro**	**pienso**	**entiendo**	**pierdo**	**prefiero**
(tú)	**cierras**	**piensas**	**entiendes**	**pierdes**	**prefieres**
(él/ella/ usted)	**cierra**	**piensa**	**entiende**	**pierde**	**prefiere**
(nosotros/as)	**cerramos**	**pensamos**	**entendemos**	**perdemos**	**preferimos**
(vosotros/as)	**cerráis**	**pensáis**	**entendéis**	**perdéis**	**preferís**
(ellos/ellas/ ustedes)	**cierran**	**piensan**	**entienden**	**pierden**	**prefieren**

➤ A few **-ir** verbs containing **-e** in the stem change this to **-i** in the present simple for all forms APART FROM the **nosotros/nosotras** and **vosotros/ vosotras** forms.

	pedir *to ask (for)*	**servir** *to serve*
(yo)	**pido**	**sirvo**
(tú)	**pides**	**sirves**
(él/ella/usted)	**pide**	**sirve**
(nosotros/as)	**pedimos**	**servimos**
(vosotros/as)	**pedís**	**servís**
(ellos/ellas/ustedes)	**piden**	**sirven**

➤ If you are not sure whether a Spanish verb belongs to this group of radical-changing verbs, you can look up the **Verb Tables** in the supplement.

Forming the present simple tense of common irregular verbs

➤ There are many other verbs that do not follow the usual patterns in Spanish. These include some very common and important verbs such as **tener** (meaning *to have*), **hacer** (meaning *to do* or *to make*) and **ir** (meaning *to go*). These verbs are shown in full below.

➤ Here are the present simple tense endings for **tener**:

	tener	Meaning: *to have*
(yo)	**tengo**	I have
(tú)	**tienes**	you have
(él/ella/usted)	**tiene**	he/she/it has, you have
(nosotros/nosotras)	**tenemos**	we have
(vosotros/vosotras)	**tenéis**	you have
(ellos/ellas/ustedes)	**tienen**	they have, you have

Tengo dos hermanas. I have two sisters.
No tengo dinero. I haven't any money.
¿Cuántos sellos tienes? How many stamps have you got?
Tiene el pelo rubio. He has blond hair.

➤ Here are the present simple tense endings for **hacer**:

	hacer	Meaning: *to do, to make*
(yo)	**hago**	I do, I make
(tú)	**haces**	you do, you make
(él/ella/usted)	**hace**	he/she/it does, he/she/it
		makes, you do, you make
(nosotros/nosotras)	**hacemos**	we do, we make
(vosotros/vosotras)	**hacéis**	you do, you make
(ellos/ellas/ustedes)	**hacen**	they do, they make, you do, you make

Hago una tortilla. I'm making an omelette.
No hago mucho deporte. I don't do a lot of sport.
¿Qué haces? What are you doing?
Hace calor. It's hot.

➤ Here are the present simple tense endings for **ir**:

	ir	**Meaning:** ***to go***
(yo)	**voy**	I go
(tú)	**vas**	you go
(él/ella/usted)	**va**	he/she/it goes, you go
(nosotros/nosotras)	**vamos**	we go
(vosotros/vosotras)	**vais**	you go
(ellos/ellas/ustedes)	**van**	they go, you go

Voy a Salamanca. — I'm going to Salamanca.
¿Adónde vas? — Where are you going?
No va al colegio. — He doesn't go to school.
No van a vender la casa. — They aren't going to sell the house.

➪ *For other irregular verbs in the present simple tense, see* ***Verb Tables*** *in the supplement.*

How to use the present simple tense in Spanish

➤ The present simple tense is often used in Spanish in the same way as it is in English, although there are some differences.

➤ As in English, you use the Spanish present simple to talk about:

- things that are generally true
  En verano hace calor. — It's hot in summer.
- things that are true now
  Viven en Francia. — They live in France.
- things that happen all the time or at certain intervals or that you do as a habit
  Marta lleva gafas. — Marta wears glasses.
  Mi tío vende mariscos. — My uncle sells shellfish.
- things that you are planning to do
  El domingo jugamos en León. — We're playing in León on Sunday.
  Mañana voy a Madrid. — I am going to Madrid tomorrow.

➤ There are some instances when you would use the present simple in Spanish, but you wouldn't use it in English:

- to talk about current projects and activities that may not actually be going on right at this very minute
  Construye una casa. — He's building a house.
- when you use certain time expressions in Spanish, especially **desde** (meaning *since*) and **desde hace** (meaning *for*), to talk about activities and states that started in the past and are still going on now
  Jaime vive aquí desde hace dos años. — Jaime has been living here for two years.
  Daniel vive aquí desde 1999. — Daniel has lived here since 1999.
  Llevo horas esperando aquí. — I've been waiting here for hours.

ser and estar

➤ In Spanish there are two irregular verbs, **ser** and **estar**, that both mean *to be*, although they are used very differently. In the present simple tense, they follow the patterns shown below.

Pronoun	ser	estar	Meaning: *to be*
(yo)	soy	estoy	I am
(tú)	eres	estás	you are
(él/ella/usted)	es	está	he/she/it is, you are
(nosotros/nosotras)	somos	estamos	we are
(vosotros/ vosotras)	sois	estáis	you are
(elllos/ellas/ustedes)	son	están	they/you are

➤ **ser** is used:

- with an adjective when talking about a characteristic or fairly permanent quality, for example, shape, size, height, colour, material, nationality.

  Mi hermano es alto. My brother is tall.
  María es inteligente. María is intelligent.
  Es rubia. She's blonde.
  Es muy guapa. She's very pretty.
  Es rojo. It's red.
  Es de algodón. It's made of cotton.
  Sus padres son italianos. His parents are Italian.
  Es joven/viejo. He's young/old.
  Son muy ricos/pobres. They're very rich/poor.

- with a following noun or pronoun that tells you what someone or something is

  Miguel es camarero. Miguel is a waiter.
  Soy yo, Enrique. It's me, Enrique.
  Madrid es la capital de España. Madrid is the capital of Spain.

- to say that something belongs to someone

  La casa es de Javier. The house belongs to Javier.
  Es mío. It's mine.

- to talk about where someone or something comes from

  Yo soy de Escocia. I'm from Scotland.
  Mi mujer es de Granada. My wife is from Granada.

- to say what time it is or what the date is

  Son las tres y media. It's half past three.
  Mañana es sábado. Tomorrow is Saturday.

- in calculations

  Tres y dos son cinco. Three and two are five.
  ¿Cuánto es? — Son dos euros. How much is it? It's two euros.

- when followed by an infinitive

  Lo importante es decir la verdad. The important thing is to tell the truth.

➪ *For more information on the **Infinitive**, see page 145.*

- to describe actions using the passive (for example *they are made*, *it is sold*)

Son fabricados en España.	They are made in Spain.

- to talk about where an event is taking place

La boda será en Madrid.	The wedding will be in Madrid.

➪ *For more information on the* ***Passive****, see page 108.*

➤ **estar** is used:

- to talk about where someone or something (other than an event) is

Estoy en Madrid.	I'm in Madrid.
¿Dónde está Burgos?	Where's Burgos?

- with an adjective when there has been a change in the condition of someone or something or to suggest that there is something unexpected about them

El café está frío.	The coffee's cold.
¡Qué guapa estás con este vestido!	How pretty you look in that dress!

- with a past participle used as an adjective, to describe the state that something is in

Las tiendas están cerradas.	The shops are closed.
No está terminado.	It isn't finished.
Está roto.	It's broken.

➪ *For more information on* ***Past participles****, see page 93.*

- when talking about someone's health

¿Cómo están ustedes?	How are you?
Estamos todos bien.	We're all well.

- to form continuous tenses such as the present continuous tense

Está comiendo.	He's eating.
Estamos aprendiendo mucho.	We are learning a great deal.

➪ *For more information on the* ***Present continuous****, see page 37.*

➤ Both **ser** and **estar** can be used with certain adjectives, but the meaning changes depending on which is used.

➤ Use **ser** to talk about permanent qualities.

Marta es muy joven.	Marta is very young.
Es delgado.	He's slim.
Viajar es cansado.	Travelling is tiring.
La química es aburrida.	Chemistry is boring.

➤ Use **estar** to talk about temporary states or qualities.

Está muy joven con ese vestido.	She looks very young in that dress.
¡Estás muy delgada!	You're looking very slim!
Hoy estoy cansado.	I'm tired today.
Estoy aburrido.	I'm bored.

➤ **ser** is used with adjectives such as **importante** (meaning *important*) and **imposible** (meaning *impossible*) when the subject is *it* in English.

Es muy interesante.	It's very interesting.
Es imposible.	It's impossible.
Es fácil.	It's easy.

➤ **ser** is used in certain set phrases.

Es igual *or* **Es lo mismo.**	It's all the same.
Es para ti.	It's for you.

➤ **estar** is also used in some set phrases.

- **estar de pie** to be standing
  Juan está de pie. — Juan is standing.
- **estar de vacaciones** to be on holiday
  ¿Estás de vacaciones? — Are you on holiday?
- **estar de viaje** to be on a trip
  Mi padre está de viaje. — My father's on a trip.
- **estar de moda** to be in fashion
  Las pantallas de plasma están de moda. — Plasma screens are in fashion.
- **estar claro** to be obvious
  Está claro que no entiendes. — It's obvious that you don't understand.

Grammar Extra!

Both **ser** and **estar** can be used with past participles. Use **ser** and the past participle in passive constructions to describe an action.

Son fabricados en España. They are made in Spain.

Use **estar** and the past participle to describe a state.

Está terminado. It's finished.

➪ For more information on ***Past participles***, see page 93.

KEY POINTS

- ✔ **ser** and **estar** both mean *to be* in English, but are used very differently.
- ✔ **ser** and **estar** are irregular verbs. You have to learn them.
- ✔ Use **ser** with adjectives describing permanent qualities or characteristics; with nouns or pronouns telling you who or what somebody or something is; with time and dates; and to form the passive.
- ✔ Use **estar** to talk about location; health; with adjectives describing a change of state; and with past participles used as adjectives to describe states.
- ✔ **estar** is also used to form present continuous tenses.
- ✔ **ser** and **estar** can sometimes be used with the same adjectives, but the meaning changes depending on which verb is used.
- ✔ **ser** and **estar** are both used in a number of set phrases.

Test yourself

Practise radical-changing verbs

35 Complete the following sentences with the correct form of the present tense of these radical-changing verbs. Refer to the verb tables in this book for help. Where it is not obvious, the subject of the verb is shown in square brackets.

a .... la tienda a las 3. **(cerrar [ellos])**

b No .... en ella. **(pensar [yo])**

c Siempre se .... con Ana en el parque. **(encontrar [él])**

d Me .... en un momento. **(vestir [yo])**

e Cuando habla rápido no la .... **(entender [ellos])**

f Siempre .... las gafas. **(perder [tú])**

g El niño .... como un angelito. **(dormir)**

h Yo le .... su número de teléfono. **(pedir)**

i Realmente, ... no contestar. **(preferir [nosotros])**

j ¿Cómo .... la caja fuerte? **(cerrar [tú])**

36 Create a sentence in the present tense using the elements given. Remember that, in Spanish, the subject of a verb is included in the verb form so it is not necessary to state it. Where it is not obvious, the subject of the verb is shown in square brackets to show you which verb form to use. Remember also that the object pronouns usually go before the verb.

a no/encontrar/mis gafas/[yo] ....

b siempre/perder/la cartera/en la calle [él]

....

c preferir/los vaqueros negros/con la camisa[yo]

....

d mis padres/dormir/la siesta/después de comer

....

e la ropa de Ana/servir/a mí. ....

f no/entender/las preguntas [ellos] ....

g pensar/lo mismo/que ellas [ellos] ....

h preferir/helado/de fresa [ella] ....

i no/dormir/bien/en verano/[ella] ....

j nunca/pedir/a vosotros/un favor/[yo]

....

Test yourself

37 Translate the following sentences into Spanish. Use a dictionary and the verb tables in this book to help you.

a They sleep in the attic. ....

b You think too much. ....

c They drive on the right. ....

d She doesn't understand the problem. ....

e If I lose my keys I can't get in.

....

f We close on Sundays. ....

g I understand you. ....

h She can't do it. ....

i They don't understand English very well. ....

j I hardly remember her. ....

38 Complete the following sentences with the correct form of the present tense of these radical-changing verbs. Refer to the verb tables in this book for help. Where it is not obvious, the subject of the verb is shown in square brackets to show you which verb form to use.

a .... llevarlos en coche. **(poder [yo])**

b Lo .... muy bien. **(recordar [yo])**

c Este cuchillo no .... para cortar. **(servir)**

d No me .... dinero aunque lo necesite. **(pedir [ella])**

e Sus alumnos no .... el tiempo en las clases. **(perder)**

f ¿Qué .... de todo esto? **(entender [tú]?)**

g No .... su nombre **(recordar [ellos])**

h ¿......................... la puerta al salir? **(cerrar [vosotros])**

i .... a las cartas los fines de semana. **(jugar [ellos])**

j ¿Cuándo .... a comer? **(empezar [ellos])**

Test yourself

39 Cross out the noun that does not go with the form of these stem-changing verbs.

a piensa	Amelia/yo/mi sobrina
b recuerdan	el abuelo/yo/los amigos
c duerme	el bebé/mis padres/los perros/el campo
d puedes	tu madre/Ina/tú
e quiero	yo/Alberto/los novios
f piden	nosotros/Ana y Luis/los hijos
g cierran	los supermercados/la tienda/la panadería
h voy	tu madre/Ina/yo
i sé	yo/Alberto/los novios
j oye	Ricardo/tú/vosotros

40 Complete the following sentences with the correct form of the present tense of these irregular verbs. Refer to the verb tables in this book when necessary. The pronoun in brackets shows you which form of the verb to use.

a Esta tarde .... tus cosas. **(traer [yo])**

b No .... sueño. **(tener [ellos])**

c ¿Cómo lo ....? **(hacer [yo])**

d Estos pantalones .... cincuenta euros. **(valer)**

e Andrea y Bernardo .... a la piscina los domingos. **(ir)**

f ¿Crees que me .... desde allí? **(oír [ellos])**

g .... a la estación. **(ir [yo])**

h La .... demasiado. **(querer [él])**

i Los domingos .... hasta tarde. **(salir [yo])**

j No .... a sus padres. **(conocer [yo])**

Test yourself

41 Create a sentence in the present tense using the elements given. Remember that, in Spanish, the subject of a verb is included in the verb form so it is not necessary to state it. Where it is not obvious, the subject of the verb is shown in square brackets to show you which verb form to use.

a primero/hacer/cama/de los niños/[yo] ....

b Bea/tener/casa/en el campo ....

c yo/poner/un poco de vinagre/en la salsa

....

d ir/a la playa/los fines de semana [ellos]

....

e no/tener/tiempo/para terminar [yo] ....

f hijos/venir/por las tardes ....

g decir/la verdad/siempre/[yo] ....

h no/oír/a ella/[yo] ....

i así/no/caerse/libros ....

42 Translate the following sentences into Spanish. Note that the translation will have irregular verbs. Use a dictionary and the verb tables in this book.

a She has two dogs. ....

b I put on the heating in the evening.

....

c I go to school. ....

d What do I do with this? ....

e How much is it? ....

f They come home every Sunday.

....

g I only say what I think. ....

h Which way do I go out? ....

i I don't know the answer. ....

j I know people from that school.

....

Test yourself

43 Complete the following sentences with the correct form of the present tense of these irregular verbs. Refer to the verb tables in this book when necessary. Where it is not obvious, the subject of the verb is shown in square brackets to show you which verb form to use.

a Siempre .... algún juego. **(traer [ellos])**

b Los miércoles .... a clase de karate. **(ir [nosotros])**

c No .... muy bien por el oído derecho. **(oír [yo])**

d ¿Qué .... con las sillas? **(hacer [yo])**

e Antonio y Lola .... a la cena. **(venir)**

f .... lo que quieres decir. **(saber [yo])**

g ¿........................ una tarta para su cumpleaños? **(hacer [yo])**

h ¿A veces .... cosas sin pensar? **(decir [yo])**

i ¿........................ a la feria? **(ir [vosotros])**

j ¿........................ amigos en Alemania? **(tener [tú])**

44 Match the two columns.

a Vale la pena.	I'm coming!.
b ¡Oye!	It's worth it.
c ¡Ya voy!	Put it on.
d No lo sé.	Listen!
e Póntelo.	I don't know.

Test yourself

Practise *ser* and *estar*

45 Complete the following sentences with the correct form of the verbs *ser* or *estar*. Remember that, in Spanish, the subject of a verb is included in the verb form, so it is not necessary to state it. Where it is not obvious, the subject of the verb is shown in square brackets to show you which verb form to use.

a Ana .... alemana. **(ser)**

b No .... muy felices en esta ciudad. **(ser [nosotros])**

c Jara .... muy guapa últimamente. **(estar)**

d El pijama .... en la maleta. **(estar)**

e ¡......................... las cuatro de la madrugada! **(ser)**

f No las cojas, no .... tuyas. **(ser)**

g Los dos hermanos .... muy altos. **(ser)**

h El parque .... a diez minutos de casa. **(estar)**

i No puedo ir a la fiesta porque .... enferma. **(estar)**

j La sopa .... caliente. **(estar)**

46 Match the two columns.

a Olga y Lola	están nerviosos.
b Laura	es de metal.
c Mis padres	están agotadas.
d La caja	está muy picante.
e La comida	es muy graciosa.

47 Match the two columns.

a Estás muy guapa.	His children are very tall.
b Sus hijos son muy altos.	You look very nice.
c Juan está aburrido.	Juan is really boring.
d Eres muy guapa.	Juan is bored.
e Juan es muy aburrido.	You are very pretty.

Test yourself

48 Translate the following sentences into Spanish.

a He's ill. ....

b She's asleep. ....

c They are very stubborn. ....

d They are at a wedding. ....

e Teresa is in Brussels all this week. ....

f His subject is very difficult. ....

g The film is quite funny. ....

h It's dinner time. ....

i How are you ***(familiar, plural)***? ....

j The CDs are Paula's. ....

49 Complete the following sentences with the correct form of *ser* or *estar*.

a María y Pedro ....novios.

b La tienda ....está abierta los domingos.

c ....demasiado cansado para salir. **[él]**

d Mi cumpleaños ....es el domingo.

e Andrea ....muy disgustada contigo.

f El lunes ....en París. **[yo]**

g ¿Dónde ....mis gafas?

h ¿Quién .... el chico de la camiseta roja?

i Nosotros ....de Mallorca.

j El juguete ....de plástico.

50 Match the two columns.

a Están de viaje.	Boots are in fashion.
b ¡Estamos de vacaciones!	We are standing.
c Las botas están de moda.	They were on their side.
d Estamos de pie.	They are on a trip.
e Estaban de lado.	We are on holiday!

Test yourself

51 Create a sentence in the present tense using the elements given. Remember that, in Spanish, the subject of a verb is included in the verb form so it is not necessary to state it. Where it is not obvious, the subject of the verb is shown in square brackets to show you which verb form to use.

a ¿dónde/estar/las camisas? ....

b ser/poco/inteligentes/[ellos] ....

c ya/no/estar/enfadado/con Luisa/[yo] ....

d mi hermana/y/yo/ser/parecidas ....

e estar/practicando/clarinete/[ellos] ....

f la tienda/estar/cerrada/los domingos

....

g ¿estar/solo/en la casa/[tú]? ....

h mermeladas/ser/fabricadas/en España

....

i ser/fundamental/llegar/a tiempo ....

j la ventana/estar/cerrada ....

The present continuous tense

➤ In Spanish, the present continuous tense is used to talk about something that is happening at this very moment.

➤ The Spanish present continuous tense is formed from the present tense of **estar** and the gerund of the verb. The gerund is the form of the verb that ends in **-ando** (for **-ar** verbs) or **-iendo** (for **-er** and **-ir** verbs) and is the same as the *-ing* form of the verb in English (for example, *walking, swimming*).

Estoy trabajando	I'm working.
No estamos comiendo.	We aren't eating.
¿Estás escribiendo?	Are you writing?

➪ *For more information on **estar** and the **Gerund**, see pages 26 and 115.*

➤ To form the gerund of an **-ar** verb, take off the **-ar** ending of the infinitive and add **-ando**:

Infinitive	**Stem Meaning**	(without **-ar**)	**Gerund**	**Meaning**
hablar	to speak	**habl-**	**hablando**	speaking
trabajar	to work	**trabaj-**	**trabajando**	working

➤ To form the gerund of an **-er** or **-ir** verb, take off the **-er** or **-ir** ending of the infinitive and add **-iendo**:

Infinitive	**Stem Meaning**	(without **-er/-ir**)	**Gerund**	**Meaning**
comer	to eat	**com-**	**comiendo**	eating
escribir	to write	**escrib-**	**escribiendo**	writing

Tip

Only use the present continuous to talk about things that are in the middle of happening right now. Use the present simple tense instead to talk about activities which are current but which may not be happening at this minute.

María trabaja en el hospital.	María works at the hospital.

➪ For more information on the ***Present simple tense***, see page 5.

KEY POINTS

✔ Only use the present continuous in Spanish for actions that are happening right now.

✔ To form the present continuous tense in Spanish, take the present tense of **estar** and add the gerund of the main verb.

Test yourself

52 Replace the highlighted verb with the present continuous form.

a **Nadamos** en el mar. ....

b **Vive** en Escocia. ....

c **Estudia** en una academia. ....

d **Aprende** música. ....

e **Compran** un coche. ....

f **Trabajo** en un hotel. ....

g **Vemos** una película. ....

h ¿Qué **miras**? ....

i **Leo** novelas históricas. ....

j **Cosen** ropa. ....

53 Match the English and the Spanish columns.

a **Están cerrando la tienda.**	You are wasting time.
b **Está haciéndose famoso.**	I'm saving a lot.
c **Estoy ahorrando mucho.**	They're closing the shop.
d **Está aprendiendo judo.**	He is getting famous.
e **Estáis perdiendo el tiempo.**	He is learning judo.

54 Complete the following sentences with the correct form of the present continuous. Remember that, in Spanish, the subject of a verb is included in the verb form, so it is not necessary to state it. Where it is not obvious, the subject of the verb is shown in square brackets to show you which form to use.

a No puedo ver la tele, ahora .... **(trabajar)**

b .... por teléfono con su novio. **(hablar [ella])**

c Mis hijos .... música en el conservatorio. **(estudiar)**

d Marc .... la cena. **(hacer)**

e No hagas ruido, los niños .... **(dormir)**

f Mi marido y yo .... la casa. **(decorar)**

g Marisa .... dinero. **(perder)**

h Ahora vienen, ... pan. **(comprar)**

i Ya voy, sólo .... el abrigo. **(ponerse)**

j Luz .... un helado. **(comer)**

Test yourself

55 Translate the following sentences into Spanish. Use a dictionary and the verb tables in this book to help you.

a The children are playing in the park.

....

b We are saving to buy a car. ....

c Are you eating? ....

d I'm not sleeping. ....

e They are watching a film. ....

f Now we are living in India.

....

g They are changing the system. ....

h They are reading the report. ....

i We are cooking a paella. ....

j They are hugging each other. ....

56 Create a sentence in the present continuous tense using the elements given. Remember that, in Spanish, the subject of a verb is included in the verb form so it is not necessary to state it. Where it is not obvious, the subject of the verb is shown in square brackets to show you which verb form to use. Use the verb tables in this book when you need to.

a María/aprender/a conducir

....

b trabajadores/hacer/huelga

....

c Jorge y yo/limpiar/cocina

....

d Nuria/cambiar/de trabajo ....

e su madre/sufrir/mucho ....

f este año/viajar/con menos frecuencia/[yo]

....

g distraerse/con el ruido [tú] ....

h desde junio/cuidar/de nuestra madre/[nosotros]

....

i no/criticar/a ella/[yo] ....

j el perro/mover/la cola ....

Test yourself

57 Complete the following sentences with the correct form of the present continuous or the present simple, depending whether the sentence refers to something which is happening at this moment or to something that is current but not happening right now. The pronoun in brackets shows you which person to use.

a ¿Ana? .... a su hermana en el salón. **(escribir [ella])**

b Ahora .... una casa. **(comprar [ellos])**

c Las maderas del suelo .... cuando las pisas. **(crujir)**

d Esta estufa .... mucho. **(calentar)**

e Un momento, ... **(vestirse [ella])**

f Nunca .... café. **(tomar [yo])**

g Llámala, te .... **(esperar [él])**

h .... sobre todo por las noches. **(leer [yo])**

i .... en este momento. **(terminar [yo])**

j .... en la costa desde pequeños. **(veranear [ellos])**

58 Fill the gaps using the present continuous form of the following verbs: *comprar, renovar, contratar, aprender, cambiar, hacer obra, trabajar.*

a Mi jefa .... la empresa para que sea más moderna.

b .... muchas nuevas máquinas.

c También .... a más trabajadores.

d Los trabajadores .... métodos más modernos y .... muchas horas.

e Además mi jefa .... en la fábrica para que sea más grande.

59 Translate the following sentences into Spanish. Use a dictionary and the verb tables in this book to help you.

a It's snowing. ....

b I'm listening. ....

c You are not behaving well. ....

d It's boiling. ....

e You are growing. ....

f It's falling. ....

g Things are changing. ....

h Are you eating right now? ....

i She is lying to us. ....

j They are selling the car. ....

60 Fill the gaps using the present continuous form of the following verbs: *pintar, esperar, celebrar, cocinar, descansar, atacar, jugar, leer, usar, estudiar.*

a Ana y yo .... un postre para la cena.

b .... el mueble de rojo. [yo]

c Jaime y su amigo .... al fútbol.

d Los aviones .... la ciudad.

e .... un método distinto al mío. [vosotros]

f Todos nosotros .... la noticia.

g Mi madre .... en el sofá.

h ¿Por qué .... sin luz?[tú]

i Alicia .... una llamada.

j .... para el examen. [ellos]

61 The present continuous refers to something which is happening at this moment whereas the present simple refers to something that is current but not happening right now. There are pairs of sentences below. Use the verb from the first sentence to fill in the gap in the second sentence to make a present continuous sentence. The first one has been done for you.

a Habla con María por teléfono todas las semanas. De hecho, *está hablando* con María por teléfono ahora mismo.

b Trabajo en finanzas. Este año .... en un banco.

c Alicia ayuda mucho a sus hijos. Ahora .... a su hija con la mudanza.

d Normalmente van a la oficina en coche. Como hay huelga de autobús .... a la oficina en metro.

e Rosa le cuenta todo a su amiga. Le .... a su amiga lo que pasó.

f ¿Lees mucho?¿ .... este libro?

g Escribo los trabajos del colegio en el ordenador. .... en el ordenador el trabajo de la semana que viene.

h Decoramos casas. Ahora .... una casa antigua.

i Vendemos electrodomésticos. Últimamente .... muchas televisiones.

j Escucha la radio a menudo, pero ahora mismo .... un CD.

The imperative

What is the imperative?
An **imperative** is a form of the verb used when giving orders and instructions, for example, *Sit down!*; *Don't go!*; *Let's start!*

Using the imperative

➤ In Spanish, the form of the imperative that you use for giving instructions depends on:

- whether you are telling someone to do something or not to do something
- whether you are talking to one person or to more than one person
- whether you are on familiar or more formal terms with the person or people

➤ These imperative forms correspond to the familiar **tú** and **vosotros/ vosotras** and to the more formal **usted** and **ustedes**, although you don't actually say these pronouns when giving instructions.

➤ There is also a form of the imperative that corresponds to *let's* in English.

Forming the imperative: instructions not to do something

➤ In orders that tell you NOT to do something and that have **no** in front of them in Spanish, the imperative forms for **tú**, **usted**, **nosotros/nosotras**, **vosotros/vosotras** and **ustedes** are all taken from a verb form called the present subjunctive. It's easy to remember because the endings for **-ar** and **-er** verbs are the opposite of what they are in the ordinary present tense.

➪ *For more information on the **Present tense** and the **Subjunctive**, see pages 5 and 132.*

➤ In regular **-ar** verbs, you take off the **-as**, **-a**, **-amos**, **-áis** and **-an** endings of the present tense and replace them with: **-es**, **-e**, **-emos**, **-éis** and **-en**.

-ar verb	**trabajar**	**to work**
tú form	**¡no trabajes!**	Don't work!
usted form	**¡no trabaje!**	Don't work!
nosotros/as form	**¡no trabajemos!**	Let's not work!
vosotros/as form	**¡no trabajéis!**	Don't work!
ustedes form	**¡no trabajen!**	Don't work!

➤ In regular **-er** verbs, you take off the **-es**, **-e**, **-emos**, **-éis** and **-en** endings of the present tense and replace them with **-as**, **-a**, **-amos**, **-áis** and **-an**.

-er verb	**comer**	**to eat**
tú form	**¡no comas!**	Don't eat!
usted form	**¡no coma!**	Don't eat!
nosotros/as form	**¡no comamos!**	Let's not eat!
vosotros/as form	**¡no comáis!**	Don't eat!
ustedes form	**¡no coman!**	Don't eat!

➤ In regular **-ir** verbs, you take off the **-es**, **-e**, **-imos**, **-ís** and **-en** endings of the present tense and replace them with **-as**, **-a**, **-amos**, **-áis** and **-an**.

-ir verb	**decidir**	**to decide**
tú form	**¡no decidas!**	Don't decide!
usted form	**¡no decida!**	Don't decide!
nosotros/as form	**¡no decidamos!**	Let's not decide!
vosotros/as form	**¡no decidáis!**	Don't decide!
ustedes form	**¡no decidan!**	Don't decide!

➤ A number of irregular verbs also have irregular imperative forms. These are shown in the table below.

	dar to give	**decir** to say	**estar** to be	**hacer** to do/make	**ir** to go
tú form	**¡no des!** don't give!	**¡no digas!** don't say!	**¡no estés!** don't be!	**¡no hagas!** don't do/make!	**¡no vayas!** don't go!
usted form	**¡no dé!** don't give!	**¡no diga!** don't say!	**¡no esté!** don't be!	**¡no haga!** don't do/make!	**¡no vaya!** don't go!
nosotros/as form	**¡no demos!** let's not give!	**¡no digamos!** let's not say!	**¡no estemos!** let's not be!	**¡no hagamos!** let's not do/make!	**¡no vayamos!** let's not go!
vosotros/as form	**¡no deis!** don't give!	**¡no digáis!** don't say!	**¡no estéis!** don't be!	**¡no hagáis!** don't do/make!	**¡no vayáis!** don't go!
ustedes form	**¡no den!** don't give!	**¡no digan!** don't say!	**¡no estén!** don't be!	**¡no hagan!** don't do/make!	**¡no vayan!** don't go!
	poner to put	**salir** to leave	**ser** to be	**tener** to have	**venir** to come
tú form	**¡no pongas!** don't put!	**¡no salgas!** don't leave!	**¡no seas!** don't be!	**¡no tengas!** don't have!	**¡no vengas!** don't come!
usted form	**¡no ponga!** don't put!	**¡no salga!** don't leave!	**¡no sea!** don't be!	**¡no tenga!** don't have!	**¡no venga!** don't come!
nosotros/as form	**¡no pongamos!** let's not put!	**¡no salgamos!** let's not leave!	**¡no seamos!** let's not be!	**¡no tengamos!** let's not have!	**¡no vengamos!** let's not come!
vosotros/as form	**¡no pongáis!** don't put!	**¡no salgáis!** don't leave!	**¡no seáis!** don't be!	**¡no tengáis!** don't have!	**¡no vengáis!** don't come!
ustedes form	**¡no pongan!** don't put!	**¡no salgan!** don't leave!	**¡no sean!** don't be!	**¡no tengan!** don't have!	**¡no vengan!** don't come!

Note that if you take the **yo** form of the present tense, take off the **-o** and add the endings to this instead for instructions NOT TO DO something, some of these irregular forms will be more predictable.

digo	*I say*	→	negative imperative stem	→	**dig-**
hago	*I do*	→	negative imperative stem	→	**hag-**
pongo	*I put*	→	negative imperative stem	→	**pong-**
salgo	*I leave*	→	negative imperative stem	→	**salg-**
tengo	*I have*	→	negative imperative stem	→	**teng-**
vengo	*I come*	→	negative imperative stem	→	**veng-**

Forming the imperative: instructions to do something

➤ In instructions telling you TO DO something, the forms for **usted**, **nosotros** and **ustedes** are exactly the same as they are in negative instructions (instructions telling you not to do something) except that there isn't a **no**.

	trabajar to work	**comer** to eat	**decidir** to decide
usted form	**¡Trabaje!**	**¡Coma!**	**¡Decida!**
nosotros/as form	**¡Trabajemos!**	**¡Comamos!**	**¡Decidamos!**
ustedes form	**¡Trabajen!**	**¡Coman!**	**¡Decidan!**

➤ There are special forms of the imperative for **tú** and **vosotros/vosotras** in positive instructions (instructions telling you to do something).

➤ The **tú** form of the imperative is the same as the **tú** form of the ordinary present simple tense, but without the final **-s**.

trabajar to work	→	**¡Trabaja!** Work!
comer to eat	→	**¡Come!** Eat!
decidir to decide	→	**¡Decide!** Decide!

➪ *For more information on the* ***Present simple tense****, see page 5.*

➤ The **vosotros/vosotras** form of the imperative is the same as the infinitive, except that you take off the final **-r** and add **-d** instead.

trabajar to work	→	**Trabajad!** Work!
comer to eat	→	**Comed!** Eat!
decidir to decide	→	**Decidid!** Decide!

➤ There are a number of imperative forms that are irregular in Spanish. The irregular imperative forms for **usted**, **nosotros/nosotras** and **ustedes** are the same as the irregular negative imperative forms without the **no**. The **tú** and **vosotros/vosotras** forms are different again.

	dar to give	**decir** to say	**estar** to be	**hacer** to do/make	**ir** to go
tú **form**	**¡da!** give!	**¡di!** say!	**¡está!** be!	**¡haz!** do/make!	**¡ve!** go!
usted **form**	**¡dé!** give!	**¡diga!** say!	**¡esté!** be!	**¡haga!** do/make!	**¡vaya!** go!
nosotros/as **form**	**¡demos!** let's give!	**¡digamos!** let's say!	**¡estemos!** let's be!	**¡hagamos!** let's do/make!	**¡vamos!** let's go!
vosotros/as **form**	**¡dad!** give!	**¡decid!** say!	**¡estad!** be!	**¡haced!** do/make!	**¡id!** go!
ustedes **form**	**¡den!** give!	**¡digan!** say!	**¡estén!** be!	**¡hagan!** do/make!	**¡vayan!** go!
	poner to put	**salir** to leave	**ser** to be	**tener** to have	**venir** to come
tú **form**	**¡pon!** put!	**¡sal!** leave!	**¡sé!** be!	**¡ten!** have!	**¡ven!** come!
usted **form**	**¡ponga!** put!	**¡salga!** leave!	**¡sea!** be!	**¡tenga!** have!	**¡venga!** come!
nosotros/as **form**	**¡pongamos!** let's put!	**¡salgamos!** let's leave!	**¡seamos!** let's be!	**¡tengamos!** let's have!	**¡vengamos!** let's come!
vosotros/as **form**	**¡poned!** put!	**¡salid!** leave!	**¡sed!** be!	**¡tened!** have!	**¡venid!** come!
ustedes **form**	**¡pongan!** put!	**¡salgan!** leave!	**¡sean!** be!	**¡tengan!** have!	**¡vengan!** come!

ℹ Note that the **nosotros/as** form for **ir** in instructions TO DO something is **vamos**; in instructions NOT TO DO something, it is **no vayamos**.

Position of object pronouns

➤ An object pronoun is a word like **me** (meaning *me* or *to me*), **la** (meaning *her/it*) or **les** (meaning *to them/to you*) that is used instead of a noun as the object of a sentence. In orders and instructions, the position of these object pronouns in the sentence changes depending on whether you are telling someone TO DO something or NOT TO DO something.

➤ If you are telling someone NOT TO DO something, the object pronouns go BEFORE the verb.

¡No me lo mandes!	Don't send it to me!
¡No me molestes!	Don't disturb me!
¡No los castigue!	Don't punish them!
¡No se la devolvamos!	Let's not give it back to him/her/them!
¡No las contestéis!	Don't answer them!

➤ If you are telling someone TO DO something, the object pronouns join on to the END of the verb. An accent is usually added to make sure that the stress in the imperative verb stays the same.

¡Explícamelo!	Explain it to me!
¡Perdóneme!	Excuse me!
¡Dígame!	Tell me!
¡Esperémosla!	Let's wait for her/it!

ℹ Note that when there are two object pronouns, the indirect object pronoun always goes before the direct object pronoun.

Other ways of giving instructions

➤ For general instructions in instruction leaflets, recipes and so on, use the infinitive form instead of the imperative.

Ver página 9.	See page 9.

➤ **vamos a** with the infinitive is often used to mean *let's*.

Vamos a ver.	Let's see.
Vamos a empezar.	Let's start.

KEY POINTS

✔ In Spanish, in instructions not to do something, the endings are taken from the present subjunctive. They are the same as the corresponding endings for **-ar** and **-er** verbs in the ordinary present tense, except that the **-e** endings go on the **-ar** verbs and the **-a** endings go on the **-er** and **-ir** verbs.

✔ For **-ar** verbs, the forms are: **no hables** (**tú** form); **no hable** (**usted** form); **no hablemos** (**nosotros/as** form); **no habléis** (**vosotros/as** form); **no hablen** (**ustedes** form).

✔ For **-er** verbs, the forms are: **no comas** (**tú** form); **no coma** (**usted** form); **no comamos** (**nosotros/as** form); **no comáis** (**vosotros/as** form); **no coman** (**ustedes** form).

✔ For **-ir** verbs, the forms are: **no decidas** (**tú** form); **no decida** (**usted** form); **no decidamos** (**nosotros/as** form); **no decidáis** (**vosotros/as** form); **no decidan** (**ustedes** form).

✔ In instructions to do something, the forms for **usted**, **nosotros/as** and **ustedes** are the same as they are in instructions not to do something.

✔ The forms for **tú** and **vosotros/as** are different:
- the **tú** form is the same as the corresponding form in the ordinary present tense, but without the final **-s**: **trabaja**; **come**; **decide**
- the **vosotros/as** form is the same as the infinitive but with a final **-d** instead of the **-r**: **trabajad**; **comed**; **decidid**

✔ A number of verbs have irregular imperative forms.

✔ The object pronouns in imperatives go before the verb when telling someone not to do something; they join onto the end of the verb when telling someone to do something.

Test yourself

62 Give orders and instructions not to do something using the present subjunctive. Use the verb tables and use the information about the present subjunctive on page 134

a ¡No .... en el sofá! **(saltar [tú])**

b ¡No .... las conversaciones de otros! **(escuchar [vosotros])**

c ¡No .... ! **(repetir [nosotros])**

d ¡No .... más caramelos! **(comer [tú])**

e ¡No .... tanto! **(trabajar [vosotros])**

f ¡No .... de ese vaso! **(beber [usted])**

g ¡No .... en la basura! **(buscar [tú])**

h ¡No .... ! **(retrasarse [tú])**

i ¡No .... las flores! **(pisar [ustedes])**

j ¡No lo .... ! **(dudar [tú])**

63 Give orders and instructions not to do something using the present subjunctive. Note that you will need to use verbs that have an irregular imperative form. Refer to page 43 and to the section on the present subjunctive on page 136 You may also need to check the verb tables.

a ¡No .... nada! **(decir [tú])**

b ¡No .... cuando llame! **(estar [vosotros])**

c ¡No .... de ahí! **(salir [ustedes])**

d ¡No .... ! **(ir [nosotros])**

e ¡No .... otra vez! **(venir [tú])**

f ¡No les .... nada! **(dar [ustedes])**

g ¡No .... tontos! **(ser [vosotros])**

h ¡No .... reparos! **(tener [usted])**

i ¡No .... la gorra! **(ponerse [tú])**

j ¡No .... a casa! **(venir [tú])**

PRACTICE PRACTICE PRACTICE PRACTICE PRACTICE PRACTICE

Test yourself

64 Complete the following sentences of instructions with the correct form of the imperative. Refer to page 45 and the verb tables. The pronoun in brackets shows you which person to use. The first one has been done for you.

a ¡......................... el ejercicio dos veces! **(repetir [tú])**

b ¡......................... con más energía! **(cantar [vosotros])**

c ¡......................... las frases del libro! **(copiar [vosotros])**

d ¡Pues entonces, ... solo! **(estudiar [tú])**

e ¡......................... con cuidado! **(copiar [ustedes])**

f ¡......................... que llega el autobús! **(correr [vosotros])**

g ¡......................... tranquilo! **(estar [usted])**

h ¡......................... todos juntos! **(viajar [nosotros])**

i ¡Por favor, ... la mano! **(soltar [tú][a mi])**

j ¡......................... un nudo bien fuerte! **(atar [vosotros])**

65 Complete the following sentences with the correct form of the imperative. Note that these verbs have irregular imperative forms. Refer to page 45 and the verb tables. The pronoun in brackets shows you which person to use. The first one has been done for you.

a ¡...*Haced*...... menos ruido! **(hacer [vosotros])**

b ¡......................... un poco de cuidado! **(tener [ustedes])**

c ¡......................... ahora mismo! **(ir [tú])**

d ¡......................... una huelga! **(hacer [nosotros])**

e ¡......................... sitio! **(hacer [ustedes])**

f ¡......................... solo! **(venir [tú])**

g ¡......................... las cosas en su sitio! **(poner [vosotros])**

h ¡......................... tranquilo! **(estar [usted])**

i ¡......................... de debajo de la mesa! **(salir [tú])**

j ¡......................... las llaves! **(dar[tú] [a mí])**

Test yourself

66 Give an instruction using the elements below. The subject pronouns are given to show who the instruction is for but remember you may not need to use them. Remember that the object pronouns usually go before the verb.

a [tú]/escucha/más atentamente ....

b [nosotros]/estudiar/la propuesta ....

c [tú]/portarse/bien ....

d [vosotros]/no/cambiar/ello ....

e [vosotros]/cerrar/la boca ....

f [nosotros]no/molestar/a la abuela ....

g [vosotros]/esperar/a mí/ahí ....

h [tú]/castigar/a ella ....

i [usedes]/mandar/callar/a ellos ....

j [vosotros]/hablar/más/alto ....

67 Translate the following instructions into Spanish using the imperative form. Sometimes you are told to use the *tú* form.

a Be quiet! ....

b Come right now! ....

c Don't give it to her! ....

d Listen to her! **[tú form]** ....

e Let's call them. ....

f Don't throw it away! ....

g Don't say that! ....

h Let's start from the beginning.

....

i Put it on there! ....

j Let's try again! ....

68 Match the two columns.

a ¡No me digas!	Pay attention!
b ¡Atiende!	You don't say!
c ¡Suelta!	Keep quiet!
d ¡Guardad silencio!	Here you are!
e ¡Tenga!	Let go!

PRACTICE PRACTICE PRACTICE PRACTICE PRACTICE PRACTICE

Test yourself

69 ***¿Me traes un vaso?* is more polite than using the imperative: *¡Tráeme un vaso!*. Change each question below into an order, remembering that the order of the pronoun may change. The first one has been done for you.**

a ¿Lees esto? ¡Lee esto!

b ¿Me atendéis, por favor? ....

c ¿Le prestas cincuenta euros a Javi?

....

d ¿Se lo das? ....

e ¿Me ayudáis? ....

f ¿Nos escuchas? ....

g ¿Acabas con el ordenador? ....

h ¿Se lo cuentas? ....

i ¿Me obedeces? ....

j ¿Vienes aquí? ....

70 **Replace the highlighted negative command with a positive command. The first one has been done for you.**

a ¡**No me llames** por teléfono! Llámame

b ¡**No lo saques** de ahí! ....

c ¡**No vengas** el último! ....

d ¡**No lo tires** todo! ....

e ¡**No me distraigas** con la música! ....

f ¡**No les dejéis** dinero! ....

g ¡**No le mires**! ....

h ¡**No la contestes** de esa forma! ....

i ¡**No lo muevas!** ....

j ¡**No los traigamos**! ....

Reflexive verbs

What is a reflexive verb?

A **reflexive verb** is one where the subject and object are the same, and where the action 'reflects back' on the subject. It is used with a reflexive pronoun such as *myself*, *yourself* and *herself* in English, for example, *I washed myself.*; *He shaved himself.*

Using reflexive verbs

➤ In Spanish, reflexive verbs are much more common than in English, and many are used in everyday language. The infinitive form of a reflexive verb has **se** attached to the end of it, for example, **secarse** (meaning *to dry oneself*). This is the way reflexive verbs are shown in dictionaries. **se** means *himself*, *herself*, *itself*, *yourself*, *themselves*, *yourselves* and *oneself*. **se** is called a reflexive pronoun.

➤ In Spanish, reflexive verbs are often used to describe things you do to yourself every day or that involve a change of some sort, for example, going to bed, sitting down, getting angry, and so on. Some of the most common reflexive verbs in Spanish are listed here.

acostarse	to go to bed
afeitarse	to shave
bañarse	to have a bath, to have a swim
dormirse	to go to sleep
ducharse	to have a shower
enfadarse	to get angry
lavarse	to wash
levantarse	to get up
llamarse	to be called
secarse	to get dried
sentarse	to sit down
vestirse	to get dressed

Me baño a las siete y media.	I have a bath at half past seven.
¡Duérmete!	Go to sleep!
Mi hermana se ducha.	My sister has a shower.
Mi madre se enfada mucho.	My mother often gets angry.
Mi hermano no se lava.	My brother doesn't wash.
Me levanto a las siete.	I get up at seven o'clock.
¿Cómo te llamas?	What's your name?
¿A qué hora os acostáis?	What time do you go to bed?
¡Sentaos!	Sit down!
Nos vestimos.	We're getting dressed.

[i] Note that **se**, **me** and so on are very rarely translated as *himself*, *myself* and so on in English. Instead of *he dresses himself* or *they bath themselves*, in English, we are more likely to say *he gets dressed* or *they have a bath*.

➤ Some Spanish verbs can be used both as reflexive verbs and as ordinary verbs (without the reflexive pronoun). When they are used as ordinary verbs, the person or thing doing the action is not the same as the person or thing receiving the action, so the meaning is different.

Me lavo.	I wash (myself).
Lavo la ropa a mano.	I wash the clothes by hand.
Me llamo Antonio.	I'm called Antonio.
¡Llama a la policía!	Call the police!
Me acuesto a las 11.	I go to bed at 11 o'clock.
Acuesta al niño.	He puts the child to bed.

Grammar Extra!

Some verbs mean ALMOST the same in the reflexive as when they are used on their own.

Duermo.	I sleep.
Me duermo.	I go to sleep.
¿Quieres ir al cine?	Do you want to go to the cinema?
Acaba de irse.	He has just left.

Forming the present tense of reflexive verbs

➤ To use a reflexive verb in Spanish, you need to decide which reflexive pronoun to use. See how the reflexive pronouns in the table on the next page correspond to the subject pronouns.

Subject pronoun	Reflexive pronoun	Meaning
(yo)	**me**	myself
(tú)	**te**	yourself
(él), (ella), (uno) **(usted)**	**se**	himself, herself, oneself, itself, yourself
(nosotros/nosotras)	**nos**	ourselves
(vosotros/vosotras)	**os**	yourselves
(ellos), (ellas) **(ustedes)**	**se**	themselves yourselves

(Yo) me levanto temprano.	I get up early.
(Él) se acuesta a las once.	He goes to bed at eleven.
Ellos no se afeitan.	They don't shave.

➤ The present tense forms of a reflexive verb work in just the same way as an ordinary verb, except that the reflexive pronoun is used as well.

➪ *For more information on the* ***Present tense****, see page 5.*

➤ The following table shows the reflexive verb **lavarse** in full.

Reflexive forms of lavarse	Meaning
(yo) **me lavo**	I wash (myself)
(tú) **te lavas**	you wash (yourself)
(él) se lava **(ella) se lava** **(uno) se lava, se lava** **(usted) se lava**	he washes (himself) she washes (herself) one washes (oneself), it washes (itself) you wash (yourself)
(nosotros/nosotras) **nos lavamos**	we wash (ourselves)
(vosotros/vosotras) os laváis	you wash (yourselves)
(ellos) **se lavan** (ellas) **se lavan** (ustedes) **se lavan**	they wash (themselves) they wash (themselves) you wash (yourselves)

➤ Some reflexive verbs, such as **acostarse**, are irregular. Some of these irregular verbs are shown in the **Verb tables** in the supplement.

Position of reflexive pronouns

➤ In ordinary tenses such as the present simple, the reflexive pronoun goes BEFORE the verb.

Me acuesto temprano. — I go to bed early.
¿Cómo se llama usted? — What's your name?

➪ *For more information on the **Present simple tense**, see page 5.*

➤ When telling someone NOT TO DO something, you also put the reflexive pronoun BEFORE the verb.

No te levantes. — Don't get up.
¡No os vayáis! — Don't leave!

➤ When telling someone TO DO something, you join the reflexive pronoun onto the end of the verb.

¡Siéntense! — Sit down!
¡Cállate! — Be quiet!

➪ *For more information on the **Imperative**, see page 42.*

Tip

When adding reflexive pronouns to the end of the imperative, you drop the final **-s** of the **nosotros** form and the final **-d** of the **vosotros** form, before the pronoun.

¡Vámonos! — Let's go!
¡Sentaos! — Sit down!

➤ You always join the reflexive pronoun onto the end of infinitives and gerunds (the **-ando** or **-iendo** forms of the verb) unless the infinitive or gerund follows another verb.

Hay que relajarse de vez en cuando.	You have to relax from time to time.
Acostándose temprano, se descansa mejor.	You feel more rested if you go to bed early.

➤ Where the infinitive or gerund follows another verb, you can put the reflexive pronoun either at the end of the infinitive or gerund or before the other verb.

Quiero bañarme *or* **Me quiero bañar.**	I want to have a bath.
Tienes que vestirte *or* **Te tienes que vestir.**	You must get dressed.
Está vistiéndose *or* **Se está vistiendo.**	She's getting dressed.
¿Estás duchándote? *or* **¿Te estás duchando?**	Are you having a shower?

➪ *For more information on **Gerunds**, see page 115.*

ⓘ Note that, when adding pronouns to the ends of verb forms, you will often have to add a written accent to preserve the stress.

Using reflexive verbs with parts of the body and clothes

➤ In Spanish, you often talk about actions to do with your body or your clothing using a reflexive verb.

Se está secando el pelo.	She's drying her hair.
Nos lavamos los dientes.	We clean our teeth.
Se está poniendo el abrigo.	He's putting on his coat.

ⓘ Note that in Spanish you do not use a possessive adjective such as *my* and *her* when talking about parts of the body. You use **el, la, los** and **las** with a reflexive verb instead.

Me estoy lavando las manos.	I'm washing my hands.

Other uses of reflexive verbs

➤ In English we often use a passive construction, for example, *goods are transported all over the world, most of our tea is imported from India and China*. In Spanish, this construction is not used so much. Instead, very often a reflexive verb with **se** is used.

Aquí se vende café.	Coffee is sold here.
Aquí se venden muchos libros.	Lots of books are sold here.
Se habla inglés.	English is spoken here.
En Suiza se hablan tres idiomas.	Three languages are spoken in Switzerland.

ⓘ Note that the verb has to be singular or plural depending on whether the noun is singular or plural.

➪ *For more information on the **Passive**, see page 108.*

➤ A reflexive verb with **se** is also used in some very common expressions.

¿Cómo <u>se dice</u> "siesta" en inglés?	How do you say "siesta" in English?
¿Cómo <u>se escribe</u> "Tarragona"?	How do you spell "Tarragona"?

➤ **se** is also used in impersonal expressions. In this case, it often corresponds to *one* (or *you*) in English.

No <u>se puede</u> entrar.	You can't go in.
No <u>se permite</u>.	You aren't *or* It isn't allowed.

➪ *For more information on **Impersonal verbs**, see page 124.*

➤ **nos**, **os** and **se** are all also used to mean *each other* and *one another*.

<u>Nos</u> escribimos.	We write to one another.
<u>Nos</u> queremos.	We love each other.
Rachel y Julie <u>se</u> odian.	Rachel and Julie hate each other.
No <u>se</u> conocen.	They don't know each other.

Key points

✔ A reflexive verb is made up of a reflexive pronoun and a verb.
✔ The reflexive pronouns are: **me, te, se, nos, os, se**.
✔ The reflexive pronoun goes before the verb, except when you are telling someone to do something and with infinitives and gerunds.

Test yourself

71 Replace the highlighted sentences with the alternative reflexive form where the pronoun is joined onto the verb. Pay attention to any accents you may need to add. The first one has been done for you.

a ¿Os queréis acostar ya? ¿Queréis acostaros ya?

b Se tiene que marchar pronto. ....

c Se está lavando el pelo. ....

d Me están esperando. ....

e Nos queremos quedar. ....

f No me quiero sentar con ella. ....

g ¿Os queréis quitar el abrigo? ....

h Se está vistiendo en este momento.

....

i Nos vamos a levantar temprano.

....

j Se están mirando todo el tiempo al espejo. ....

72 Change the following instructions into the negative. The first one has been done for you.

a ¡Márchate! No te marches.

b ¡Levántate! ....

c Péinate. ....

d ¡Muévete! ....

e ¡Callaos! ....

f Dúchate ahora. ....

g Quítate los zapatos. ....

h Bébete la leche. ....

i Súbete la manga. ....

j ¡Quítate de ahí! ....

73 The following English sentences all contain actions connected with the body or clothing. Translate them into Spanish using reflexive verbs. Remember that Spanish does not use *mi*, *tu*, *su*, etc when referring to parts of your body or to your clothes. Use a dictionary and the verb tables in this book to help you.

a She is brushing her teeth. ....

b Clara and Jorge, put on your coats. ....

Test yourself

c They have a shower in the evenings. ....

d You've got to wash your hair. ....

e Don't you take your gloves off? ....

f Wash your hands with soap and water. ....

g Tie your shoe laces. ....

h Are you getting dressed? ....

i The children always have a bath before going to bed.

....

j Better put on your boots. ....

74 Replace the highlighted verbs with the alternative passive reflexive *se* + verb form. Pay attention to whether the verb is singular or plural by checking whether the noun that follows is singular or plural. The first one has been done for you.

a Aquí **hablamos** inglés. *Aquí se habla inglés.* ....

b **Venden** muchos libros en el supermercado.

....

c En el garaje **compran** coches viejos.

....

d En Alemania **fabrican** coches. ....

e **Reparamos** ordenadores ....

f Desde allí **exportan** por toda Europa.

....

g En esa casa **alquilan** un piso ....

h **Hacemos** fotocopias. ....

i En el kiosko **venden** periódicos. ....

j **Compramos y vendemos.** ....

75 Complete the following sentences with the reflexive form *se* + verb to say whether something is allowed or not, by using either *se prohíbe* or *se permite*. The first one has been done for you.

a *Se prohíbe* .... fumar en el avión. **(prohibir)**

b No .... usar el móvil. **(permitir)**

c .... mirar el diccionario en el examen. **(permitir)**

d No .... entrar en la sala. **(permitir)**

Test yourself

e .... correr por los pasillos. **(prohibir)**

f No .... tocar los cuadros. **(permitir)**

g No........................ tirar papeles al suelo. **(permitir)**

h .... sacar fotos. **(prohibir)**

i .... dormir en la playa. **(permite)**

j No .... hacer fuego. **(prohibir)**

76 Translate the following sentences into Spanish using the passive reflexive *se* + verb. Pay attention whether the verb is singular or plural by checking whether the subject is singular or plural. The first one has been done for you.

a It is covered with plastic to protect it.
Se cubre con un plástico para protegerlo.

b The clothes are manufactured in India. ....

c Three languages are taught in the school. ....

d Then it's protected with a special code. ....

e The food is distributed throughout the country.
....

f The table is painted with a special paint. ....

g It is made with good materials. ....

h Every part is checked. ....

i All the documents are revised. ....

j Afterwards the vegetables are washed. ....

77 Create a sentence using the elements given. Remember that the reflexive pronoun will go before the verb unless the verb is in the infinitive or gerund forms. The subject of the verb is shown, if necessary, in square brackets to show you which verb form to use. The first one has been done for you.

a lavarse/la herida/cada día/[yo] *Me lavo la herida cada día.*

b levantarse/antes/de las 8/[ella] ....

c ahora/cansarse/con facilidad/ [ella] ....

d sentarse/en un sofá/viejo/[nosotros] ....

e no/disgustarse/con ella[tú] ....

f reirse/mucho/con la película/[nosotros] ....

g los niños/disfrazarse/de payasos/con ropas viejas
....

h enfadarse/por nada[vosotros] ....

i el pequeño/ya/ponerse/los calcetines/solo ....

j ¿cómo/llamarse/tu novia? ....

78 **The reflexive is also used in Spain to mean 'each other'. Translate the following sentences into Spanish. Use a dictionary and the verb tables to help you. The first one has been done for you.**

a They love each other. *Se aman.*

b They phone each other often. ....

c We know each other well. ....

d My daughters fight a lot. ....

e Victoria and Chus rarely talk to each other. ....

f They text each other. ....

g They don't recognise each other. ....

h We hate each other. ....

i They don't respect each other. ....

j Lorenzo and Gabi always help each other. ....

79 **Some verbs have a different meaning when they are used in the reflexive. Match each sentence below with the correct meaning.**

a **Duerme en el sofá.**	I'm leaving.
b **Yo me voy.**	I fall asleep on the sofa watching TV.
c **La puerta se abre.**	I'm coming.
d **Yo voy.**	The door opens.
e **Me duermo en el sofá viendo la tele.**	She sleeps on the sofa.

80 **Fill in the gaps using following reflexive verbs: *ducharse, reírse, tomarse, levantarse, irse, prepararse, afeitarse, beberse*. The first one has been done for you.**

a Antonio *se levanta* a las 7 de la mañana.

b Va al baño, ... y ....

c Antonio, ... el desayuno mientras escucha la radio y .... con las bromas del programa.

d .... un café rápidamente y .... una tostada.

e Luego, ... a coger el autobús para ir al trabajo.

The future tense

> **What is the future tense?**
>
> The **future** tense is a verb tense used to talk about something that will happen or will be true in the future, for example, *He'll be here soon; I'll give you a call; What will you do?; It will be sunny tomorrow.*

Ways of talking about the future

➤ In Spanish, just as in English, you can often use the present tense to refer to something that is going to happen in the future.

Cogemos el tren de las once.	We're getting the eleven o'clock train.
Mañana voy a Madrid.	I am going to Madrid tomorrow.

➤ In English we often use *going to* with an infinitive to talk about the immediate future or our future plans. In Spanish, you can use the present tense of **ir** followed by **a** and an infinitive.

Va a perder el tren.	He's going to miss the train.
Va a llevar una media hora.	It's going to take about half an hour.
Voy a hacerlo mañana.	I'm going to do it tomorrow.

Forming the future tense

➤ In English we can form the future tense by putting *will* or its shortened form *'ll* before the verb. In Spanish you have to change the verb endings. So, just as **hablo** means *I speak*, **hablaré** means *I will speak* or *I shall speak*.

➤ To form the future tense of regular **-ar, -er** and **-ir** verbs, add the following endings to the infinitive of the verb: **-é, -ás, -á, -emos, -éis, -án**.

➤ The following table shows the future tense of three regular verbs: **hablar** (meaning *to speak*), **comer** (meaning *to eat*) and **vivir** (meaning *to live*).

(yo)	**hablaré**	**comeré**	**viviré**	I'll speak/eat/live
(tú)	**hablarás**	**comerás**	**vivirás**	you'll speak/eat/live
(él) **(ella)** **(usted)**	**hablará**	**comerá**	**vivirá**	he'll speak/eat/live she'll speak/eat/live it'll speak/eat/live you'll speak/eat/live
(nosotros/ nosotras)	**hablaremos**	**comeremos**	**viviremos**	we'll speak/eat/live
(vosotros/ vosotras)	**hablaréis**	**comeréis**	**viviréis**	you'll speak/eat/live
(ellos/ellas/ ustedes)	**hablarán**	**comerán**	**vivirán**	they'll/you'll speak/eat/live

Hablaré con ella.	I'll speak to her.
Comeremos en casa de José.	We'll eat at José's.

No volverá. He won't come back.
¿Lo entenderás? Will you understand it?

ℹ Note that in the future tense only the **nosotros/nosotras** form doesn't have an accent.

Tip
Remember that Spanish has no direct equivalent of the word *will* in verb forms like *will* rain or *will* look and so on. You change the Spanish verb ending instead to form the future tense.

Grammar Extra!
In English, we sometimes use *will* with the meaning of be *willing* to rather than simply to express the future, for example, *Will you wait for me a moment?* In Spanish you don't use the future tense to say this; you use the verb **querer** (meaning to want) instead.

¿Me quieres esperar un momento, por favor? Will you wait for me a moment, please?

Verbs with irregular stems in the future tense

➤ There are a few verbs that DO NOT use their infinitives as the stem for the future tense. Here are some of the most common.

Verb	Stem	(yo)	(tú)	(él) (ella) (usted)	(nosotros) (nosotras)	(vosotros) (vosotras)	(ellos) (ellas) (ustedes)
decir to say	**dir-**	**diré**	**dirás**	**dirá**	**diremos**	**diréis**	**dirán**
haber to have	**habr-**	**habré**	**habrás**	**habrá**	**habremos**	**habréis**	**habrán**
hacer to do/ make	**har-**	**haré**	**harás**	**hará**	**haremos**	**haréis**	**harán**
poder to be able to	**podr-**	**podré**	**podrás**	**podrá**	**podremos**	**podréis**	**podrán**
poner to put	**pondr-**	**pondré**	**pondrás**	**pondrá**	**pondremos**	**pondréis**	**pondrán**
querer to want	**querr-**	**querré**	**querrás**	**querrá**	**querremos**	**querréis**	**querrán**
saber to know	**sabr-**	**sabré**	**sabrás**	**sabrá**	**sabremos**	**sabréis**	**sabrán**
salir to leave	**saldr-**	**saldré**	**saldrás**	**saldrá**	**saldremos**	**saldréis**	**saldrán**
tener to have	**tendr-**	**tendré**	**tendrás**	**tendrá**	**tendremos**	**tendréis**	**tendrán**
venir to come	**vendr-**	**vendré**	**vendrás**	**vendrá**	**vendremos**	**vendréis**	**vendrán**

Lo haré mañana.	I'll do it tomorrow.
No podremos hacerlo.	We won't be able to do it.
Lo pondré aquí.	I'll put it here.
Saldrán por la mañana.	They'll leave in the morning.
¿A qué hora vendrás?	What time will you come?

ℹ Note that the verb **haber** is only used when forming other tenses, such as the perfect tense, and in the expression **hay** (meaning *there is* or *there are*).

➪ *For more information on the **Perfect tense** and on **hay**, see pages 93 and 125.*

Reflexive verbs in the future tense

➤ The future tense of reflexive verbs is formed in just the same way as for ordinary verbs, except that you have to remember to give the reflexive pronoun (**me, te, se, nos, os, se**).

Me levantaré temprano.	I'll get up early.

Key points

- ✔ You can use a present tense in Spanish to talk about something that will happen or be true, just as in English.
- ✔ You can use **ir a** with an infinitive to talk about things that will happen in the immediate future.
- ✔ In Spanish there is no direct equivalent of the word *will* in verb forms like *will rain* and *will look*. You change the verb endings instead.
- ✔ To form the future tense, add the endings **-é, -ás, á, -emos, -éis, -án** to the infinitive.
- ✔ Some verbs have irregular stems in the future tense. It is worth learning these.

Test yourself

81 Replace the highlighted verb with the future tense using the *ir a* construction.

a **Están visitando** a sus abuelos. ....

b **Escuchan** las noticias. ....

c ¿**Puedes** ayudarme? ....

d **Cocinamos** paella. ....

e ¿**Vamos** al teatro? ....

f **Renuevan** una casa en el pueblo. ....

g **Aprende** a montar en bicicleta. ....

h ¿No **queréis** quedaros? ....

i ¿**Hacen** una merienda en el campo? ....

j ¿**Comemos** en un banco? ....

82 Complete the following sentences with the correct form of future. The pronoun in brackets shows you which person to use.

a Lo .... mañana. **(encontrar [tú])**

b .... si no lo metes en el congelador. **(derretirse [ello])**

c Claro que .... **(ayudar [él] [a ti])**

d Lo .... en el trabajo. **(imprimir [yo])**

e ¿Mañana .... más pronto? **(levantarse [vosotros])**

f Nos .... por teléfono esta noche. **(llamar [ellos])**

g .... toda la noche. **(trabajar [yo])**

h Vamos a visitar Londres y.................... cerca del centro. **(quedarse [nosotros])**

i .... para correr el maratón. **(prepararse [ella])**

j No te preocupes, ... el problema. **(resolver [nosotros])**

83 Each question below has two sentences using the same verb. In one sentence something will happen in the future and in the other something will happen in the immediate future (using the structure *ir a + inf*). One sentence has a gap where the verb is missing. Fill in the missing verbs. The first one is done for you.

a Por fín lo voy a conocer. Algún día lo *conoceré*....................

b Voy a comprar una casa en el campo. Cuando trabaje .... una casa en el campo.

c Iré a visitarlos a Argentina. El próximo mes .... a Argentina.

d Mis padres dormirán en la cama grande. Mis padres ya se....................

Test yourself

e Mañana hablaré con Lourdes. No me molestes, ... con Lourdes.

f ¿Vas a usar el ordenador ahora? ¿........................ el ordenador para hacer el trabajo?

g Saldré a las tres. .... a salir ahora.

h Me iré a comer más tarde. Hoy .... a comer más tarde.

i Este fin de semana voy a sembrar tulipanes. En verano .... pensamientos.

j No te preocupes, lo arreglaré. Tranquila, ... enseguida.

84 **Match the two columns.**

a Nosotros	van a ir de vacaciones a la playa.
b Mis vecinos	hablaremos con Lucía.
c También yo	van a jugar en el salón.
d Mi primo y tú	estaré esperando.
e Los niños	os veréis en Navidad.

85 **Create a sentence in the future using the elements given. Note that you will need verbs that are irregular in the future. Remember that, in Spanish, the subject of a verb is included in the verb form so it is not necessary to state it. Where it is not obvious, the subject of the verb is shown in square brackets to show you which verb form to use.**

a no/poder hacerlo/sola[yo] ....

b ¿a/qué hora/salir/de casa/[nosotros]? ....

c ¿no/salir/ este domingo/[vosotros]? ....

d querer/algo/todo/para ella [ella] ....

e Pedro y María/hacer/la comida/para el cumpleaños

....

f ponerse/el vestido nuevo/para Navidad/[tú] ....

....

g decir/la verdad/a él [yo] ....

h Pilar/ponerse en contacto/con Luis

....

i ¿venir/a verme/año próximo/[vosotros]?

....

j leer/el periódico/en el viaje/[yo] ....

Test yourself

86 Complete the following sentences with the correct form of the future tense. Note that you will need verbs that are irregular in the future. The pronoun in brackets shows you which person to use.

a ¿......................... con Carlos en el coche? **(ir [vosotros])**

b ¿......................... la leche en la nevera? **(poner [tú])**

c Sonia .... lo que hay que hacer. **(decir)**

d El sábado .... con sus amigas. **(salir [ella])**

e No .... molestar. **(querer [ellos])**

f El lunes ya......................... el coche. **(tener [yo])**

g Mis amigos .... todos a mi fiesta de cumpleaños. **(venir)**

h ¿Cuándo .... del colegio? **(salir [ellos])**

i Ya .... terminado para entonces. **(haber [yo])**

j .... todo lo posible. **(hacer [ellos])**

87 Translate these sentences into Spanish. Use the *tú* form for 'you' unless otherwise stated.

a I'll say it again. ....

b I won't be able to see it. ....

c We'll leave at three. ....

d She is going to try to fix it. ....

e I'll come to see you. ....

f She'll leave in the morning ....

g She's going to do it again. ....

h They won't have money to buy it. ....

i It's going to rain tomorrow. ....

j When will they phone? ....

k Will you go skiing this Christmas? ....

l Will you [***ustedes*** form] be at home this afternoon?

....

Test yourself

88 Complete the following sentences of instructions for a mystery trip with the correct form of the future tense of the following verbs: *estar, hablar, salir, coger, llevar, sentarse, ir*. Use the *tú* form.

a .... del trabajo a las 5.

b .... a la estación de tren y .... el tren a Edimburgo de las 5.54.

c En el tren......................... en el asiento 3b del vagón G.

d No......................... con nadie.

e Al llegar a Edimburgo, te ....esperando un hombre con un paraguas rojo y él te .... a tu destino.

The conditional

What is the conditional?

The **conditional** is a verb form used to talk about things that would happen or that would be true under certain conditions, for example, *I would help you if I could*. It is also used to say what you would like or need, for example, *Could you give me the bill?*

Using the conditional

➤ You can often recognize a conditional in English by the word *would* or its shortened form *'d*.

I would be sad if you left.
If you asked him, he'd help you.

➤ You use the conditional for:

- saying what you would like to do
  Me gustaría conocerlo. — I'd like to meet him.
- making suggestions
  Podrías alquilar una bici. — You could hire a bike.
- giving advice
  Deberías hacer más ejercicio. — You should do more exercise.
- saying what you would do
  Le dije que le ayudaría. — I said I would help him.

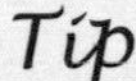

There is no direct Spanish translation of would in verb forms like *would be*, *would like*, *would help* and so on. You change the Spanish verb ending instead.

Forming the conditional

➤ To form the conditional of regular **-ar, -er,** and **-ir** verbs, add the following endings to the infinitive of the verb: **-ía, -ías, -ía, -íamos, -íais, -ían.**

➤ The following table shows the conditional tense of three regular verbs: **hablar** (meaning *to speak*), **comer** (meaning *to eat*) and **vivir** (meaning *to live*).

(yo)	**hablar<u>ía</u>**	**comer<u>ía</u>**	**vivir<u>ía</u>**	I would speak/eat/live
(tú)	**hablar<u>ías</u>**	**comer<u>ías</u>**	**vivir<u>ías</u>**	you would speak/eat/live
(él) **(ella)** **(usted)**	**hablar<u>ía</u>**	**comer<u>ía</u>**	**vivir<u>ía</u>**	he would speak/eat/live she would speak/eat/live it would speak/eat/live you would speak/eat/live
(nosotros/ nosotras) **(vosotros/ vosotras)** **(ellos/ellas)** **(ustedes)**	**hablar<u>íamos</u>** **hablar<u>íais</u>** **hablar<u>ían</u>**	**comer<u>íamos</u>** **comer<u>íais</u>** **comer<u>ían</u>**	**vivir<u>íamos</u>** **vivir<u>íais</u>** **vivir<u>ían</u>**	we would speak/eat/live you would speak/eat/live they would speak/eat/live you would speak/eat/live

Me <u>gustaría</u> ir a China. — I'd like to go to China.
Dije que <u>hablaría</u> con ella. — I said that I would speak to her.
<u>Debería</u> llamar a mis padres. — I should ring my parents.

Tip

Don't forget to put an accent on the **í** in the conditional.

Note that the endings in the conditional tense are identical to those of the <u>imperfect tense</u> for **-er** and **-ir** verbs. The only difference is that they are added to a different stem.

➪ *For more information on the **Imperfect tense**, see page 84.*

Verbs with irregular stems in the conditional

➤ To form the conditional of irregular verbs, use the same stem as for the future tense, then add the usual endings for the conditional. The same verbs that are irregular in the future tense are irregular in the conditional.

Verb	Stem	(yo)	(tú)	(él) (ella) (usted)	(nosotros) (nosotras)	(vosotros) (vosotras)	(ellos) (ellas) (ustedes)
decir to say	**dir-**	**diría**	**dirías**	**diría**	**diríamos**	**diríais**	**dirían**
haber to have	**habr-**	**habría**	**habrías**	**habría**	**habríamos**	**habríais**	**habrían**
hacer to do/ make	**har-**	**haría**	**harías**	**haría**	**haríamos**	**haríais**	**harían**
poder to be able to	**podr-**	**podría**	**podrías**	**podría**	**podríamos**	**podríais**	**podrían**
poner to put	**pondr-**	**pondría**	**pondrías**	**pondría**	**pondríamos**	**pondríais**	**pondrían**
querer to want	**querr-**	**querría**	**querrías**	**querría**	**querríamos**	**querríais**	**querrían**
saber to know	**sabr-**	**sabría**	**sabrías**	**sabría**	**sabríamos**	**sabríais**	**sabrían**
salir to leave	**saldr-**	**saldría**	**saldrías**	**saldría**	**saldríamos**	**saldríais**	**saldrían**
tener to have	**tendr-**	**tendría**	**tendrías**	**tendría**	**tendríamos**	**tendríais**	**tendrían**
venir to come	**vendr-**	**vendría**	**vendrías**	**vendría**	**vendríamos**	**vendríais**	**vendrían**

➪ *For more information on the* **Future tense**, *see page 60.*

¿Qué harías tú en mi lugar? — What would you do if you were me?
¿Podrías ayudarme? — Could you help me?
Yo lo pondría aquí. — I would put it here.

[i] Note that the verb **haber** is only used when forming other tenses, such as the perfect tense, and in the expression **hay** (meaning *there is/there are*).

➪ *For more information on the* **Perfect tense** *and on* **hay**, *see pages 93 and 125.*

Reflexive verbs in the conditional

➤ The conditional of reflexive verbs is formed in just the same way as for ordinary verbs, except that you have to remember to give the reflexive pronoun (**me, te, se, nos, os, se**).

Le dije que me levantaría temprano. I told him I would get up early.

Key points

✔ In Spanish, there is no direct equivalent of the word *would* in verb forms like *would go* and *would look* and so on. You change the verb ending instead.

✔ To form the conditional tense, add the endings **-ía, ías, -ía, -íamos, -íais, -ían** to the infinitive. The conditional uses the same stem as for the future.

✔ Some verbs have irregular stems which are used for both the conditional and the future. It is worth learning these.

Test yourself

89 Complete the following sentences with the correct form of the conditional. The pronoun in brackets shows you which person to use.

a Ella .... con la casa. **(quedarse)**

b Os dije que .... un poco en terminar. **(tardar)**

c ¿Te .... tener un perro? **(gustar)**

d ¡Tengo un hambre! .... un buen filete. **(comerme)**

e Por él, ... de estudiar. **(dejar)**

f Si me tocase la lotería, ... por todo el mundo. **(viajar)**

g Él .... todos los aparatos nuevos. **(comprarse)**

h Si pudiese, ... en el campo. **(vivir [ella])**

i .... con gusto este trabajo. **(Dejar)**

j Todos .... ser más amables con ellos **(deber [nosotros])**

90 Create a sentence in the conditional tense using the elements given. Remember that, in Spanish, the subject of a verb is included in the verb form so it is not necessary to state it. Where it is not obvious, the subject of the verb is shown in square brackets to show you which verb form to use.

a Ana/cambiar/el color ....

b su padre/escuchar/a ella/más ....

c los alumnos/deber estudiar/más/para el examen

....

d poder comprar/una cama/más grande/[vosotros]

....

e no/comer/en ese restaurante/[yo]

....

f deber intentar/tranquilizarse/un poco/ [él]

....

g yo/no/llamar/a ella ....

h poder hacer ejercicio/más a menudo [vosotros]

....

i ¿cómo/hablar/del tema/con Marisa/[tú]?

....

j mis hermanos /preferir/venir/enseguida

....

PRACTICE PRACTICE PRACTICE PRACTICE PRACTICE PRACTICE

Test yourself

91 Complete the following sentences with the correct form of the conditional. Note that you will be using verbs that are irregular in the conditional. The pronoun in brackets shows you which person to use if necessary.

a Él .... qué hacer. **(saber)**

b .... ir a correr al parque. **(poder [tú])**

c ¡Si pudiese, ... de esta ciudad! **(salir [yo])**

d Sé que tú lo .... de otra forma. **(hacer)**

e Yo no .... dudas. **(tener)**

f ¿......................... sujetarme esto? **(poder [tú])**

g Yo .... la televisión más cerca. **(poner)**

h ¿Qué .... que es esto? **(decir [tú])**

i No .... molestarlos. **(querer [yo])**

j Yo .... que no. **(decir)**

92 Match the two columns.

a Alejandro	podríais ir juntas.
b ¿Os	debería cambiar de trabajo.
c Yo si heredase,	lo pasarían bien.
d Vosotras dos	compraríais esta casa?
e Aquí ellos	dejaría de trabajar.

93 Translate the following sentences into Spanish using the conditional. Use the *tú* form for 'you' where appropriate.

a You ought to pay attention in class. ....

b They would like to meet you. ....

c Would you do it? ....

d They shouldn't spend so much. ....

e You could visit the castle. ....

f With that money, I would buy a boat. ....

g I wouldn't mind. ....

h The dog wouldn't eat that. ....

i I wouldn't worry about it. ....

j They should ask first. ....

Test yourself

94 Match the two columns.

a What should they do?	Les gustaría ir al cine.
b What would they like to do?	Deberían asegurarse primero.
c What would you do?	Preferirían comer carne.
d What could we do on holiday?	Yo no se lo diría.
e What would they prefer?	Podríais ir a la playa.

95 Replace the highlighted infinitive with the relevant conditional form. The first one has been done for you.

a ¿Os **importar** esperar aquí? importaría

b Ana **tener** que haber preguntado. ....

c Gustavo **saber** la respuesta. ....

d Les **encantar** venir al concierto. ....

e A Luz le **gustar** conocerte. ....

f Arantxa **ser** la persona ideal. ....

g Me **tener** que preparar. ....

h ¿Os **gustar** intentarlo?. ....

i Eso no **importar**. ....

j Yo no **irse** a vivir allí. ....

The preterite

What is the preterite?

The **preterite** is a form of the verb that is used to talk about actions that were completed in the past in Spanish. It often corresponds to the simple past in English, as in *I bought a new bike; Mary went to the shops on Friday; I typed two reports yesterday*.

Using the preterite

➤ In English, we use the simple past tense to talk about actions:

- that were completed at a certain point in the past
  I bought a dress yesterday.
- that were part of a series of events
  I went to the beach, undressed and put on my swimsuit.
- that went on for a certain amount of time
  The war lasted three years.

➤ In English, we also use the simple past tense to describe actions which happened frequently (*Our parents took us swimming in the holidays*), and to describe settings (*It was a dark and stormy night*).

➤ In Spanish, the preterite is the most common tense for talking about the past. You use the preterite for actions:

- that were completed at a certain point in the past
  Ayer compré un vestido. — I bought a dress yesterday.
- that were part of a series of events
  Fui a la playa, me quité la ropa y me puse el bañador. — I went to the beach, undressed and put on my swimsuit.
- that went on for a certain amount of time
  La guerra duró tres años. — The war lasted three years.

➤ However, you use the imperfect tense for actions that happened frequently (where you could use *used to* in English) and for descriptions of settings.

➪ *For more information on the **Imperfect tense**, see page 84.*

Forming the preterite of regular verbs

➤ To form the preterite of any regular **-ar** verb, you take off the **-ar** ending to form the stem, and add the endings: **-é, -aste, -ó, -amos, -asteis, -aron**.

➤ To form the preterite of any regular **-er** or **-ir** verb, you also take off the **-er** or **-ir** ending to form the stem and add the endings: **-í, -iste, -ió, -imos, -isteis, -ieron**.

➤ The following table shows the preterite of three regular verbs: **hablar** (meaning *to speak*), **comer** (meaning *to eat*) and **vivir** (meaning *to live*).

(yo)	**habl<u>é</u>**	**com<u>í</u>**	**viv<u>í</u>**	I spoke/ate/lived
(tú)	**habl<u>aste</u>**	**com<u>iste</u>**	**viv<u>iste</u>**	you spoke/ate/lived
(él) **(ella)** **(usted)**	**habl<u>ó</u>**	**com<u>ió</u>**	**viv<u>ió</u>**	he spoke/ate/lived she spoke/ate/lived it spoke/ate/lived you spoke/ate/lived
(nosotros nosotras)	**habl<u>amos</u>**	**com<u>imos</u>**	**viv<u>imos</u>**	we spoke/ate/lived
(vosotros/ vosotras)	**hablast<u>eis</u>**	**comist<u>eis</u>**	**vivist<u>eis</u>**	you spoke/ate/lived
(ellos/ellas) **(ustedes)**	**habl<u>aron</u>**	**com<u>ieron</u>**	**viv<u>ieron</u>**	they spoke/ate/lived you spoke/ate/lived

<u>Bailé</u> con mi hermana.	I danced with my sister.
No <u>hablé</u> con ella.	I didn't speak to her.
<u>Comimos</u> en un restaurante.	We had lunch in a restaurant.
¿<u>Cerraste</u> la ventana?	Did you close the window?

ℹ Note that Spanish has no direct translation of *did* or *didn't* in questions or negative sentences. You simply use a past tense and make it a question by making your voice go up at the end or changing the word order; you make it negative by adding **no**.

Tip

Remember the accents on the **yo** and **él/ella/usted** forms of regular verbs in the preterite. Only an accent shows the difference, for example, between **hablo** I <u>speak</u> and **habló** <u>he spoke</u>.

Irregular verbs in the preterite

➤ A number of verbs have very irregular forms in the preterite. The table shows some of the most common.

Verb	(yo)	(tú)	(él) (ella) (usted)	(nosotros) (nosotras)	(vosotros) (vosotras)	(ellos) (ellas) (ustedes)
andar to walk	**anduve**	**anduviste**	**anduvo**	**anduvimos**	**anduvisteis**	**anduvieron**
conducir to drive	**conduje**	**condujiste**	**condujo**	**condujimos**	**condujisteis**	**condujeron**
dar to give	**di**	**diste**	**dio**	**dimos**	**disteis**	**dieron**
decir to say	**dije**	**dijiste**	**dijo**	**dijimos**	**dijisteis**	**dijeron**
estar to be	**estuve**	**estuviste**	**estuvo**	**estuvimos**	**estuvisteis**	**estuvieron**
hacer to do, to make	**hice**	**hiciste**	**hizo**	**hicimos**	**hicisteis**	**hicieron**
ir to go	**fui**	**fuiste**	**fue**	**fuimos**	**fuisteis**	**fueron**
poder to be able to	**pude**	**pudiste**	**pudo**	**pudimos**	**pudisteis**	**pudieron**
poner to put	**puse**	**pusiste**	**puso**	**pusimos**	**pusisteis**	**pusieron**
querer to want	**quise**	**quisiste**	**quiso**	**quisimos**	**quisisteis**	**quisieron**
saber to know	**supe**	**supiste**	**supo**	**supimos**	**supisteis**	**supieron**
ser to be	**fui**	**fuiste**	**fue**	**fuimos**	**fuisteis**	**fueron**
tener to have	**tuve**	**tuviste**	**tuvo**	**tuvimos**	**tuvisteis**	**tuvieron**
traer to bring	**traje**	**trajiste**	**trajo**	**trajimos**	**trajisteis**	**trajeron**
venir to come	**vine**	**viniste**	**vino**	**vinimos**	**vinisteis**	**vinieron**
ver to see	**vi**	**viste**	**vio**	**vimos**	**visteis**	**vieron**

i Note that **hizo** (the **él/ella/usted** form of **hacer**) is spelt with a **z.**

Fue a Madrid.	He went to Madrid.
Te vi en el parque.	I saw you in the park.
No vinieron.	They didn't come.
¿Qué hizo?	What did she do?
Se lo di a Teresa.	I gave it to Teresa.
Fue en 1999.	It was in 1999.

Tip

The preterite forms of **ser** (meaning *to be*) are the same as the preterite forms of **ir** (meaning *to go*).

➤ Some other verbs are regular EXCEPT FOR the **él/ella/usted** and **ellos/ellas/ustedes** forms (*third persons singular and plural*). In these forms the stem vowel changes.

Verb	(yo)	(tú)	(él) (ella) (usted)	(nosotros) (nosotras)	(vosotros) (vosotras)	(ellos) (ellas) (ustedes)
dormir to sleep	**dormí**	**dormiste**	**durmió**	**dormimos**	**dormisteis**	**durmieron**
morir to die	**morí**	**moriste**	**murió**	**morimos**	**moristeis**	**murieron**
pedir to ask for	**pedí**	**pediste**	**pidió**	**pedimos**	**pedisteis**	**pidieron**
reír to laugh	**reí**	**reíste**	**rio**	**reímos**	**reísteis**	**rieron**
seguir to follow	**seguí**	**seguiste**	**siguió**	**seguimos**	**seguisteis**	**siguieron**
sentir to feel	**sentí**	**sentiste**	**sintió**	**sentimos**	**sentisteis**	**sintieron**

Antonio durmió diez horas.	Antonio slept for ten hours.
Murió en 1066.	He died in 1066.
Pidió paella.	He asked for paella.
¿Los siguió?	Did she follow them?
Sintió un dolor en la pierna.	He felt a pain in his leg.
Nos reímos mucho.	We laughed a lot.
Juan no se rio.	Juan didn't laugh.

➤ **caer** (meaning *to fall*) and **leer** (meaning *to read*) have an accent in all persons apart from the **ellos/ellas/ustedes** form (*third person plural*). In addition, the vowel changes to **y** in the **él/ella/usted** and **ellos/ellas/ ustedes** forms (*third persons singular and plural*).

Verb	(yo)	(tú)	(él) (ella) (usted)	(nosotros) (nosotras)	(vosotros) (vosotras)	(ellos) (ellas) (ustedes)
caer to fall	**caí**	**caíste**	**cayó**	**caímos**	**caísteis**	**cayeron**
construir to build	**construí**	**construiste**	**construyó**	**construimos**	**construisteis**	**construyeron**
leer to read	**leí**	**leíste**	**leyó**	**leímos**	**leísteis**	**leyeron**

[i] Note that **construir** also changes to **y** in the **él/ella/usted** and **ellos/ellas/ustedes** forms (*third persons singular and plural*), but only has accents in the **yo** and **él/ella/usted** forms.

Se cayó por la ventana. He fell out of the window.
Ayer leí un artículo muy interesante. I read a very interesting article yesterday.
Construyeron una nueva autopista. They built a new motorway.

Other spelling changes in the preterite

➤ Spanish verbs that end in -**zar**, -**gar** and -**car** in the infinitive change the **z** to **c**, the **g** to **gu** and the **c** to **qu** in the **yo** form (*first person singular*).

Verb	(yo)	(tú)	(él) (ella) (usted)	(nosotros) (nosotras)	(vosotros) (vosotras)	(ellos) (ellas) (ustedes)
cruzar to cross	**crucé**	**cruzaste**	**cruzó**	**cruzamos**	**cruzasteis**	**cruzaron**
empezar to begin	**empecé**	**empezaste**	**empezó**	**empezamos**	**empezasteis**	**empezaron**
pagar to pay for	**pagué**	**pagaste**	**pagó**	**pagamos**	**pagasteis**	**pagaron**
sacar to follow	**saqué**	**sacaste**	**sacó**	**sacamos**	**sacasteis**	**sacaron**

Crucé el río. I crossed the river.
Empecé a hacer mis deberes. I began doing my homework.
No pagué la cuenta. I didn't pay the bill.
Me saqué las llaves del bolsillo. I took my keys out of my pocket.

[i] *Note that the change from* **g** *to* **gu** *and* **c** *to* **qu** *before* **e** *is to keep the sound hard.*

Reflexive verbs in the preterite

➤ The preterite of reflexive verbs is formed in just the same way as for ordinary verbs, except that you have to remember to give the reflexive pronoun (**me, te, se, nos, os, se**).

Me levanté a las siete. — I got up at seven.

Key points

✔ The preterite is the most common way to talk about the past in Spanish.

✔ To form the preterite of regular **-ar** verbs, take off the **-ar** ending and add the endings: **-é**, **-aste**, **-ó**, **-amos**, **-asteis**, **-aron**.

✔ To form the preterite of regular **-er** and **-ir** verbs, take off the **-er** and **-ir** endings and add the endings: **-í**, **-iste**, **-ió**, **-imos**, **-isteis**, **-ieron**.

✔ There are a number of verbs which are irregular in the preterite. These forms have to be learnt.

✔ With some verbs, the accents and spelling change in certain forms.

Test yourself

96 Complete the following sentences with the correct form of the preterite. If necessary, the pronoun in square brackets will show you which person to use.

a El concierto .... tarde. **(terminar)**

b Mis padres .... al nacer yo. **(separarse)**

c ¿Cuándo .... Manu a casa? **(llegar)**

d El verano pasado .... la montaña. **(subir [ellos])**

e ¿Sabes si Elena .... ayer con el inspector? **(hablar)**

f Jaime .... con Lidia. **(romper)**

g ¿Quién .... los refrescos? **(comprar)**

h ¿En que año ....? **(casarse [vosotros])**

i No se lo .... **(preguntar [yo])**

j Nuria y Gabi .... juntos. **(trabajar)**

97 Complete the following sentences with the correct form of the preterite paying attention to any verbs that are irregular. If necessary, the pronoun in square brackets will show you which person to use.

a Los niños .... en el parque toda la tarde. **(estar)**

b Se lo .... a él. **(decir [yo])**

c El piso se lo .... sus padres. **(dar)**

d Irma y Pau .... por el centro de la ciudad. **(andar)**

e Nosotros .... las cervezas. **(traer)**

f Ayer .... a visitar a mis tíos. **(ir [yo])**

g No .... hasta los 21 años. **(conducir [yo])**

h Sonia no .... buena suerte con los negocios. **(tener)**

i ¿Cómo lo ....? **(hacer [vosotros])**

j Mis padres no lo .... hasta ayer. **(saber)**

Test yourself

98 Complete the following sentences with the correct form of the preterite. Note that you will use verbs that may change their stems in the preterite.

a ¿Os .... mucho con la comedia? **(reir)**

b La policía .... el rastro de los ladrones. **(seguir)**

c Le .... consejo. **(pedir [yo])**

d La pequeña .... abrazada a su muñeco. **(dormirse)**

e Lo .... mucho. **(sentir [yo])**

f Camen y tú .... lo mismo. **(pedir)**

g Mi abuela .... a los 89 años. **(morir)**

h .... una cosa fría en la espalda. **(sentir [yo])**

i Nos .... los apuntes de clase. **(pedir [ellos])**

j Los .... por la calle. **(seguir [nosotros])**

99 Create a sentence in the preterite using the elements given. Remember that, in Spanish, the subject of a verb is included in the verb form so it is not necessary to state it. Where it is not obvious, the subject of the verb is shown in square brackets to show you which verb form to use.

a Toni/hacer/un castillo de arena/en la playa

....

b decir/a María/la verdad/[yo] ....

c Pedro y yo/ir/en barco/a Barcelona

....

d ¿cómo/poder/cruzar/a nado[tú]? ....

e ¿Qué/decir/a ellos/en la reunión/[vosotros]?

....

f la ambulancia/conducir/a toda velocidad

....

g estar/muy tranquilo/toda la tarde[tú]

....

h ¿dónde/poner/dinero/[vosotros]? ....

i dar/a ellos/los documentos/[tú] ....

j traer/a mí/el maletín/[ellos] ....

Test yourself

100 Fill in the gap in the second sentence, using the same verb as the first sentence but in the preterite, to describe something specific that happened at a certain point in the past. The first one has been done for you. Note that you will be using verbs that are irregular in the preterite.

a Yo sacaba dinero todos los meses. Yo ....saqué........ dinero para pagaros.

b Construían apartamentos para vender. .... unos apartamentos junto al río.

c Siempre pagaban sus deudas. .... todas sus deudas y dejaron la ciudad.

d Andrés conducía un autobús para trabajar. En el viaje .... Andrés.

e No podían venir mucho a vernos. No .... venir a vernos aquel domingo.

f Yo empezaba a salir un poco por las noches. .... a salir cuando tenía diecisiete años.

g Cruzaban la calle todos los días. Ayer .... la calle solos.

h Sabías lo que había pasado. .... lo que había pasado mucho después.

i No querían molestarnos. No .... molestarnos y se fueron.

j Siempre traías buenas noticias. Aquel día .... buenas noticias.

101 Create sentences using the required form of the preterite. Note that you will be using verbs that are irregular in the preterite. The first one has been done for you.

a andar de noche Anduvisteis de noche. .... **[vosotros]**

b decir la verdad .... **[tú]**

c ir solo .... **[tú]**

d poder entrar .... **[usted]**

e querer probar .... **[vosotros]**

f saber esperar .... **[ustedes]**

g dar dinero .... **[tú]**

h ponerse el abrigo .... **[vosotros]**

i tener valor .... **[tú]**

j querer preguntar .... **[ustedes]**

Test yourself

102 Complete the following sentences with the correct form of the preterite. If necessary, the pronoun in square brackets will show you which person to use.

a Se .... de calle cuando me .... **(cruzarse; ver [él])**

b ¿Cuándo .... a jugar? **(empezar [vosotros])**

c Los romanos .... el acueducto. **(construir)**

d ¿Cuánto .... ayer? **(leer [tú])**

e Se .... en la calle por correr. **(caer [ellos])**

f Le .... hasta el último céntimo. **(pagar [yo])**

g Yo .... el móvil y .... a sacar fotos. **(sacar; ponerse)**

h Lo .... en voz alta. **(leer [ellos])**

i .... de un primer piso sobre un arbusto. **(caer [yo])**

j Anoche .... una película. **(ver [nosotros])**

103 Translate the following sentences into Spanish.

a I found it under the bed. ....

b They lost the match. ....

c I lost my keys in the street. ....

d They went out again. ....

e She bought some books and some CDs. ....

f They ordered coffee. ....

g I had a problem. ....

h Pilar brought some games. ....

i The minister resigned yesterday. ....

j I drove all the time. ....

The imperfect tense

What is the imperfect tense?

The **imperfect tense** is one of the verb tenses used to talk about the past, especially in descriptions, and to say what was happening or used to happen, for example, *It was sunny at the weekend; We were living in Spain at the time; I used to walk to school.*

Using the imperfect tense

➤ In Spanish, the imperfect tense is used:

- to describe what things were like and how people felt in the past

Hacía calor.	It was hot.
No teníamos mucho dinero.	We didn't have much money.
Tenía hambre.	I was hungry.

- to say what used to happen or what you used to do regularly in the past

Cada día llamaba a su madre.	He used to ring his mother every day.

- to describe what was happening or what the situation was when something else took place

Tomábamos café.	We were having coffee.
Me caí cuando cruzaba la carretera.	I fell over when I was crossing the road.

Grammar Extra!

Sometimes, instead of the ordinary imperfect tense being used to describe what was happening at a given moment in the past when something else occurred interrupting it, the continuous form is used. This is made up of the imperfect tense of **estar** (**estaba**, **estabas** and so on), followed by the **-ando/-iendo** form of the main verb. The other verb – the one that relates the event that occurred – is in the preterite.

Montse miraba la televisión *or* **Montse estaba mirando la televisión cuando sonó el teléfono.**	Montse was watching television when the telephone rang.

➪ For further information on the ***Preterite***, see page 74.

Forming the imperfect tense

➤ To form the imperfect of any regular **-ar** verb, you take off the **-ar** ending of the infinitive to form the stem and add the endings: **-aba, -abas, -aba,-ábamos, -abais, -aban.**

➤ The following table shows the imperfect tense of one regular **-ar** verb: **hablar** (meaning *to speak*).

(yo)	**hablaba** I used to speak	I spoke, I was speaking,
(tú)	**hablabas**	you spoke, you were speaking, you used to speak
(él/ella/usted)	**hablaba**	he/she/it/you spoke, he/she/it was speaking, you were speaking , he/she/it/you used to speak
(nosotros/nosotras)	**hablábamos**	we spoke, we were speaking, we used to speak
(vosotros/vosotras)	**hablabais**	you spoke, you were speaking, you used to speak
(ellos/ellas/ustedes)	**hablaban**	they/you spoke, they/ you were speaking, they/ you used to speak

Note that in the imperfect tense of **-ar** verbs, the only accent is on the **nosotros/nosotras** form

Hablaba francés e italiano.	He spoke French and Italian.
Cuando era joven, mi tío trabajaba mucho.	My uncle worked hard when he was young.
Estudiábamos matemáticas e inglés.	We were studying maths and English.

➤ To form the imperfect of any regular **-er** or **-ir** verb, you take off the **-er** or **-ir** ending of the infinitive to form the stem and add the endings: **-ía, -ías, -ía, -íamos, -íais, -ían.**

➤ The following table shows the imperfect of two regular verbs: **comer** (meaning *to eat*) and **vivir** (meaning *to live*).

(yo)	**comía**	**vivía**	I ate/lived, I was eating/living, I used to eat/live
(tú)	**comías**	**vivías**	you ate/lived, you were eating/living, you used to eat/live
(él/ella/ usted)	**comía**	**vivía**	he/she/it/you ate/lived, he/she/it was eating/living, you were eating/living, he/she/it was eating/living, you were eating/living
(nosotros/ nosotras)	**comíamos**	**vivíamos**	we ate/lived, we were eating/living, we used to eat/live
(vosotros/ vosotras)	**comíais**	**vivíais**	you ate/lived, you were eating/living, you used to eat/live
(ellos/ellas/ ustedes)	**comían**	**vivían**	they/you ate/lived, they/you were eating/living, they/you used to eat/live

i Note that in the imperfect tense of **-er** and **-ir** verbs, there's an accent on all the endings.

A veces, <u>comíamos</u> en casa de Pepe.	We sometimes used to eat at Pepe's.
<u>Vivía</u> en un piso en la Avenida de Barcelona.	She lived in a flat in Avenida de Barcelona.
Cuando llegó el médico, ya se <u>sentían</u> mejor.	They were already feeling better when the doctor arrived.

Tip

The imperfect endings for **-er** and **-ir** verbs are the same as the endings used to form the conditional for all verbs. The only difference is that, in the conditional, the endings are added to the future stem.

➪ *For more information on the **Conditional**, see page 67.*

Irregular verbs in the imperfect tense

➤ **ser, ir** and **ver** are irregular in the imperfect tense.

	ser	**Meaning:** ***to be***
(yo)	**era**	I was
(tú)	**eras**	you were
(él/ella/usted)	**era**	he/she/it was, you were
(nosotros/nosotras)	**éramos**	we were
(vosotros/vosotras)	**erais**	you were
(ellos/ellas/ustedes)	**eran**	they were/you were

<u>Era</u> un chico muy simpático.	He was a very nice boy.
Mi madre <u>era</u> profesora.	My mother was a teacher.

	ir	**Meaning:** ***to go***
(yo)	**iba**	I went/used to go/was going
(tú)	**ibas**	you went/used to go/were going
(él/ella/usted)	**iba**	he/she/it went/used to go/was going, you went/used to go/were going
(nosotros/nosotras)	**íbamos**	we went/used to go/were going
(vosotros/vosotras)	**ibais**	you went/used to go/were going
(ellos/ellas/ustedes)	**iban**	they/you went/used to go/were going

<u>Iba</u> a la oficina cada día.	Every day he would go to the office.
¿Adónde <u>iban</u>?	Where were they going?

	ver	**Meaning:** ***to see/to watch***
(yo)	**veía**	I saw/used to see, I watched/used to watch/was watching
(tú)	**veías**	you saw/used to see, you watched/ used to watch/were watching
(él/ella/usted)	**veía**	he/she/it saw/used to see, he/she/it watched/used to watch/was watching, you saw/used to see, you watched/ used to watch/were watching
(nosotros/nosotras)	**veíamos**	we saw/used to see, we watched/ used to watch/were watching
(vosotros/vosotras)	**veíais**	you saw/used to see, you watched/ used to watch/were watching
(ellos/ellas/ustedes)	**veían**	they/you saw/used to see, they/you watched/used to watch/were watching

Los sábados, siempre lo veíamos. — We always used to see him on Saturdays.
Veía la televisión cuando llegó mi tío. — I was watching television when my uncle arrived.

Reflexive verbs in the imperfect tense

➤ The imperfect of reflexive verbs is formed in just the same way as for ordinary verbs, except that you have to remember to give the reflexive pronoun (**me, te, se, nos, os, se**).

Antes se levantaba temprano. — He used to get up early.

Grammar Extra!

In Spanish, you also use the imperfect tense with certain time expressions, in particular with **desde** (meaning *since*), **desde hacía** (meaning *for*) and **hacía ... que** (meaning *for*) to talk about activities and states that had started previously and were still going on at a particular point in the past:

Estaba enfermo desde 2000. — He had been ill since 2000.
Conducía ese coche desde hacía tres meses. — He had been driving that car for three months.
Hacía mucho tiempo que salían juntos. — They had been going out together for a long time.
Hacía dos años que vivíamos en Madrid. — We had been living in Madrid for two years.

Compare the use of **desde, desde hacía** and **hacía ... que** with the imperfect with that of **desde, desde hace,** and **hace ... que** with the present.

Key points

- ✔ To form the imperfect tense of **-ar** verbs, take off the **-ar** ending and add the endings: **-aba**, **-abas**, **-aba**, **-ábamos**, **-abais**, **-aban**.
- ✔ To form the imperfect tense of **-er** and **-ir** verbs, take off the **-er** and **-ir** endings and add the endings: **-ía**, **-ías**, **-ía**, **-íamos**, **-íais**, **-ían**.
- ✔ **ser**, **ir** and **ver** are irregular in the imperfect.

Test yourself

104 Complete the following sentences with the correct form of the imperfect tense. If necessary, the pronoun in square brackets will show you which person to use.

a Los alumnos .... diez minutos hasta llegar al colegio. **(caminar)**

b No me culpes, yo no lo .... **(saber [yo])**

c ¿Tú antes no .... desde casa? **(trabajabar)**

d Aunque .... , se portaron bien. **(aburrirse)**

e ¿De qué .... tan en secreto? **(hablar [vosotros])**

f Se empezó a sentir enfermo y .... a menudo. **(estornudar)**

g Su forma de hablar .... sus sentimientos. **(herir)**

h De pequeña, ... por nada. **(llorar [tú])**

i Llegó cuando yo .... comiendo **(estar)**

j Me dijo que no .... nada. **(necesitar [tú])**

105 Complete the following sentences with the correct form of the imperfect tense. Note that you will need verbs that are irregular in the imperfect. Where it is not obvious, the subject of the verb is shown in square brackets.

a Todas las mañanas .... lo mismo. **(ser)**

b ¿Adónde .... tan deprisa? **(ir [ellos])**

c Cuando llegó Juan .... una película. **(ver [nosotros])**

d Todos sus perros .... de raza. **(ser)**

e Antonio .... al trabajo en autobús. **(ir)**

f Antes .... a los nietos más. **(ver [nosotros])**

g El pueblo .... muy tranquilo. **(ser)**

h ¿No .... amigos? **(ser [vosotros])**

i Fui al médico porque lo .... todo muy borroso. **(ver)**

j No los .... a llamar hasta la tarde. **(ir [yo])**

106 Create a sentence in the imperfect tense using the elements given. Remember that, in Spanish, the subject of a verb is included in the verb form so it is not necessary to state it. Where it is not obvious, the subject of the verb is shown in square brackets to show you which verb form to use.

a Felix/merecer/ganar/el premio ....

b los niños/obedecer/pero/también/protestar/a menudo ....
....

Test yourself

c en el pueblo/normalmente/refrescar/por las noches

....

d siempre/regalar/a nosotros/ropa/[ella] ....

e no/hablar/con/Nerea/ desde el verano/[yo]

....

f antes/pensar/diferente/[tú] ....

g en la casa/todos/temer/malas noticias/[nosotros]

....

h Ana/ montar/a caballo/desde/los 7 años

....

i sentirse/acomplejada/porque/ser/muy baja/[ella]

....

j ¿curarse/de la enfermedad/[tú]? ....

107 Translate the following sentences into Spanish.

a Were you living in England then? ....

b My mum picked me up from school every day.

....

c When I was little, I didn't have many friends.

....

d They felt lonely in the big city. ....

e They were always winning. ....

f She read his letter every night. ....

g We didn't have much time. ....

h They were exhausted. ....

i What were you doing? ....

j There were more than thirty of us. ....

Test yourself

108 The imperfect is used to describe something that used to happen regularly in the past. In each of the pairs of sentences below, the first sentence describes something that happened at a given time in the past. Fill in the gap in the second sentence, using the same verb as the first sentence but in the imperfect form, to describe something that used to happen regularly in the past. The first one has been done for you.

a Salimos al cine el domingo pasado. ...Salíamos.... al cine todos los domingos.

b Aquella mañana desayuné deprisa porque llegaba tarde al trabajo. Normalmente .... deprisa para no llegar tarde al trabajo.

c Vivieron tres meses en Argentina. .... en Argentina desde pequeños.

d El verano pasado fuimos a la playa. .... a la playa todos los veranos.

e Anoche cenamos pronto. En mi familia .... pronto.

f Se sintió ignorada en la fiesta. Constantemente .... ignorada.

g Vimos a Clara la semana pasada. A menudo .... a Clara.

h Juan trabajó con ellos tres meses. Juan .... con ellos frecuentemente.

i Ayer se compró unos pantalones nuevos. Normalmente se .... poca ropa.

j El fin de semana pasado vieron una película con unos amigos. .... una película todas las noches.

109 Translate these sentences into Spanish using the time expressions *desde...* and *hacía...*. Remember that in Spanish you would use the imperfect rather than the pluperfect tense. The first one has been done for you.

a He had been ill for three years. Hacía tres años que estaba enfermo/ Estaba enfermo desde hacia tres años.

b I hadn't seen her since school. ....

c We had been living in London for a while. ....

....

d They had been playing in the group for three years. ....

....

e I had had the same car for a long time. ....

....

f I hadn't eaten since breakfast. ....

g We hadn't talked since university. ....

....

Test yourself

h She had done the same job for ten years. ....

....

i Iván hadn't been on holiday for two years. ....

....

j I hadn't tidied the room for months. ....

....

110 Create a sentence in the imperfect tense using the elements given. Note that you will need verbs that are irregular in the imperfect. Remember that, in Spanish, the subject of a verb is included in the verb form so it is not necessary to state it. Where it is not obvious, the subject of the verb is shown in square brackets to show you which verb form to use.

a María/no/oír/ello/bien ....

b Luis y Antonio/ser/amigos/desde la infancia

....

c narrar/la historia/con música[ella] ....

d el zorro/escarbar/en el suelo ....

e a los tres años/ya/gatear[él] ....

f ir/poco/de fiesta/[ellos] ....

g ¿no/ir/muy deprisa/en la moto/[vosotros]?

....

h Pilar/leer/ellos/con interés ....

i ver/las montañas/desde/mi habitación/[yo]

....

j ayudar/a ellos/a pagar/el piso[ellos] ....

111 Match the two columns.

a Desde hacía cinco años	íbamos mucho a bailar.
b De jóvenes	mientras me vestía.
c Oí el ruido	cuando la llamaron.
d Estaba dormida	para ir a trabajar.
e Me levantaba a las 7	no iban a esquiar.

The perfect tense

What is the perfect tense?

The **perfect** tense is a verb form used to talk about what has or hasn't happened; for example, *I've broken my glasses*; *We haven't spoken about it*.

Using the perfect tense

➤ In English, we use the perfect tense (*have*, *has* or their shortened forms *'ve* and *'s* followed by a past participle such as *spoken*, *eaten*, *lived*, *been*) to talk about what has or hasn't happened today, this week, this year or in our lives up to now.

➤ The Spanish perfect tense is used in a similar way.

He terminado el libro.	I've finished the book.
¿Has fregado el suelo?	Have you washed the floor?
Nunca ha estado en Bolivia.	He's never been to Bolivia.
Ha vendido su caballo.	She has sold her horse.
Todavía no hemos comprado un ordenador.	We still haven't bought a computer.
Ya se han ido.	They've already left.

Grammar Extra!

You may also come across uses of the perfect tense in Spanish to talk about actions completed in the very recent past. In English, we'd use the past simple tense in such cases.

¿Lo has visto?	Did you see that?

Forming the perfect tense

➤ As in English, the perfect tense in Spanish has two parts to it. These are:

- the present tense of the verb **haber** (meaning *to have*)
- a part of the main verb called the past participle.

Forming the past participle

➤ To form the past participle of regular **-ar** verbs, take off the **-ar** ending of the infinitive and add **-ado**.

hablar (*to speak*)	→	**hablado** (*spoken*)

➤ To form the past participle of regular **-er** or **-ir** verbs, take off the **-er** or **-ir** ending of the infinitive and add **-ido**.

comer (*to eat*)	→	**comido** (*eaten*)
vivir (*to live*)	→	**vivido** (*lived*)

The perfect tense of some regular verbs

➤ The following table shows how you can combine the present tense of **haber** with the past participle of any verb to form the perfect tense. In this case, the past participles are taken from the following regular verbs: **hablar** (meaning *to speak*); **trabajar** (meaning *to work*); **comer** (meaning *to eat*); **vender** (meaning *to sell*); **vivir** (meaning *to live*); **decidir** (meaning *to decide*).

	Present of haber	Past participle	Meaning
(yo)	**he**	**hablado**	I have spoken
(tú)	**has**	**trabajado**	you have worked
(él/ella/usted)	**ha**	**comido**	he/she/it has eaten, you have eaten
(nosotros/ nosotras)	**hemos**	**vendido**	we have sold
(vosotros/ vosotras)	**habéis**	**vivido**	you have lived
(ellos/ellas/ ustedes)	**han**	**decidido**	they/you have decided

<u>Has trabajado</u> mucho. — You've worked hard.
No <u>he comido</u> nada. — I haven't eaten anything.

ⓘ Note that you should not confuse **haber** with **tener.** Even though they both mean *to have*, **haber** is only used for forming tenses and in certain impersonal expressions such as **hay** and **había** meaning *there is*, *there are*, *there was*, *there were*, and so on.

➪ *For further information on **Impersonal verbs**, see page 124.*

Verbs with irregular past participles

➤ Some past participles are irregular. There aren't too many, so try to learn them.

abrir (*to open*) → **abierto** (*opened*)
cubrir (*to cover*) → **cubierto** (*covered*)
decir (*to say*) → **dicho** (*said*)
escribir (*to write*) → **escrito** (*written*)
freír (*to fry*) → **frito** (*fried*)
hacer (*to do, to make*) → **hecho** (*done, made*)
morir (*to die*) → **muerto** (*died*)
oír (*to hear*) → **oído** (*heard*)
poner (*to put*) → **puesto** (*put*)
romper (*to break*) → **roto** (*broken*)
ver (*to see*) → **visto** (*seen*)
volver (*to return*) → **vuelto** (*returned*)

<u>He abierto</u> una cuenta en el banco. — I've opened a bank account.
No <u>ha dicho</u> nada. — He hasn't said anything.
Hoy <u>he hecho</u> muchas cosas. — I've done a lot today.
Todavía no <u>he hecho</u> los deberes. — I haven't done my homework yet.
<u>Han muerto</u> tres personas. — Three people have died.

¿Dónde <u>has puesto</u> mis zapatos? Where have you put my shoes?
Carlos <u>ha roto</u> el espejo. Carlos has broken the mirror.
Jamás <u>he visto</u> una cosa parecida. I've never seen anything like it.
¿<u>Ha vuelto</u> Ana? Has Ana come back?

Tip

he/has/ha and so on must <u>NEVER</u> be separated from the past participle. Any object pronouns go before the form of **haber** being used, and <u>NOT</u> between the form of **haber** and the past participle.

No <u>lo</u> he visto. I haven't seen it.
¿<u>Lo</u> has hecho ya? Have you done it yet?

Reflexive verbs in the perfect tense

➤ The perfect tense of reflexive verbs is formed in the same way as for ordinary verbs. The reflexive pronouns (**me**, **te**, **se**, **nos**, **os**, **se**) come before **he**, **has**, **ha**, and so on. The table below shows the perfect tense of **lavarse** in full.

(Subject pronoun)	Reflexive pronoun	Present tense of haber	Past Participle	Meaning
(yo)	**me**	**he**	**lavado**	I have washed
(tú)	**te**	**has**	**lavado**	you have washed
(él) **(ella)** **(uno)** **(usted)**	**se**	**ha**	**lavado**	he has washed she has washed one has washed it has washed you have washed
(nosotros) **(nosotras)**	**nos**	**hemos**	**lavado**	we have washed we have washed
(vosotros) **(vosotras)**	**os**	**habéis**	**lavado**	you have washed you have washed
(ellos) **(ellas)** **(ustedes)**	**se**	**han**	**lavado**	they have washed they have washed you have washed

---

Grammar Extra!

Don't use the perfect tense with **desde, desde hace** and **hace ... que** when talking about how long something has been going on for. Use the present tense instead.

Está enfermo desde julio.	He has been ill since July.
Conduce ese coche desde hace tres meses.	He has been driving that car for three months.
Hace mucho tiempo que salen juntos.	They have been going out together for a long time.

➪ For more information on the ***Present tense***, see page 5.

➤ In European Spanish you CAN use the perfect tense in the negative with **desde** and **desde hace**.

No lo he visto desde hace mucho tiempo.	I haven't seen him for a long time.

Key points

- ✔ The Spanish perfect tense is formed using the present tense of **haber** and a past participle.
- ✔ In Spanish, the perfect tense is used very much as it is in English.
- ✔ The past participle of regular **-ar** verbs ends in **-ado**, and the past participle of regular **-er** and **-ir** verbs ends in **-ido**.
- ✔ Make sure you know the following irregular past participle forms: **abierto**, **cubierto**, **dicho**, **escrito**, **frito**, **hecho**, **muerto**, **oído**, **puesto**, **roto**, **visto**, **vuelto**.

Test yourself

112 Complete the following sentences with the correct form of the perfect tense. Note that you will be using verbs that have an irregular form in the past participle. The pronoun in brackets shows you which person to use.

a Por fín .... el trabajo. **(terminar [ellos])**

b No .... nunca en su casa. **(estar [nosotros])**

c Le .... a Juan mi batería. **(vender [yo])**

d ¿Qué .... de comida? **(hacer [vosotros])**

e Esta película ya la .... **(ver [nosotros])**

f .... tu abrigo en el armario. **(poner [yo])**

g ¿Qué te .... en el trabajo? **(decir [ellos])**

h Este libro no lo .... aún. **(leer [yo])**

i .... al niño con una manta porque hace frío. **(cubrir [yo])**

j No .... aún del trabajo. **(volver [ellos])**

113 Create a sentence in the perfect tense using the elements given. Note that you will be using verbs that have an irregular form in the past participle. Remember that, in Spanish, the subject of a verb is included in the verb form so it is not necessary to state it. Where it is not obvious, the subject of the verb is shown in square brackets to show you which verb form to use.

a ¿estar/en Suecia/ya/[vosotros]? ....

b ¿qué/hacer/con el coche viejo/[tú] ....

c Arturo/ir/de vacaciones/a Francia

....

d tomar/demasiado/café [yo] ....

e ¿no/oír/la noticia/[vosotros]? ....

f montar/negocio/de ordenadores/en el pueblo [ellos]

....

g cientos de personas/morir/en el terremoto

....

h los dos países/romper/relaciones ....

i Carmen/poner/un bar ....

j hoy/ver/a él/en la estación/[yo] ....

Test yourself

114 Replace the highlighted section with an object pronoun and make sure you place it in the right position. The first one has been done for you.

a Me he comprado **las botas**. *Me las he comprado.*

b María ha regado **las plantas** esta mañana. ....

c Ya he leído **el periódico**. ....

d Los directivos han reunido **a los trabajadores**. ....

e ¿Habéis pintado **las paredes** otra vez? ....

f Me he encontrado **a Lucía** en la calle. ....

g Han roto **el jarrón**. ....

h Ha sacado una foto **a las niñas**. ....

i He terminado **el informe**. ....

j Ha vendido **el coche**. ....

115 Complete the following sentences with the correct past participle.

a Los hemos .... en seguida. **(coger)**

b Los han .... desde el año pasado. **(usar)**

c Han .... en muchas partes de España. **(vivir)**

d He .... la ventana un poco. **(abrir)**

e ¿Quién te ha .... eso? **(decir)**

f Está todo .... de nieve. **(cubrir)**

g ¿Quién ha .... eso? **(hacer)**

h ¿Dónde has .... las llaves? **(poner)**

i Ya han .... de las vacaciones. **(volver)**

j Esa película ya la hemos .... **(ver)**

116 Cross out the names that do not go with the verbs.

a hemos comido	Alberto/el perro/María y yo
b han estudiado	los profesores/el alumno/los estudiantes
c habéis vuelto	vosotros/mi hemana/Pedro y tú
d he hecho	Cristina/yo/las dos amigas
e hemos escrito	Nuria y yo/nosotras/Andrea
f ha puesto	Ana/el perro/los abuelos

g han cogido ustedes/mis primos/Lorenzo

h hemos recibido nosotros tres/los carteros/María y yo

i has salido tú/los abuelos/Cristina

j he querido los profesores/yo/Alberto

117 Respond to the following sentences using the structure *Ya* + reflexive pronoun + the verb in the perfect tense. The first one has been done for you.

a Tienes que **ducharte**. Ya me he duchado.

b ¿Van a **sentarse**? ....

c ¿Cuándo va a **acostarse**? ....

d Coge una toalla para **secarte**.. ....

e ¿No va a **afeitarse**? ....

f ¿Van a **enfadarse** con nosotros? ....

g ¿Crees que va a **dormirse** pronto? ....

h ¿Cuándo va a **irse** de casa? ....

i ¿Van a **repetirlo**? ....

j ¿Cómo vas a **disfrazarte**? ....

118 Sometimes Spanish uses the perfect tense to talk about actions that have taken place very recently. Translate the following sentences into English.

a ¿Has notado eso? ....

b ¿Has visto la forma en que la mira?

....

c ¿Has corrido para llegar aquí? ....

d Se ha ido ahora mismo. ¿Lo has visto?

....

e ¿Has visto su cara cuando lo oyó?

....

Test yourself

119 Translate these English sentences into Spanish. Remember that, when talking about how long something has been going on, Spanish does not use the perfect tense like English does. The first one is done for you.

a I have been ill since January. *Estoy enfermo desde enero.*

b We've known him since the summer. ....

c They have been living here since last year.

....

d She has been painting for five years. ....

e He has had the bike for a long time.

....

f He has been working at the hospital since last year.

....

g Since when have you been interested in my work?

....

h She has done ballet since she was little. ....

i I have been studying French for three years.

....

j They have using the same system for years.

....

120 Translate the following sentences into Spanish.

a We haven't finished it. ....

b We've already seen it. ....

c She has changed a lot. ....

d Who has eaten the cake? ....

e I have forgotten your name ....

f Have you done it yet? ....

g Have you opened the file? ....

h He hasn't said much. ....

i I haven't done my homework yet. ....

j I haven't eaten yet. ....

The pluperfect or past perfect tense

What is the pluperfect tense?
The **pluperfect** is a verb tense that is used to talk about what had happened or had been true at a point in the past, for example, *I'd forgotten to finish my homework.*

Using the pluperfect tense

➤ When talking about the past, we sometimes refer to things that had happened previously. In English, we often use *had* followed by a past participle such as *spoken*, *eaten*, *lived* or *been* to do this. This tense is known as the pluperfect or past perfect tense.

➤ The Spanish pluperfect tense is used and formed in a similar way.

Ya habíamos comido cuando llegó. We'd already eaten when he arrived.
Nunca lo había visto antes de aquella noche. I'd never seen it before that night.

Forming the pluperfect tense

➤ Like the perfect tense, the pluperfect tense in Spanish has two parts to it:

- the imperfect tense of the verb **haber** (meaning *to have*)
- the past participle.

➪ *For more information on the* ***Imperfect tense*** *and* ***Past participles****, see pages 84 and 93.*

➤ The table below shows how you can combine the imperfect tense of **haber** with the past participle of any verb to form the pluperfect tense. Here, the past participles are taken from the following regular verbs: **hablar** (meaning *to speak*); **trabajar** (meaning *to work*); **comer** (meaning *to eat*); **vender** (meaning *to sell*); **vivir** (meaning *to live*); **decidir** (meaning *to decide*).

(Subject pronoun)	Imperfect of haber	Past Participle	Meaning
(yo)	había	hablado	I had spoken
(tú)	habías	trabajado	you had worked
(él/ella/usted)	había	comido	he/she/it/you had eaten
(nosotros/ nosotras)	habíamos	vendido	we had sold
(vosotros/ vosotras)	habíais	vivido	you had lived
(ellos/ellas/ ustedes)	habían	decidido	they/you had decided

No había trabajado antes. He hadn't worked before.
Había vendido su caballo. She had sold her horse.

➤ Remember that some very common verbs have irregular past participles.

abrir (*to open*) → **abierto** (*opened*)
cubrir (*to cover*) → **cubierto** (*covered*)
decir (*to say*) → **dicho** (*said*)
escribir (*to write*) → **escrito** (*written*)
freír (*to fry*) → **frito** (*fried*)
hacer (*to do, to make*) → **hecho** (*done, made*)
morir (*to die*) → **muerto** (*died*)
oír (*to hear*) → **oído** (*heard*)
poner (*to put*) → **puesto** (*put*)
romper (*to break*) → **roto** (*broken*)
ver (*to see*) → **visto** (*seen*)
volver (*to return*) → **vuelto** (*returned*)

No <u>había dicho</u> nada. He hadn't said anything.
Tres personas <u>habían muerto</u>. Three people had died.

Tip

había/habías/habían and so on must <u>NEVER</u> be separated from the past participle. Any object pronouns go before the form of **haber** being used, and <u>NOT</u> between the form of **haber** and the past participle.

No lo había visto. I hadn't seen it.

Reflexive verbs in the pluperfect tense

➤ The pluperfect tense of reflexive verbs is formed in the same way as for ordinary verbs. The reflexive pronouns (**me**, **te**, **se**, **nos**, **os**, **se**) come before **había**, **habías**, **había**, and so on. The table below shows the pluperfect tense of **lavarse** in full.

(Subject pronoun)	Reflexive pronoun	Imperfect tense of haber	Past Participle	Meaning
(yo)	me	había	lavado	I had washed
(tú)	te	habías	lavado	you had washed
(él) (ella) (uno) (usted)	se	había	lavado	he had washed she had washed one had washed it had washed you had washed
(nosotros) (nosotras)	nos	habíamos	lavado	we had washed we had washed
(vosotros) (vosotras)	os	habíais	lavado	you had washed you had washed
(ellos) (ellas) (ustedes)	se	habían	lavado	they had washed they had washed you had washed

Grammar Extra!

Don't use the pluperfect with **desde**, **desde hacía** and **hacía ... que** when talking about how long something had been going on for. Use the imperfect instead.

Estaba enfermo desde 2000.	He had been ill since 2000.
Conducía ese coche desde hacía tres meses.	He had been driving that car for three months.
Hacía mucho tiempo que salían juntos.	They had been going out together for a long time.

➪ For more information on the ***Imperfect tense***, see page 84.

In European Spanish you CAN use the pluperfect tense in the negative with **desde** and **desde hacía**.

No lo había visto desde hacía mucho tiempo.	I hadn't seen him for a long time.

Key points

- ✔ The Spanish pluperfect tense is formed using the imperfect tense of **haber** and a past particple.
- ✔ In Spanish, the pluperfect tense is used very much as it is in English.
- ✔ The past participle of regular **-ar** verbs ends in **-ado**, while that of regular **-er** and **-ir** verbs ends in **-ido**.
- ✔ Make sure you know the irregular forms: **abierto**, **cubierto**, **dicho**, **escrito**, **frito**, **hecho**, **muerto**, **oído**, **puesto**, **roto**, **visto**, **vuelto**.

PRACTICE PRACTICE PRACTICE PRACTICE PRACTICE PRAC

Test yourself

121 Complete the following sentences with the correct form of the pluperfect tense. The pronoun in brackets shows you which person to use. The first one has been done for you.

a *Habían probado*...... todo tipo de métodos. **(probar [ellos])**

b Los dos exploradores lo .... sin ayuda. **(conseguir)**

c Tanto sufrimiento la .... mucho. **(marcar)**

d .... el dinero entre todos los vecinos. **(reunir)**

e Sus antepasados .... fuera de Europa. **(nacer)**

f Marta .... un collar para su madre. **(comprar)**

g ¿No lo .... todavía? **(ordenar [tú])**

h No .... conmigo. **(hablar [ellos])**

i Cuando llegaron, ya .... la cena. **(preparar [nosotros])**

j Lo .... de verde. **(pintar [ellos])**

122 Create a sentence in the pluperfect tense using the elements given. Note that you will be using verbs that have an irregular past participle. Remember that, in Spanish, the subject of a verb is included in the verb form so it is not necessary to state it. Where it is not obvious, the subject of the verb is shown in square brackets to show you which verb form to use. The first one has been done for you.

a el niño/poner/los juguetes/debajo de la cama

El niño había puesto los juguetes debajo de la cama...........................

b ¿qué/decidir/vosotros/antes de hablar/con él?

....

c yo/sospechar/la verdad/desde el principio

....

d el dueño/morir/en 1965 ....

e ellos/ya/oír/la sirena ....

f no/ver/a ellos/desde la semana anterior/[yo]

....

g nunca/decir/nada malo/de ella/[nosotros]

....

h Emilio/no/molestarse/en absoluto/por eso

....

i ¿dónde/guardar/el dinero/Gloria?

....

j Elena/ya/ponerse/en contacto/conmigo

....

123 Replace the highlighted verbs with the perfect tense. Note that you will be using verbs that have an irregular past participle. The first one has been done for you.

a Mis padres no **oyeron** el teléfono. habían oído

b Mi madre **frió** el pescado para la cena. ....

c Mara lo **hizo** todo sola. ....

d Sus padres **volvieron** a vivir al pueblo. ....

e Ana **escribió** una carta de queja. ....

f Los policías **pusieron** unas barreras. ....

g Tú lo **rompiste**. ....

h La nieve **cubrió** el campo. ....

i Los profesores **dijeron** que no. ....

j Yo **abrí** la puerta ....

124 Replace the highlighted section with an object pronoun and make sure you place it in the right position. The first one has been done for you.

a Aún no habían leído **el informe**. Aún no lo habían leído.

b Se había comprado **una moto**. ....

c Los padres habían organizado **una fiesta**.

....

d Habían construido **un muro** entre las dos casas.

....

e Se había encontrado **a su profesora** en el concierto.

....

f Ana había plantado **los tomates** esa tarde. ....

g Carolina había hecho unos vestidos **a las niñas.**

....

h Habían terminado toda **la tarta**. ....

i Habíamos pintado de nuevo **la casa**. ....

j Mis padres habían comprado **unas tierras** cerca.

Test yourself

125 Respond to the following sentences using the structure *Ya* + reflexive pronoun + the pluperfect tense. The first one has been done for you.

a Tenía que **escribirlo**. *Ya los había escrito.*

b ¿Ibais a **hacerlo**?

c ¿Cuándo ibais a **acostaros**?

d Tenían que **ponerse** de pie.

e ¿No ibas a **afeitarte**?

f ¿Iban a **veros**?

g ¿Iba a **morirse**?

h ¿Cuándo iban a **salir**?

i Tenía que **destruir** las pruebas.

j Esperaba **oír** la señal.

126 Translate the following into Spanish.

a They hadn't finished it.

b Laura hadn't changed since then.

c I had not decided to go.

d Had you already got up at that time? [***vosotros*** form]

e Had you told your parents?

f She had never skied before.

g We had never visit the cathedral.

h He still hadn't been to see that film.

i She'd already decided to leave him.

j They had already started the exam.

127 Translate these sentences into Spanish. Remember to use the imperfect tense. The first one has been done for you.

a She had been abroad since May. *Estaba en el extranjero desde mayo.*

b We had known him since the Autumn.

c He had been writing since his youth.

d She had been riding a horse since she was little.

e We had been working at the project since last year.

....

f They had been going out for a while. ....

g They had been writing to each other for months.

....

h They had been getting ready for a year. ....

i We had loved each other for years. ....

j I had been looking at her for a while. ....

128 Match the two columns.

a What had he done?	Habían ido a París.
b How had you do it?	Habíamos acordado dividirlo entre las dos.
c Where had they gone?	Habíamos tardado una hora.
d What had you and Laura agreed?	Había roto el jarrón.
e How long had we taken?	Había usado pinturas.

129 Create a sentence in the pluperfect tense using the elements below. Where the subject of the sentence is unclear, it is shown in square brackets. Pay attention to the order of pronouns where these are required. The first one has been done for you.

a Marta/ya/decir/a nosotros/lo de la pelea
Marta ya nos había dicho lo de la pelea.

b yo/ya/escribir/a él/con la respuesta ....

c por qué/no/hacer/ello/mejor/[vosotros]

....

d ¿cómo/romper/ello/[tú]? ....

e ¿quién/escribir/el mensaje?

....

f primera vez/no/oír/[yo] ....

g freír/patatas/para la cena [yo] ....

h Teresa/poner/móvil/en el bolso ....

i ponerse/muy gordos/[vosotros] ....

j no/volver/a casa/desde/la pelea/[ella] ....

The passive

What is the passive?

The **passive** is a verb form that is used when the subject of the verb is the person or thing that is affected by the action, for example, *Mary is liked by everyone; Two children were hurt in an accident; The house was sold*.

Using the passive

- Verbs can be either active or passive.
- In a normal or active sentence, the subject of the verb is the person or thing doing the action described by the verb. The object of the verb is the person or thing that the verb most directly affects.
  Peter (*subject*) wrote (*active verb*) a letter (*object*).
  Ryan (*subject*) hit (*active verb*) me (*object*).
- Provided the verb has an object, in English, as in Spanish, you can turn an active sentence round to make it a passive sentence by using *to be* followed by a past participle. In this case the person or thing directly affected by the action becomes the subject of the verb.
  A letter (*subject*) was written (*passive verb*).
  I (*subject*) was hit (*passive verb*).
- To show who or what is responsible for the action in a passive construction, in English you use *by*.
  I (*subject*) was hit (*passive verb*) by Ryan.
- You use the passive rather than the active when you want to focus attention on the person or thing affected by the action rather than the person or thing that carries it out.
  John was injured in an accident.
- You can also use the passive when you don't know who is responsible for the action.
  Several buses were vandalized.

Forming the passive

- In English we use the verb *to be* with a past participle (*was painted, were seen, are made*) to form the passive. In Spanish, the passive is formed in exactly the same way, using the verb **ser** (meaning *to be*) and a past participle. When you say who the action is or was done by, you use the preposition **por** (meaning *by*).

➪ *For more information on the **Past participle**, see page 93.*

Son fabricados en España.	They're made in Spain.
Es hecho a mano.	It's made by hand *or* It's handmade.
Fue escrito por JK Rowling.	It was written by JK Rowling.
La casa fue construida en 1956.	The house was built in 1956.

El cuadro <u>fue pintado</u> por mi padre. The picture was painted by my father.
El colegio va a <u>ser modernizado</u>. The school is going to be modernized.

Note that the ending of the past participle agrees with the subject of the verb **ser** in exactly the same way as an adjective would.

➤ Here is the preterite of the **-ar** verb **enviar** (meaning *to send*) in its passive form.

(Subject pronoun)	Preterite of ser	Past Participle	Meaning
(yo)	fui	**enviado** (masculine) **enviada** (feminine)	I was sent
(tú)	fuiste	**enviado** (masculine) **enviada** (feminine)	you were sent
(él) (ella) (usted)	fue	**enviado** **enviada** **enviado** (masculine) **enviada** (feminine)	he was sent she was sent you were sent
(nosotros) (nosotras)	fuimos fuimos	**enviados** **enviadas**	we were sent we were sent
(vosotros) (vosotras)	fuisteis	**enviados** **enviadas**	you were sent you were sent
(ellos) (ellas) (ustedes)	fueron	**enviados** **enviadas** **enviados** (masculine) **enviadas** (feminine)	they were sent they were sent you were sent you were sent

➤ You can form other tenses in the passive by changing the tense of the verb **ser**.
Future: **Serán enviados.** They will be sent.
Perfect: **Han sido enviados.** They have been sent.

➤ Irregular past participles are the same as they are in the perfect tense.

*For more information on **Irregular past participles**, see page 94.*

Avoiding the passive

➤ Passives are not as common in Spanish as they are in English. Spanish native speakers usually prefer to avoid using the passive by:

- using the active construction instead of the passive
  La policía <u>interrogó</u> al sospechoso. The suspect was interrogated by the police.
  Su madre le regaló un libro. He was given a book by his mother.

- using an active verb in the third person plural
  <u>Ponen</u> demasiados anuncios en la televisión. Too many adverts are shown on television.

- using a reflexive construction (as long as you don't need to say who the action is done by)

Se fabrican en España.	They're made in Spain.
Se hace a mano.	It's made by hand.
La casa se construyó en 1956.	The house was built in 1956.
Todos los libros se han vendido.	All the books have been sold.

➪ *For more information on **Reflexive verbs**, see page 51.*

- using an impersonal **se** construction

Se cree que va a morir.	It is thought he will die.

➪ *For more information on the impersonal **se** construction, see page 127.*

Tip

Active verbs often have both a direct object and an indirect object.
He gave me (*indirect object*) a book (*direct object*).

In English, both of these objects can be made the subject of a passive verb; *I was given a book*. or *A book was given to me*.

In Spanish, an indirect object can NEVER become the subject of a passive verb.

Key points

✔ The passive is formed using **ser** + past participle, sometimes followed by **por** (meaning *by*).
✔ The past participle must agree with the subject of **ser**.
✔ Passive constructions are not as common as they are in English. You can often avoid the passive by using the third person plural of the active verb or by using a reflexive construction.

Test yourself

130 Create a passive sentence in the past (*fui, fuiste* etc + participle) using the elements below. Remember that some verbs have irregular past participles. The first one has been done for you.

a el poema/escribir/su abuelo *El poema fue escrito por su abuelo.*

b la casa/construir/un famoso arquitecto

....

c el proyecto/revisar/el ingeniero

....

d la calle/cerrar/la policía ....

e muchos/herir/la bomba ....

f el reloj/fabricar/en Suiza ....

g la escultura/crear/Giacometti ....

h la escena/rodar/en directo ....

i el cuadro/comprar/un magnate

....

j los derechos/adquirir/la editorial

....

131 Complete the following sentences with the correct form of the passive in the past tense. Remember that some verbs have irregular past participles. The first one has been done for you.

a La ventana *fue abierta* por la fuerza. **(abrir)**

b Los expertos .... sobre el problema. **(consultar)**

c Dicen que los rehenes .... por sus secuestradores. **(maltratar)**

d Todos invitados .... a sus habitaciones. **(llevar)**

e Los sospechosos .... en libertad. **(poner)**

f Todas las propuestas .... en el Parlamento. **(debatir)**

g El ladrón .... por una mujer. **(ver)**

h Según la leyenda, la ciudad .... por un terremoto. **(destruir)**

i Todos los obstáculos .... **(eliminar)**

j .... varias estatuas del museo. **(robar)**

Test yourself

132 Replace the highlighted passive form in the past with a passive in the future: *será*, *serás* etc + participle. The first example has been done for you.

a El edificio **fue construido** cerca del río. *será construido*

b El coche **fue fabricado** en Alemania. ......

c La decisión **fue anunciada** en televisión. ......

d Los bienes **fueron repartidos** entre los herederos. ......

e La película **fue rodada** en Madrid. ......

f El sospechoso **fue interrogado** por la policía. ......

g El nacimiento **fue celebrado** por todos. ......

h El edificio **fue renovado** totalmente. ......

i Las obras **fueron donadas** por un magnate. ......

j Los alimentos **fueron empaquetados** en el almacén. ......

133 Replace the highlighted passive form with passive in the past perfect: *ha*, *has* etc + *sido* + participle. The first one has been done for you.

a El metal **fue recubierto** con oro. *ha sido recubierto*

b Las propuestas **fueron rechazadas** en el Congreso. ......

c **Fui traicionado** por mis enemigos. ......

d El paquete **fue enviado** con urgencia. ......

e El acontecimiento **fue celebrado** con solemnidad. ......

f El documento **fue escrito** en árabe. ......

g Los rebeldes **fueron derrotados** . ...

h Todos los problemas **fueron eliminados**. ......

i Los experimentos **fueron realizados** en el laboratorio. ......

j **Fueron tratados** con respeto. ......

Test yourself

134 Replace the highlighted passive form with the more common reflexive construction using *se*. The first one has been done for you.

a La sala **fue renovada** hace tres años. *se renovó*

b **Fueron construidos** en Portugal. ......

c El espectáculo **fue cancelado** anoche. ......

d Los alimentos **serán distribuidos** por todo el territorio. ......

e El documento **fue redactado** la semana pasa. ......

f El problema **fue analizado** en la reunión. ......

g Las conclusiones **serán explicadas** durante el programa. ......

h La finca **fue adquirida** hace poco. ......

i El motor **será reparado** en breve. ......

j Los productos **serán empaquetado** antes de mandarlos. ......

135 Match the two columns.

a Empaquetado en Grecia.	Flat for sale.
b Es hecho a mano.	We buy gold.
c Se vende piso.	It's handmade.
d Se compra oro.	It's made in Spain.
e Se fabrica en España.	Packed in Greece.

Test yourself

136 Translate the following passive sentences into Spanish using a reflexive construction. The first one has been done for you.

a The shoes are manufactured in Mallorca.
Los zapatos se fabrican en Mallorca.

b The series is being filmed in Argentina.
....

c Too much time has been wasted. ....

d All the money has been spent. ....

e New trees have been planted opposite the museum.
....

f The flats were sold very quickly. ....

g It was invented in 1993. ....

h It was done with care. ....

i It was bought with money from the company.
....

j They were carefully revised. ....

137 Translate the following passive sentences into Spanish using an active construction. The first one has been done for you.

a The players were taken to the hotel. *Llevaron a los jugadores al hotel.*

b We were served dinner by the waiter. ....

c We were taken to a secret place. ....

d The plan is being revised by the committee.
....

e They were surprised by the police. ....

f She was pushed. ....

g He was given a warning by his boss. ....

h It was carefully examined. ....

i We were invited on Sunday. ....

j It was written by a friend. ....

The gerund

What is a gerund?

The **gerund** is a verb form ending in *-ing* which is used to form verb tenses, and which in English may also be used as an adjective and a noun, for example, *What are you doing?; the setting sun; Swimming is easy!*

Using the gerund

➤ In Spanish, the gerund is a form of the verb that usually ends in **-ando** or **-iendo** and is used to form continuous tenses.

Estoy trabajando.	I'm working.
Estamos comiendo.	We are eating.

➤ It is used with **estar** to form continuous tenses such as:

- the present continuous

Está fregando los platos.	He's washing the dishes.
Estoy escribiendo una carta.	I'm writing a letter.

➪ *For more information on the **Present continuous**, see page 37.*

- the imperfect continuous

Estaba reparando el coche.	She was fixing the car.
Estaban esperándonos.	They were waiting for us.

[i] Note that continuous tenses should only be used in Spanish to describe action that is or was happening at the time you are talking about.

Grammar Extra!

Sometimes another verb, such as **ir** or **venir** is used instead of **estar** with a gerund in continuous tenses. These verbs emphasize the gradualness or the slowness of the process.

Iba anocheciendo.	It was getting dark.
Eso lo vengo diciendo desde hace tiempo.	That's what I've been saying all along.

➤ The gerund is also used after certain other verbs:

- **seguir haciendo algo** and **continuar haciendo algo** are both used with the meaning of *to go on doing something* or *to continue doing something*.

Siguió cantando *or* **Continuó cantando.**	He went on singing *or* He continued singing.
Siguieron leyendo *or* **Continuaron leyendo.**	They went on reading *or* They continued reading.

- **llevar** with a time expression followed by the gerund is used to talk about how long someone has been doing something:

Lleva dos años estudiando inglés.	He's been studying English for two years.
Llevo una hora esperando aquí.	I've been waiting here for an hour.

Note that the present tense of **llevar** followed by a gerund means the same as the English *have/has been + -ing*.

➤ **pasar(se)** with a time expression followed by the gerund is used to talk about how long you've spent doing something.

Pasé *or* **Me pasé el fin de semana estudiando.**	I spent the weekend studying.
Pasamos *or* **Nos pasamos el día leyendo.**	We spent the day reading.

➤ Verbs of movement, such as **salir** (meaning *to come out* or *to go out*), **entrar** (meaning *to come in* or *to go in*), and **irse** (meaning *to leave*) are sometimes followed by a gerund such as **corriendo** (meaning *running*) or **cojeando** (meaning *limping*). The English equivalent of **salir corriendo**, **entrar corriendo** or **irse cojeando**, would be *to run out*, *to run in* or *to limp off* in such cases.

Salió corriendo.	He ran out.
Se fue cojeando.	He limped off.

Tip

Use a past participle not a gerund to talk about physical position.

Estaba tumbado en el sofá.	He was lying on the sofa.
Estaba sentada.	She was sitting down.
Lo encontré tendido en el suelo.	I found him lying on the floor.
La escalera estaba apoyada contra la pared.	The ladder was leaning against the wall.

➪ For more information on the ***Past participles,*** see page 93.

➤ You will also come across the gerund used in other ways. For example:

Los vimos jugando al fútbol.	We saw them playing football.
Estudiando, aprobarás.	By studying, *or* If you study, you'll pass.

Forming the gerund of regular verbs

➤ To form the gerund of regular **-ar** verbs, take off the **-ar** ending of the infinitive to form the stem, and add **-ando.**

Infinitive	Stem	Gerund
hablar	habl-	hablando
trabajar	trabaj-	trabajando

➤ To form the gerund of regular **-er** and **-ir** verbs, take off the **-er** and **-ir** ending of the infinitive to form the stem, and add **-iendo.**

Infinitive	Stem	Gerund
comer	**com-**	**comiendo**
vivir	**viv-**	**viviendo**

The gerund of irregular verbs

➤ Some verbs have an irregular gerund form. You have to learn these.

Infinitives	Meaning	Gerund	Meaning
decir	to say	**diciendo**	saying
dormir	to sleep	**durmiendo**	sleeping
freír	to fry	**friendo**	frying
morir	to die	**muriendo**	dying
pedir	to ask for	**pidiendo**	asking for
poder	to be able to	**pudiendo**	being able to
reír	to laugh	**riendo**	laughing
seguir	to follow	**siguiendo**	following
sentir	to feel	**sintiendo**	feeling
venir	to come	**viniendo**	coming
vestir	to dress	**vistiendo**	dressing

➤ In the next group of verbs there is a **y** rather than the normal **i**.

Infinitives	Meaning	Gerund	Meaning
caer	to fall	**cayendo**	falling
creer	to believe	**creyendo**	believing
leer	to read	**leyendo**	reading
oír	to hear	**oyendo**	hearing
traer	to bring	**trayendo**	bringing
ir	to go	**yendo**	going

Tip

In English, we often use *-ing* forms as adjectives, for example, *running water*, *shining eyes*, *the following day*. In Spanish, you cannot use the **-ando** and **-iendo** forms like this. Instead, there are sometimes corresponding forms ending in **-ante** and **-iente** that can be used as adjectives.

agua corriente	running water
ojos brillantes	shining eyes
Al día siguiente, visitamos Toledo.	The following day we visited Toledo.

Similarly, in English, we often use the *-ing* forms as nouns. In Spanish you have to use the infinitive instead.

Fumar es malo para la salud.	Smoking is bad for you.

Position of pronouns with the gerund

➤ Object pronouns and reflexive pronouns are usually attached to the end of the gerund, although you can also often put them before **estar** in continuous tenses.

Estoy hablándote *or* **Te estoy hablando.**	I'm talking to you.
Está vistiéndose *or* **Se está vistiendo.**	He's getting dressed.
Estaban mostrándoselo *or* **Se lo estaban mostrando.**	They were showing it to him/her/them/you.

ℹ Note that you will always have to add an accent to keep the stress in the same place when adding pronouns to the end of a gerund.

KEY POINTS

- ✔ Use the gerund in continuous tenses with **estar** as well as after **seguir** and **continuar.**
- ✔ Gerunds for **-ar** verbs add **-ando** to the stem of the verb.
- ✔ Gerunds for **-er** and **-ir** verbs usually add **-iendo** to the stem of the verb.
- ✔ **-ando** and **-iendo** gerunds cannot be used as adjectives or nouns.
- ✔ You can attach pronouns to the end of the gerund, or sometimes put them before the previous verb.

For further explanation of grammatical terms, please see pages viii-x.

Test yourself

138 Complete the following sentences with the gerund. The first one has been done for you.

a Tenía fiebre y estaba ..estornudando..... sin parar. **(estornudar)**

b ¿Por qué estabas .... tanto? **(chillar)**

c Sus amigos la están .... mucho en el colegio. **(ayudar)**

d El pánico se fue .... entre la población. **(extenderse)**

e Llevo dos años .... alemán. **(estudiando)**

f Los dos iban .... tonterías. **(cantar)**

g Los organizadores estaban .... la sala. **(preparar)**

h Cuando los vi se estaban .... **(bañar)**

i Ya estoy .... la maleta para irme. **(hacer)**

j Llevo veinte minutos .... **(esperar)**

139 Complete the following sentences with the gerund. Note that you will need verbs that are irregular in the gerund. The first one has been done for you.

a Sigamos ..leyendo........ solare los verbos. **(leer)**

b Estamos .... en el campo. **(vivir)**

c Continuó .... que no era cierto. **(creer)**

d Me estoy .... de frío. **(morir)**

e Estamos .... a trabajar en autobús. **(ir)**

f ¿Qué estáis .... ? **(decir)**

g ¡Me estoy .... de aquí! **(caer)**

h Estaban .... la tele. **(ver)**

i Todavía siguen .... **(dormir)**

j Te lo estoy .... por favor. **(pedir)**

140 Replace the highlighted section with the structure *seguir* + gerund. Make sure you match the tense of the highlighted verb. The first sentence has been done for you.

a Ana **leía** en el sofa. Ana seguía leyendo en el sofá. ....

b Los chicos **duermen** todavía. ....

c Mi tía **hablaba** por teléfono. ....

d Los invitados **comen**. ....

Test yourself

e Patxi **insiste** en que él no lo hizo.

....

f ¿Vosotros **estudiáis** en la biblioteca?

....

g **Escribe** con pluma. ....

h **Iba** al trabajo en bicicleta. ....

i Nuria y Julia **eran** amigas. ....

j **Conducía** un coche rojo. ....

141 Create a sentence using *llevar* + gerund with the elements given, to express how long something lasted or has lasted. Make the sentence in the present or in the past (imperfect) as indicated. The subject of the verb is shown in square brackets when necessary. The first two have been done for you.

a tres días/trabajar/sin descanso/[yo] ***(imperfect)***

Llevaba tres días trabajando sin descanso.

b Nerea y Pablo/un año/estudiar/japonés/***(present)***

Nerea y Pablo llevan un año estudiando japonés.

c dos semanas/sin saber/de ellos/[nosotros] ***(imperfect)***

....

d Alicia/una hora/esperar/en el café/ ***(present)***

....

e Juan/tres años/trabajar/en la misma empresa ***(present)***

....

f tres noches/dormir/en el sofá/[él] ***(imperfect)***

....

g Jorge/tres horas/jugar/al ordenador ***(present)***

....

h una hora/quejarse/[tú] ***(present)***

....

i cuánto/tiempo/Toni/estudiar ***(present)***

....

j ya/cinco años/vivir/en Mallorca/[nosotros] ***(imperfect)***

....

Test yourself

142 Create a sentence to show how long someone has been doing something using *pasarse* + gerund and the elements given. Make the sentence in the present or in the past (preterite) as indicated. The subject of the verb is shown in square brackets when necessary. The first two have been done for you.

a todo el día/estudiar/[yo] ***(preterite)***
Me pasé todo el día estudiando.

b las horas/sin/hacer/nada/[ellos] ***(present)***
Se pasan las horas sin hacer nada.

c obreros/tres días/quitar/basura ***(preterite)***

....

d Clara/la tarde/maquillarse ***(preterite)***

....

e el pobre chico/los fines de semana/ver/la tele ***(present)***

....

f Juan y Luis/la mañana/arreglar/el coche ***(preterite)***

....

g Mar y Eva/las horas/hablar/por teléfono ***(present)***

....

h la semana/correr/de un lado para otro/[yo] ***(present)***

....

i tres días/en la cárcel/[él] ***(preterite)***

....

j mis hijos y yo/la vida/discutir ***(present)***

....

Test yourself

143 Complete the gaps to create sentences of movement using *salir/entrar/ir* + gerund with the verbs shown in brackets. Make the sentences in the past tense. The first one has been done for you.

a El ladrón ..*salió corriendo*..... del bar **(correr [salir])**

b La niña .... en la habitación. **(saltar [entrar])**

c Los pájaros .... **(volar [irse])**

d El tronco .... por la cuesta. **(rodar [bajar])**

e La pelota .... por la calle. **(botar [ir])**

f Yo .... porque llegaba tarde. **(correr [irse])**

g Los participantes en la carrera de sacos .... al sonar la señal. **(botar [salir])**

h Ana y yo .... para coger el autobús. **(correr [ir])**

i Pedro .... **(arrastrarse [salir])**

j Los actores .... al escenario. **(corriendo [entrar])**

144 Translate the following sentences into Spanish. Remember that when English uses the gerund '–ing' form as a noun, Spanish uses the infinitive. The first one has been done for you.

a Smoking is bad for your health *Fumar es malo para la salud.*..................

b Running twice a week is a good exercise.

....

c Reading is her favourite hobby. ....

d Eating too much salt is not good. ....

e Crying is not going to solve anything ....

f Revising a bit before the exam is a good idea.

....

g Arguing with him won't help. ....

h Cleaning the house is not something I like.

....

i Watching too much TV becomes boring.

....

j Listening to them is always good. ....

Test yourself

145 Create sentences using the reflexive pronoun + the gerund in the present tense. The first one has been done for you.

a estar vistiéndose **(Luis)** *Luis se está visitiendo./Luis está visitiéndose.*

b estar besándose **(los novios)** ....

c estar maquillándose **(la actriz)** ....

d estar insultándose **(los políticos)** ....

e estar despertándose **(el bebé)** ....

f estar duchándose **(Carmen)** ....

g estar acostándose **(Antonio)** ....

h estar secándose **(la ropa)** ....

i estar enfadándose **(yo)** ....

j estar confundiendose **(tú)** ....

146 Translate the following into Spanish.

a We like playing tennis. ....

b We were listening to music. ....

c I spend my life waiting for you. ....

d No littering. ....

e Do you like travelling? ....

f They were lying down. ....

g She's getting dressed. ....

h They were crossing the street. ....

i I'm reading a novel. ....

j Walking is a good habit. ....

Impersonal verbs

> **What is an impersonal verb?**
> An **impersonal verb** is a verb whose subject is *it*, but this '*it*' does not refer to any specific thing; for example, *It's going to rain; It's nine o'clock.*

Verbs that are always used impersonally

➤ There are some verbs such as **llover** (meaning *to rain*) and **nevar** (meaning *to snow*), that are only used in the '*it*' form, the infinitive, and as a gerund (the *-ing* form of the verb). These are called impersonal verbs because there is no person, animal or thing performing the action.

Llueve.	It's raining.
Está lloviendo.	It's raining.
Va a llover.	It's going to rain.
Nieva.	It's snowing.
Está nevando.	It's snowing.
Nevaba.	It was snowing.
Estaba nevando.	It was snowing.
Mañana nevará.	It will snow tomorrow.

Verbs that are sometimes used impersonally

➤ There are also some other very common verbs that are sometimes used as impersonal verbs, for example **hacer**, **haber** and **ser**.

➤ **hacer** is used in a number of impersonal expressions relating to the weather:

Hace frío/calor.	It's cold/hot.
Ayer hacía mucho frío/calor.	It was very cold/hot yesterday.
Hace sol/viento.	It's sunny/windy.
Va a hacer sol/viento.	It's going to be sunny/windy.
Hace un tiempo estupendo/horrible.	It's a lovely/horrible day.

➤ **hacer** is also used in combination with **que** and **desde** in impersonal time expressions, to talk about how long something has been going on for or how long it is since something happened.

Hace seis meses que vivo aquí. *or* **Vivo aquí desde hace seis meses.**	I've been living here for six months.
Hace tres años que estudio español *or* **Estudio español desde hace tres años.**	I've been studying Spanish for three years.
Hace mucho tiempo que no la veo *or* **No la veo desde hace mucho tiempo.**	I haven't seen her for ages *or* It is ages since I saw her.
Hace varias semanas que no voy por allí *or* **No voy por allí desde hace varias semanas.**	I haven't been there for several weeks *or* It is several weeks since I went there.

ℹ Note the use of the present simple in Spanish in the above examples where in English we'd use the perfect tense or the past tense.

➤ **hacer** is also used impersonally in the expression (**me/te/le**) **hace falta**, which means *it is necessary* (*for me/you/him*).

Si hace falta, voy.	I'll go if necessary.
No hace falta llamar.	We/You/I needn't call.
Me hace falta otro vaso más.	I need another glass.
No hace falta ser un experto.	You don't need to be an expert.
No hacía falta.	It wasn't necessary.

ℹ Note that not all impersonal expressions in Spanish are translated into English using impersonal expressions.

➤ **haber** too can be used impersonally with the meaning *there is/there are, there was/there were, there will be*, and so on. It has the special form **hay** in the present. For the other tenses, you take the third person singular (the *'it'* form) of **haber** in the appropriate tense.

Hay un cine cerca de aquí.	There's a cinema near here.
Hay dos supermercados.	There are two supermarkets.
No hay bares.	There are no bars.
Había mucho ruido.	There was a lot of noise.
Había muchos coches.	There were a lot of cars
Hubo un accidente.	There was an accident.
Hubo varios problemas.	There were several problems.
¿Habrá tiempo?	Will there be time?
¿Habrá suficientes sillas?	Will there be enough chairs?

ℹ Note that you should ALWAYS use the singular form (never the plural), no matter how many things there are.

➤ **haber** is used in the construction **hay que** with an infinitive to talk about actions that need to be taken.

Hay que trabajar más.	We/You need to work harder.
Hay que ser respetuoso.	You/We/One must be respectful.
Habrá que decírselo.	We'll/You'll have to tell him.

➤ **ser** can be used in certain impersonal constructions with adjectives, for example:

- **es/era/fue** + adjective + infinitive

Es importante ahorrar dinero.	It's important to save money.
Fue torpe hacer eso.	It was silly to do that.
Sería mejor esperar.	It would be better to wait.

- **es/era/fue** + adjective + **que** + verb

Es cierto que tengo problemas.	It's true that I've got problems.
Es verdad que trabaja mucho.	It's true that he works hard.

ℹ Note that when they are used in the negative (**no es cierto que...**; **no es verdad que...**), these expressions have to be followed by the subjunctive.

➪ *For more information on the* ***Subjunctive****, see page* 132.

Grammar Extra!

When impersonal expressions that don't state facts are followed by **que** (meaning *that*) and a verb, this verb must be in the subjunctive. For this reason, the following non-factual impersonal expressions are all followed by the subjunctive:

- **Es posible que...** — It's possible that... / ...might...
  Es posible que ganen. — They might win.
- **Es imposible que...** — It's impossible that... / ...can't possibly...
  Es imposible que lo sepan. — They can't possibly know.
- **Es necesario que...** — It's necessary that.../ ...need to...
  No es necesario que vengas. — You don't need to come.
- **Es mejor que...** — ...be better to...
  Es mejor que lo pongas aquí. — You'd better put it here.

➪ *For more information on the* ***Subjunctive****, see page 132.*

➤ **ser** is also used impersonally with **de día** and **de noche** to say whether it's day or night.

Era de noche cuando llegamos. — It was night when we arrived.
Todavía es de día allí. — It's still day there.

➪ *For other time expressions with* ***ser****, see page 26.*

➤ **basta con** is used impersonally:

- with a following infinitive to mean *it's enough to/all you need do is*
  Basta con telefonear para reservar un asiento. — All you need do is phone to reserve a seat.
  Basta con dar una vuelta por la ciudad para... — You only need to take a walk round the city to ...
- with a noun or pronoun to mean *all you need is* or *all it takes is*
  Basta con un error para que todo se estropee. — All it takes is one mistake to ruin everything.

➤ **(me) parece que** is used to give opinions.

Parece que va a llover. — It looks as if it's going to rain.
Me parece que estás equivocado. — I think that you are wrong.

[i] Note that when **(me) parece que** is used in the negative, the following verb has to be in the subjunctive.

➪ *For more information on the* ***Subjunctive****, see page 132.*

➤ **vale la pena** is used to talk about what's worth doing.

Vale la pena.	It's worth it.
No vale la pena.	It's not worth it.
Vale la pena hacer el esfuerzo.	It's worth making the effort.
No vale la pena gastar tanto dinero.	It's not worth spending so much money.

Grammar Extra!

se is often used in impersonal expressions, especially with the verbs **creer, decir, poder,** and **tratar**. In such cases it often corresponds to *it*, *one* or *you* in English.

• **Se cree que...**	It is thought *or* People think that...
Se cree que es un mito.	It is thought to be a myth.
• **Se dice que...**	It is said *or* People say that...
Se dice que es rico.	He is said to be rich.
• **Se puede...**	One can.../People can.../You can...
Aquí se puede aparcar.	One can park here.
• **Se trata de...**	It's a question of.../It's about...
No se trata de dinero.	It isn't a question of money.
Se trata de resolverlo.	We must solve it.

➪ *For more information on* ***Reflexive verbs****, see page 51.*

KEY POINTS

✔ Impersonal verbs and expressions can only be used in the *'it'* form, the infinitive and the gerund.

✔ Impersonal expressions relating to the weather are very common.

✔ Although in English we use *there is* or *there are* depending on the number of people or things that there are, in Spanish **hay**, **había**, **hubo** and so on are used in the singular form only.

✔ Some very common ordinary verbs are also used as impersonal verbs.

PRACTICE PRACTICE PRACTICE PRACTICE PRACTICE PRACTICE

Test yourself

147 Translate the following sentences into Spanish.

a It was raining hard. ....

b It was very cold. ....

c It's going to snow tomorrow. ....

d The weather is terrible. ....

e It's snowing. ....

f It's going be sunny. ....

g It was very hot. ....

h What was the weather like? ....

i Last week it was very hot. ....

j It's going to be windy. ....

148 Create a sentence in the present tense using the impersonal expression *(me/te/le) hace falta* and the elements given. Remember to put the object pronoun in the right place. The first sentence has been done for you.

a hacer falta/a mí/cincuenta euros *Me hacen falta cincuenta euros.*

b hacer falta/a Isabel/unas botas ....

c hacer falta/a nosotros/un cuchillo/para el pan

....

d hacer falta/tener/paciencia ....

e no/ hacer falta/enfadarse ....

f hacer falta/a nosotros/un manual ....

g hacer falta/más sal/en la sopa ....

h no/hacer falta/a ellos/un coche ....

i hacer falta/a mi madre/una batidora ....

j hace falta/a mí/un ordenador/más rápido ....

149 Replace the highlighted section of the text with the construction *hay/hubo/habrá/habría que* + infinitive. Match the tense that is indicated. The first one has been done for you.

a **comprar** más pan ***(present)*** *Hay que comprar más pan.*

b **decírselo** a Miguel ***(preterite)*** ....

c **solucionarlo** pronto ***(present)*** ....

d **intentarlo** ***(future)*** ....

e **respetar** las costumbres ***(present)*** ....

f **decírselo *(conditional)*** ....

g **revisarlo** otra vez ***(conditional)*** ....

h **consultar** con un experto ***(present)*** ....

i **salir** corriendo ***(preterite)*** ....

j **esperar** un poco ***(future)*** ....

150 Translate the following sentences into Spanish using the structure *es/era/fue/sera/sería* + adjective + infinitive. The first one has been done for you.

a It's good to laugh. Es bueno reír.

b It was dangerous to go. ....

c It was important to meet with them. ....

d It was very useful to ask him. ....

e It is good to walk. ....

f It would be useful to see it. ....

g It's not healthy to eat too many sweets. ....

h It'll be strange not to see you. ....

i It won't be too tiring. ....

j It would be ideal to see it. ....

151 Translate these sentences into Spanish using the time expressions *desde...* or *desde hace....* Remember that in Spanish you would use the present rather than the perfect tense. Use a dictionary and the verb tables in this book. The first one has been done for you.

a They have been away for six months. Están fuera desde hace seis meses/ Hace seis meses que están fuera.

b We haven't talked for ages. ....

....

c We have been living here for the last two years. ....

....

d She hasn't seen him for two weeks. ....

....

e María has had the house for three years. ....

Test yourself

f I haven't been to the theatre for a long time. ....

....

g How long have you been married? ....

....

h They have been together for three months. ....

....

i I've been studying German for five years. ....

....

j We have been waiting for two hours.

....

152 Complete the following sentences with the construction *se cree/piensa/dice... + que* or *se trata... + de*. The first one has been done for you.

a ....Se cree que.... la mató. **(creerse que)**

b .... un poco de dinero. **(tratarse de)**

c .... van a fracasar. **(pensarse que)**

d .... va a dimitir. **(creerse que)**

e .... lo robó. **(sospecharse que)**

f .... es millonario. **(decirse que)**

g .... lo han comprado. **(comentarse que)**

h .... un momento. **(tratarse de)**

i .... se han separado. **(rumorearse que)**

j .... es un fraude. **(piensa que)**

153 Complete the following sentences with the construction *vale/merece la pena*, either in the present or the imperfect, as indicated. The first one has been done for you.

a No ....vale la pena.... esperar. ***(present)*** **(valer la pena)**

b Por algo así .... pagar un poco más. ***(imperfect)*** **(merecer la pena)**

c No .... enfadarse por eso. ***(present)*** **(merecer la pena)**

d .... intentarlo. ***(imperfect)*** **(valer la pena)**

e Sí que .... visitarlo. ***(imperfect)*** **(valer la pena)**

f Os .... comprar un ordenador. ***(present)*** **(merecer la pena)**

g .... estudiar. ***(present)*** **(valer la pena)**

h Las casas .... ***(present)*** **(merecer la pena)**

i Era una película que .... *(imperfect)* **(merecer la pena)**

j Sus novelas .... *(present)* **(valer la pena)**

154 Create a sentence using the impersonal expression *(me/te/le) parece que* and the elements given. Use the tense that is indicated. Remember to put the object pronoun in the right place. The first sentence has been done for you.

a parecer /a mí/que/ser tarde ***(present)*** Me parece que es tarde.

b ¿parecer/a vosotros/que/este reloj/ser mejor? ***(present)***

....

c parecer/a mí/que/Ana/no querer ***(present)*** ....

d ¿parecer/a ellos/que/ser útil? ***(imperfect)*** ....

e así/parecer/que/ser/una mariposa ***(present)*** ....

f parecer/a nosotros/que/no/ser/buena idea ***(imperfect)***

....

g parecer/a él/que/tú/estar/equivocado ***(imperfect)***

....

h parecer/a mí/que/Juan/estar/borracho ***(present)***

....

i eso/parecer/a mí/que ser/diferente ***(present)*** ....

j parecer/a nosotros/difícil ***(present)*** ....

155 Translate the following sentences into Spanish.

a There isn't a boss, really. ....

b There were many people who doubt it.

....

c There was a new child in the school. ....

d There will be protests. ....

e There's a new cinema in the area. ....

f There are papers on the floor. ....

g There wasn't a lot of noise. ....

h Were there many guests? ....

i In the end, there wasn't enough money.

....

j Will there be enough time?. ....

The subjunctive

What is the subjunctive?

The **subjunctive** is a verb form that is used in certain circumstances especially when expressing some sort of feeling or when there is doubt about whether something will happen or whether something is true. It is only used occasionally in modern English, for example, *If I were you, ...; So be it.; I wish you were here.*

Using the subjunctive

➤ Although you may not know it, you will already be familiar with many of the forms of the present subjunctive, as it is used when giving orders and instructions not to do something as well as in the **usted**, **ustedes** and **nosotros** forms of instructions to do something. For example, if you phone someone in Spain, they will probably answer with **¡diga!** or **¡dígame!**, an imperative form taken from the present subjunctive of **decir**.

➪ *For more information on **Imperatives**, see page 42.*

➤ In Spanish, the subjunctive is used after certain verbs and conjunctions when two parts of a sentence have different subjects.

Tengo miedo de que le ocurra algo.	I'm afraid something may (*subjunctive*) happen to him.

(The subject of the first part of the sentence is *I*; the subject of the second part of the sentence is *something*.).

➤ In English, in a sentence like *We want him/José to be happy*, we use an infinitive (*to be*) for the second verb even though *want* and *be happy* have different subjects (*we* and *him/José*).

➤ In Spanish you cannot do this. You have to use the subjunctive for the second verb.

Queremos que él sea feliz.	We want him to be happy.
Queremos que José sea feliz.	We want José to be happy.

➤ You CAN use an infinitive for the second verb in Spanish when the subject of both verbs is the same.

Queremos ser felices.	We want to be happy.

Coming across the subjunctive

➤ The subjunctive has several tenses, the main ones being the present subjunctive and the imperfect subjunctive. The tense used for the subjunctive verb depends on the tense of the previous verb.

➪ *For more information on **Tenses with the subjunctive**, see page 137.*

➤ In sentences containing two verbs with different subjects, you will find that the second verb is in the subjunctive when the first verb:

- expresses a wish

Quiero que vengan.	I want them to come.
Quiero que se vaya.	I want him/her to leave.
Deseamos que tengan éxito.	We want them to be successful.

- expresses an emotion

Siento mucho que no puedas venir.	I'm very sorry that you can't come.
Espero que venga.	I hope he comes.
Me sorprende que no esté aquí.	I'm surprised that he isn't here.
Me alegro de que te gusten.	I'm pleased that you like them.

➤ If the subject of both verbs is the same, an infinitive is used as the second verb instead of a subjunctive.

➤ Compare the following examples. In the examples on the left, both the verb expressing the wish or emotion and the second verb have the same subject, so the second verb is an infinitive. In the examples on the right, each verb has a different subject, so the second verb is in the subjunctive.

Infinitive construction	**Subjunctive construction**
Quiero estudiar. I want to study.	**Quiero que José estudie.** I want José to study.
Maite quiere irse. Maite wants to leave.	**Maite quiere que me vaya.** Maite wants me to leave.
Siento no poder venir. I'm sorry I can't come.	**Siento que no puedas venir.** I'm sorry that you can't come.
Me alegro de poder ayudar. I'm pleased to be able to help.	**Me alegro de que puedas ayudar.** I'm pleased you can help.

➤ You will also come across the verb + **que** + subjunctive construction (often with a personal object such as **me**, **te** and so on) when the first verb is one you use to ask or advise somebody to do something.

Solo te pido que tengas cuidado.	I'm only asking you to be careful.
Te aconsejo que no llegues tarde.	I'd advise you not to be late.

➤ You will also come across the subjunctive in the following cases:

- after verbs expressing doubt or uncertainty, and verbs saying what you think about something that are used with **no**

Dudo que tenga tiempo.	I doubt I'll have time.
No creo que venga.	I don't think she'll come.
No pienso que esté bien.	I don't think it's right.

- in impersonal constructions that show a need to do something

¿Hace falta que vaya Jaime?	Does Jaime need to go?
No es necesario que vengas.	You don't need to come.

- in impersonal constructions that do not express facts

Es posible que tengan razón.	They may be right.

➪ *For more information on **Impersonal verbs**, see page 124.*

Grammar Extra!

Use the indicative (that is, any verb form that isn't subjunctive) after impersonal expressions that state facts provided they are NOT in the negative.

Es verdad que es interesante.	It's true that it's interesting.
Es cierto que me gusta el café.	It's true I like coffee.
Parece que se va a ir.	It seems that he's going to go.

➤ The subjunctive is used after **que** to express wishes.

¡Que lo pases bien!	Have a good time!
¡Que te diviertas!	Have fun!

➤ The subjunctive is also used after certain conjunctions linking two parts of a sentence which each have different subjects.

- **antes de que** before

¿Quieres decirle algo antes de que se vaya?	Do you want to say anything to him before he goes?

- **para que** so that

Es para que te acuerdes de mí.	It's so that you'll remember me.

- **sin que** without

Salimos sin que nos vieran.	We left without them seeing us.

Tip

Use **para**, **sin** and **antes de** with the infinitive when the subject of both verbs is the same.

Fue en taxi para no llegar tarde.	He went by taxi so that he wouldn't be late.
Pedro se ha ido sin esperarnos.	Pedro's gone without waiting for us.
Cenamos antes de ir al teatro.	We had dinner before we went to the theatre.

Forming the present subjunctive

➤ To form the present subjunctive of most verbs, take off the **-o** ending of the **yo** form of the present simple, and add a fixed set of endings.

➤ For **-ar** verbs, the endings are: **-e**, **-es**, **-e**, **-emos**, **-éis**, **-en**.

➤ For both **-er** and **-ir** verbs, the endings are: **-a**, **-as**, **-a**, **-amos**, **-áis**, **-an**.

For further explanation of grammatical terms, please see pages viii-x.

➤ The following table shows the present subjunctive of three regular verbs: **hablar** (meaning *to speak*), **comer** (meaning *to eat*) and **vivir** (meaning *to live*).

Infinitive	**(yo)**	**(tú)**	**(él) (ella) (usted)**	**(nosotros) (nosotras)**	**(vosotros) (vosotras)**	**(ellos) (ellas) (ustedes)**
hablar to speak	**hable**	**hables**	**hable**	**hablemos**	**habléis**	**hablen**
comer to eat	**coma**	**comas**	**coma**	**comamos**	**comáis**	**coman**
vivir to live	**viva**	**vivas**	**viva**	**vivamos**	**viváis**	**vivan**

Quiero que comas algo. I want you to eat something.
Me sorprende que no hable inglés. I'm surprised he doesn't speak English.
No es verdad que trabajen aquí. It isn't true that they work here.

➤ Some verbs have very irregular **yo** forms in the ordinary present tense and these irregular forms are reflected in the stem for the present subjunctive.

Infinitive	**(yo)**	**(tú)**	**(él) (ella) (usted)**	**(nosotros) (nosotras)**	**(vosotros) (vosotras)**	**(ellos) (ellas) (ustedes)**
decir to say	**diga**	**digas**	**diga**	**digamos**	**digáis**	**digan**
hacer to do/make	**haga**	**hagas**	**haga**	**hagamos**	**hagáis**	**hagan**
poner to put	**ponga**	**pongas**	**ponga**	**pongamos**	**pongáis**	**pongan**
salir to leave	**salga**	**salgas**	**salga**	**salgamos**	**salgáis**	**salgan**
tener to have	**tenga**	**tengas**	**tenga**	**tengamos**	**tengáis**	**tengan**
venir to come	**venga**	**vengas**	**venga**	**vengamos**	**vengáis**	**vengan**

Voy a limpiar la casa antes de que vengan. I'm going to clean the house before they come.

ℹ Note that only the **vosotros** form has an accent.

Tip

The present subjunctive endings are the opposite of what you'd expect, as **-ar** verbs have endings starting with **-e**, and **-er** and **-ir** verbs have endings starting with **-a**.

Forming the present subjunctive of irregular verbs

➤ The following verbs have irregular subjunctive forms:

Infinitive	(yo)	(tú)	(él) (ella) (usted)	(nosotros) (nosotras)	(vosotros) (vosotras)	(ellos) (ellas) (ustedes)
dar to give	**dé**	**des**	**dé**	**demos**	**deis**	**den**
estar to be	**esté**	**estés**	**esté**	**estemos**	**estéis**	**estén**
haber to have	**haya**	**hayas**	**haya**	**hayamos**	**hayáis**	**hayan**
ir to go	**vaya**	**vayas**	**vaya**	**vayamos**	**vayáis**	**vayan**
saber to know	**sepa**	**sepas**	**sepa**	**sepamos**	**sepáis**	**sepan**
ser to be	**sea**	**seas**	**sea**	**seamos**	**seáis**	**sean**

No quiero que te vayas. — I don't want you to go.
Dudo que esté aquí. — I doubt if it's here.
No piensan que sea él. — They don't think it's him.
Es posible que haya problemas. — There may be problems.

➤ Verbs that change their stems (radical-changing verbs) in the ordinary present usually change them in the same way in the present subjunctive.

➪ *For more information on* ***radical-changing verbs****, see page 11.*

Infinitive	(yo)	(tú)	(él) (ella) (usted)	(nosotros) (nosotras)	(vosotros) (vosotras)	(ellos) (ellas) (ustedes)
pensar to think	**piense**	**pienses**	**piense**	**pensemos**	**penséis**	**piensen**
entender to understand	**entienda**	**entiendas**	**entienda**	**entendamos**	**entendáis**	**entiendan**
poder to be able	**pueda**	**puedas**	**pueda**	**podamos**	**podáis**	**puedan**
querer to want	**quiera**	**quieras**	**quiera**	**queramos**	**queráis**	**quieran**
volver to return	**vuelva**	**vuelvas**	**vuelva**	**volvamos**	**volváis**	**vuelvan**

No hace falta que vuelvas. — There's no need for you to come back.
Es para que lo entiendas. — It's so that you understand.
Me alegro de que puedas venir. — I'm pleased you can come.

➤ Sometimes the stem of the **nosotros** and **vosotros** forms isn't the same as it is in the ordinary present tense.

Infinitive	(yo)	(tú)	(él) (ella) (usted)	(nosotros) (nosotras)	(vosotros) (vosotras)	(ellos) (ellas) (ustedes)
dormir to sleep	**duerma**	**duermas**	**duerma**	**durmamos**	**durmáis**	**duerman**
morir to die	**muera**	**mueras**	**muera**	**muramos**	**muráis**	**mueran**
pedir to ask for	**pida**	**pidas**	**pida**	**pidamos**	**pidáis**	**pidan**
seguir to follow	**siga**	**sigas**	**siga**	**sigamos**	**sigáis**	**sigan**
sentir to feel	**sienta**	**sientas**	**sienta**	**sintamos**	**sintáis**	**sientan**

Queremos hacerlo antes de que nos muramos. We want to do it before we die.
Vendré a veros cuando os sintáis mejor. I'll come and see you when you feel better.

Tenses with the subjunctive

➤ If the verb in the first part of the sentence is in the present, future or imperative, the second verb will usually be in the present subjunctive.

Quiero *(present)* **que lo hagas** *(present subjunctive)*. I want you to do it.
Iremos *(future)* **por aquí para que no nos vean** *(present subjunctive)*. We'll go this way so that they won't see us.

➤ If the verb in the first part of the sentence is in the conditional or a past tense, the second verb will usually be in the imperfect subjunctive.

Me gustaría (*conditional*) **que llegaras** (*imperfect subjunctive*) **temprano.**
I'd like you to arrive early.
Les pedí (*preterite*) **que me esperaran** (*imperfect subjunctive*).
I asked them to wait for me.

Indicative or subjunctive?

➤ Many expressions are followed by the indicative (the ordinary form of the verb) when they state facts, and by the subjunctive when they refer to possible or intended future events and outcomes.

➤ Certain conjunctions relating to time such as **cuando** (meaning *when*), **hasta que** (meaning *until*), **en cuanto** (meaning *as soon as*) and **mientras** (meaning *while*) are used with the indicative when the action has happened or when talking about what happens regularly.

¿Qué dijo cuando te vio? What did he say when he saw you?
Siempre lo compro cuando voy a España. I always buy it when I go to Spain.
Me quedé allí hasta que volvió Antonio. I stayed there until Antonio came back.

➤ The same conjunctions are followed by the subjunctive when talking about a vague future time.

¿Qué quieres hacer cuando <u>seas</u> mayor?	What do you want to do when yougrow up? *(but you're not grown up yet)*
¿Por qué no te quedas aquí hasta que <u>vuelva</u> Antonio?	Why don't you stay here until Antonio comes back? *(but Antonio hasn't come back yet)*
Lo haré en cuanto <u>pueda</u> *or* **tan pronto como <u>pueda</u>.**	I'll do it as soon as I can. *(but I'm not able to yet)*

Grammar Extra!

aunque is used with the <u>indicative</u> (the ordinary verb forms) when it means *although* or *even though*. In this case, the second part of the sentence is stating a fact.

Me gusta el francés aunque <u>prefiero</u> el alemán.	I like French although I prefer German.
Seguí andando aunque me <u>dolía</u> la pierna.	I went on walking even though my leg hurt.

aunque is used with the <u>subjunctive</u> when it means *even if*. Here, the second part of the sentence is not yet a fact.

Te llamaré cuando vuelva aunque <u>sea</u> tarde.	I'll ring you when I get back, even if it's late.

Forming the imperfect subjunctive

➤ For all verbs, there are <u>two</u> imperfect subjunctive forms that are exactly the same in meaning.

➤ The stem for both imperfect subjunctive forms is the same: you take off the **-aron** or **-ieron** ending of the **ellos** form of the preterite and add a fixed set of endings to what is left.

➪ *For more information on the* **Preterite**, *see page 74.*

➤ For **-ar** verbs, the endings are: **-ara**, **-aras**, **-ara**, **-áramos**, **-arais**, **-aran** or **-ase**, **-ases**, **-ase**, **-ásemos**, **-aseis**, **-asen**. The first form is more common.

➤ For **-er** and **-ir** verbs, the endings are: **-iera**, **-ieras**, **-iera**, **-iéramos**, **-ierais**, **-ieran** *or* **-iese**, **-ieses**, **-iese**, **-iésemos**, **-ieseis**, **-iesen**. The first form is more common.

➤ The following table shows the imperfect subjunctive of three regular verbs: **hablar** (meaning *to speak*), **comer** (meaning *to eat*) and **vivir** (meaning *to live*).

Infinitive	**(yo)**	**(tú)**	**(él) (ella) (usted)**	**(nosotros) (nosotras)**	**(vosotros) (vosotras)**	**(ellos) (ellas) (ustedes)**
hablar to speak	**hablara** **hablase**	**hablaras** **hablases**	**hablara** **hablase**	**habláramos** **hablásemos**	**hablarais** **hablaseis**	**hablaran** **hablasen**
comer to eat	**comiera** **comiese**	**comieras** **comieses**	**comiera** **comiese**	**comiéramos** **comiésemos**	**comierais** **comieseis**	**comieran** **comiesen**
vivir to live	**viviera** **viviese**	**vivieras** **vivieses**	**viviera** **viviese**	**viviéramos** **viviésemos**	**vivierais** **vivieseis**	**vivieran** **viviesen**

➤ Many verbs have irregular preterite forms which are reflected in the stem for the imperfect subjunctive. For example:

Infinitive	**(yo)**	**(tú)**	**(él) (ella) (usted)**	**(nosotros) (nosotras)**	**(vosotros) (vosotras)**	**(ellos) (ellas) (ustedes)**
dar to give	**diera** **diese**	**dieras** **dieses**	**diera** **diese**	**diéramos** **diésemos**	**dierais** **dieseis**	**dieran** **diesen**
estar to be	**estuviera** **estuviese**	**estuvieras** **estuvieses**	**estuviera** **estuviese**	**estuviéramos** **estuviésemos**	**estuvierais** **estuvieseis**	**estuvieran** **estuviesen**
hacer to do/make	**hiciera** **hiciese**	**hicieras** **hicieses**	**hiciera** **hiciese**	**hiciéramos** **hiciésemos**	**hicierais** **hicieseis**	**hicieran** **hiciesen**
poner to put	**pusiera** **pusiese**	**pusieras** **pusieses**	**pusiera** **pusiese**	**pusiéramos** **pusiésemos**	**pusierais** **pusieseis**	**pusieran** **pusiesen**
tener to have	**tuviera** **tuviese**	**tuvieras** **tuvieses**	**tuviera** **tuviese**	**tuviéramos** **tuviésemos**	**tuvierais** **tuvieseis**	**tuvieran** **tuviesen**
ser to be	**fuera** **fuese**	**fueras** **fueses**	**fuera** **fuese**	**fuéramos** **fuésemos**	**fuerais** **fueseis**	**fueran** **fuesen**
venir to come	**viniera** **viniese**	**vinieras** **vinieses**	**viniera** **viniese**	**viniéramos** **viniésemos**	**vinierais** **vinieseis**	**vinieran** **viniesen**

Forming the imperfect subjunctive of some irregular -ir verbs

➤ In some irregular **-ir** verbs – the ones that don't have an **i** in the **ellos** form of the preterite – **-era**, **-eras**, **-era**, **-éramos**, **-erais**, **-eran** *or* **-ese**, **-eses**, **-ese**, **-ésemos**, **-eseis**, **-esen** are added to the preterite stem instead of **-iera** and **-iese** and so on.

➪ *For more information on the **Preterite**, see page 74.*

Infinitive	**(yo)**	**(tú)**	**(él) (ella) (usted)**	**(nosotros) (nosotras)**	**(vosotros) (vosotras)**	**(ellos) (ellas) (ustedes)**
decir to say	**dijera** **dijese**	**dijeras** **dijeses**	**dijera** **dijese**	**dijéramos** **dijésemos**	**dijerais** **dijeseis**	**dijeran** **dijesen**
ir to go	**fuera** **fuese**	**fueras** **fueses**	**fuera** **fuese**	**fuéramos** **fuésemos**	**fuerais** **fueseis**	**fueran** **fuesen**

[i] Note that the imperfect subjunctive forms of **ir** and **ser** are identical.

Teníamos miedo de que se fuera.	We were afraid he might leave.
No era verdad que fueran ellos.	It wasn't true that it was them.

Present indicative or imperfect subjunctive after si

➤ Like some other conjunctions, **si** (meaning *if*) is sometimes followed by the ordinary present tense (the present indicative) and sometimes by the imperfect subjunctive.

➤ **si** is followed by the present indicative when talking about likely possibilities.

Si quieres, te dejo el coche.	If you like, I'll lend you the car. *(and you may well want to borrow the car)*
Compraré un bolígrafo si tienen.	I'll buy a pen if they have any. *(and there may well be some pens)*

➤ **si** is followed by the imperfect subjunctive when talking about unlikely or impossible conditions.

Si tuviera más dinero, me lo compraría.	If I had more money, I'd buy it. *(but I haven't got more money)*
Si yo fuera tú, lo compraría.	If I were you, I'd buy it. *(but I'm not you)*

Tip

You probably need the imperfect subjunctive in Spanish after **si** if the English sentence has would in it.

KEY POINTS

- ✔ After certain verbs you have to use a subjunctive in Spanish when there is a different subject in the two parts of the sentence.
- ✔ A subjunctive is also found after impersonal expressions, as well as after certain conjunctions.
- ✔ Structures with the subjunctive can often be avoided if the subject of both verbs is the same. An infinitive can often be used instead.
- ✔ The endings of the present subjunctive in regular **-ar** verbs are: -**e**, **-es**, **-e**, **-emos**, **-éis**, **-en**.
- ✔ The endings of the present subjunctive in regular **-er** and **-ir** verbs are: -**a**, **-as**, **-a**, **-amos**, **-áis**, **-an**.
- ✔ The endings of the imperfect subjunctive in regular **-ar** verbs are: -**ara**, **-aras**, **-ara**, **-áramos**, **-arais**, **-aran** or **-ase**, **-ases**, **-ase**, **-ásemos**, **-aseis**, **-asen**.
- ✔ The endings of the imperfect subjunctive in regular **-er** and **-ir** verbs are: **-iera**, **-ieras**, **-iera**, **-iéramos**, **-ierais**, **-ieran** or -**iese**, **-ieses**, **-iese**, **-iésemos**, **-ieseis**, **-iesen**.
- ✔ Some verbs have irregular subjunctive forms.

Test yourself

156 Complete the following with the correct form of the present subjunctive. The first one has been done for you.

a que vosotros ......*habléis*...... **(hablar)**

b que yo .... **(poder)**

c que ellos .... **(estudiar)**

d que él .... **(vivir)**

e que tú .... **(comer)**

f que yo .... **(tener)**

g que vosotros .... **(decir)**

h que ellos .... **(venir)**

i que ellas .... **(salir)**

j que tú .... **(hacer)**

k que ustedes .... **(tener)**

157 Complete the following sentences with the correct form of the present subjunctive. The pronoun in brackets shows you which person to use. The first one has been done for you.

a Deseamos ...*te mejores*... pronto **(mejorarse [tú])**

b Quiero que .... aquí. **(esperar [él])**

c Dicen que .... en coche. **(ir [nosotros])**

d Me sorprende que no .... aún. **(haber llegado [ellos])**

e Toni quiere que .... a la fiesta. **(ir [tú])**

f El profesor duda mucho que .... adivinarlo. **(poder [vosotros])**

g Les extraña un poco que .... fuera. **(estar [nosotros])**

h Se alegran mucho de que .... **(haber ganado [tú])**

i No creo que .... a tanto. **(atreverse [él])**

j Dudo que .... tan tarde. **(salir [ellos])**

158 Replace the highlighted section with the structure *que* + present subjunctive, using the noun indicated. The first example has been done for you.

a Quiere **ganar. (Marta)** *Quiere que Marta gane.*......................................

b Espero **ayudarte. (tus padres)** ....

c Nos alegramos de **estar** aquí. **(tu amiga)** ....

Test yourself

d Siento **molestar**. **(los perros)** ....

e Le gusta **cantar**. **(Nuria)** ....

f Sentimos **llegar** tarde. **(los pasajeros)** ....

g Se alegran de **tener tiempo**. **(tú)** ....

h Quiero **ir** de vacaciones con mis padres. **(los niños)** ....

i Preferimos **no enterarnos. (mi madre)** ....

j Quieren **salir** pronto. **(los alumnos)** ....

159 Cross out the nouns that don't go with the verb.

a pongamos	Miguel y yo/la policía/nosotros
b tenga	mis primas/Ana/el coche
c estéis	tus padres y tú/tus hermanos/sus profesores
d sea	la reunión/las niñas/la madre
e entienda	el profesor/los alumnos/los políticos
f estés	tu perro/un amigo/tú
g dé	Miguel/los empleados/yo
h coman	los animales/la invitada/Ana
i vivamos	María y mi amiga/las palomas/Susana y yo
j salgáis	la policía/vosotros/mis hermanas

160 Complete the following sentences with the correct form of the subjunctive. The first one has been done for you.

a No creo que mi hermana ....*venga*........ a cenar. **(venir)**

b Es posible que ya lo .... todos. **(saber)**

c No hace falta que .... tan pronto. **(ir [tú])**

d Prefiero que .... un rato. **(quedarse [vosotros])**

e Que yo .... , nadie se ha quejado. **(saber)**

f ¡No se lo .... aún! **(decir [tú])**

g Espero que los niños .... los disfraces. **(ponerse)**

h Cuando .... mayor quiere ser médico. **(ser [ella])**

i Hazlo cuando .... **(poder [tú])**

j Espero que les .... la sorpresa. **(gustar)**

Test yourself

161 Complete the following with the correct form of the imperfect subjunctive. Remember that the imperfect subjunctive has two forms in Spanish. Please show both of them. Note that some verbs will show a change in the stem. The first question has been done for you.

a que yo *comiese/comiese* **(comer)**

b que nosotros .... **(volver)**

c que tú .... **(pensar)**

d que él .... **(salir)**

e que yo .... **(hacer)**

f que ellos .... **(tener)**

g que ellas .... **(haber)**

h que tú .... **(dar)**

i que ella .... **(ser)**

j que nosotros .... **(estar)**

162 Complete the following sentences with the correct form of the imperfect subjunctive. The pronoun in brackets shows you which person to use. The first one has been done for you.

a Si yo *pudiera/pudiese* viajaría más. **(poder)**

b Me gustaría que .... a vernos. **(venir [ellos])**

c .... un libro de poemas, por favor. **(querer [yo])**

d Trabajé tanto para que .... suficiente dinero. **(tener [nosotros])**

e Me tratas como si yo .... tonta. **(ser)**

f ¡Qué rabia que no .... venir. **(querer [ellos])**

g ¡Ojalá .... volver! **(poder [yo])**

h Me gustaría que .... un rato a pasear. **(salir [nosotros])**

i ¿Iríais si .... tiempo? **(tener [vosotros])**

j Dudo mucho que lo .... hacer. **(poder [nosotros])**

Test yourself

163 Match the infinitive and subjunctive forms.

a **saber**	salga
b **ir**	vaya
c **ser**	supiera
d **poder**	seáis
e **salir**	puedan

164 Match each subjunctive form to the infinitive form of the verb.

a **haber**	supieran
b **saber**	hiciera
c **hacer**	hayamos
d **ser**	dieran
e **dar**	fuera

PRACTICE PRACTICE PRACTICE PRACTICE PRACTICE PRACTICE PRACTICE PRACTICE

The Infinitive

What is the infinitive?
The **infinitive** is a form of the verb that hasn't had any endings added to it and doesn't relate to any particular tense. In English, the infinitive is usually shown with *to*, as in *to speak*, *to eat*, *to live*.

Using the infinitive

➤ In English, the infinitive is usually thought of as being made up of two words, for example, *to speak*. In Spanish, the infinitive consists of one word and is the verb form that ends in **-ar**, **-er** or **-ir**, for example, **hablar**, **comer**, **vivir**.

➤ When you look up a verb in the dictionary, you will find that information is usually listed under the infinitive form.

➤ In Spanish, the infinitive is often used in the following ways:

- after a preposition such as **antes de** (meaning *before*), **después de** (meaning *after*)

Después de comer, fuimos a casa de Pepe.	After eating, we went round to Pepe's.
Salió sin hacer ruido.	She went out without making a noise.
Siempre veo la tele antes de acostarme.	I always watch TV before going to bed.

[i] Note that in English we always use the *-ing* form of the verb after a preposition, for example, *before going*. In Spanish you have to use the infinitive form after a preposition.

- in set phrases, particularly after adjectives or nouns

Estoy encantada de poder ayudarte.	I'm delighted to be able to help you.
Está contento de vivir aquí.	He's happy living here.
Tengo ganas de salir.	I feel like going out.
No hace falta comprar leche.	We/You don't need to buy any milk.
Me dio mucha alegría verla.	I was very pleased to see her.
Me da miedo cruzar la carretera.	I'm afraid of crossing the road.

- after another verb, sometimes as the object of it

Debo llamar a casa.	I must phone home.
Prefiero esquiar.	I prefer skiing.
Me gusta escuchar música.	I like listening to music.
Nos encanta nadar.	We love swimming.
¿Te apetece ir al cine?	Do you fancy going to the cinema?

[i] Note that, when it comes after another verb, the Spanish infinitive often corresponds to the *-ing* form in English.

- in instructions that are aimed at the general public – for example in cookery books or on signs

Cocer a fuego lento.	Cook on a low heat.
Prohibido pisar el césped.	Don't walk on the grass.

- as a noun, where in English we would use the *-ing* form of the verb

  Lo importante es intentarlo. — Trying is the important thing.

ℹ Note that, when the infinitive is the subject of another verb, it may have the article **el** before it, particularly if it starts the sentence.

El viajar tanto me resulta cansado. — I find so much travelling tiring.

> *Tip*
>
> Be especially careful when translating the English *-ing* form. It is often translated by the infinitive in Spanish.

Linking two verbs together

➤ There are three ways that verbs can be linked together when the second verb is an infinitive:

- with no linking word in between

¿Quieres venir?	Do you want to come?
Necesito hablar contigo.	I need to talk to you.

- with a preposition

ir a hacer algo	to be going to do something
aprender a hacer algo	to learn to do something
dejar de hacer algo	to stop doing something
Voy a comprarme un móvil.	I'm going to buy a mobile.
Aprendimos a esquiar.	We learnt to ski.
Quiere dejar de fumar.	He wants to stop smoking.

ℹ Note that you have to learn the preposition required for each verb.

- in set structures

tener que hacer algo	to have to do something
Tengo que salir.	I've got to go out.
Tendrías que comer más.	You should eat more.
Tuvo que devolver el dinero.	He had to pay back the money.

Verbs followed by the infinitive with no preposition

➤ Some Spanish verbs and groups of verbs can be followed by an infinitive with no preposition:

- **poder** (meaning *to be able to, can, may*), **saber** (meaning *to know how to, can*), **querer** (meaning *to want*) and **deber** (meaning *to have to, must*)

No puede venir.	He can't come.
¿Sabes esquiar?	Can you ski?
Quiere estudiar medicina.	He wants to study medicine.
Debes hacerlo.	You must do it.

- verbs like **gustar**, **encantar** and **apetecer**, where the infinitive is the subject of the verb

Me gusta estudiar.	I like studying.
Nos encanta bailar.	We love dancing.
¿Te apetece ir al cine?	Do you fancy going to the cinema?

For further explanation of grammatical terms, please see pages viii-x.

- verbs that relate to seeing or hearing, such as **ver** (meaning *to see*) and **oír** (meaning *to hear*)

Nos ha visto llegar.	He saw us arrive.
Te he oído cantar.	I heard you singing.

- the verbs **hacer** (meaning *to make*) and **dejar** (meaning *to let*)

¡No me hagas reír!	Don't make me laugh!
Mis padres no me dejan salir por la noche.	My parents don't let me go out at night.

- the following common verbs

decidir	to decide
desear	to wish, want
esperar	to hope
evitar	to avoid
necesitar	to need
odiar	to hate
olvidar	to forget
pensar	to think
preferir	to prefer
recordar	to remember
sentir	to regret

Han decidido comprarse una casa.	They've decided to buy a house.
No desea tener más hijos.	She doesn't want to have any more children.
Espero poder ir.	I hope to be able to go.
Evita gastar demasiado dinero.	He avoids spending too much money.
Necesito salir un momento.	I need to go out for a moment.
Olvidó dejar su dirección.	She forgot to leave her address.
Pienso hacer una paella.	I'm thinking of making a paella.
Siento molestarte.	I'm sorry to bother you.

➤ Some of these verbs combine with infinitives to make set phrases with a special meaning:

- **querer decir** to mean

¿Qué quiere decir eso?	What does that mean?

- **dejar caer** to drop

Dejó caer la bandeja.	She dropped the tray.

Verbs followed by the preposition a and the infinitive

➤ The following verbs are the most common ones that can be followed by **a** and the infinitive:

- verbs relating to movement such as **ir** (meaning *to go*) and **venir** (meaning *to come*)

Se va a comprar un caballo.	He's going to buy a horse.
Viene a vernos.	He's coming to see us.

- the following common verbs

aprender a hacer algo	to learn to do something
comenzar a hacer algo	to begin to do something
decidirse a hacer algo	to decide to do something
empezar a hacer algo	to begin to do something

llegar a hacer algo	to manage to do something
llegar a ser algo	to become something
probar a hacer algo	to try to do something
volver a hacer algo	to do something again

Me gustaría aprender a nadar.	I'd like to learn to swim.
No llegó a terminar la carrera.	He didn't manage to finish his degree course.
Llegó a ser primer ministro.	He became prime minister.
No vuelvas a hacerlo nunca más.	Don't ever do it again.

➤ The following verbs can be followed by **a** and a person's name or else by **a** and a noun or pronoun referring to a person, and then by another **a** and an infinitive.

ayudar a alguien a hacer algo	to help someone to do something
enseñar a alguien a hacer algo	to teach someone to do something
invitar a alguien a hacer algo	to invite someone to do something

¿Le podrías ayudar a Antonia a fregar los platos?	Could you help Antonia do the dishes?
Le enseñó a su hermano a nadar.	He taught his brother to swim.
Los he invitado a tomar unas copas en casa.	I've invited them over for drinks.

Verbs followed by the preposition de and the infinitive

➤ The following verbs are the most common ones that can be followed by **de** and the infinitive:

aburrirse de hacer algo	to get bored with doing something
acabar de hacer algo	to have just done something
acordarse de haber hecho/ de hacer algo	to remember having done/ doing something
alegrarse de hacer algo	to be glad to do something
dejar de hacer algo	to stop doing something
tener ganas de hacer algo	to want to do something
tratar de hacer algo	to try to do something

Me aburría de no poder salir de casa.	I was getting bored with not being able to leave the house.
Acabo de comprar un móvil.	I've just bought a mobile.
Acababan de llegar cuando...	They had just arrived when...
Me alegro de verte.	I'm glad to see you.
¿Quieres dejar de hablar?	Will you stop talking?
Tengo ganas de volver a España.	I want to go back to Spain.

Verbs followed by the preposition con and the infinitive

➤ The following verbs are the most common ones that can be followed by **con** and the infinitive:

amenazar con hacer algo	to threaten to do someting
soñar con hacer algo	to dream about doing something
Amenazó con denunciarlos.	He threatened to report them.
Sueño con vivir en España.	I dream about living in Spain.

Verbs followed by the preposition en and the infinitive

➤ The verb **quedar** is the most common one that can be followed by **en** and the infinitive:

quedar <u>en</u> hacer algo	to agree to do something
Habíamos quedado <u>en</u> encontrarnos a las ocho.	We had agreed to meet at eight.

Key points

- ✔ Infinitives are found after prepositions, set phrases and in instructions to the general public.
- ✔ They can also function as the subject or object of a verb, when the infinitive corresponds to the *-ing* form in English.
- ✔ Many Spanish verbs can be followed by another verb in the infinitive.
- ✔ The two verbs may be linked by nothing at all, or by **a**, **de** or another preposition.
- ✔ The construction in Spanish does not always match the English. It's best to learn these constructions when you learn a new verb.

Test yourself

165 Complete the following sentences with a verb in the infinitive that fits the meaning. The first letter of the missing verb has been given as a clue.

a Fuimos a .... una película. **(v...)**

b Aprendí a .... sobre hielo. **(p...)**

c Me puse a .... una canción. **(c...)**

d Suele .... de la cama a las ocho. **(l...)**

e ¿Quieres .... un refresco? **(b...)**

f Le encanta .... libros. **(l...)**

g Les gusta mucho .... en el ordenador. **(j...)**

h ¿Os apetece .... a cenar? **(s...)**

i Hace falta ir a .... pan. **(c...)**

j ¿Puedes .... la dirección en este papel? **(e...)**

166 Rewrite these instructions changing the highlighted verb into the infinitive.

a Primero **pesa** la harina y la mantequilla. ....

b **Mezcla** la harina y la mantequilla con los dedos.

....

c Luego **añade** un poco de agua. ....

d **Forma** una masa mezclando la harina y la mantequilla con el agua.

....

e Por otro lado, **pela y corta** en trozos las manzanas.

....

f **Extiende** la masa con el rodillo. ....

g **Pon** la masa extendida en un molde. ....

h **Coloca** las manzanas sobre la masa. ....

i **Mete** al horno caliente durante una hora. ....

j **Saca** del horno y deja enfriar. ....

167 Match the two columns.

a aprender hacer algo	to start doing something
b empezar a hacer algo	to manage to do something
c llegar a hacer algo	to do something again
d volver a hacer algo	to try to do something
e probar a hacer algo	to learn to do something

Test yourself

168 Replace the highlighted text with the verb in brackets in the infinitive.

a Aprendí a **hacer algo**.[cociné] ....

b Probamos a **hacer algo**.[buceamos] ....

c Empezamos a **hacer algo**.[cantamos] ....

d Llegaron a **hacer algo**.[subieron la montaña] ....

e Conseguimos **hacer algo**.[lo entendimos] ....

f Volviste a **hacer algo**.[lo intentó] ....

g ¿Os decidísteis a **hacer algo?**[lo comprásteis] ....

h Comenzaron a **hacer algo**.[trabajaron] ....

i Decidieron **hacer algo**.[llamaron] ....

j Olvidamos **hacer algo**.[lo cerramos] ....

169 Change the sentence so that the highlighted text is used in the infinitive after the first verb in the sentence. The first one has been done for you.

a Lo hemos decidido: **nos compramos** un barco.
Hemos decidido comprarnos un barco. ....

b Lo prefieren: **no vuelven** a su pueblo. ....

c Lo siento; **te hago enfadar**. ....

d Me apetece: **me voy** a bailar. ....

e Le gusta; **cocina** los fines de semana. ....

f **Me compro** un ordenador; lo necesito. ....

g Lo han decidido: **dejan** de fumar. ....

h Lo prefiero: no **voy**. ....

i Lo ha decidido: **abre** un restaurante. ....

j **Recibimos** muchas visitas: nos gusta. ....

PRACTICE PRACTICE PRACTICE PRACTICE PRACTICE

Test yourself

170 Complete the following sentences with a verb in the infinitive that fits the meaning. The first letter of the missing verb has been given as a clue.

a Tiene prohibido .... por la noche. **(s...)**

b No les deja .... a la cama muy tarde. **(i...)**

c Prohibido .... basura. **(t...)**

d Te prohíbo .... esas palabras. **(d...)**

e Mi padre no nos deja .... alcohol. **(b...)**

f Debes .... por teléfono a tus padres. **(ll...)**

g Me ha prohibido .... más ropa. **(c...)**

h En verano, prefieren .... cerveza. **(t...)**

i ¿Nos dejas .... en el ordenador? **(j...)**

j Mis padres nos dejan .... una fiesta en casa. **(h...)**

171 Match the Spanish and English.

a Dejó caer el boli.	I hope to be able to go.
b Espero poder ir.	I must try.
c ¿Qué quieres decir?	He dropped the pen.
d Debo intentarlo.	He became a doctor.
e Llegó a ser médico.	What do you mean?

172 Translate the following sentences into Spanish.

a I would like to go on holiday. ....

b They are going to learn Arabic. ....

c Can you play the bass? ....

d We helped him find the way.

....

e Sometimes they forget to switch off the computer.

....

f We didn't manage to visit Costa Rica ....

g She is going to buy a motorbike. ....

h They have to buy their tickets. ....

i I want to learn to drive. ....

j He taught me to ride a bike. ....

Test yourself

173 Complete the following sentences with the prepositions *a*, *de*, or *con*.

a Iba .... dárselo.

b Se cansaron .... ver la película.

c Comenzó .... chillar.

d Me acordé .... cerrar la puerta.

e Se alegró .... haber venido.

f Acaban .... empezar.

g Soñaba .... conocerla.

h Deja .... repetirlo.

i Basta .... pedirlo por favor.

j Tenía ganas .... comer.

Prepositions after verbs

➤ In English, there are some phrases which are made up of verbs and prepositions, for example, *to accuse somebody of something*, *to look forward to something* and *to rely on something*.

➤ In Spanish there are also lots of set phrases made up of verbs and prepositions. Often the prepositions in Spanish are not the same as they are in English, so you will need to learn them. Listed below are phrases using verbs and some common Spanish prepositions.

➪ *For more information on verbs used with a preposition and the infinitive, see page 148.*

Verbs followed by a

➤ **a** is often the equivalent of the English word *to* when it is used with an indirect object after verbs like **enviar** (meaning *to send*), **dar** (meaning *to give*) and **decir** (meaning *to say*).

dar algo a alguien	to give something to someone
decir algo a alguien	to say something to someone
enviar algo a alguien	to send something to someone
escribir algo a alguien	to write something to someone
mostrar algo a alguien	to show something to someone

Tip

There is an important difference between Spanish and English with this type of verb. In English, you can say either *to give something to someone* or *to give someone something*.

You can NEVER miss out **a** in Spanish in the way that you can sometimes miss out *to* in English.

➤ Here are some verbs taking **a** in Spanish that have a different construction in English.

asistir a algo	to attend something, to be at something
dirigirse a (un lugar)	to head for (a place)
dirigirse a alguien	to address somebody
jugar a algo	to play something *(sports/games)*
llegar a (un lugar)	to arrive at (a place)
oler a algo	to smell of something
parecerse a alguien/algo	to look like somebody/something
subir(se) a un autobús/un coche	to get on a bus/into a car
subir(se) a un árbol	to climb a tree
tener miedo a alguien	to be afraid of somebody
Este perfume huele a jazmín.	This perfume smells of jasmine.
¡De prisa, sube al coche!	Get into the car, quick!
Nunca tuvieron miedo a su padre.	They were never afraid of their father.

➪ *For verbs such as **gustar**, **encantar** and **faltar**, see **Verbal idioms** on page 159.*

Verbs followed by de

➤ Here are some verbs taking **de** in Spanish that have a different construction in English:

acordarse de algo/alguien	to remember something/somebody
alegrarse de algo	to be glad about something
bajarse de un autobús/un coche	to get off a bus/out of a car
darse cuenta de algo	to realize something
depender de algo/alguien	to depend on something/somebody
despedirse de alguien	to say goodbye to somebody
preocuparse de algo/alguien	to worry about something/somebody
quejarse de algo	to complain about something
reírse de algo/alguien	to laugh at something/somebody
salir de (un cuarto/un edificio)	to leave (a room/a building)
tener ganas de algo	to want something
trabajar de (camarero/secretario)	to work as (a waiter/secretary)
tratarse de algo/alguien	to be a question of something/ to be about somebody

Nos acordamos muy bien de aquellas vacaciones.	We remember that holiday very well.
Se bajó del coche.	He got out of the car.
No depende de mí.	It doesn't depend on me.
Se preocupa mucho de su apariencia.	He worries a lot about his appearance.

Verbs followed by con

➤ Here are some verbs taking **con** in Spanish that have a different construction in English:

contar con alguien/algo	to rely on somebody/something
encontrarse con alguien	to meet somebody (*by chance*)
enfadarse con alguien	to get annoyed with somebody
hablar con alguien	to talk to somebody
soñar con alguien/algo	to dream about somebody/something

Cuento contigo.	I'm relying on you.
Me encontré con ella al entrar en el banco.	I met her as I was going into the bank.
¿Puedo hablar con usted un momento?	May I talk to you for a moment?

Verbs followed by en

➤ Here are some verbs taking **en** in Spanish that have a different construction in English:

entrar en (un edificio/un cuarto)	to enter, go into (a building/a room)
pensar en algo/alguien	to think about something/somebody
No quiero pensar en eso.	I don't want to think about that.

Verbs followed by por

➤ Here are some verbs taking **por** in Spanish that have a different construction in English:

interesarse por algo/alguien	to ask about something/somebody
preguntar por alguien	to ask for/about somebody
preocuparse por algo/alguien	to worry about something/somebody
Me interesaba mucho por la arqueología.	I was very interested in archaeology.
Se preocupa mucho por su apariencia.	He worries a lot about his appearance.

Verbs taking a direct object in Spanish but not in English

➤ In English there are a few verbs that are followed by *at*, *for* or *to* which, in Spanish, are not followed by any preposition other than the personal **a**.

mirar algo/a alguien	to look at something/somebody
escuchar algo/a alguien	to listen to something/somebody
buscar algo/a alguien	to look for something/somebody
pedir algo	to ask for something
esperar algo/a alguien	to wait for something/somebody
pagar algo	to pay for something
Mira esta foto.	Look at this photo.
Me gusta escuchar música.	I like listening to music.
Estoy buscando las gafas.	I'm looking for my glasses.
Pidió una taza de té.	He asked for a cup of tea.
Estamos esperando el tren.	We're waiting for the train.
Ya he pagado el billete.	I've already paid for my ticket.
Estoy buscando a mi hermano.	I'm looking for my brother.

KEY POINTS

- ✔ The prepositions used with Spanish verbs are often very different from those used in English, so make sure you learn common expressions involving prepositions in Spanish.
- ✔ The most common prepositions used with verbs in Spanish are **a**, **de**, **con**, **en** and **por**.
- ✔ Some Spanish verbs are not followed by a preposition, but are used with a preposition in English.

For further explanation of grammatical terms, please see pages viii-x.

Test yourself

174 Complete the following sentences with the correct form of *a* or *de*. Remember that *a + el = al* and *de + el = del*. The first one has been done for you.

a De repente me acordé ...de... Antonio.

b Dale .... esta tecla para que funcione.

c Se bajaron .... autobús.

d No me parezco .... mi hermana.

e En el verano, trabajé .... recepcionista.

f ¿Vamos .... tomar un café?

g ¿Te alegras .... verme?

h Asistieron .... la comida.

i Sube .... tercer piso.

j Se despidieron .... nosotros.

175 Complete the following sentences with the correct form of *a* or *con*. Remember that *a + el = al*.

a Huele .... café.

b Contamos .... vosotros.

c Nos dirigimos .... la entrada.

d Se encontró .... una sorpresa.

e Los fines de semana jugamos .... las cartas.

f Juega .... tu hermana.

g ¿Cuándo llegas .... aeropuerto?

h Nunca cuenta .... su marido.

i Se subieron .... coche.

j Estuvimos hablando .... el jefe.

176 Complete the following sentences with the correct form of *de*, *en*, or *por*. Remember that *de + el = del*. The first one has been done for you.

a No se dio cuenta ...del... error.

b Se ríen .... nosotros.

c Entré .... el grupo hace cinco años.

d Tengo muchas ganas .... verte.

e Se interesan mucho .... sus hijos.

f Eso depende .... ti.

Test yourself

g Preguntamos .... el encargado.

h Se quejan .... ruido.

i Estoy pensando .... tí.

j Se trata .... un momento.

177 Complete the following sentences with the prepositions *con*, *en* or *por*. The first one has been done for you.

a Estamos contentos ....con..... el resultado.

b Se preocupan .... su enfermedad.

c Siempre está pensando .... divertirse.

d No preguntaron .... Marta.

e Tuvimos que salir .... la ventana.

f Sueña .... vivir cerca del mar.

g Tenía que hablar .... la profesora.

h Hay que contar .... ellos.

i Entraron .... su casa.

j Se enfadó .... su novio.

178 Some verbs are followed by a preposition in English but not in Spanish. Translate the following sentences into Spanish.

a She was looking for her glasses. ....

b We were looking at the menu. ....

c She was looking at me. ....

d We paid for the meal. ....

e We listened to the news. ....

f They are waiting for you. ....

g He asked for a pen. ....

h What are you looking for? ....

i We are not asking for money. ....

j Listen to me! ....

Verbal Idioms

Present tense of gustar

➤ You will probably already have come across the phrase **me gusta...** meaning *I like...*. Actually, **gustar** means literally *to please*, and if you remember this, you will be able to use **gustar** much more easily.

Me gusta el chocolate.	I like chocolate. (*literally: chocolate pleases me*)
Me gustan los animales.	I like animals. (*literally: animals please me*)
Nos gusta el español.	We like Spanish. (*literally: Spanish pleases us*)
Nos gustan los españoles.	We like Spanish people. (*literally: Spanish people please us*)

➤ Even though **chocolate**, **animales**, and so on, come after **gustar**, they are the subject of the verb (the person or thing performing the action) and therefore the endings of **gustar** change to agree with them.

➤ When the thing that you like is singular, you use **gusta** (*third person singular*), and when the thing that you like is plural, you use **gustan** (*third person plural*).

Le gusta Francia.	He/She likes France. (*literally: France pleases him/her*)
Le gustan los caramelos.	He/She likes sweets. (*literally: Sweets please him/her*)

ℹ Note that **me**, **te**, **le**, **nos**, **os** and **les**, which are used with **gustar**, are indirect object pronouns.

Other tenses of gustar

➤ You can use **gustar** in other tenses in Spanish.

Les gustó la fiesta.	They liked the party.
Les gustaron los fuegos artificiales.	They liked the fireworks.
Te va a gustar la película.	You'll like the film.
Te van a gustar las fotos.	You'll like the photos.
Les ha gustado mucho el museo.	They really liked the museum.
Les han gustado mucho los cuadros.	They really liked the paintings.

➤ You can also use **más** with **gustar** to say what you prefer.

A mí me gusta más el rojo.	I prefer the red one. (*literally: the red one pleases me more*)
A mí me gustan más los rojos.	I prefer the red ones. (*literally: the red ones please me more*)

Other verbs like gustar

➤ There are several other verbs which behave in the same way as **gustar**:

- encantar

Me encanta el flamenco.	I love flamenco.
Me encantan los animales.	I love animals.

- faltar

Le faltaba un botón.	He had a button missing.
Le faltaban tres dientes.	He had three teeth missing.

- quedar

No les queda nada.	They have nothing left.
Solo nos quedan dos kilómetros.	We've only got two kilometres left.

- doler

Le dolía la cabeza.	His head hurt.
Le dolían las muelas.	His teeth hurt.

- interesar

Te interesará el libro.	The book will interest you.
Te interesarán sus noticias.	His news will interest you.

- importar

No me importa la lluvia.	The rain doesn't matter to me. *or* I don't mind the rain.
Me importan mucho mis estudios.	My studies matter to me a lot.

- hacer falta

Nos hace falta un ordenador.	We need a computer.
Nos hacen falta libros.	We need books.

Grammar Extra!

All the examples given above are in the third persons singular and plural as these are by far the most common. However, it is also possible to use these verbs in other forms.

Creo que le gustas. I think he likes you. (*literally: I think you please him*)

Verbal idioms used with another verb

➤ In English you can say *I like playing football*, *we love swimming* and so on, and in Spanish you can also use another verb with most of the verbs like **gustar**. However, the verb form you use for the second verb in Spanish is the infinitive.

Le gusta jugar al fútbol.	He/She likes playing football.
No me gusta bailar.	I don't like dancing.
Nos encanta estudiar.	We love studying.
No me importa tener que esperar.	I don't mind having to wait.

➪ *For more information on the **Infinitive**, see page 145.*

Key points

✔ There are a number of common verbs in Spanish which are used in the opposite way to English, for example, **gustar**, **encantar**, **hacer falta**, and so on. With all these verbs, the object of the English verb is the subject of the Spanish verb.

✔ The endings of these verbs change according to whether the thing liked or needed and so on is singular or plural.

✔ All these verbs can be followed by another verb in the infinitive.

Test yourself

179 Cross out the subjects that the verb cannot refer to.

a me gusta la película/el fútbol/los pasteles/las cortinas

b os gustan las novelas/el vino/el toreo/leer/las deportivas

c ¿le gustó la obra/el castillo/los juegos/las zapatillas/la sortija?

d ¿os gustaron la casa/los pasteles/los pantalones/París/el reportaje

e no nos han gustado las uvas/los barcos/el ruido/el hotel

f le van a gustar mi amigo/las vacaciones/las asignaturas/sus opiniones/mi bolso

g les ha gustado la comida/el trabajo/los poemas/la fiesta

h ¿te gustaron las rosquillas/los colores/mi coche/las fotos/el chocolate?

i me ha gustado verte/la tienda/los americanos/leer/el zoo

j ¿les gustaba bailar/los bombones/cocinar/el marisco/los libros?

180 Match the two parts of the sentence.

a Le duele unas botas.

b Me hacen falta la pierna.

c ¿Os importa los animales.

d No le hace falta esperar?

e Me encantan dinero.

181 Complete the following sentences with the correct form of the present tense replacing the object shown in brackets with the structure *me, te, le...* + verb. The first one has been done for you.

a ...No me importa... repetirlo. **(importar [a mí])**

b .... mucho las patatas fritas. **(gustar [a él])**

c .... tres informes por revisar. **(quedar [a nosotros])**

d ¿.................................. más que el viejo? **(gustar [a ti])**

e .... el estómago. **(doler [a ella])**

f ¿No .... el campo? **(encantar [a vosotros])**

g .... vasos. **(faltar [a nosotros])**

h No .... grande. **(quedar [a mí])**

i .... más tiempo. **(hacer falta [a nosotros])**

j .... informarte. **(interesar [a ti])**

PRACTICE PRACTICE PRACTICE PRACTICE PRACTICE PRACTICE PRACTICE PRACTICE

Test yourself

182 Translate the following sentences into Spanish. Use a dictionary and the verb tables in this book.

a I love the beach. ....

b We've got no food left. ....

c You are going to like this game. ....

d It matters to me what you do. ....

e They need books in the school. ....

f She had a tooth missing. ....

g Do you prefer the big ones? ....

h I had a headache. ....

i We have only got three more exercises left.

....

j We need milk. ....

Solutions

1
a entr-
b decid-
c escrib-
d com-
e escuch-
f obr-
g celebr-
h beb-
i ayud-
j romp-

2
a salir
b ir/estar
c haber
d conducir
e poner
f caer
g ser
h ir
i venir
j dar

3
a -ar
b -er
c -ar
d -ir
e -ar
f -ar
g -ir
h -er
i -ar
j -ir

4
a ¿Cómo te llamas?
b Trabajo en un colegio.
c Vive en Barcelona.
d Se llama Clara.
e ¿Hablas inglés?
f Mi casa no está lejos.
g Ana tiene quince años
h Hace sol.
i Vivo con unos amigos.
j Es muy alto.

5
a Ana **tiene un perro**.
b Sus padres **llegan por la tarde**.
c Yo **no entiendo nada**.
d Nosotros **vamos en autobús**.
e Vosotros **termináis en diez minutos**.

6
a Los alumnos **repasan la lección**.
b Mi amiga **trabaja por las noches**.
c La película **dura dos horas**.
d Salimos **los dos a la vez**.
e ¿Cuándo **estudias**?

7
a Nieva
b pinta
c solucionas
d Habla
e Estudian
f dominan
g estiro
h peláis
i Gasta
j planean

8
a ¿Estudias francés?
b Habla con Laura todas las semanas.
c La película empieza a las nueve.
d Siempre viaja en coche.
e Limpio la casa los viernes.
f Odia el pop.
g Canto en un coro.
h Llegan por la mañana.
i ¿Cómo te llamas?
j ¿Desayunáis todos en la cocina?

9
a Exageras mucho.
b Alicia la espera en la parada del autobús.
c Los dos pintan muebles.
d Muchos jóvenes emigran pronto al extranjero.
e ¿Dónde filman la película?
f ¿Por dónde entráis a la casa?
g Sólo cocinamos los fines de semana.
h Los domingos miramos la televisión.
i Por la noche siempre los arropo.
j Aitana siempre repasa la lección antes del examen.

10
a el secuestrador
b el perro/yo/Luis
c las estufas
d tú/María y tú
e los turistas/el guía
f el deportista
g la señora de la limpieza/ mi padre
h el coche/Andrés
i un amigo/las dudas/ muchas personas
j los jefes/los conferenciantes

11
a cultiva
b evolucionan
c adivinas
d Admiro
e bucean
f complicáis
g copiamos
h Suman
i ganan
j ordena

12
a doblamos
b dibujamos
c cortamos
d Rellenamos
e pegamos

13
a laváis
b cortan
c cavo
d fumamos
e cultivan
f escapa
g miráis
h gastas
i nado
j dibuja

14
a Corta
b Brilla
c Quema
d Lava
e adorna
f Funciona
g Cocina
h Ilumina
i Ahorra
j graba

15
a Estas flores **crecen en el campo**.
b El autobús **recorre toda la costa**.
c El niño **tose un poco**.
d Comemos **los dos juntos**.
e Te **veo más tarde**.

16
a comprendo
b Comen
c deben
d bebes
e lee
f ofende
g Venden
h depende
i Entendéis
j accedes

17
a ¿Dónde metemos las cajas?

Solutions

- **b** No comprendo los ejercicios.
- **c** Los alumnos leen cada día en clase.
- **d** Las raíces absorben el agua.
- **e** ¿A cuánto vendéis los tomates?
- **f** Lucía ve las películas en el ordenador.
- **g** Así no ofendo a nadie.
- **h** No entiende a Susana.
- **i** Primero respondemos a tus preguntas.
- **j** Mi madre se mete en la cama a las diez.

18
- **a** aprende
- **b** Coge
- **c** come bebe
- **d** debe
- **e** Hace responde

19
- **a** comes
- **b** bebemos
- **c** cosen
- **d** vende
- **e** aprende
- **f** metes
- **g** tejéis
- **h** recorren
- **i** sabemos
- **j** debemos

20
- **a** Toses
- **b** prometo
- **c** come
- **d** vendemos
- **e** coses
- **f** Comprendo
- **g** Teméis
- **h** sorprenden
- **i** metéis
- **j** suspendemos

21
- **a** ¿Venden aquí baterías para el móvil?
- **b** Barro la cocina todos los días.
- **c** No bebo alcohol.
- **d** Pablo aprende chino en el colegio.
- **e** No meto la mermelada en la nevera.
- **f** Lee libros en la biblioteca.
- **g** ¿Le debéis todos dinero?.
- **h** Veo a Ana en la universidad.
- **i** ¿Lo conoces?
- **j** Ven muy poco la tele.

22
- **a** Crecimos **los dos en el mismo pueblo**.
- **b** Creo **que no es cierto**.
- **c** ¿Vosotros **bebéis leche en el desayuno**?
- **d** Los niños **temen a su padre**.
- **e** ¿En el supermercado **venden ropa**?

23
- **a** aprenden
- **b** Debe
- **c** Arde
- **d** prometo
- **e** Absorbe
- **f** Recorre
- **g** Teje
- **h** accedes
- **i** Venden
- **j** suspenden

24
- **a** ¿Cómo las conoces?
- **b** Luis la ve todas las semanas.
- **c** No lo comprendo.
- **d** Os lo prometemos.
- **e** Mi madre los mete antes en agua.
- **f** Lo ves en la pantalla.
- **g** Siempre la sorprendemos.
- **h** ¿A cuánto lo vendemos?
- **i** La entiendo.
- **j** ¿Por qué no lo coméis?

25
- **a** compartimos
- **b** vive
- **c** escriben
- **d** subís
- **e** permiten
- **f** interrumpes
- **g** abrimos
- **h** parto
- **i** recibimos
- **j** imprimo

26
- **a** Siempre insisto en ello.
- **b** Viven juntos.
- **c** Recibo fotos en mi móvil.
- **d** Dividen las tareas entre los tres.
- **e** ¿Cómo escribes tu nombre?
- **f** ¿Viven cerca?
- **g** No lo permiten.
- **h** Lo cubro con una tela.
- **i** ¿Por qué insistes?
- **j** Estas plantas sobreviven condiciones muy extremas.

27
- **a** Alicia no sube nunca en ascensor.
- **b** Mis padres no me permiten fumar en casa.
- **c** ¿Los subes por la escalera?
- **d** Todas las mañanas los visto.
- **e** Los profesores no nos permiten móviles en clase.
- **f** Siempre reciben muchos regalos.
- **g** Nunca interrumpimos a la profesora.
- **h** ¿Cuándo recibís la paga?
- **i** ¿Por qué me interrumpes?

28
- **a** vivo
- **b** Comparto
- **c** recibo
- **d** Escribo imprimo
- **e** recibo

29
- **a** subimos
- **b** abren
- **c** escribís
- **d** sobrevivimos
- **e** imprime
- **f** parto
- **g** aplaudes
- **h** recibís
- **i** unimos
- **j** interrumpes

30
- **a** permiten
- **b** Imprime
- **c** recibe
- **d** Parte
- **e** aplauden
- **f** añade
- **g** crujen
- **h** Abre
- **i** discuten
- **j** comparten

31
- **a** viven
- **b** Ocurre
- **c** recibe
- **d** Escribes
- **e** Suben
- **f** divides
- **g** compartimos
- **h** gruñe

Solutions

i recibo
j abres

32 a la profesora/la policía
b una historia/un accidente
c el portero
d tú
e el león
f mis amigos
g mi primo/mi novia
h Ana/el médico
i mi profesor
j el obrero

33 a Ocurre **en las mejores familias**.
b Los problemas **unen a los amigos**.
c Si me gusta el espectáculo, **aplaudo mucho**.
d Mi novia y yo **vivimos en el campo**.
e Mi móvil **no recibe mensajes**.

34 a No vive con sus padres.
b Nunca abro tus cartas.
c ¿Dónde viven tus padres?
d Unes las dos partes con esto.
e El profesor de deportes siempre divide a la clase en tres grupos.
f Este animal sobrevive con poca agua.
g Suben a verme a menudo.
h Aquí no recibo llamadas.
i Todos los días subo tres pisos.
j Nunca discute con ella.

35 a Cierran
b pienso
c encuentra
d visto
e entienden
f pierdes
g duerme
h pido
i preferimos
j cierras

36 a No encuentro mis gafas.
b Siempre pierde la cartera en la calle.
c Prefiero los vaqueros negros con la camisa.
d Mis padres duermen la siesta después de comer.
e La ropa de Ana me sirve.
f No entienden las preguntas.
g Piensan lo mismo que ellas.
h Prefiere el helado de fresa.
i No duerme bien en verano.
j Nunca os pido un favor.

37 a Duermen en el ático.
b Piensas demasiado.
c Conducen por la derecha.
d No entiende el problema.
e Si pierdo las llaves no puedo entrar.
f Cerramos los domingos.
g Te entiendo.
h No puede hacerlo.
i No entienden muy bien inglés.
j Apenas la recuerdo.

38 a Puedo
b recuerdo
c sirve
d pide
e pierden
f entiendes
g recuerdan
h Cerráis
i Juegan
j empiezan

39 a yo
b el abuelo/yo
c mis padres/los perros
d tu madre/Ina
e Alberto/los novios
f nosotros
g la tienda/la panadería
h tu madre/Ina
i Alberto/los novios
j tú/vosotros

40 a traigo
b tienen
c hago
d valen
e van
f oyen
g Voy
h quiere
i salgo
j conozco

41 a Primero hago la cama de los niños.
b Bea tiene una casa en el campo.
c Yo pongo un poco de vinagre en la salsa.
d Van a la playa los fines de semana.
e No tengo tiempo para terminar.
f Los hijos vienen por las tardes.
g Digo la verdad siempre.
h No la oigo.
i Así no se caen los libros.

42 a Tiene dos perros.
b Pongo la calefacción por la noche.
c Voy al colegio.
d ¿Qué hago con esto?
e ¿Cuánto es?
f Vienen a casa todos los domingos.
g Sólo digo lo que pienso.
h ¿Por dónde salgo?
i No sé la respuesta.
j Conozco a gente de ese colegio.

43 a traen
b vamos
c oigo
d hago
e vienen
f Sé
g Hago
h digo
i Vais
j Tienes

44 a Vale la pena. **It's worth it.**
b ¡Oye! **Listen!**
c ¡Ya voy! **I'm coming!**
d No lo sé. **I don't know.**
e Póntelo. **Put it on.**

45 a es
b somos
c está
d está
e Son
f son
g son
h está
i estoy
j está

46 a Olga y Lola **están agotadas**.

Solutions

b Laura **es muy graciosa**.
c Mis padres **están nerviosos**.
d La caja **es de metal**.
e La comida **está muy picante**.

47 **a** Estás muy guapa. **You look very nice.**
b Sus hijos son muy altos. **His children are very tall.**
c Juan está aburrido. **Juan is bored.**
d Eres muy guapa. **You are very pretty.**
e Juan es muy aburrido. **Juan is really boring.**

48 **a** Está enfermo.
b Está dormida.
c Son muy cabezotas.
d Están en una boda.
e Teresa está Brussels toda esta semana.
f Su asignatura es muy difícil.
g La película es bastante divertida.
h Es hora de cenar.
i ¿Cómo estáis?
j Los CDs son de Paula.

49 **a** son
b está
c Está
d es
e está
f estoy
g están
h es
i somos
j es

50 **a** Están de viaje. **They are on a trip.**
b ¡Estamos de vacaciones! **We are on holiday!**
c Las botas están de moda. **Boots are in fashion.**
d Estamos de pie. **We are standing.**
e Estaban de lado. **They were on their side.**

51 **a** ¿Dónde están las camisas?
b Son poco inteligentes.
c Ya no estoy enfadado con Luisa.
d Mi hermana y yo somos parecidas.
e Están practicando el clarinete.
f La tienda está cerrada los domingos.
g ¿Estás sólo en la casa?
h Las mermeladas son fabricadas en España
i Es fundamental llegar a tiempo.
j La ventana está cerrada.

52 **a** Estamos nadando
b Está viviendo
c Está estudiando
d Está aprendiendo
e Están comprando
f Estoy trabajando
g Estamos viendo
h estás mirando
i Estoy leyendo
j Están cosiendo

53 **a** Están cerrando la tienda. **They're closing the shop.**
b Está haciéndose famoso. **He is getting famous.**
c Estoy ahorrando mucho. **I'm saving a lot.**
d Está aprendiendo judo. **He is learning judo.**
e Estáis perdiendo el tiempo. **You are wasting time.**

54 **a** estoy trabajando
b Está hablando
c están estudiando
d está haciendo
e están durmiendo
f estamos decorando
g está perdiendo
h están comprando
i estoy poniéndome
j está comiendo

55 **a** Los niños están jugando en el parque.
b Estamos ahorrando para comprar un coche.
c ¿Estás comiendo?
d No estoy durmiendo.
e Están viendo una película.
f Ahora estamos viviendo en la India.
g Están cambiando el sistema.
h Están leyendo el informe.
i Estamos haciendo una paella.
j Están abrazándose.

56 **a** María está aprendiendo a conducir.
b Los trabajadores están haciendo huelga.
c Jorge y yo estamos limpiando la cocina.
d Nuria está cambiando de trabajo.
e Su madre está sufriendo mucho.
f Este año estoy viajando con menos frecuencia.
g Estás distrayéndote con el ruido.
h Desde junio estamos cuidando de nuestra madre.
i No estoy criticándola.
j El perro está moviendo la cola.

57 **a** Está escribiendo
b están comprando
c crujen
d calienta
e está vistiéndose
f tomo
g está esperando
h Leo
i Estoy terminando
j Veranean

58 **a** está renovando
b Está comprando
c está contratando
d están aprendiendo están trabajando
e está haciendo obra

59 **a** Está nevando.
b Estoy escuchando.
c No te estás portando bien.
d Está hirviendo.
e Estás creciendo.
f Se está cayendo.
g Las cosas están cambiando.
h ¿Estás comiendo ahora mismo?
i Nos está mintiendo.
j Están vendiendo el coche.

Solutions

60 **a** estámos cocinando **b** Estoy pintando **c** están jugando **d** están atacando **e** Estáis usando **f** estamos celebrando **g** está descansando **h** estás leyendo **i** está esperando **j** Están estudiando

61 **a** está hablando **b** estoy trabajando **c** está ayudando **d** están yendo **e** está contando **f** Estás leyendo **g** Estoy escribiendo **h** estamos decorando **i** estamos vendiendo **j** está escuchando

62 **a** saltes **b** escuchéis **c** repitamos **d** comas **e** trabajéis **f** beba **g** busques **h** te retrases **i** pisen **j** dudes

63 **a** digas **b** estéis **c** salgan **d** vayamos **e** vengas **f** den **g** seáis **h** tenga **i** te pongas **j** vengas

64 **a** Repite **b** Cantad **c** Copiad **d** estudia **e** Copien **f** Corred **g** Esté **h** Viajemos **i** suéltame **j** Atad

65 **a** Haced **b** Tengan **c** Ve **d** Hagamos **e** Hagan **f** Ven **g** Poned **h** Esté **i** Sal **j** Dáme

66 **a** ¡Escucha más atentamente! **b** ¡Estudiemos la propuesta! **c** ¡Pórtate bien! **d** ¡No lo cambiéis! **e** ¡Cerrad la boca! **f** ¡No molestemos a la abuela! **g** ¡Esperadme ahí! **h** ¡Castígala! **i** ¡Mándelos callar! **j** ¡Hablad más alto!

67 **a** ¡Cállate! **b** ¡Ven ahora mismo! **c** ¡No se lo des (a ella)! **d** ¡Escúchala! **e** Llamémoslos. **f** ¡No lo tires! **g** ¡No digas eso! **h** Empecemos desde el principio. **i** ¡Ponlo ahí encima! **j** ¡Intentémoslo otra vez!

68 **a** ¡No me digas! **You don't say!** **b** ¡Atiende! **Pay attention!** **c** ¡Suelta! **Let go!** **d** ¡Guardad silencio! **Keep quiet!** **e** ¡Tenga! **Here you are!**

69 **a** ¡Lee esto! **b** ¡Atendedme, por favor! **c** ¡Préstale cincuenta euros a Javi! **d** ¡Dáselo! **e** ¡Ayudadme! **f** ¡Escúchanos! **g** ¡Acaba con el ordenador! **h** ¡Cuéntaselo! **i** ¡Obedéceme! **j** ¡Ven aquí!

70 **a** Llámame **b** Sácalo **c** Ven **d** Tíralo **e** Distráeme **f** Dejadles **g** Mírale **h** Contéstala **i** Muévelo **j** Traigámoslos

71 **a** ¿Queréis acostaros ya? **b** Tiene que marcharse pronto. **c** Está lavándose el pelo. **d** Están esperándome. **e** Queremos quedarnos. **f** No quiero sentarme con ella. **g** ¿Queréis quitaros el abrigo? **h** Está vistiéndose en este momento. **i** Vamos a levantarnos temprano. **j** Están mirándose todo el tiempo al espejo.

72 **a** No te marches. **b** No te levantes. **c** No te peines. **d** No te muevas. **e** No os calléis. **f** No te duches ahora. **g** No te quites los zapatos. **h** No te bebas la leche. **i** No te subas la manga. **j** No te quites de ahí.

73 **a** Se está lavando los dientes. **b** Clara y Jorge, poneos el abrigo. **c** Se duchan por la noche. **d** Tienes que lavarte el pelo **e** ¿No te quitas los guantes? **f** Lávate las manos con agua y jabón. **g** Átate los cordones de los zapatos **h** ¿Te estás vistiendo? **i** Los niños siempre se bañan antes de irse a la cama **j** Mejor ponte las botas.

74 **a** Aquí se habla inglés. **b** Se venden muchos libros en el supermercado. **c** Se compran coches viejos en el garaje. **d** Se fabrican coches en Alemania. **e** Se reparan ordenadores. **f** Desde allí se exporta por toda Europa. **g** En esa casa se alquila un piso. **h** Se hacen fotocopias.

Solutions

- i En el kiosko se venden periódicos.
- j Se compra y se vende.

75
- **a** Se prohíbe
- **b** se permite
- **c** Se permite
- **d** se permite
- **e** Se prohíbe
- **f** se permite
- **g** se permite
- **h** Se prohíbe
- **i** Se permite
- **j** se prohíbe

76
- **a** Se cubre con un plástico para protegerlo.
- **b** La ropa se fabrica en la India.
- **c** Se enseñan tres idiomas en el colegio.
- **d** Luego se protege con un código especial.
- **e** La comida se distribuye por el país.
- **f** La mesa se pinta con una pintura especial.
- **g** Se hace con buenos materiales.
- **h** Se comprueban todas las piezas/partes.
- **i** Todos los documentos se revisan.
- **j** Después se lavan las verduras.

77
- **a** Me lavo la herida cada día.
- **b** Se levanta antes de las 8.
- **c** Ahora se cansa con facilidad.
- **d** Nos sentamos en un sofá viejo.
- **e** No te disgustes con ella.
- **f** Nos reímos mucho con la película.
- **g** Los niños se disfrazan de payasos con ropas viejas.
- **h** Os enfadáis por nada.
- **i** El pequeño ya se pone los calcetines solo.
- **j** ¿Cómo se llama tu novia?

78
- **a** Se aman.
- **b** Se llaman a menudo.
- **c** Nos conocemos bien.
- **d** Mis hijas se pelean mucho.
- **e** Victoria y Chus apenas se hablan.
- **f** Se mandan mensajes de móvil.
- **g** No se reconocen
- **h** Nos odiamos.
- **i** No se respetan
- **j** Lorenzo y Gabi se ayudan siempre.

79
- **a** Duerme en el sofá. **She sleeps on the sofa.**
- **b** Yo me voy. **I'm leaving.**
- **c** La puerta se abre. **The door opens.**
- **d** Yo voy. **I'm coming.**
- **e** Me duermo en el sofá viendo la tele. **I fall asleep on the sofa watching TV.**

80
- **a** se levanta
- **b** se ducha
  se afeita
- **c** se prepara
  se ríe
- **d** Se bebe
  se come
- **e** se va

81
- **a** Van a visitar
- **b** Van a escuchar
- **c** Vas a poder
- **d** Vamos a cocinar
- **e** Vamos a ir
- **f** Van a renovar
- **g** Va a aprender
- **h** váis a querer
- **i** Van a hacer
- **j** Vamos

82
- **a** encontrarás
- **b** Se derretirá
- **c** te ayudará
- **d** imprimiré
- **e** os levantareis
- **f** llamarán
- **g** Trabajaré
- **h** nos quedaremos
- **i** Se preparará
- **j** resolveremos

83
- **a** conoceré
- **b** compraré
- **c** voy a visitarlos
- **d** van a dormir
- **e** voy a hablar
- **f** Usarás
- **g** Voy a
- **h** voy a irme
- **i** sembraré
- **j** voy a arreglarlo

84
- **a** Nosotros **hablaremos con Lucía**.
- **b** Mis vecinos **van a ir de vacaciones a la playa**.
- **c** También yo **estaré esperando**.
- **d** Mi primo y tú **os veréis en Navidad**.
- **e** Los niños **van a jugar en el salón**

85
- **a** No podré hacerlo sola.
- **b** ¿A qué hora saldremos de casa?
- **c** ¿No saldréis este domingo?
- **d** Lo querrá todo para ella.
- **e** Pedro y María harán la comida para el cumpleaños.
- **f** ¿Te pondrás el vestido nuevo para Navidad?
- **g** Le diré la verdad.
- **h** Pilar se pondrá en contacto con Luis.
- **i** ¿Vendréis a verme el año próximo?
- **j** Leeré el periódico en el viaje.

86
- **a** Iréis
- **b** Pondrás
- **c** dirá
- **d** saldrá
- **e** querrán
- **f** tendré
- **g** vendrán
- **h** saldrán
- **i** habré
- **j** Harán

87
- **a** Lo diré otra vez.
- **b** No podré verlo.
- **c** Saldremos a las tres.
- **d** Va a intentar arreglarlo.
- **e** Vendré a verte.
- **f** Saldrá por la mañana.
- **g** Va a hacerlo otra vez.
- **h** No tendrán dinero para comprarlo.
- **i** Mañana va a llover.
- **j** ¿Cuándo llamarán?
- **k** ¿Irás a esquiar estas Navidades?
- **l** ¿Estarán esta tarde en casa?

88
- **a** Saldrás
- **b** Irás
  cogerás

Solutions

c te sentarás
d hablarás
e estará
llevará

89 a se quedaría
b tardaría
c gustaría
d Me comería
e dejaría
f viajaría
g se compraría
h viviría
i Dejaría
j deberíamos

90 a Ana cambiaría el color.
b Su padre la escucharía más.
c Los alumnos deberían estudiar más para el examen.
d Podríais comprar una cama más grande.
e No comería en ese restaurante.
f Debería intentar tranquilizarse un poco.
g Yo no la llamaría.
h Podríais hacer ejercicio más a menudo.
i ¿Cómo hablarías del tema con Marisa?
j Mis hermanos preferirían venir enseguida.

91 a sabría
b Podrías
c saldría
d harías
e tendría
f Podrías
g pondría
h dirías
i querría
j diría

92 a Alejandro **debería cambiar de trabajo**.
b ¿Os **compraríais esta casa**?
c Yo si heredase, **dejaría de trabajar**.
d Vosotras dos **podríais ir juntas**.
e Aquí ellos **lo pasarían bien**.

93 a Deberías atender más en clase.
b Les gustaría conocerte.
c ¿Tú lo harías?
d No deberían gastar tanto.
e Podrías visitar el castillo.
f Con ese dinero, compraría un barco.
g No me importaría.
h El perro no se comería eso.
i Yo no me preocuparía.
j Deberían preguntar primero.

94 a What should they do? **Deberían asegurarse primero.**
b What would they like to do? **Les gustaría ir al cine.**
c What would you do? **Yo no se lo diría.**
d What could we do on holiday? **Podríais ir a la playa.**
e What would they prefer? **Preferirían comer carne.**

95 a importaría
b tendría
c sabría
d encantaría
e gustaría
f sería
g tendría
h gustaría
i importaría
j me iría

96 a terminó
b se separaron
c llegó
d subieron
e habló
f rompió
g compró
h os casasteis
i pregunté
j trabajaron

97 a estuvieron
b dije
c dieron
d anduvieron
e trajimos
f fui
g conduje
h tuvo
i hicísteis
j supieron

98 a reísteis
b siguió
c pedí
d se durmió
e sentí
f pedisteis
g murió
h Sentí
i pidieron
j seguimos

99 a Toni hizo un castillo de arena en la playa.
b Le dije a María la verdad
c Pedro y yo fuimos en barco a Barcelona.
d ¿Cómo pudiste cruzar a nado?
e ¿Qué les dijisteis en la reunión?
f La ambulancia condujo a toda velocidad.
g Estuviste muy tranquilo toda la tarde.
h ¿Dónde pusisteis el dinero?
i ¿Les distes los documentos?
j Me trajeron el maletín.

100 a saqué
b Construyeron
c Pagaron
d condujo
e pudieron
f Empecé
g cruzaron
h Supiste
i quisieron
j trajiste

101 a Anduvisteis de noche.
b Dijiste la verdad.
c Fuiste solo.
d Pudo entrar.
e Quisisteis probar.
f Supieron esperar.
g Distes dinero.
h Os pusisteis el abrigo.
i Tuviste valor.
j Quisieron preguntar.

102 a cruzó
vió
b empezasteis
c construyeron
d leíste
e cayeron
f pagué

Solutions

g saqué
me puse
h leyeron
i Caí
j vimos

103 **a** Lo encontré debajo de la cama.
b Perdieron el partido.
c Perdí las llaves en la calle.
d Salieron otra vez.
e Compró unos libros y unos CDs.
f Pidieron café.
g Tuve un problema.
h Pilar trajo unos juegos.
i El ministro dimitió ayer.
j Conduje todo el tiempo.

104 **a** caminaban
b sabía
c trabajabas
d se aburrían
e hablábais
f estornudaba
g hería
h llorabas
i estaba
j necesitabas

105 **a** era
b iban
c veíamos
d eran
e iba
f veíamos
g era
h erais
i veía
j iba

106 **a** Felix merecía ganar el premio.
b Los niños obedecían pero también protestaban a menudo.
c En el pueblo normalmente refrescaba por las noches.
d Siempre nos regalaba ropa.
e No hablaba con Nerea desde el verano.
f Antes pensabas diferente.
g En la casa todos temíamos malas noticias.
h Ana montaba a caballo desde los 7 años.
i Se sentía acomplejada porque era muy baja.
j ¿Te curaste de la enfermedad?

107 **a** ¿Vivías entonces en Inglaterra?
b Todos los días mi madre me recogía del colegio.
c Cuando era pequeño, no tenía muchos amigos.
d Se sentían solos en la gran ciudad.
e Siempre ganaban.
f Todas las noches leía su carta.
g No teníamos mucho tiempo.
h Estaban agotados.
i ¿Qué hacías?
j Éramos más de treinta.

108 **a** Salíamos
b desayunaba
c Vivían
d Íbamos
e cenábamos
f se sentía
g veíamos
h trabajaba
i compraba
j Veían

109 **a** Hacía tres años que estaba enfermo/Estaba enfermo desde hacía tres años.
b No la veía desde el colegio.
c Hacía un tiempo que vivíamos en Londres./ Vivíamos en Londres desde hacía un tiempo.
d Hacía tres años que tocaban en el grupo./ Tocaban en el grupo desde hacía tres años.
e Hacía mucho tiempo que tenía el mismo coche./Tenía el mismo coche desde hacía mucho tiempo.
f No había comido desde el desayuno.
g No nos hablábamos desde la universidad.
h Hacía diez años que hacía el mismo trabajo./ Hacía el mismo trabajo desde hacía diez años.
i Hacía dos años que Iván no iba de vacaciones./ Iván no iba de vacaciones desde hacía dos años.
j Hacía tres meses que ordenaba la habitación./ No había ordenado la habitación desde hacía meses.

110 **a** María no lo oía bien.
b Luis y Antonio eran amigos desde la infancia.
c Narraba la historia con música.
d El zorro escarbaba en el suelo.
e A los tres años ya gateaba.
f Iban poco de fiesta.
g ¿No ibais muy deprisa en la moto?
h Pilar los leía con interés.
i Veía las montañas desde mi habitación.
j Los ayudaban a pagar el piso.

111 **a** Desde hacía cinco años **no iban a esquiar**.
b De jóvenes **íbamos mucho a bailar**.
c Oí el ruido **mientras me vestía**.
d Estaba dormida **cuando la llamaron**.
e Me levantaba a las 7 **para ir a trabajar**.

112 **a** han terminado
b hemos estado
c he vendido
d habéis hecho
e hemos visto
f He puesto
g han dicho
h he leído
i He cubierto
j han vuelto

113 **a** ¿Habéis estado en Suecia ya?
b ¿Qué has hecho con el coche viejo?
c Arturo ha ido de vacaciones a Francia.
d He tomado demasiado café.
e ¿No habéis oído la noticia?
f Han montado un

Solutions

negocio de ordenadores en el pueblo.
- **g** Cientos de personas han muerto en el terremoto.
- **h** Los dos países han roto relaciones.
- **i** Carmen ha puesto un bar.
- **j** Hoy lo he visto en la estación.

114
- **a** Me las he comprado.
- **b** María las ha regado esta mañana.
- **c** Ya lo he leído.
- **d** Los directivos los han reunido.
- **e** ¿Las habéis pintado otra vez?
- **f** Me la he encontrado en la calle.
- **g** Lo han roto.
- **h** Les ha sacado una foto.
- **i** Lo he terminado.
- **j** Lo ha vendido.

115
- **a** Ya me he duchado
- **b** Ya se han sentado.
- **c** Ya se ha acostado
- **d** Ya me he secado.
- **e** Ya se ha afeitado
- **f** Ya se han enfadado.
- **g** Ya se ha dormido.
- **h** Ya se ha ido.
- **i** Ya lo han repetido.
- **j** ¡Ya me he disfrazado!

116
- **a** Alberto/el perro
- **b** el alumno
- **c** mi hemana
- **d** Cristina/las dos amigas
- **e** Andrea
- **f** los abuelos
- **g** Lorenzo
- **h** los carteros
- **i** los abuelos/Cristina
- **j** los profesores/Alberto

117
- **a** cogido
- **b** usado
- **c** vivido
- **d** abierto
- **e** dicho
- **f** cubierto
- **g** hecho
- **h** puesto
- **i** vuelto
- **j** visto

118
- **a** Did you notice that?
- **b** Did you see the way he looked at her?
- **c** Did you run to come here?
- **d** He's gone just now. Did you see him?
- **e** Did you see his face when he heard?

119
- **a** Estoy enfermo desde enero.
- **b** Lo conocemos desde el verano.
- **c** Viven aquí desde el año pasado.
- **d** Pinta desde hace cinco años.
- **e** Tiene la bici desde hace mucho tiempo.
- **f** Trabaja en el hospital desde el año pasado.
- **g** ¿Desde cuándo te interesa mi trabajo?
- **h** Hace ballet desde que era pequeña
- **i** Estudio francés desde hace tres años.
- **j** Usan el mismo sistema desde hace años.

120
- **a** No lo hemos terminado.
- **b** Ya lo hemos visto.
- **c** Ha cambiado mucho.
- **d** ¿Quién se ha comido el pastel?
- **e** He olvidado tu nombre.
- **f** ¿Lo has hecho ya?
- **g** ¿Has abierto el archivo?
- **h** No ha dicho mucho.
- **i** Aún no he hecho los deberes.
- **j** Aún no he comido.

121
- **a** Habían probado
- **b** habían conseguido
- **c** había marcado
- **d** Habían reunido
- **e** habían nacido
- **f** había comprado
- **g** habías ordenado
- **h** habían hablado
- **i** habíamos preparado
- **j** habían pintado

122
- **a** El niño había puesto los juguetes debajo de la cama.
- **b** ¿Qué habíais decidido vosotros antes de hablar con él?
- **c** Yo había sospechado la verdad desde el principio.
- **d** El dueño había muerto en 1965.
- **e** Ellos ya habían oído la sirena.
- **f** No les había visto desde la semana anterior.
- **g** Nunca habíamos dicho nada malo de ella.
- **h** Emilio no se había molestado en absoluto por eso.
- **i** ¿Dónde había guardado el dinero Gloria?
- **j** Elena ya se había puesto en contacto conmigo.

123
- **a** habían oído
- **b** había frito
- **c** había hecho
- **d** habían vuelto
- **e** había escrito
- **f** habían puesto
- **g** habías roto
- **h** había cubierto
- **i** habían dicho
- **j** había abierto

124
- **a** Aún no lo habían leído.
- **b** Se la había comprado.
- **c** Los padres la habían organizado.
- **d** Lo habían construido entre las dos casas.
- **e** Se la había encontrado en el concierto.
- **f** Ana los había plantado esa tarde.
- **g** Carolina les había hecho unos vestidos.
- **h** La habían terminado toda.
- **i** La habíamos pintado de nuevo.
- **j** Mis padres las habían comprado cerca.

125
- **a** Ya los había escrito.
- **b** Ya lo habíamos hecho.
- **c** Ya nos habíamos acostado.
- **d** Ya se habían puesto de pie.
- **e** Ya me había afeitado
- **f** Ya nos habían visto.
- **g** Ya se había muerto.
- **h** Ya habían salido.
- **i** Ya las había destruido.
- **j** Ya la había oído.

126
- **a** No lo habían terminado.
- **b** Laura no había

Solutions

cambiado desde entonces.
- **c** No había decidido ir.
- **d** ¿Os habíais levantado ya a esa hora?
- **e** ¿Se lo habías dicho a tus padres?
- **f** Nunca había esquiado antes.
- **g** Nunca habíamos visitado la catedral.
- **h** Todavía no había ido a ver esa película.
- **i** Ya había decidido dejarlo.
- **j** Ya habían empezado el examen.

127
- **a** Estaba en el extranjero desde mayo.
- **b** Lo conocíamos desde el otoño.
- **c** Escribía desde joven.
- **d** Montaba a caballo desde pequeña.
- **e** Trabajábamos en el proyecto desde el año pasado.
- **f** Salían juntos desde hacía un tiempo.
- **g** Se escribían desde hacía meses.
- **h** Se preparaban desde hacía un año.
- **i** Nos amábamos desde hacía años.
- **j** La miraba desde hacía un rato.

128
- **a** What had he done? **Había roto el jarrón.**
- **b** How had you do it? **Había usado pinturas.**
- **c** Where had they gone? **Habían ido a París.**
- **d** What had you and Laura agreed? **Habíamos acordado dividirlo entre las dos.**
- **e** How long had we taken? **Habíamos tardado una hora.**

129
- **a** Marta ya nos había dicho lo de la pelea.
- **b** Yo ya le había escrito con la respuesta.
- **c** ¿Por qué no lo habíais hecho mejor?
- **d** ¿Cómo lo habías roto?
- **e** ¿Quién había escrito el mensaje?
- **f** La primera vez no lo había oído.
- **g** Había frito unas patatas para la cena.
- **h** Teresa había puesto el móvil en el bolso.
- **i** Os habéis puesto muy gordos
- **j** No había vuelto a casa desde la pelea.

130
- **a** El poema fue escrito por su abuelo.
- **b** La casa fue construida por un famoso arquitecto.
- **c** El proyecto fue revisado por el ingeniero.
- **d** La calle fue cerrada por la policía.
- **e** Muchos fueron heridos por la bomba.
- **f** El reloj fue fabricado en Suiza.
- **g** La escultura fue creada por Giacometti.
- **h** La escena fue rodada en directo.
- **i** El cuadro fue comprado por un magnate.
- **j** Los derechos fueron adquiridos por la editorial.

131
- **a** fue abierta
- **b** fueron consultados
- **c** fueron maltratados
- **d** fueron llevados
- **e** fueron puestos
- **f** fueron debatidas
- **g** fue visto
- **h** fue destruida
- **i** fueron eliminados
- **j** Fueron robadas

132
- **a** será construido
- **b** será fabricado
- **c** será anunciada
- **d** serán repartidos
- **e** será rodada
- **f** será interrogado
- **g** será celebrado
- **h** será renovado
- **i** serán donadas
- **j** serán empaquetados

133
- **a** ha sido recubierto
- **b** han sido rechazadas
- **c** He sido traicionado
- **d** ha sido enviado
- **e** ha sido celebrado
- **f** ha sido escrito
- **g** han sido derrotados
- **h** han sido eliminados
- **i** han sido realizados
- **j** Han sido tratados

134
- **a** se renovó
- **b** Se construyeron
- **c** se canceló
- **d** se distribuirán
- **e** se redactó
- **f** se analizó
- **g** se explicarán
- **h** se adquirió
- **i** se reparará
- **j** se empaquetarán

135
- **a** Empaquetado en Grecia. **Packed in Greece.**
- **b** Es hecho a mano.
- **b** **It's handmade.**
- **c** Se vende piso. **Flat for sale.**
- **d** Se compra oro. **We buy gold.**
- **e** Se fabrica en España.
- **f** **It's made in Spain.**

136
- **a** Los zapatos se fabrican en Mallorca.
- **b** La serie se está rodando en Argentina.
- **c** Se ha perdido demasiado tiempo.
- **d** Se ha gastado todo el dinero.
- **e** Se han plantado nuevos árboles frente al museo.
- **f** Los pisos se vendieron muy rápido.
- **g** Se inventó en 1993.
- **h** Se hizo con cuidado.
- **i** Se compró con dinero de la empresa.
- **j** Se revisaron con cuidado.

137
- **a** Llevaron a los jugadores al hotel.
- **b** El camarero nos sirvió la comida.
- **c** Nos llevaron a un lugar secreto.
- **d** El comité está revisando el plan.
- **e** La policía los sorprendió.
- **f** La empujaron.
- **g** Su jefe le dio un aviso.

Solutions

h Lo examinaron cuidadosamente.
i Nos invitaron/Nos invitó el domingo.
j Lo escribió un amigo.

138 a estornudando
b chillando
c ayudando
d extendiendo
e estudiando
f cantando
g preparando
h bañando
i haciendo
j esperando

139 a leyendo
b viviendo
c creyendo
d muriendo
e estudiando
f diciendo
g cayendo
h viendo
i durmiendo
j pidiendo

140 a Ana seguía leyendo en el sofá.
b Los chicos siguen durmiendo todavía.
c Mi tía seguía hablando por teléfono.
d Los invitados siguen comiendo.
e Patxi sigue insistiendo en que él no lo hizo.
f ¿Vosotros seguís estudiando en la biblioteca?
g Sigue escribiendo con pluma.
h Seguía yendo al trabajo en bicicleta.
i Nuria y Julia seguían siendo amigas.
j Seguía conduciendo un coche rojo.

141 a Llevaba tres días trabajando sin descanso.
b Nerea y Pablo llevan un año estudiando japonés.
c Llevábamos dos semanas sin saber de ellos.
d Alicia lleva una hora esperando en el café.
e Juan lleva tres años en la misma empresa.
f Llevaba tres noches durmiendo en el sofá.
g Jorge lleva tres horas jugando al ordenador.
h Llevas una hora quejándote.
i ¿Cuánto tiempo lleva Toni estudiando?
j Ya/llevábamos cinco años viviendo en Mallorca.

142 a Me pasé todo el día estudiando.
b Se pasan las horas sin hacer nada.
c Los obreros se pasaron tres días quitando basura.
d Clara se pasó la tarde maquillándose.
e El pobre chico se pasa los fines de semana viendo la tele.
f Juan y Luis se pasaron la mañana arreglando el coche.
g Mar y Eva se pasan las horas hablando por teléfono.
h Me paso la semana corriendo de un lado para otro.
i Se pasó tres días en la cárcel.
j Mis hijos y yo nos pasamos la vida discutiendo.

143 a salió corriendo
b entró saltando
c se fueron volando
d bajar rodando
e fue botando
f me fui corriendo
g salieron botando
h fuimos corriendo
i salió arrastrándose
j entraron corriendo

144 a Fumar es malo para la salud.
b Correr dos veces a la semana es un buen ejercicio.
c Leer es su pasatiempo favorito.
d Tomar demasiada sal no es bueno.
e Llorar no va a solucionar nada.
f Repasar un poco antes del examen es una buena idea.
g Discutir con él no va a ayudar.
h Limpiar la casa no es algo que me guste.
i Ver la tele demasiado se hace aburrido.
j Siempre es bueno escucharlos.

145 a Luis se está vistiendo./ Luis está vistiéndose.
b Los novios se están besando./Los novios están besándose.
c La actriz se está maquillando./ La actriz está maquillándose.
d Los políticos se están insultando./Los políticos están insultándose.
e El bebé se está despertando./ El bebé estar despertándose.
f Carmen se está duchando./Carmen está duchándose.
g Antonio se está acostando/Antonio está acostándose.
h La ropa se está secando./ La ropa está secándose.
i Me estoy enfadando./ Estoy enfadándome.
j Te estás confundiendo./ Estás confundiéndote.

146 a Nos gusta jugar al tenis.
b Estábamos escuchando música.
c Me paso la vida esperándote.
d Prohibido tirar basura.
e ¿Te gusta viajar?
f Estaban tumbados.
g Se está vistiendo./Está vistiéndose.
h Estaban cruzando la calle.
i Estoy leyendo una novela.
j Andar es una buena costumbre.

SOLUTIONS SOLUTIONS SOLUTIONS SOLUTIONS

Solutions

147
- **a** Llovía mucho.
- **b** Hacía mucho frío.
- **c** Mañana va a nevar.
- **d** Hace un tiempo horrible.
- **e** Nieva./Está nevando.
- **f** Va a hacer sol.
- **g** Hacía mucho calor.
- **h** ¿Qué tiempo hizo?
- **i** La semana pasada hizo mucho calor.
- **j** Va a hacer viento.

148
- **a** Me hacen falta cincuenta euros.
- **b** A Isabel le hacen falta unas botas.
- **c** Nos hace falta un cuchillo para el pan.
- **d** Hace falta tener paciencia.
- **e** No hace falta enfadarse.
- **f** Nos hace falta un manual.
- **g** Hace falta más sal en la sopa.
- **h** No les hace falta un coche.
- **i** A mi madre le hace falta una batidora.
- **j** Me hace falta un ordenador más rápido.

149
- **a** Hay que comprar más pan.
- **b** Hubo que decírselo a Miguel.
- **c** Hay que solucionarlo pronto.
- **d** Habrá que intentarlo.
- **e** Hay que respetar las costumbres.
- **f** Habría que decírselo.
- **g** Habría que revisarlo otra vez.
- **h** Hay que consultar con un experto.
- **i** Hubo que salir corriendo.
- **j** Habrá que esperar un poco.

150
- **a** Es bueno reír.
- **b** Era peligroso ir.
- **c** Era importante reunirse con ellos.
- **d** Fue muy útil preguntarle.
- **e** Es bueno andar.
- **f** Sería útil verlo.
- **g** No es saludable comer muchos dulces.
- **h** Será extraño no verte.
- **i** No será demasiado cansado.
- **j** Sería ideal verlo.

151
- **a** Están fuera desde hace seis meses/Hace seis meses que están fuera.
- **b** No nos hablamos desde hace mucho tiempo/ Hace mucho tiempo que no nos hablamos.
- **c** Vivimos aquí desde hace dos años./Hace dos años que vivimos aquí.
- **d** No lo ve desde hace dos semanas./ Hace dos semanas que no lo ve.
- **e** María tiene la casa desde hace tres años./ Hace tres años que María tiene la casa.
- **f** No voy al teatro desde hace mucho tiempo./ Hace mucho que no voy al teatro.
- **g** ¿Desde cuándo estáis casados?/¿Cuánto tiempo hace que estáis casados?
- **h** Están juntos desde hace tres meses./Hace tres meses que están juntos.
- **i** Estudio alemán desde hace cinco años/ Hace cinco años que estudio alemán.
- **j** Estamos esperando desde hace dos horas./ Hace dos horas que estamos esperando.

152
- **a** Se cree que
- **b** Se trata de
- **c** Se piensa que
- **d** Se cree que
- **e** Se sospecha que
- **f** Se dice que
- **g** Se comenta que
- **h** Se trata de
- **i** Se rumorea que
- **j** Se piensa que

153
- **a** No vale la pena
- **b** merecía la pena
- **c** merece la pena
- **d** Valía la pena
- **e** valía la pena
- **f** merece la pena
- **g** Vale la pena
- **h** merecen la pena
- **i** merecía la pena
- **j** valen la pena

154
- **a** Me parece que es tarde
- **b** ¿Os parece que este reloj es mejor?
- **c** Me parece que Ana no quiere.
- **d** ¿Les parecía que era útil?
- **e** Así parece que es una mariposa.
- **f** Nos parecía que no era buena idea.
- **g** Le parecía que estás equivocado.
- **h** Me parece que Juan está borracho.
- **i** Eso me parece que es diferente.
- **j** Nos parece difícil.

155
- **a** Realmente no hay un jefe.
- **b** Había/Hubo mucha gente que lo dudó.
- **c** Había un niño nuevo en el colegio.
- **d** Habrá protestas.
- **e** Hay un cine nuevo en la zona.
- **f** Hay papeles en el suelo.
- **g** No había/hubo mucho ruido.
- **h** ¿Había/hubo muchos invitados?
- **i** Al final, no había/hubo dinero suficiente.
- **j** ¿Habrá tiempo suficiente?

156
- **a** habléis
- **b** pueda
- **c** estudien
- **d** viva
- **e** comas
- **f** tenga
- **g** digáis
- **h** vengan
- **i** salgan
- **j** hagas
- **k** tengan

157
- **a** te mejores
- **b** espere
- **c** vayamos
- **d** hayan llegado
- **e** vayas
- **f** podáis
- **g** estemos
- **h** hayas ganado

Solutions

i se atreva
j salgan

158 a Quiere que Marta gane.
b Espero que tus padres te ayuden.
c Nos alegramos de que tu amiga esté aquí.
d Siento que los perros molesten.
e Le gusta que Nuria cante.
f Sentimos que los pasajeros lleguen tarde.
g Se alegran de que (tú) tengas tiempo.
h Quiero que los niños vayan de vacaciones con mis padres.
i Preferimos que mi madre no se entere.
j Quieren que los alumnos salgan pronto.

159 a la policía
b mis primas
c tus hermanos/sus profesores
d las niñas
e los alumnos/los políticos
f tu perro/un amigo
g los empleados
h la invitada/Ana
i María y mi amiga/las palomas
j mis hermanas

160 a venga
b sepan
c vayas
d os quedéis
e sepa
f digas
g se pongan
h sea
i puedas
j guste

161 a comiera/comiese
b volviéramos/volviésemos
c pensaras/pensases
d saliera/saliese
e hiciera/hiciese
f tuvieran/tuviesen
g hubieran/hubiesen
h dieras/dieses
i fuera/fuese
j estuviéramos/estuviésemos

162 a pudiera/pudiese
b vinieran/viniesen
c Quisiera
d tuviéramos/tuviésemos
e fuera/fuese
f quisieran/quisiesen
g pudiera/pudiese
h saliéramos/saliésemos
i tuvierais/tuvieseis
j pudiéramos/pudiésemos

163 a saber **supiera**
b ir **vaya**
c ser **seáis**
d poder **puedan**
e salir **salga**

164 a haber **hayamos**
b saber **supieran**
c hacer **hiciera**
d ser **fuera**
e dar **dieran**

165 a ver
b patinar
c cantar
d levantarse
e beber
f leer
g jugar
h salir
i comprar
j escribir

166 a Primero pesar la harina y la mantequilla.
b Mezclar la harina y la mantequilla.
c Luego añadir un poco de agua.
d Formar una masa mezclando la harina y la mantequilla con el agua.
e Por otro lado, pelar y cortar en trozos las manzanas.
f Extender la masa con el rodillo.
g Poner la masa extendida en un molde.
h Colocar las manzanas sobre la masa.
i Meter al horno caliente durante una hora.
j Sacar del horno y dejar enfriar.

167 a aprender hacer algo **to learn to do something**
b empezar a hacer algo **to start doing something**
c llegar a hacer algo **to manage to do something**
d volver a hacer algo **to do something again**
e probar a hacer algo **to try to do something**

168 a Aprendí a cocinar.
b Probamos a bucear.
c Empezamos a cantar.
d Llegaron a subir la montaña.
e Conseguimos entenderlo.
f Volviste a intentarlo.
g ¿Os decidisteis a comprarlo?
h Comenzaron a trabajar.
i Decidieron llamar.
j Olvidamos cerrarlo.

169 a Hemos decidido comprarnos un barco.
b Prefieren no volver a su pueblo.
c Siento hacerte enfadar.
d Me apetece irme a bailar.
e Le gusta cocinar los fines de semana.
f Necesito comprarme un ordenador.
g Han decidido dejar de fumar.
h Prefiero no ir.
i Ha decidido abrir un restaurante.
j Nos gusta recibir muchas visitas.

170 a salir
b irse
c tirar
d decir
e beber
f llamar
g comprar
h tomar
i jugar
j hacer

171 a Dejó caer el boli. **He dropped the pen.**
b Espero poder ir. **I hope to be able to go.**
c ¿Qué quieres decir? **What do you mean?**

Solutions

- **d** Debo intentarlo. **I must try.**
- **e** Llegó a ser médico. **He became a doctor.**

172
- **a** Me gustaría irme de vacaciones.
- **b** Van a aprender árabe.
- **c** ¿Sabes tocar el bajo?
- **d** Le ayudamos a encontrar el camino.
- **e** A veces se olvidan de apagar el ordenador.
- **f** No llegamos a visitar Costa Rica.
- **g** Se va a comprar una moto.
- **h** Tienen que comprar los billetes.
- **i** Quiero aprender a conducir.
- **j** Me enseño a montar en bici.

173
- **a** a
- **b** de
- **c** a
- **d** de
- **e** de
- **f** de
- **g** con
- **h** de
- **i** con
- **j** de

174
- **a** de
- **b** a
- **c** del
- **d** a
- **e** de
- **f** a
- **g** de
- **h** a
- **i** al
- **j** de

175
- **a** a
- **b** con
- **c** a
- **d** con
- **e** a
- **f** con
- **g** al
- **h** con
- **i** al
- **j** con

176
- **a** del
- **b** de
- **c** en
- **d** de
- **e** por
- **f** de
- **g** por
- **h** del
- **i** en
- **j** de

177
- **a** con
- **b** por
- **c** en
- **d** por
- **e** por
- **f** con
- **g** con
- **h** con
- **i** en
- **j** con

178
- **a** Buscaba sus gafas.
- **b** Mirábamos el menú.
- **c** Me estaba mirando.
- **d** Pagamos la comida.
- **e** Escuchamos las noticias.
- **f** Te están esperando.
- **g** Pidió un boli.
- **h** ¿Qué estás buscando?
- **i** No estamos pidiendo dinero.
- **j** ¡Escúchame!

179
- **a** los pasteles/las cortinas
- **b** el vino/el toreo/leer
- **c** los juegos/las zapatillas
- **d** la casa/París/el reportaje
- **e** el ruido/el hotel
- **f** mi amigo/mi bolso
- **g** los poemas
- **h** mi coche/las fotos/el chocolate
- **i** los americanos
- **j** los bombones/los libros

180
- **a** Le duele **la pierna**.
- **b** Me hacen falta **unas botas**.
- **c** ¿Os importa **esperar**?
- **d** No le hace falta **dinero**.
- **e** Me encantan **los animales**.

181
- **a** No me importa
- **b** Le gustan
- **c** Nos quedan
- **d** Te gusta
- **e** Le duele
- **f** os encanta
- **g** Nos faltan
- **h** me queda
- **i** Nos hace falta
- **j** Te interesa

182
- **a** Me encanta la playa.
- **b** No nos queda comida.
- **c** Te va a gustar este juego.
- **d** Me importa lo que haces.
- **e** En el colegio hacen falta libros.
- **f** Le faltaba un diente.
- **g** ¿Prefieres los grandes?
- **h** Me dolía la cabeza.
- **i** Sólo nos quedan tres ejercicios.
- **j** Nos hace falta leche.

main index

Index

verb tables

Introduction

The **Verb Tables** in the following section contain 120 tables of Spanish verbs (some regular and some irregular) in alphabetical order. Each table shows you the following forms: **Present, Present Perfect, Preterite, Imperfect, Future, Conditional, Present Subjunctive, Imperfect Subjunctive, Imperative** and the **Past Participle** and **Gerund**. For more information on these tenses and how they are formed you should refer to the main text.

In order to help you use the verbs shown in the **Verb Tables** correctly, there are also a number of example phrases on each page to show the verb as it is used in context.

In Spanish there are both **regular** verbs (their forms follow the normal rules) and **irregular** verbs (their forms do not follow the normal rules). The regular verbs in these tables that you can use as models for other regular verbs are:

hablar (regular **-ar** verb, Verb Table 60)
comer (regular **-er** verb, Verb Table 27)
vivir (regular **-ir** verb, Verb Table 118)

The irregular verbs are shown in full.

The **Verb Index** at the end of this section contains over 1200 verbs, each of which is cross-referred to one of the verbs given in the Verb Tables. The table shows the patterns that the verb listed in the index follows.

abolir (to abolish)

	PRESENT	PRESENT PERFECT
(yo)		**he abolido**
(tú)		**has abolido**
(él/ella/usted)		**ha abolido**
(nosotros/as)	**abolimos**	**hemos abolido**
(vosotros/as)	**abolís**	**habéis abolido**
(ellos/ellas/ ustedes)		**han abolido**

Present tense only used in persons shown

	PRETERITE	IMPERFECT
(yo)	**abolí**	**abolía**
(tú)	**aboliste**	**abolías**
(él/ella/usted)	**abolió**	**abolía**
(nosotros/as)	**abolimos**	**abolíamos**
(vosotros/as)	**abolisteis**	**abolíais**
(ellos/ellas/ ustedes)	**abolieron**	**abolían**

GERUND	PAST PARTICIPLE
aboliendo	**abolido**

	FUTURE	CONDITIONAL
(yo)	**aboliré**	**aboliría**
(tú)	**abolirás**	**abolirías**
(él/ella/usted)	**abolirá**	**aboliría**
(nosotros/as)	**aboliremos**	**aboliríamos**
(vosotros/as)	**aboliréis**	**aboliríais**
(ellos/ellas/ ustedes)	**abolirán**	**abolirían**

	PRESENT SUBJUNCTIVE	IMPERFECT SUBJUNCTIVE
(yo)	not used	**aboliera** or **aboliese**
(tú)		**abolieras** or **abolieses**
(él/ella/usted)		**aboliera** or **aboliese**
(nosotros/as)		**aboliéramos** or **aboliésemos**
(vosotros/as)		**abolierais** or **abolieseis**
(ellos/ellas/ ustedes)		**abolieran** or **aboliesen**

IMPERATIVE

abolid

EXAMPLE PHRASES

Hay que **abolirlo**.
It ought to be abolished.

¿Por qué no **abolimos** esta ley?
Why don't we abolish this law?

Han abolido la pena de muerte.
They have abolished the death penalty.

Abolieron la esclavitud.
They abolished slavery.

Sólo unidos **aboliremos** la injusticia.
We will only abolish injustice if we stand together.

Prometieron que **abolirían** la censura.
They promised they'd abolish censorship.

Si lo **abolieran**, se producirían disturbios.
There would be riots if it were abolished.

Remember that subject pronouns are not used very often in Spanish.

abrir (to open)

	PRESENT	PRESENT PERFECT
(yo)	**abro**	**he abierto**
(tú)	**abres**	**has abierto**
(él/ella/usted)	**abre**	**ha abierto**
(nosotros/as)	**abrimos**	**hemos abierto**
(vosotros/as)	**abrís**	**habéis abierto**
(ellos/ellas/ ustedes)	**abren**	**han abierto**

	PRETERITE	IMPERFECT
(yo)	**abrí**	**abría**
(tú)	**abriste**	**abrías**
(él/ella/usted)	**abrió**	**abría**
(nosotros/as)	**abrimos**	**abríamos**
(vosotros/as)	**abristeis**	**abríais**
(ellos/ellas/ ustedes)	**abrieron**	**abrían**

GERUND	PAST PARTICIPLE
abriendo	**abierto**

	FUTURE	CONDITIONAL
(yo)	**abriré**	**abriría**
(tú)	**abrirás**	**abrirías**
(él/ella/usted)	**abrirá**	**abriría**
(nosotros/as)	**abriremos**	**abriríamos**
(vosotros/as)	**abriréis**	**abriríais**
(ellos/ellas/ ustedes)	**abrirán**	**abrirían**

	PRESENT SUBJUNCTIVE	IMPERFECT SUBJUNCTIVE
(yo)	**abra**	**abriera** or **abriese**
(tú)	**abras**	**abrieras** or **abrieses**
(él/ella/usted)	**abra**	**abriera** or **abriese**
(nosotros/as)	**abramos**	**abriéramos** or **abriésemos**
(vosotros/as)	**abráis**	**abrierais** or **abrieseis**
(ellos/ellas/ ustedes)	**abran**	**abrieran** or **abriesen**

IMPERATIVE

abre / abrid

Use the present subjunctive in all cases other than these **tú** and **vosotros** affirmative forms.

EXAMPLE PHRASES

Hoy **se abre** el plazo de matrícula.
Registration begins today.

Han abierto un restaurante cerca de aquí.
They've opened a new restaurant near here.

¿Quién **abrió** la ventana?
Who opened the window?

La llave **abría** el armario.
The key opened the cupboard.

Abrirán todas las puertas de la catedral.
They'll open all the doors of the cathedral.

Me dijo que hoy **abrirían** sólo por la tarde.
He told me that they'd only be open in the evening.

No creo que **abran** un nuevo supermercado por aquí.
I don't think they'll open a new supermarket here.

No **abras** ese grifo.
Don't turn on that tap.

Remember that subject pronouns are not used very often in Spanish.

actuar (to act)

	PRESENT	PRESENT PERFECT
(yo)	**actúo**	**he actuado**
(tú)	**actúas**	**has actuado**
(él/ella/usted)	**actúa**	**ha actuado**
(nosotros/as)	**actuamos**	**hemos actuado**
(vosotros/as)	**actuáis**	**habéis actuado**
(ellos/ellas/ ustedes)	**actúan**	**han actuado**

	PRETERITE	IMPERFECT
(yo)	**actué**	**actuaba**
(tú)	**actuaste**	**actuabas**
(él/ella/usted)	**actuó**	**actuaba**
(nosotros/as)	**actuamos**	**actuábamos**
(vosotros/as)	**actuasteis**	**actuabais**
(ellos/ellas/ ustedes)	**actuaron**	**actuaban**

	GERUND	PAST PARTICIPLE
	actuando	**actuado**

	FUTURE	CONDITIONAL
(yo)	**actuaré**	**actuaría**
(tú)	**actuarás**	**actuarías**
(él/ella/usted)	**actuará**	**actuaría**
(nosotros/as)	**actuaremos**	**actuaríamos**
(vosotros/as)	**actuaréis**	**actuaríais**
(ellos/ellas/ ustedes)	**actuarán**	**actuarían**

	PRESENT SUBJUNCTIVE	IMPERFECT SUBJUNCTIVE
(yo)	**actúe**	**actuara** or **actuase**
(tú)	**actúes**	**actuaras** or **actuases**
(él/ella/usted)	**actúe**	**actuara** or **actuase**
(nosotros/as)	**actuemos**	**actuáramos** or **actuásemos**
(vosotros/as)	**actuéis**	**actuarais** or **actuaseis**
(ellos/ellas/ ustedes)	**actúen**	**actuaran** or **actuasen**

IMPERATIVE

actúa / actuad

Use the present subjunctive in all cases other than these **tú** and **vosotros** affirmative forms.

EXAMPLE PHRASES

Actúa de una forma muy rara.
He's acting very strangely.

Ha actuado siguiendo un impulso.
He acted on impulse.

Actuó en varias películas.
He was in several films.

Actuaba como si no supiera nada.
She was behaving as if she didn't know anything about it.

¿Quién **actuará** en su próxima película?
Who will be in his next film?

Yo nunca **actuaría** así.
I'd never behave like that.

Si **actuara** de forma más lógica, sería más fácil atraparle.
It would be easier to catch him if he behaved in a more logical way.

Actuad como mejor os parezca.
Do as you think best.

Remember that subject pronouns are not used very often in Spanish.

adquirir (to acquire)

	PRESENT	PRESENT PERFECT
(yo)	**adquiero**	**he adquirido**
(tú)	**adquieres**	**has adquirido**
(él/ella/usted)	**adquiere**	**ha adquirido**
(nosotros/as)	**adquirimos**	**hemos adquirido**
(vosotros/as)	**adquirís**	**habéis adquirido**
(ellos/ellas/ ustedes)	**adquieren**	**han adquirido**

	PRETERITE	IMPERFECT
(yo)	**adquirí**	**adquiría**
(tú)	**adquiriste**	**adquirías**
(él/ella/usted)	**adquirió**	**adquiría**
(nosotros/as)	**adquirimos**	**adquiríamos**
(vosotros/as)	**adquiristeis**	**adquiríais**
(ellos/ellas/ ustedes)	**adquirieron**	**adquirían**

GERUND	PAST PARTICIPLE
adquiriendo	**adquirido**

	FUTURE	CONDITIONAL
(yo)	**adquiriré**	**adquiriría**
(tú)	**adquirirás**	**adquirirías**
(él/ella/usted)	**adquirirá**	**adquiriría**
(nosotros/as)	**adquiriremos**	**adquiriríamos**
(vosotros/as)	**adquiriréis**	**adquiriríais**
(ellos/ellas/ ustedes)	**adquirirán**	**adquirirían**

	PRESENT SUBJUNCTIVE	IMPERFECT SUBJUNCTIVE
(yo)	**adquiera**	**adquiriera** or **adquiriese**
(tú)	**adquieras**	**adquirieras** or **adquirieses**
(él/ella/usted)	**adquiera**	**adquiriera** or **adquiriese**
(nosotros/as)	**adquiramos**	**adquiriéramos** or **adquiriésemos**
(vosotros/as)	**adquiráis**	**adquirierais** or **adquirieseis**
(ellos/ellas/ ustedes)	**adquieran**	**adquirieran** or **adquiriesen**

IMPERATIVE
adquiere / adquirid

Use the present subjunctive in all cases other than these **tú** and **vosotros** affirmative forms.

EXAMPLE PHRASES

Adquiere cada vez mayor importancia.
It's becoming more and more important.

Está adquiriendo una reputación que no merece.
It's getting a reputation it doesn't deserve.

Hemos adquirido una colección de sellos.
We've bought a stamp collection.

Con el tiempo **adquirió** cierta madurez.
Over the years he gained a certain maturity.

Al final **adquirirán** los derechos de publicación.
They will get the publishing rights in the end.

¿Lo **adquirirías** por ese precio?
Would you buy it for that price?

Adquiera o no la nacionalidad, podrá permanecer en el país.
She'll be able to stay in the country whether she becomes naturalized or not.

Tenía gran interés en que **adquiriera** el cuadro.
He was very keen that she should buy the picture.

Remember that subject pronouns are not used very often in Spanish.

advertir (to warn; to notice)

	PRESENT	PRESENT PERFECT
(yo)	**advierto**	**he advertido**
(tú)	**adviertes**	**has advertido**
(él/ella/usted)	**advierte**	**ha advertido**
(nosotros/as)	**advertimos**	**hemos advertido**
(vosotros/as)	**advertís**	**habéis advertido**
(ellos/ellas/ustedes)	**advierten**	**han advertido**

	PRETERITE	IMPERFECT
(yo)	**advertí**	**advertía**
(tú)	**advertiste**	**advertías**
(él/ella/usted)	**advirtió**	**advertía**
(nosotros/as)	**advertimos**	**advertíamos**
(vosotros/as)	**advertisteis**	**advertíais**
(ellos/ellas/ustedes)	**advirtieron**	**advertían**

GERUND	PAST PARTICIPLE
advirtiendo	**advertido**

	FUTURE	CONDITIONAL
(yo)	**advertiré**	**advertiría**
(tú)	**advertirás**	**advertirías**
(él/ella/usted)	**advertirá**	**advertiría**
(nosotros/as)	**advertiremos**	**advertiríamos**
(vosotros/as)	**advertiréis**	**advertiríais**
(ellos/ellas/ustedes)	**advertirán**	**advertirían**

	PRESENT SUBJUNCTIVE	IMPERFECT SUBJUNCTIVE
(yo)	**advierta**	**advirtiera** or **advirtiese**
(tú)	**adviertas**	**advirtieras** or **advirtieses**
(él/ella/usted)	**advierta**	**advirtiera** or **advirtiese**
(nosotros/as)	**advirtamos**	**advirtiéramos** or **advirtiésemos**
(vosotros/as)	**advirtáis**	**advirtierais** or **advirtieseis**
(ellos/ellas/ustedes)	**adviertan**	**advirtieran** or **advirtiesen**

IMPERATIVE

advierte / advertid

Use the present subjunctive in all cases other than these **tú** and **vosotros** affirmative forms.

EXAMPLE PHRASES

Te **advierto** que no va a ser nada fácil.
I must warn you that it won't be at all easy.

No **he advertido** nada extraño en su comportamiento.
I haven't noticed anything strange about his behaviour.

Ya te **advertí** que no intervinieras.
I warned you not to get involved.

Las señales **advertían** del peligro.
The signs warned of danger.

Si **advirtiera** algún cambio, llámenos.
If you should notice any change, give us a call.

Adviértele del riesgo que entraña.
Warn him about the risk involved.

Remember that subject pronouns are not used very often in Spanish.

almorzar (to have lunch)

	PRESENT	PRESENT PERFECT
(yo)	**almuerzo**	**he almorzado**
(tú)	**almuerzas**	**has almorzado**
(él/ella/usted)	**almuerza**	**ha almorzado**
(nosotros/as)	**almorzamos**	**hemos almorzado**
(vosotros/as)	**almorzáis**	**habéis almorzado**
(ellos/ellas/ ustedes)	**almuerzan**	**han almorzado**

	PRETERITE	IMPERFECT
(yo)	**almorcé**	**almorzaba**
(tú)	**almorzaste**	**almorzabas**
(él/ella/usted)	**almorzó**	**almorzaba**
(nosotros/as)	**almorzamos**	**almorzábamos**
(vosotros/as)	**almorzasteis**	**almorzabais**
(ellos/ellas/ ustedes)	**almorzaron**	**almorzaban**

GERUND	PAST PARTICIPLE
almorzando	**almorzado**

	FUTURE	CONDITIONAL
(yo)	**almorzaré**	**almorzaría**
(tú)	**almorzarás**	**almorzarías**
(él/ella/usted)	**almorzará**	**almorzaría**
(nosotros/as)	**almorzaremos**	**almorzaríamos**
(vosotros/as)	**almorzaréis**	**almorzaríais**
(ellos/ellas/ ustedes)	**almorzarán**	**almorzarían**

	PRESENT SUBJUNCTIVE	IMPERFECT SUBJUNCTIVE
(yo)	**almuerce**	**almorzara** or **almorzase**
(tú)	**almuerces**	**almorzaras** or **almorzases**
(él/ella/usted)	**almuerce**	**almorzara** or **almorzase**
(nosotros/as)	**almorcemos**	**almorzáramos** or **almorzásemos**
(vosotros/as)	**almorcéis**	**almorzarais** or **almorzaseis**
(ellos/ellas/ ustedes)	**almuercen**	**almorzaran** or **almorzasen**

IMPERATIVE

almuerza / almorzad

Use the present subjunctive in all cases other than these **tú** and **vosotros** affirmative forms.

EXAMPLE PHRASES

¿Dónde vais a **almorzar**?
Where are you going to have lunch?

¿A qué hora **almuerzas**?
What time do you have lunch?

Ya **hemos almorzado**.
We've already had lunch.

Almorcé en un bar.
I had lunch in a bar.

Siempre **almorzaba** un bocadillo.
He always had a sandwich for lunch.

Mañana **almorzaremos** todos juntos.
We'll all have lunch together tomorrow.

Almuerce o no siempre me entra sueño a esta hora.
I always feel sleepy at this time of the day, regardless of whether I've had lunch or not.

Si **almorzara** así todos los días, estaría mucho más gordo.
I'd be much fatter if I had this sort of lunch every day.

Remember that subject pronouns are not used very often in Spanish.

amanecer (to get light; to wake up)

	PRESENT	PRESENT PERFECT
(yo)	**amanezco**	**he amanecido**
(tú)	**amaneces**	**has amanecido**
(él/ella/usted)	**amanece**	**ha amanecido**
(nosotros/as)	**amanecemos**	**hemos amanecido**
(vosotros/as)	**amanecéis**	**habéis amanecido**
(ellos/ellas/ ustedes)	**amanecen**	**han amanecido**

	PRETERITE	IMPERFECT
(yo)	**amanecí**	**amanecía**
(tú)	**amaneciste**	**amanecías**
(él/ella/usted)	**amaneció**	**amanecía**
(nosotros/as)	**amanecimos**	**amanecíamos**
(vosotros/as)	**amanecisteis**	**amanecíais**
(ellos/ellas/ ustedes)	**amanecieron**	**amanecían**

GERUND	PAST PARTICIPLE
amaneciendo	**amanecido**

	FUTURE	CONDITIONAL
(yo)	**amaneceré**	**amanecería**
(tú)	**amanecerás**	**amanecerías**
(él/ella/usted)	**amanecerá**	**amanecería**
(nosotros/as)	**amaneceremos**	**amaneceríamos**
(vosotros/as)	**amaneceréis**	**amaneceríais**
(ellos/ellas/ ustedes)	**amanecerán**	**amanecerían**

	PRESENT SUBJUNCTIVE	IMPERFECT SUBJUNCTIVE
(yo)	**amanezca**	**amaneciera** or **amaneciese**
(tú)	**amanezcas**	**amanecieras** or **amanecieses**
(él/ella/usted)	**amanezca**	**amaneciera** or **amaneciese**
(nosotros/as)	**amanezcamos**	**amaneciéramos** or **amaneciésemos**
(vosotros/as)	**amanezcáis**	**amanecierais** or **amanecieseis**
(ellos/ellas/ ustedes)	**amanezcan**	**amanecieran** or **amaneciesen**

IMPERATIVE

amanece / amaneced

Use the present subjunctive in all cases other than these **tú** and **vosotros** affirmative forms.

EXAMPLE PHRASES

Siempre **amanece** nublado.
The day always starts off cloudy.

Justo en ese momento **estaba amaneciendo**.
Just then, dawn was breaking.

Hoy **ha amanecido** a las ocho.
Today it got light at eight o'clock.

La ciudad **amaneció** desierta.
In the morning, the town was deserted.

Amanecía de un humor de perros.
She would wake up in a really bad mood.

Pronto **amanecerá**.
It will soon be daylight.

Saldremos en cuanto **amanezca**.
We'll set off as soon as it gets light.

Si **amanecieras** con fiebre, toma una de estas pastillas.
If you should wake up with a temperature, take one of these pills.

Remember that subject pronouns are not used very often in Spanish.

andar (to walk)

	PRESENT	PRESENT PERFECT
(yo)	**ando**	**he andado**
(tú)	**andas**	**has andado**
(él/ella/usted)	**anda**	**ha andado**
(nosotros/as)	**andamos**	**hemos andado**
(vosotros/as)	**andáis**	**habéis andado**
(ellos/ellas/ ustedes)	**andan**	**han andado**

	PRETERITE	IMPERFECT
(yo)	**anduve**	**andaba**
(tú)	**anduviste**	**andabas**
(él/ella/usted)	**anduvo**	**andaba**
(nosotros/as)	**anduvimos**	**andábamos**
(vosotros/as)	**anduvisteis**	**andabais**
(ellos/ellas/ ustedes)	**anduvieron**	**andaban**

GERUND	PAST PARTICIPLE
andando	**andado**

	FUTURE	CONDITIONAL
(yo)	**andaré**	**andaría**
(tú)	**andarás**	**andarías**
(él/ella/usted)	**andará**	**andaría**
(nosotros/as)	**andaremos**	**andaríamos**
(vosotros/as)	**andaréis**	**andaríais**
(ellos/ellas/ ustedes)	**andarán**	**andarían**

	PRESENT SUBJUNCTIVE	IMPERFECT SUBJUNCTIVE
(yo)	**ande**	**anduviera** or **anduviese**
(tú)	**andes**	**anduvieras** or **anduvieses**
(él/ella/usted)	**ande**	**anduviera** or **anduviese**
(nosotros/as)	**andemos**	**anduviéramos** or **anduviésemos**
(vosotros/as)	**andéis**	**anduvierais** or **anduvieseis**
(ellos/ellas/ ustedes)	**anden**	**anduvieran** or **anduviesen**

IMPERATIVE

anda / andad

Use the present subjunctive in all cases other than these **tú** and **vosotros** affirmative forms.

EXAMPLE PHRASES

Andar es un ejercicio muy sano.
Walking is very good exercise.

Hemos andado todo el camino hasta aquí.
We walked all the way here.

Anduvimos al menos 10 km.
We walked at least 10 km.

Por aquel entonces **andaban** mal de dinero.
Back then they were short of money.

Voy **andando** al trabajo todos los días.
I walk to work every day.

Andará por los cuarenta.
He must be about forty.

Yo **me andaría** con pies de plomo.
I'd tread very carefully.

El médico le ha aconsejado que **ande** varios kilómetros al día.
The doctor has advised him to walk several kilometres a day.

Si **anduvieras** con más cuidado, no te pasarían esas cosas.
If you were more careful, this sort of thing wouldn't happen to you.

Remember that subject pronouns are not used very often in Spanish.

apoderarse (to take possession)

	PRESENT	PRESENT PERFECT
(yo)	**me apodero**	**me he apoderado**
(tú)	**te apoderas**	**te has apoderado**
(él/ella/usted)	**se apodera**	**se ha apoderado**
(nosotros/as)	**nos apoderamos**	**nos hemos apoderado**
(vosotros/as)	**os apoderáis**	**os habéis apoderado**
(ellos/ellas/ ustedes)	**se apoderan**	**se han apoderado**

	PRETERITE	IMPERFECT
(yo)	**me apoderé**	**me apoderaba**
(tú)	**te apoderaste**	**te apoderabas**
(él/ella/usted)	**se apoderó**	**se apoderaba**
(nosotros/as)	**nos apoderamos**	**nos apoderábamos**
(vosotros/as)	**os apoderasteis**	**os apoderabais**
(ellos/ellas/ ustedes)	**se apoderaron**	**se apoderaban**

GERUND	PAST PARTICIPLE
apoderando	**apoderado**

	FUTURE	CONDITIONAL
(yo)	**me apoderaré**	**me apoderaría**
(tú)	**te apoderarás**	**te apoderarías**
(él/ella/usted)	**se apoderará**	**se apoderaría**
(nosotros/as)	**nos apoderaremos**	**nos apoderaríamos**
(vosotros/as)	**os apoderaréis**	**os apoderaríais**
(ellos/ellas/ ustedes)	**se apoderarán**	**se apoderarían**

	PRESENT SUBJUNCTIVE	IMPERFECT SUBJUNCTIVE
(yo)	**me apodere**	**me apoderara** or **apoderase**
(tú)	**te apoderes**	**te apoderaras** or **apoderases**
(él/ella/usted)	**se apodere**	**se apoderara** or **apoderase**
(nosotros/as)	**nos apoderemos**	**nos apoderáramos** or **apoderásemos**
(vosotros/as)	**os apoderéis**	**os apoderarais** or **apoderaseis**
(ellos/ellas/ ustedes)	**se apoderen**	**se apoderaran** or **apoderasen**

IMPERATIVE

apodérate / apoderaos

Use the present subjunctive in all cases other than these **tú** and **vosotros** affirmative forms.

EXAMPLE PHRASES

En esas situaciones, el miedo **se apodera** de mí.
In situations like that, I find myself gripped by fear.

Poco a poco **se han ido apoderando** de las riquezas del país.
Little by little, they've seized the country's riches.

Se apoderaron de las joyas y huyeron.
They ran off with the jewels.

El desánimo **se apoderaba** de nosotros por momentos.
We were feeling more and more discouraged by the minute.

No dejes que la curiosidad **se apodere** de ti.
Don't let curiosity get the better of you.

Remember that subject pronouns are not used very often in Spanish.

aprobar (to pass; to approve of)

	PRESENT	PRESENT PERFECT
(yo)	**apruebo**	**he aprobado**
(tú)	**apruebas**	**has aprobado**
(él/ella/usted)	**aprueba**	**ha aprobado**
(nosotros/as)	**aprobamos**	**hemos aprobado**
(vosotros/as)	**aprobáis**	**habéis aprobado**
(ellos/ellas/ ustedes)	**aprueban**	**han aprobado**

	PRETERITE	IMPERFECT
(yo)	**aprobé**	**aprobaba**
(tú)	**aprobaste**	**aprobabas**
(él/ella/usted)	**aprobó**	**aprobaba**
(nosotros/as)	**aprobamos**	**aprobábamos**
(vosotros/as)	**aprobasteis**	**aprobabais**
(ellos/ellas/ ustedes)	**aprobaron**	**aprobaban**

GERUND	PAST PARTICIPLE
aprobando	**aprobado**

	FUTURE	CONDITIONAL
(yo)	**aprobaré**	**aprobaría**
(tú)	**aprobarás**	**aprobarías**
(él/ella/usted)	**aprobará**	**aprobaría**
(nosotros/as)	**aprobaremos**	**aprobaríamos**
(vosotros/as)	**aprobaréis**	**aprobaríais**
(ellos/ellas/ ustedes)	**aprobarán**	**aprobarían**

	PRESENT SUBJUNCTIVE	IMPERFECT SUBJUNCTIVE
(yo)	**apruebe**	**aprobara** or **aprobase**
(tú)	**apruebes**	**aprobaras** or **aprobases**
(él/ella/usted)	**apruebe**	**aprobara** or **aprobase**
(nosotros/as)	**aprobemos**	**aprobáramos** or **aprobásemos**
(vosotros/as)	**aprobéis**	**aprobarais** or **aprobaseis**
(ellos/ellas/ ustedes)	**aprueben**	**aprobaran** or **aprobasen**

IMPERATIVE

aprueba / aprobad

Use the present subjunctive in all cases other than these **tú** and **vosotros** affirmative forms.

EXAMPLE PHRASES

No **apruebo** esa conducta.
I don't approve of that sort of behaviour.

Este año lo **estoy aprobando** todo.
So far this year I've passed everything.

Han aprobado una ley antitabaco.
They've passed an anti-smoking law.

¿**Aprobaste** el examen?
Did you pass the exam?

La decisión **fue aprobada** por mayoría.
The decision was approved by a majority.

Remember that subject pronouns are not used very often in Spanish.

arrancar (to pull up)

	PRESENT	PRESENT PERFECT
(yo)	**arranco**	**he arrancado**
(tú)	**arrancas**	**has arrancado**
(él/ella/usted)	**arranca**	**ha arrancado**
(nosotros/as)	**arrancamos**	**hemos arrancado**
(vosotros/as)	**arrancáis**	**habéis arrancado**
(ellos/ellas/ ustedes)	**arrancan**	**han arrancado**

	PRETERITE	IMPERFECT
(yo)	**arranqué**	**arrancaba**
(tú)	**arrancaste**	**arrancabas**
(él/ella/usted)	**arrancó**	**arrancaba**
(nosotros/as)	**arrancamos**	**arrancábamos**
(vosotros/as)	**arrancasteis**	**arrancabais**
(ellos/ellas/ ustedes)	**arrancaron**	**arrancaban**

GERUND	PAST PARTICIPLE
arrancando	**arrancado**

	FUTURE	CONDITIONAL
(yo)	**arrancaré**	**arrancaría**
(tú)	**arrancarás**	**arrancarías**
(él/ella/usted)	**arrancará**	**arrancaría**
(nosotros/as)	**arrancaremos**	**arrancaríamos**
(vosotros/as)	**arrancaréis**	**arrancaríais**
(ellos/ellas/ ustedes)	**arrancarán**	**arrancarían**

	PRESENT SUBJUNCTIVE	IMPERFECT SUBJUNCTIVE
(yo)	**arranque**	**arrancara** or **arrancase**
(tú)	**arranques**	**arrancaras** or **arrancases**
(él/ella/usted)	**arranque**	**arrancara** or **arrancase**
(nosotros/as)	**arranquemos**	**arrancáramos** or **arrancásemos**
(vosotros/as)	**arranquéis**	**arrancarais** or **arrancaseis**
(ellos/ellas/ ustedes)	**arranquen**	**arrancaran** or **arrancasen**

IMPERATIVE

arranca / arrancad

Use the present subjunctive in all cases other than these **tú** and **vosotros** affirmative forms.

EXAMPLE PHRASES

Lo tienes que **arrancar** de raíz.
You must pull it up by its roots.

Estaba arrancando malas hierbas.
I was pulling up weeds.

Me **has arrancado** un botón.
You've pulled off one of my buttons.

El viento **arrancó** varios árboles.
Several trees were uprooted in the wind.

No **arranques** hojas del cuaderno.
Don't go tearing pages out of the exercise book.

Arranca y vámonos.
Start the engine and let's get going.

Remember that subject pronouns are not used very often in Spanish.

arrepentirse (to be sorry)

	PRESENT	PRESENT PERFECT
(yo)	**me arrepiento**	**me he arrepentido**
(tú)	**te arrepientes**	**te has arrepentido**
(él/ella/usted)	**se arrepiente**	**se ha arrepentido**
(nosotros/as)	**nos arrepentimos**	**nos hemos arrepentido**
(vosotros/as)	**os arrepentís**	**os habéis arrepentido**
(ellos/ellas/ ustedes)	**se arrepienten**	**se han arrepentido**

	PRETERITE	IMPERFECT
(yo)	**me arrepentí**	**me arrepentía**
(tú)	**te arrepentiste**	**te arrepentías**
(él/ella/usted)	**se arrepintió**	**se arrepentía**
(nosotros/as)	**nos arrepentimos**	**nos arrepentíamos**
(vosotros/as)	**os arrepentisteis**	**os arrepentíais**
(ellos/ellas/ ustedes)	**se arrepintieron**	**se arrepentían**

GERUND	PAST PARTICIPLE
arrepintiéndose, etc	**arrepentido**

	FUTURE	CONDITIONAL
(yo)	**me arrepentiré**	**me arrepentiría**
(tú)	**te arrepentirás**	**te arrepentirías**
(él/ella/usted)	**se arrepentirá**	**se arrepentiría**
(nosotros/as)	**nos arrepentiremos**	**nos arrepentiríamos**
(vosotros/as)	**os arrepentiréis**	**os arrepentiríais**
(ellos/ellas/ ustedes)	**se arrepentirán**	**se arrepentirían**

	PRESENT SUBJUNCTIVE	IMPERFECT SUBJUNCTIVE
(yo)	**me arrepienta**	**me arrepintiera** or **arrepintiese**
(tú)	**te arrepientas**	**te arrepintieras** or **arrepintieses**
(él/ella/usted)	**se arrepienta**	**se arrepintiera** or **arrepintiese**
(nosotros/as)	**nos arrepintamos**	**nos arrepintiéramos** or **arrepintiésemos**
(vosotros/as)	**os arrepintáis**	**os arrepintierais** or **arrepintieseis**
(ellos/ellas/ ustedes)	**se arrepientan**	**se arrepintieran** or **arrepintiesen**

IMPERATIVE

arrepiéntete / arrepentíos

Use the present subjunctive in all cases other than these **tú** and **vosotros** affirmative forms.

EXAMPLE PHRASES

¡**Te** vas a **arrepentir** de esto!
You'll be sorry you did that!

No **me arrepiento** de nada.
I don't regret anything.

Arrepintiéndote en serio, seguro que te perdonarán.
If you're truly sorry, I'm sure they'll forgive you.

Se arrepintieron y decidieron no vender la casa.
They changed their minds and decided not to sell the house.

Algún día **se arrepentirá** de no haber estudiado una carrera.
One day he'll be sorry he didn't go to university.

No **te arrepientas** nunca de haber dicho la verdad.
Don't ever regret having told the truth.

Remember that subject pronouns are not used very often in Spanish.

atravesar (to cross; to go through)

	PRESENT	PRESENT PERFECT
(yo)	**atravieso**	**he atravesado**
(tú)	**atraviesas**	**has atravesado**
(él/ella/usted)	**atraviesa**	**ha atravesado**
(nosotros/as)	**atravesamos**	**hemos atravesado**
(vosotros/as)	**atravesáis**	**habéis atravesado**
(ellos/ellas/ ustedes)	**atraviesan**	**han atravesado**

	PRETERITE	IMPERFECT
(yo)	**atravesé**	**atravesaba**
(tú)	**atravesaste**	**atravesabas**
(él/ella/usted)	**atravesó**	**atravesaba**
(nosotros/as)	**atravesamos**	**atravesábamos**
(vosotros/as)	**atravesasteis**	**atravesabais**
(ellos/ellas/ ustedes)	**atravesaron**	**atravesaban**

GERUND	PAST PARTICIPLE
atravesando	**atravesado**

	FUTURE	CONDITIONAL
(yo)	**atravesaré**	**atravesaría**
(tú)	**atravesarás**	**atravesarías**
(él/ella/usted)	**atravesará**	**atravesaría**
(nosotros/as)	**atravesaremos**	**atravesaríamos**
(vosotros/as)	**atravesaréis**	**atravesaríais**
(ellos/ellas/ ustedes)	**atravesarán**	**atravesarían**

	PRESENT SUBJUNCTIVE	IMPERFECT SUBJUNCTIVE
(yo)	**atraviese**	**atravesara** or **atravesase**
(tú)	**atravieses**	**atravesaras** or **atravesases**
(él/ella/usted)	**atraviese**	**atravesara** or **atravesase**
(nosotros/as)	**atravesemos**	**atravesáramos** or **atravesásemos**
(vosotros/as)	**atraveséis**	**atravesarais** or **atravesaseis**
(ellos/ellas/ ustedes)	**atraviesen**	**atravesaran** or **atravesasen**

IMPERATIVE

atraviesa / atravesad

Use the present subjunctive in all cases other than these **tú** and **vosotros** affirmative forms.

EXAMPLE PHRASES

Atravesamos un mal momento.
We're going through a bad patch.

En este momento **está atravesando** la ciudad en un coche descubierto.
Right now he's driving through the city in an open-topped vehicle.

Hemos atravesado el río a nado.
We swam across the river.

La bala le **atravesó** el cráneo.
The bullet went through his skull.

Un camión **se** nos **atravesó** en la carretera.
A lorry pulled out in front of us on the road.

El túnel **atravesará** la montaña.
The tunnel will go through the mountain.

Remember that subject pronouns are not used very often in Spanish.

aunar (to join together)

	PRESENT	PRESENT PERFECT
(yo)	**aúno**	**he aunado**
(tú)	**aúnas**	**has aunado**
(él/ella/usted)	**aúna**	**ha aunado**
(nosotros/as)	**aunamos**	**hemos aunado**
(vosotros/as)	**aunáis**	**habéis aunado**
(ellos/ellas/ ustedes)	**aúnan**	**han aunado**

	PRETERITE	IMPERFECT
(yo)	**auné**	**aunaba**
(tú)	**aunaste**	**aunabas**
(él/ella/usted)	**aunó**	**aunaba**
(nosotros/as)	**aunamos**	**aunábamos**
(vosotros/as)	**aunasteis**	**aunabais**
(ellos/ellas/ ustedes)	**aunaron**	**aunaban**

GERUND	PAST PARTICIPLE
aunando	**aunado**

	FUTURE	CONDITIONAL
(yo)	**aunaré**	**aunaría**
(tú)	**aunarás**	**aunarías**
(él/ella/usted)	**aunará**	**aunaría**
(nosotros/as)	**aunaremos**	**aunaríamos**
(vosotros/as)	**aunaréis**	**aunaríais**
(ellos/ellas/ ustedes)	**aunarán**	**aunarían**

	PRESENT SUBJUNCTIVE	IMPERFECT SUBJUNCTIVE
(yo)	**aúne**	**aunara** or **aunase**
(tú)	**aúnes**	**aunaras** or **aunases**
(él/ella/usted)	**aúne**	**aunara** or **aunase**
(nosotros/as)	**aunemos**	**aunáramos** or **aunásemos**
(vosotros/as)	**aunéis**	**aunarais** or **aunaseis**
(ellos/ellas/ ustedes)	**aúnen**	**aunaran** or **aunasen**

IMPERATIVE

aúna / aunad

Use the present subjunctive in all cases other than these **tú** and **vosotros** affirmative forms.

EXAMPLE PHRASES

En esta obra **se han aunado** imaginación y técnica.
This play combines imagination and technique.

Aunaron esfuerzos.
They joined forces.

La pintura barroca **aunaba** conocimientos de geometría y anatomía.
Baroque painting brought knowledge of geometry and anatomy together.

Remember that subject pronouns are not used very often in Spanish.

avergonzar (to shame)

	PRESENT	PRESENT PERFECT
(yo)	**avergüenzo**	**he avergonzado**
(tú)	**avergüenzas**	**has avergonzado**
(él/ella/usted)	**avergüenza**	**ha avergonzado**
(nosotros/as)	**avergonzamos**	**hemos avergonzado**
(vosotros/as)	**avergonzáis**	**habéis avergonzado**
(ellos/ellas/ ustedes)	**avergüenzan**	**han avergonzado**

	PRETERITE	IMPERFECT
(yo)	**avergoncé**	**avergonzaba**
(tú)	**avergonzaste**	**avergonzabas**
(él/ella/usted)	**avergonzó**	**avergonzaba**
(nosotros/as)	**avergonzamos**	**avergonzábamos**
(vosotros/as)	**avergonzasteis**	**avergonzabais**
(ellos/ellas/ ustedes)	**avergonzaron**	**avergonzaban**

GERUND	PAST PARTICIPLE
avergonzando	**avergonzado**

	FUTURE	CONDITIONAL
(yo)	**avergonzaré**	**avergonzaría**
(tú)	**avergonzarás**	**avergonzarías**
(él/ella/usted)	**avergonzará**	**avergonzaría**
(nosotros/as)	**avergonzaremos**	**avergonzaríamos**
(vosotros/as)	**avegonzaréis**	**avergonzaríais**
(ellos/ellas/ ustedes)	**avergonzarán**	**avergonzarían**

	PRESENT SUBJUNCTIVE	IMPERFECT SUBJUNCTIVE
(yo)	**avergüence**	**avergonzara** or **avergonzase**
(tú)	**avergüences**	**avergonzaras** or **avergonzases**
(él/ella/usted)	**avergüence**	**avergonzara** or **avergonzase**
(nosotros/as)	**avergoncemos**	**avergonzáramos** or **avergonzásemos**
(vosotros/as)	**avergoncéis**	**avergonzarais** or **avergonzaseis**
(ellos/ellas/ ustedes)	**avergüencen**	**avergonzaran** or **avergonzasen**

IMPERATIVE

avergüenza / avergonzad

Use the present subjunctive in all cases other than these **tú** and **vosotros** affirmative forms.

EXAMPLE PHRASES

Tendrías que **avergonzarte**.
You should be ashamed of yourself.

Le **avergüenza** no tener dinero.
He's ashamed of having no money.

Cuando me lo dijo **me avergoncé**.
I was embarrassed when he told me.

Se avergonzaba de su familia.
He was ashamed of his family.

Avergonzándote no arreglas nada.
Being ashamed doesn't solve anything.

Si hubiera sabido que **te avergonzarías** tanto, no te lo habría dicho.
I wouldn't have told you if I'd known you'd be so embarrassed.

Si de verdad **se avergonzaran**, no se comportarían así.
They wouldn't behave like that if they were really ashamed.

Remember that subject pronouns are not used very often in Spanish.

averiguar (to find out)

	PRESENT	PRESENT PERFECT
(yo)	**averiguo**	**he averiguado**
(tú)	**averiguas**	**has averiguado**
(él/ella/usted)	**averigua**	**ha averiguado**
(nosotros/as)	**averiguamos**	**hemos averiguado**
(vosotros/as)	**averiguáis**	**habéis averiguado**
(ellos/ellas/ustedes)	**averiguan**	**han averiguado**

	PRETERITE	IMPERFECT
(yo)	**averigüé**	**averiguaba**
(tú)	**averiguaste**	**averiguabas**
(él/ella/usted)	**averiguó**	**averiguaba**
(nosotros/as)	**averiguamos**	**averiguábamos**
(vosotros/as)	**averiguasteis**	**averiguabais**
(ellos/ellas/ustedes)	**averiguaron**	**averiguaban**

GERUND	PAST PARTICIPLE
averiguando	**averiguado**

	FUTURE	CONDITIONAL
(yo)	**averiguaré**	**averiguaría**
(tú)	**averiguarás**	**averiguarías**
(él/ella/usted)	**averiguará**	**averiguaría**
(nosotros/as)	**averiguaremos**	**averiguaríamos**
(vosotros/as)	**averiguaréis**	**averiguaríais**
(ellos/ellas/ustedes)	**averiguarán**	**averiguarían**

	PRESENT SUBJUNCTIVE	IMPERFECT SUBJUNCTIVE
(yo)	**averigüe**	**averiguara** or **averiguase**
(tú)	**averigües**	**averiguaras** or **averiguases**
(él/ella/usted)	**averigüe**	**averiguara** or **averiguase**
(nosotros/as)	**averigüemos**	**averiguáramos** or **averiguásemos**
(vosotros/as)	**averigüéis**	**averiguarais** or **averiguaseis**
(ellos/ellas/ustedes)	**averigüen**	**averiguaran** or **averiguasen**

IMPERATIVE

averigua / averiguad

Use the present subjunctive in all cases other than these **tú** and **vosotros** affirmative forms.

EXAMPLE PHRASES

Trataron de **averiguar** su paradero.
They tried to find out his whereabouts.

Poco a poco van **averiguando** más cosas sobre su vida.
They're gradually finding out more about his life.

¿Cómo **has averiguado** dónde vivo?
How did you find out where I lived?

¿Cuándo lo **averiguaron**?
When did they find out?

Lo **averiguaré** pronto.
I'll find out soon.

Dijo que si le dábamos tiempo lo **averiguaría**.
She said that she'd find out if we gave her time.

En cuanto lo **averigüe** te lo digo.
I'll tell you as soon as I find out.

¡**Averígualo** inmediatamente!
Check it out immediately!

Remember that subject pronouns are not used very often in Spanish.

bendecir (to bless)

	PRESENT	PRESENT PERFECT
(yo)	**bendigo**	**he bendecido**
(tú)	**bendices**	**has bendecido**
(él/ella/usted)	**bendice**	**ha bendecido**
(nosotros/as)	**bendecimos**	**hemos bendecido**
(vosotros/as)	**bendecís**	**habéis bendecido**
(ellos/ellas/ ustedes)	**bendicen**	**han bendecido**

	PRETERITE	IMPERFECT
(yo)	**bendije**	**bendecía**
(tú)	**bendijiste**	**bendecías**
(él/ella/usted)	**bendijo**	**bendecía**
(nosotros/as)	**bendijimos**	**bendecíamos**
(vosotros/as)	**bendijisteis**	**bendecíais**
(ellos/ellas/ ustedes)	**bendijeron**	**bendecían**

	GERUND	PAST PARTICIPLE
	bendiciendo	**bendecido**

	FUTURE	CONDITIONAL
(yo)	**bendeciré**	**bendeciría**
(tú)	**bendecirás**	**bendecirías**
(él/ella/usted)	**bendecirá**	**bendeciría**
(nosotros/as)	**bendeciremos**	**bendeciríamos**
(vosotros/as)	**bendeciréis**	**bendeciríais**
(ellos/ellas/ ustedes)	**bendecirán**	**bendecirían**

	PRESENT SUBJUNCTIVE	IMPERFECT SUBJUNCTIVE
(yo)	**bendiga**	**bendijera** or **bendijese**
(tú)	**bendigas**	**bendijeras** or **bendijeses**
(él/ella/usted)	**bendiga**	**bendijera** or **bendijese**
(nosotros/as)	**bendigamos**	**bendijéramos** or **bendijésemos**
(vosotros/as)	**bendigáis**	**bendijerais** or **bendijeseis**
(ellos/ellas/ ustedes)	**bendigan**	**bendijeran** or **bendijesen**

IMPERATIVE

bendice / bendecid

Use the present subjunctive in all cases other than these **tú** and **vosotros** affirmative forms.

EXAMPLE PHRASES

Su padre **bendice** siempre la mesa.
His father always says grace.

La vida me **ha bendecido** con unos hijos maravillosos.
I've been blessed with wonderful children.

Jesús **bendijo** los panes y los peces.
Jesus blessed the fish and the bread.

Bendecía el día en que lo conoció.
She blessed the day she met him.

El Papa **bendecirá** a los fieles desde el balcón.
The Pope will bless the faithful from the balcony.

Quieren que sea él quien **bendiga** su unión.
They want him to marry them.

Pidieron a un sacerdote que **bendijera** su nueva casa.
They asked a priest to bless their new house.

Remember that subject pronouns are not used very often in Spanish.

caber (to fit)

	PRESENT	PRESENT PERFECT
(yo)	**quepo**	**he cabido**
(tú)	**cabes**	**has cabido**
(él/ella/usted)	**cabe**	**ha cabido**
(nosotros/as)	**cabemos**	**hemos cabido**
(vosotros/as)	**cabéis**	**habéis cabido**
(ellos/ellas/ ustedes)	**caben**	**han cabido**

	PRETERITE	IMPERFECT
(yo)	**cupe**	**cabía**
(tú)	**cupiste**	**cabías**
(él/ella/usted)	**cupo**	**cabía**
(nosotros/as)	**cupimos**	**cabíamos**
(vosotros/as)	**cupisteis**	**cabíais**
(ellos/ellas/ ustedes)	**cupieron**	**cabían**

GERUND	PAST PARTICIPLE
cabiendo	**cabido**

	FUTURE	CONDITIONAL
(yo)	**cabré**	**cabría**
(tú)	**cabrás**	**cabrías**
(él/ella/usted)	**cabrá**	**cabría**
(nosotros/as)	**cabremos**	**cabríamos**
(vosotros/as)	**cabréis**	**cabríais**
(ellos/ellas/ ustedes)	**cabrán**	**cabrían**

	PRESENT SUBJUNCTIVE	IMPERFECT SUBJUNCTIVE
(yo)	**quepa**	**cupiera** or **cupiese**
(tú)	**quepas**	**cupieras** or **cupieses**
(él/ella/usted)	**quepa**	**cupiera** or **cupiese**
(nosotros/as)	**quepamos**	**cupiéramos** or **cupiésemos**
(vosotros/as)	**quepáis**	**cupierais** or **cupieseis**
(ellos/ellas/ ustedes)	**quepan**	**cupieran** or **cupiesen**

IMPERATIVE

cabe / cabed

Use the present subjunctive in all cases other than these **tú** and **vosotros** affirmative forms.

EXAMPLE PHRASES

No te preocupes, que va a **caber**.
Don't worry, it will fit.

Aquí no **cabe**.
There isn't enough room for it here.

Al final **ha cabido** todo.
In the end everything went in.

No le **cupo** la menor duda.
She wasn't in any doubt.

No **cabía** en sí de gozo.
She was beside herself with joy.

¿Crees que **cabrá**?
Do you think there will be enough room for it?

Cabría cuestionarse si es la mejor solución.
We should ask ourselves whether it's the best solution.

Hizo lo imposible para que le **cupiera** la redacción en una página.
He did everything he could to fit the composition onto one page.

Remember that subject pronouns are not used very often in Spanish.

caer (to fall)

	PRESENT	PRESENT PERFECT
(yo)	**caigo**	**he caído**
(tú)	**caes**	**has caído**
(él/ella/usted)	**cae**	**ha caído**
(nosotros/as)	**caemos**	**hemos caído**
(vosotros/as)	**caéis**	**habéis caído**
(ellos/ellas/ ustedes)	**caen**	**han caído**

	PRETERITE	IMPERFECT
(yo)	**caí**	**caía**
(tú)	**caíste**	**caías**
(él/ella/usted)	**cayó**	**caía**
(nosotros/as)	**caímos**	**caíamos**
(vosotros/as)	**caísteis**	**caíais**
(ellos/ellas/ ustedes)	**cayeron**	**caían**

GERUND	PAST PARTICIPLE
cayendo	**caído**

	FUTURE	CONDITIONAL
(yo)	**caeré**	**caería**
(tú)	**caerás**	**caerías**
(él/ella/usted)	**caerá**	**caería**
(nosotros/as)	**caeremos**	**caeríamos**
(vosotros/as)	**caeréis**	**caeríais**
(ellos/ellas/ ustedes)	**caerán**	**caerían**

	PRESENT SUBJUNCTIVE	IMPERFECT SUBJUNCTIVE
(yo)	**caiga**	**cayera** or **cayese**
(tú)	**caigas**	**cayeras** or **cayeses**
(él/ella/usted)	**caiga**	**cayera** or **cayese**
(nosotros/as)	**caigamos**	**cayéramos** or **cayésemos**
(vosotros/as)	**caigáis**	**cayerais** or **cayeseis**
(ellos/ellas/ ustedes)	**caigan**	**cayeran** or **cayesen**

IMPERATIVE

cae / caed

Use the present subjunctive in all cases other than these **tú** and **vosotros** affirmative forms.

EXAMPLE PHRASES

Su cumpleaños **cae** en viernes.
Her birthday falls on a Friday.

Ese edificio se **está cayendo**.
That building's falling down.

Se me **ha caído** un guante.
I've dropped one of my gloves.

Me **caí** por las escaleras.
I fell down the stairs.

Me **caía** muy bien.
I really liked him.

Tarde o temprano, **caerá** en manos del enemigo.
Sooner or later, it will fall into enemy hands.

Yo me **caería** con esos tacones.
I'd fall over if I wore heels like those.

Seguirá adelante **caiga** quien **caiga**.
She'll go ahead no matter how many heads have to roll.

No **caigas** tan bajo.
Don't stoop so low.

Remember that subject pronouns are not used very often in Spanish.

cambiar (to change)

	PRESENT	PRESENT PERFECT
(yo)	**cambio**	**he cambiado**
(tú)	**cambias**	**has cambiado**
(él/ella/usted)	**cambia**	**ha cambiado**
(nosotros/as)	**cambiamos**	**hemos cambiado**
(vosotros/as)	**cambiáis**	**habéis cambiado**
(ellos/ellas/ ustedes)	**cambian**	**han cambiado**

	PRETERITE	IMPERFECT
(yo)	**cambié**	**cambiaba**
(tú)	**cambiaste**	**cambiabas**
(él/ella/usted)	**cambió**	**cambiaba**
(nosotros/as)	**cambiamos**	**cambiábamos**
(vosotros/as)	**cambiasteis**	**cambiabais**
(ellos/ellas/ ustedes)	**cambiaron**	**cambiaban**

GERUND	PAST PARTICIPLE
cambiando	**cambiado**

	FUTURE	CONDITIONAL
(yo)	**cambiaré**	**cambiaría**
(tú)	**cambiarás**	**cambiarías**
(él/ella/usted)	**cambiará**	**cambiaría**
(nosotros/as)	**cambiaremos**	**cambiaríamos**
(vosotros/as)	**cambiaréis**	**cambiaríais**
(ellos/ellas/ ustedes)	**cambiarán**	**cambiarían**

	PRESENT SUBJUNCTIVE	IMPERFECT SUBJUNCTIVE
(yo)	**cambie**	**cambiara** or **cambiase**
(tú)	**cambies**	**cambiaras** or **cambiases**
(él/ella/usted)	**cambie**	**cambiara** or **cambiase**
(nosotros/as)	**cambiemos**	**cambiáramos** or **cambiásemos**
(vosotros/as)	**cambiéis**	**cambiarais** or **cambiaseis**
(ellos/ellas/ ustedes)	**cambien**	**cambiaran** or **cambiasen**

IMPERATIVE

cambia / cambiad

Use the present subjunctive in all cases other than these **tú** and **vosotros** affirmative forms.

EXAMPLE PHRASES

Necesito **cambiar** de ambiente.
I need a change of scene.

Te **cambio** mi bolígrafo por tu goma.
I'll swap my pen for your rubber.

He cambiado de idea.
I've changed my mind.

Cambié varias veces de trabajo.
I changed jobs several times.

Cambiaban de coche cada año.
They changed their car every year.

Cuando la conozcas, **cambiarás** de idea.
You'll change your mind when you meet her.

Si pudiéramos, **nos cambiaríamos** de casa.
If we could, we'd move house.

No quiero que **cambies**.
I don't want you to change.

Cámbiate, que se nos hace tarde.
Get changed, it's getting late.

Remember that subject pronouns are not used very often in Spanish.

cazar (to hunt; to shoot)

	PRESENT	PRESENT PERFECT
(yo)	**cazo**	**he cazado**
(tú)	**cazas**	**has cazado**
(él/ella/usted)	**caza**	**ha cazado**
(nosotros/as)	**cazamos**	**hemos cazado**
(vosotros/as)	**cazáis**	**habéis cazado**
(ellos/ellas/ustedes)	**cazan**	**han cazado**

	PRETERITE	IMPERFECT
(yo)	**cacé**	**cazaba**
(tú)	**cazaste**	**cazabas**
(él/ella/usted)	**cazó**	**cazaba**
(nosotros/as)	**cazamos**	**cazábamos**
(vosotros/as)	**cazasteis**	**cazabais**
(ellos/ellas/ustedes)	**cazaron**	**cazaban**

GERUND	PAST PARTICIPLE
cazando	**cazado**

	FUTURE	CONDITIONAL
(yo)	**cazaré**	**cazaría**
(tú)	**cazarás**	**cazarías**
(él/ella/usted)	**cazará**	**cazaría**
(nosotros/as)	**cazaremos**	**cazaríamos**
(vosotros/as)	**cazaréis**	**cazaríais**
(ellos/ellas/ustedes)	**cazarán**	**cazarían**

	PRESENT SUBJUNCTIVE	IMPERFECT SUBJUNCTIVE
(yo)	**cace**	**cazara** or **cazase**
(tú)	**caces**	**cazaras** or **cazases**
(él/ella/usted)	**cace**	**cazara** or **cazase**
(nosotros/as)	**cacemos**	**cazáramos** or **cazásemos**
(vosotros/as)	**cacéis**	**cazarais** or **cazaseis**
(ellos/ellas/ustedes)	**cacen**	**cazaran** or **cazasen**

IMPERATIVE

caza / cazad

Use the present subjunctive in all cases other than these **tú** and **vosotros** affirmative forms.

EXAMPLE PHRASES

Salieron a **cazar** ciervos.
They went deer-hunting.

Caza las cosas al vuelo.
She's very quick on the uptake.

No **he cazado** nada de lo que ha dicho.
I didn't understand a word he said.

Los **cacé** robando.
I caught them stealing.

Cazaban con lanza.
They hunted with spears.

¡Quién **cazara** a un millonario!
I wish I could land myself a millionaire!

Remember that subject pronouns are not used very often in Spanish.

cerrar (to close)

	PRESENT	PRESENT PERFECT
(yo)	**cierro**	**he cerrado**
(tú)	**cierras**	**has cerrado**
(él/ella/usted)	**cierra**	**ha cerrado**
(nosotros/as)	**cerramos**	**hemos cerrado**
(vosotros/as)	**cerráis**	**habéis cerrado**
(ellos/ellas/ ustedes)	**cierran**	**han cerrado**

	PRETERITE	IMPERFECT
(yo)	**cerré**	**cerraba**
(tú)	**cerraste**	**cerrabas**
(él/ella/usted)	**cerró**	**cerraba**
(nosotros/as)	**cerramos**	**cerrábamos**
(vosotros/as)	**cerrasteis**	**cerrabais**
(ellos/ellas/ ustedes)	**cerraron**	**cerraban**

GERUND	PAST PARTICIPLE
cerrando	**cerrado**

	FUTURE	CONDITIONAL
(yo)	**cerraré**	**cerraría**
(tú)	**cerrarás**	**cerrarías**
(él/ella/usted)	**cerrará**	**cerraría**
(nosotros/as)	**cerraremos**	**cerraríamos**
(vosotros/as)	**cerraréis**	**cerraríais**
(ellos/ellas/ ustedes)	**cerrrarán**	**cerrarían**

	PRESENT SUBJUNCTIVE	IMPERFECT SUBJUNCTIVE
(yo)	**cierre**	**cerrara** or **cerrase**
(tú)	**cierres**	**cerraras** or **cerrases**
(él/ella/usted)	**cierre**	**cerrara** or **cerrase**
(nosotros/as)	**cerremos**	**cerráramos** or **cerrásemos**
(vosotros/as)	**cerréis**	**cerrarais** or **cerraseis**
(ellos/ellas/ ustedes)	**cierren**	**cerraran** or **cerrasen**

IMPERATIVE

cierra / cerrad

Use the present subjunctive in all cases other than these **tú** and **vosotros** affirmative forms.

EXAMPLE PHRASES

No puedo **cerrar** la maleta.
I can't shut my suitcase.

No **cierran** al mediodía.
They don't close at lunchtime.

Ha cerrado la puerta con llave.
She's locked the door.

Cerró el libro.
He closed the book.

Se le **cerraban** los ojos.
She couldn't keep her eyes open.

No dejes que **se cierre** la puerta de golpe.
Don't let the door slam shut.

No **cierres** la ventana.
Don't close the window.

Cierra el grifo.
Turn off the tap.

Remember that subject pronouns are not used very often in Spanish.

cocer (to boil; to cook)

	PRESENT	PRESENT PERFECT
(yo)	**cuezo**	**he cocido**
(tú)	**cueces**	**has cocido**
(él/ella/usted)	**cuece**	**ha cocido**
(nosotros/as)	**cocemos**	**hemos cocido**
(vosotros/as)	**cocéis**	**habéis cocido**
(ellos/ellas/ustedes)	**cuecen**	**han cocido**

	PRETERITE	IMPERFECT
(yo)	**cocí**	**cocía**
(tú)	**cociste**	**cocías**
(él/ella/usted)	**coció**	**cocía**
(nosotros/as)	**cocimos**	**cocíamos**
(vosotros/as)	**cocisteis**	**cocíais**
(ellos/ellas/ustedes)	**cocieron**	**cocían**

GERUND	PAST PARTICIPLE
cociendo	**cocido**

	FUTURE	CONDITIONAL
(yo)	**coceré**	**cocería**
(tú)	**cocerás**	**cocerías**
(él/ella/usted)	**cocerá**	**cocería**
(nosotros/as)	**coceremos**	**coceríamos**
(vosotros/as)	**coceréis**	**coceríais**
(ellos/ellas/ustedes)	**cocerán**	**cocerían**

	PRESENT SUBJUNCTIVE	IMPERFECT SUBJUNCTIVE
(yo)	**cueza**	**cociera** or **cociese**
(tú)	**cuezas**	**cocieras** or **cocieses**
(él/ella/usted)	**cueza**	**cociera** or **cociese**
(nosotros/as)	**cozamos**	**cociéramos** or **cociésemos**
(vosotros/as)	**cozáis**	**cocierais** or **cocieseis**
(ellos/ellas/ustedes)	**cuezan**	**cocieran** or **cociesen**

IMPERATIVE

cuece / coced

Use the present subjunctive in all cases other than these **tú** and **vosotros** affirmative forms.

EXAMPLE PHRASES

Las gambas **se cuecen** en un momento.
Prawns take no time to cook.

Aquí nos **estamos cociendo**.
It's boiling in here.

He cocido todo junto.
I've cooked everything together.

Coció el pan en el horno.
He baked the bread in the oven.

Así se **cocerá** antes.
This way it will be ready sooner.

Te dije que lo **cocieras** tapado.
I told you to cook it with the lid on.

No lo **cuezas** demasiado.
Don't overcook it.

Cuécelo a fuego lento.
Cook it over a gentle heat.

Remember that subject pronouns are not used very often in Spanish.

coger (to catch; to take)

	PRESENT	PRESENT PERFECT
(yo)	**cojo**	**he cogido**
(tú)	**coges**	**has cogido**
(él/ella/usted)	**coge**	**ha cogido**
(nosotros/as)	**cogemos**	**hemos cogido**
(vosotros/as)	**cogéis**	**habéis cogido**
(ellos/ellas/ ustedes)	**cogen**	**han cogido**

	PRETERITE	IMPERFECT
(yo)	**cogí**	**cogía**
(tú)	**cogiste**	**cogías**
(él/ella/usted)	**cogió**	**cogía**
(nosotros/as)	**cogimos**	**cogíamos**
(vosotros/as)	**cogisteis**	**cogíais**
(ellos/ellas/ ustedes)	**cogieron**	**cogían**

	GERUND	PAST PARTICIPLE
	cogiendo	**cogido**

	FUTURE	CONDITIONAL
(yo)	**cogeré**	**cogería**
(tú)	**cogerás**	**cogerías**
(él/ella/usted)	**cogerá**	**cogería**
(nosotros/as)	**cogeremos**	**cogeríamos**
(vosotros/as)	**cogeréis**	**cogeríais**
(ellos/ellas/ ustedes)	**cogerán**	**cogerían**

	PRESENT SUBJUNCTIVE	IMPERFECT SUBJUNCTIVE
(yo)	**coja**	**cogiera** or **cogiese**
(tú)	**cojas**	**cogieras** or **cogieses**
(él/ella/usted)	**coja**	**cogiera** or **cogiese**
(nosotros/as)	**cojamos**	**cogiéramos** or **cogiésemos**
(vosotros/as)	**cojáis**	**cogierais** or **cogieseis**
(ellos/ellas/ ustedes)	**cojan**	**cogieran** or **cogiesen**

IMPERATIVE

coge / coged

Use the present subjunctive in all cases other than these **tú** and **vosotros** affirmative forms.

EXAMPLE PHRASES

¿Por qué no **coges** el tren de las seis?
Why don't you get the six o'clock train?

Estuvimos cogiendo setas.
We were picking mushrooms.

Le **he cogido** cariño al gato.
I've grown fond of the cat.

La **cogí** entre mis brazos.
I took her in my arms.

Cogía el metro todos los días.
I used to take the tube every day.

Se cogerá un resfriado.
He'll catch a cold.

Yo **cogería** el azul.
I'd take the blue one.

No le **cojas** los juguetes a tu hermana.
Don't take your sister's toys.

Coja la primera calle a la derecha.
Take the first street on the right.

Remember that subject pronouns are not used very often in Spanish.

colgar (to hang)

	PRESENT	PRESENT PERFECT
(yo)	**cuelgo**	**he colgado**
(tú)	**cuelgas**	**has colgado**
(él/ella/usted)	**cuelga**	**ha colgado**
(nosotros/as)	**colgamos**	**hemos colgado**
(vosotros/as)	**colgáis**	**habéis colgado**
(ellos/ellas/ ustedes)	**cuelgan**	**han colgado**

	PRETERITE	IMPERFECT
(yo)	**colgué**	**colgaba**
(tú)	**colgaste**	**colgabas**
(él/ella/usted)	**colgó**	**colgaba**
(nosotros/as)	**colgamos**	**colgábamos**
(vosotros/as)	**colgasteis**	**colgabais**
(ellos/ellas/ ustedes)	**colgaron**	**colgaban**

	GERUND	PAST PARTICIPLE
	colgando	**colgado**

	FUTURE	CONDITIONAL
(yo)	**colgaré**	**colgaría**
(tú)	**colgarás**	**colgarías**
(él/ella/usted)	**colgará**	**colgaría**
(nosotros/as)	**colgaremos**	**colgaríamos**
(vosotros/as)	**colgaréis**	**colgaríais**
(ellos/ellas/ ustedes)	**colgarán**	**colgarían**

	PRESENT SUBJUNCTIVE	IMPERFECT SUBJUNCTIVE
(yo)	**cuelgue**	**colgara** or **colgase**
(tú)	**cuelgues**	**colgaras** or **colgases**
(él/ella/usted)	**cuelgue**	**colgara** or **colgase**
(nosotros/as)	**colguemos**	**colgáramos** or **colgásemos**
(vosotros/as)	**colguéis**	**colgarais** or **colgaseis**
(ellos/ellas/ ustedes)	**cuelguen**	**colgaran** or **colgasen**

IMPERATIVE
cuelga / colgad

Use the present subjunctive in all cases other than these **tú** and **vosotros** affirmative forms.

EXAMPLE PHRASES

Cada día **cuelgan** el cartel de "no hay billetes".
Every day the "sold out" sign goes up.

Hay telarañas **colgando** del techo.
There are cobwebs hanging from the ceiling.

Te **he colgado** la chaqueta en la percha.
I've hung your jacket on the hanger.

Me **colgó** el teléfono.
He hung up on me.

De la pared **colgaba** un espejo.
There was a mirror hanging on the wall.

Colgaremos el cuadro en esa pared.
We'll hang the picture on that wall.

¡Que lo **cuelguen**!
Hang him!

No **cuelgue**, por favor.
Please don't hang up.

¡**Cuelga**, por favor, que quiero hacer una llamada!
Please hang up.
I want to use the phone!

Remember that subject pronouns are not used very often in Spanish.

comer (to eat)

	PRESENT	PRESENT PERFECT
(yo)	**como**	**he comido**
(tú)	**comes**	**has comido**
(él/ella/usted)	**come**	**ha comido**
(nosotros/as)	**comemos**	**hemos comido**
(vosotros/as)	**coméis**	**habéis comido**
(ellos/ellas/ustedes)	**comen**	**han comido**

	PRETERITE	IMPERFECT
(yo)	**comí**	**comía**
(tú)	**comiste**	**comías**
(él/ella/usted)	**comió**	**comía**
(nosotros/as)	**comimos**	**comíamos**
(vosotros/as)	**comisteis**	**comíais**
(ellos/ellas/ustedes)	**comieron**	**comían**

GERUND	PAST PARTICIPLE
comiendo	**comido**

	FUTURE	CONDITIONAL
(yo)	**comeré**	**comería**
(tú)	**comerás**	**comerías**
(él/ella/usted)	**comerá**	**comería**
(nosotros/as)	**comeremos**	**comeríamos**
(vosotros/as)	**comeréis**	**comeríais**
(ellos/ellas/ustedes)	**comerán**	**comerían**

	PRESENT SUBJUNCTIVE	IMPERFECT SUBJUNCTIVE
(yo)	**coma**	**comiera** or **comiese**
(tú)	**comas**	**comieras** or **comieses**
(él/ella/usted)	**coma**	**comiera** or **comiese**
(nosotros/as)	**comamos**	**comiéramos** or **comiésemos**
(vosotros/as)	**comáis**	**comierais** or **comieseis**
(ellos/ellas/ustedes)	**coman**	**comieran** or **comiesen**

IMPERATIVE
come / comed

Use the present subjunctive in all cases other than these **tú** and **vosotros** affirmative forms.

EXAMPLE PHRASES

No **come** carne.
He doesn't eat meat.

Se lo **ha comido** todo.
He's eaten it all.

Comimos en un restaurante.
We had lunch in a restaurant.

Siempre **comían** demasiado.
They always ate too much.

Me lo **comeré** yo.
I'll eat it.

Si no fuera por mí, no **comeríamos**.
We wouldn't eat if it weren't for me.

Si **comieras** más, no estarías tan delgado.
You wouldn't be so thin if you ate more.

No **comas** tan deprisa.
Don't eat so fast.

Remember that subject pronouns are not used very often in Spanish.

conducir (to drive; to lead)

	PRESENT	PRESENT PERFECT
(yo)	**conduzco**	**he conducido**
(tú)	**conduces**	**has conducido**
(él/ella/usted)	**conduce**	**ha conducido**
(nosotros/as)	**conducimos**	**hemos conducido**
(vosotros/as)	**conducís**	**habéis conducido**
(ellos/ellas/ ustedes)	**conducen**	**han conducido**

	PRETERITE	IMPERFECT
(yo)	**conduje**	**conducía**
(tú)	**condujiste**	**conducías**
(él/ella/usted)	**condujo**	**conducía**
(nosotros/as)	**condujimos**	**conducíamos**
(vosotros/as)	**condujisteis**	**conducíais**
(ellos/ellas/ ustedes)	**condujeron**	**conducían**

	GERUND	PAST PARTICIPLE
	conduciendo	**conducido**

	FUTURE	CONDITIONAL
(yo)	**conduciré**	**conduciría**
(tú)	**conducirás**	**conducirías**
(él/ella/usted)	**conducirá**	**conduciría**
(nosotros/as)	**conduciremos**	**conduciríamos**
(vosotros/as)	**conduciréis**	**conduciríais**
(ellos/ellas/ ustedes)	**conducirán**	**conducirían**

	PRESENT SUBJUNCTIVE	IMPERFECT SUBJUNCTIVE
(yo)	**conduzca**	**condujera** or **condujese**
(tú)	**conduzcas**	**condujeras** or **condujeses**
(él/ella/usted)	**conduzca**	**condujera** or **condujese**
(nosotros/as)	**conduzcamos**	**condujéramos** or **condujésemos**
(vosotros/as)	**conduzcáis**	**condujerais** or **condujeseis**
(ellos/ellas/ ustedes)	**conduzcan**	**condujeran** or **condujesen**

IMPERATIVE

conduce / conducid

Use the present subjunctive in all cases other than these **tú** and **vosotros** affirmative forms.

EXAMPLE PHRASES

No sé **conducir**.
I can't drive.

Conduces muy bien.
You're a very good driver.

Enfadarte no te **ha conducido** a nada.
Getting angry hasn't got you anywhere.

La pista nos **condujo** hasta él.
The clue led us to him.

¿**Conducías** tú?
Was it you driving?

El camarero les **conducirá** a su mesa.
The waiter will show you to your table.

Si bebes, no **conduzcas**.
Don't drink and drive.

Le pedí que **condujera** más despacio.
I asked him to drive more slowly.

Conduzca con cuidado.
Drive carefully.

Remember that subject pronouns are not used very often in Spanish.

conocer (to know)

	PRESENT	PRESENT PERFECT
(yo)	**conozco**	**he conocido**
(tú)	**conoces**	**has conocido**
(él/ella/usted)	**conoce**	**ha conocido**
(nosotros/as)	**conocemos**	**hemos conocido**
(vosotros/as)	**conocéis**	**habéis conocido**
(ellos/ellas/ ustedes)	**conocen**	**han conocido**

	PRETERITE	IMPERFECT
(yo)	**conocí**	**conocía**
(tú)	**conociste**	**conocías**
(él/ella/usted)	**conoció**	**conocía**
(nosotros/as)	**conocimos**	**conocíamos**
(vosotros/as)	**conocisteis**	**conocíais**
(ellos/ellas/ ustedes)	**conocieron**	**conocían**

GERUND	PAST PARTICIPLE
conociendo	**conocido**

	FUTURE	CONDITIONAL
(yo)	**conoceré**	**conocería**
(tú)	**conocerás**	**conocerías**
(él/ella/usted)	**conocerá**	**conocería**
(nosotros/as)	**conoceremos**	**conoceríamos**
(vosotros/as)	**conoceréis**	**conoceríais**
(ellos/ellas/ ustedes)	**conocerán**	**conocerían**

	PRESENT SUBJUNCTIVE	IMPERFECT SUBJUNCTIVE
(yo)	**conozca**	**conociera** or **conociese**
(tú)	**conozcas**	**conocieras** or **conocieses**
(él/ella/usted)	**conozca**	**conociera** or **conociese**
(nosotros/as)	**conozcamos**	**conociéramos** or **conociésemos**
(vosotros/as)	**conozcáis**	**conocierais** or **conocieseis**
(ellos/ellas/ ustedes)	**conozcan**	**conocieran** or **conociesen**

IMPERATIVE

conoce / conoced

Use the present subjunctive in all cases other than these **tú** and **vosotros** affirmative forms.

EXAMPLE PHRASES

Conozco un restaurante donde se come bien.
I know a restaurant where the food is very good.

Nunca **he conocido** a nadie así.
I've never met anybody like that.

La **conocí** en una fiesta.
I met her at a party.

Nos conocíamos desde hacía años.
We'd known each other for years.

No sé si la **conocerás** cuando la veas.
I don't know if you'll recognize her when you see her.

No quiero que mis padres le **conozcan**.
I don't want my parents to meet him.

Si no la **conociera**, pensaría que lo hizo queriendo.
If I didn't know her better, I'd think she had done it on purpose.

Remember that subject pronouns are not used very often in Spanish.

construir (to build)

	PRESENT	PRESENT PERFECT
(yo)	**construyo**	**he construido**
(tú)	**construyes**	**has construido**
(él/ella/usted)	**construye**	**ha construido**
(nosotros/as)	**construimos**	**hemos construido**
(vosotros/as)	**construís**	**habéis construido**
(ellos/ellas/ustedes)	**construyen**	**han construido**

	PRETERITE	IMPERFECT
(yo)	**construí**	**construía**
(tú)	**construiste**	**construías**
(él/ella/usted)	**construyó**	**construía**
(nosotros/as)	**construimos**	**construíamos**
(vosotros/as)	**construisteis**	**construíais**
(ellos/ellas/ustedes)	**construyeron**	**construían**

GERUND	PAST PARTICIPLE
construyendo	**construido**

	FUTURE	CONDITIONAL
(yo)	**construiré**	**construiría**
(tú)	**construirás**	**construirías**
(él/ella/usted)	**construirá**	**construiría**
(nosotros/as)	**construiremos**	**construiríamos**
(vosotros/as)	**construiréis**	**construiríais**
(ellos/ellas/ustedes)	**construirán**	**construirían**

	PRESENT SUBJUNCTIVE	IMPERFECT SUBJUNCTIVE
(yo)	**construya**	**construyera** or **construyese**
(tú)	**construyas**	**construyeras** or **construyeses**
(él/ella/usted)	**construya**	**construyera** or **construyese**
(nosotros/as)	**construyamos**	**construyéramos** or **construyésemos**
(vosotros/as)	**construyáis**	**construyerais** or **construyeseis**
(ellos/ellas/ustedes)	**construyan**	**construyeran** or **construyesen**

IMPERATIVE

construye / construid

Use the present subjunctive in all cases other than these **tú** and **vosotros** affirmative forms.

EXAMPLE PHRASES

Construyen casas de madera.
They build wooden houses.

Están construyendo una escuela.
They're building a new school.

Ha construido la casa él solo.
He built the house on his own.

Lo **construyó** sin planos.
He built it without any plans.

Su empresa **construía** puentes.
His company built bridges.

Aquí **construirán** una autopista.
They're going to build a new motorway here.

Yo **construiría** la oración de otra forma.
I'd construct the sentence differently.

Le pedí que lo **construyera** así.
I asked him to build it like this.

Remember that subject pronouns are not used very often in Spanish.

contar (to tell; to count)

	PRESENT	PRESENT PERFECT
(yo)	**cuento**	**he contado**
(tú)	**cuentas**	**has contado**
(él/ella/usted)	**cuenta**	**ha contado**
(nosotros/as)	**contamos**	**hemos contado**
(vosotros/as)	**contáis**	**habéis contado**
(ellos/ellas/ ustedes)	**cuentan**	**han contado**

	PRETERITE	IMPERFECT
(yo)	**conté**	**contaba**
(tú)	**contaste**	**contabas**
(él/ella/usted)	**contó**	**contaba**
(nosotros/as)	**contamos**	**contábamos**
(vosotros/as)	**contasteis**	**contabais**
(ellos/ellas/ ustedes)	**contaron**	**contaban**

	GERUND	PAST PARTICIPLE
	contando	**contado**

	FUTURE	CONDITIONAL
(yo)	**contaré**	**contaría**
(tú)	**contarás**	**contarías**
(él/ella/usted)	**contará**	**contaría**
(nosotros/as)	**contaremos**	**contaríamos**
(vosotros/as)	**contaréis**	**contaríais**
(ellos/ellas/ ustedes)	**contarán**	**contarían**

	PRESENT SUBJUNCTIVE	IMPERFECT SUBJUNCTIVE
(yo)	**cuente**	**contara** or **contase**
(tú)	**cuentes**	**contaras** or **contases**
(él/ella/usted)	**cuente**	**contara** or **contase**
(nosotros/as)	**contemos**	**contáramos** or **contásemos**
(vosotros/as)	**contéis**	**contarais** or **contaseis**
(ellos/ellas/ ustedes)	**cuenten**	**contaran** or **contasen**

IMPERATIVE

cuenta / contad

Use the present subjunctive in all cases other than these **tú** and **vosotros** affirmative forms.

EXAMPLE PHRASES

Sabe **contar** hasta diez.
She can count up to ten.

Estoy contando los días.
I'm counting the days.

¿**Has contado** el dinero?
Have you counted the money?

Nos **contó** un secreto.
He told us a secret.

Para él sólo **contaba** su carrera.
The only thing that mattered to him was his career.

Prométeme que no se lo **contarás** a nadie.
Promise you won't tell anyone.

Quiero que me **cuente** exactamente qué pasó.
I want you to tell me exactly what happened.

Quería que le **contara** un cuento.
She wanted me to tell her a story.

No **cuentes** conmigo.
Don't count on me.

Venga, **cuéntamelo**.
Come on, tell me.

Remember that subject pronouns are not used very often in Spanish.

crecer (to grow)

	PRESENT	PRESENT PERFECT
(yo)	**crezco**	**he crecido**
(tú)	**creces**	**has crecido**
(él/ella/usted)	**crece**	**ha crecido**
(nosotros/as)	**crecemos**	**hemos crecido**
(vosotros/as)	**crecéis**	**habéis crecido**
(ellos/ellas/ustedes)	**crecen**	**han crecido**

	PRETERITE	IMPERFECT
(yo)	**crecí**	**crecía**
(tú)	**creciste**	**crecías**
(él/ella/usted)	**creció**	**crecía**
(nosotros/as)	**crecimos**	**crecíamos**
(vosotros/as)	**crecisteis**	**crecíais**
(ellos/ellas/ustedes)	**crecieron**	**crecían**

GERUND	PAST PARTICIPLE
creciendo	**crecido**

	FUTURE	CONDITIONAL
(yo)	**creceré**	**crecería**
(tú)	**crecerás**	**crecerías**
(él/ella/usted)	**crecerá**	**crecería**
(nosotros/as)	**creceremos**	**creceríamos**
(vosotros/as)	**creceréis**	**creceríais**
(ellos/ellas/ustedes)	**crecerán**	**crecerían**

	PRESENT SUBJUNCTIVE	IMPERFECT SUBJUNCTIVE
(yo)	**crezca**	**creciera** or **creciese**
(tú)	**crezcas**	**crecieras** or **crecieses**
(él/ella/usted)	**crezca**	**creciera** or **creciese**
(nosotros/as)	**crezcamos**	**creciéramos** or **creciésemos**
(vosotros/as)	**crezcáis**	**crecierais** or **crecieseis**
(ellos/ellas/ustedes)	**crezcan**	**crecieran** or **creciesen**

IMPERATIVE

crece / creced

Use the present subjunctive in all cases other than these **tú** and **vosotros** affirmative forms.

EXAMPLE PHRASES

Esas plantas **crecen** en Chile.
Those plants grow in Chile.

¡Cómo **has crecido**!
Haven't you grown!

Crecimos juntos.
We grew up together.

La ciudad **crecía** a pasos agigantados.
The city was growing by leaps and bounds.

Sigue **creciendo** la inflación.
Inflation is still going up.

Este año la economía **crecerá** un 2%.
The economy will grow by 2% this year.

Crecería mejor en un ambiente húmedo.
It would grow better in a humid environment.

Cuando **crezca**, ya verás.
When he grows up, you'll see.

Quería que sus hijos **crecieran** en otro ambiente.
She wanted her children to grow up in a different environment.

Remember that subject pronouns are not used very often in Spanish.

cruzar (to cross)

	PRESENT	PRESENT PERFECT
(yo)	**cruzo**	**he cruzado**
(tú)	**cruzas**	**has cruzado**
(él/ella/usted)	**cruza**	**ha cruzado**
(nosotros/as)	**cruzamos**	**hemos cruzado**
(vosotros/as)	**cruzáis**	**habéis cruzado**
(ellos/ellas/ustedes)	**cruzan**	**han cruzado**

	PRETERITE	IMPERFECT
(yo)	**crucé**	**cruzaba**
(tú)	**cruzaste**	**cruzabas**
(él/ella/usted)	**cruzó**	**cruzaba**
(nosotros/as)	**cruzamos**	**cruzábamos**
(vosotros/as)	**cruzasteis**	**cruzabais**
(ellos/ellas/ustedes)	**cruzaron**	**cruzaban**

GERUND	PAST PARTICIPLE
cruzando	**cruzado**

	FUTURE	CONDITIONAL
(yo)	**cruzaré**	**cruzaría**
(tú)	**cruzarás**	**cruzarías**
(él/ella/usted)	**cruzará**	**cruzaría**
(nosotros/as)	**cruzaremos**	**cruzaríamos**
(vosotros/as)	**cruzaréis**	**cruzaríais**
(ellos/ellas/ustedes)	**cruzarán**	**cruzarían**

	PRESENT SUBJUNCTIVE	IMPERFECT SUBJUNCTIVE
(yo)	**cruce**	**cruzara** or **cruzase**
(tú)	**cruces**	**cruzaras** or **cruzases**
(él/ella/usted)	**cruce**	**cruzara** or **cruzase**
(nosotros/as)	**crucemos**	**cruzáramos** or **cruzásemos**
(vosotros/as)	**crucéis**	**cruzarais** or **cruzaseis**
(ellos/ellas/ustedes)	**crucen**	**cruzaran** or **cruzasen**

IMPERATIVE
cruza / cruzad

Use the present subjunctive in all cases other than these **tú** and **vosotros** affirmative forms.

EXAMPLE PHRASES

Hace tiempo que no **me cruzo** con él.
I haven't seen him for a long time.

La caravana **está cruzando** el desierto.
The caravan is crossing the dessert.

Se me **han cruzado** los cables.
I got mixed up.

Cruzaron el puente.
They crossed the bridge.

La carretera **cruzaba** la urbanización.
The road went through the housing estate.

Cruzarán varias especies distintas.
They'll cross several different species.

Crucemos los dedos.
Let's keep our fingers crossed.

Le dije que **cruzara** por el paso de cebra.
I told her to cross at the pedestrian crossing.

No **cruces** la calle con el semáforo en rojo.
Don't cross the road when the lights are red.

Remember that subject pronouns are not used very often in Spanish.

cubrir (to cover)

	PRESENT	PRESENT PERFECT
(yo)	**cubro**	**he cubierto**
(tú)	**cubres**	**has cubierto**
(él/ella/usted)	**cubre**	**ha cubierto**
(nosotros/as)	**cubrimos**	**hemos cubierto**
(vosotros/as)	**cubrís**	**habéis cubierto**
(ellos/ellas/ ustedes)	**cubren**	**han cubierto**

	PRETERITE	IMPERFECT
(yo)	**cubrí**	**cubría**
(tú)	**cubriste**	**cubrías**
(él/ella/usted)	**cubrió**	**cubría**
(nosotros/as)	**cubrimos**	**cubríamos**
(vosotros/as)	**cubristeis**	**cubríais**
(ellos/ellas/ ustedes)	**cubrieron**	**cubrían**

	GERUND	PAST PARTICIPLE
	cubriendo	**cubierto**

	FUTURE	CONDITIONAL
(yo)	**cubriré**	**cubriría**
(tú)	**cubrirás**	**cubrirías**
(él/ella/usted)	**cubrirá**	**cubriría**
(nosotros/as)	**cubriremos**	**cubriríamos**
(vosotros/as)	**cubriréis**	**cubriríais**
(ellos/ellas/ ustedes)	**cubrirán**	**cubrirían**

	PRESENT SUBJUNCTIVE	IMPERFECT SUBJUNCTIVE
(yo)	**cubra**	**cubriera** or **cubriese**
(tú)	**cubras**	**cubrieras** or **cubrieses**
(él/ella/usted)	**cubra**	**cubriera** or **cubriese**
(nosotros/as)	**cubramos**	**cubriéramos** or **cubriésemos**
(vosotros/as)	**cubráis**	**cubrierais** or **cubrieseis**
(ellos/ellas/ ustedes)	**cubran**	**cubrieran** or **cubriesen**

IMPERATIVE

cubre / cubrid

Use the present subjunctive in all cases other than these **tú** and **vosotros** affirmative forms.

EXAMPLE PHRASES

Esto no **cubre** los gastos.
This isn't enough to cover expenses.

Le **han cubierto** con una manta.
They've covered him with a blanket.

Se cubrió la cara con las manos.
She covered her face with her hands.

La nieve **cubría** la montaña.
The mountain was covered in snow.

Los corredores **cubrirán** una distancia de 2 km.
The runners will cover a distance of 2 km.

¿Quién **cubriría** la vacante?
Who'd fill the vacancy?

Quiero que **cubras** la noticia.
I want you to cover the story.

Remember that subject pronouns are not used very often in Spanish.

dar (to give)

	PRESENT	PRESENT PERFECT
(yo)	**doy**	**he dado**
(tú)	**das**	**has dado**
(él/ella/usted)	**da**	**ha dado**
(nosotros/as)	**damos**	**hemos dado**
(vosotros/as)	**dais**	**habéis dado**
(ellos/ellas/ustedes)	**dan**	**han dado**

	PRETERITE	IMPERFECT
(yo)	**di**	**daba**
(tú)	**diste**	**dabas**
(él/ella/usted)	**dio**	**daba**
(nosotros/as)	**dimos**	**dábamos**
(vosotros/as)	**disteis**	**dabais**
(ellos/ellas/ustedes)	**dieron**	**daban**

GERUND	PAST PARTICIPLE
dando	**dado**

	FUTURE	CONDITIONAL
(yo)	**daré**	**daría**
(tú)	**darás**	**darías**
(él/ella/usted)	**dará**	**daría**
(nosotros/as)	**daremos**	**daríamos**
(vosotros/as)	**daréis**	**daríais**
(ellos/ellas/ustedes)	**darán**	**darían**

	PRESENT SUBJUNCTIVE	IMPERFECT SUBJUNCTIVE
(yo)	**dé**	**diera** or **diese**
(tú)	**des**	**dieras** or **dieses**
(él/ella/usted)	**dé**	**diera** or **diese**
(nosotros/as)	**demos**	**diéramos** or **diésemos**
(vosotros/as)	**deis**	**dierais** or **dieseis**
(ellos/ellas/ustedes)	**den**	**dieran** or **diesen**

IMPERATIVE

da / dad

Use the present subjunctive in all cases other than these **tú** and **vosotros** affirmative forms.

EXAMPLE PHRASES

Me **da** miedo la oscuridad.
I'm afraid of the dark.

Le **han dado** varios premios a su película.
His film has been awarded several prizes.

Nos **dieron** un par de entradas gratis.
They gave us a couple of free tickets.

Mi ventana **daba** al jardín.
My window looked out on the garden.

Te **daré** el número de mi móvil.
I'll give you my mobile phone number.

Me **daría** mucha alegría volver a verla.
It would be really good to see her again.

Quiero que me lo **des** ahora mismo.
I want you to give it to me right now.

Déme 2 kilos.
2 kilos please.

Remember that subject pronouns are not used very often in Spanish.

decir (to say; to tell)

	PRESENT	PRESENT PERFECT
(yo)	**digo**	**he dicho**
(tú)	**dices**	**has dicho**
(él/ella/usted)	**dice**	**ha dicho**
(nosotros/as)	**decimos**	**hemos dicho**
(vosotros/as)	**decís**	**habéis dicho**
(ellos/ellas/ ustedes)	**dicen**	**han dicho**

	PRETERITE	IMPERFECT
(yo)	**dije**	**decía**
(tú)	**dijiste**	**decías**
(él/ella/usted)	**dijo**	**decía**
(nosotros/as)	**dijimos**	**decíamos**
(vosotros/as)	**dijisteis**	**decíais**
(ellos/ellas/ ustedes)	**dijeron**	**decían**

GERUND	PAST PARTICIPLE
diciendo	**dicho**

	FUTURE	CONDITIONAL
(yo)	**diré**	**diría**
(tú)	**dirás**	**dirías**
(él/ella/usted)	**dirá**	**diría**
(nosotros/as)	**diremos**	**diríamos**
(vosotros/as)	**diréis**	**diríais**
(ellos/ellas/ ustedes)	**dirán**	**dirían**

	PRESENT SUBJUNCTIVE	IMPERFECT SUBJUNCTIVE
(yo)	**diga**	**dijera** or **dijese**
(tú)	**digas**	**dijeras** or **dijeses**
(él/ella/usted)	**diga**	**dijera** or **dijese**
(nosotros/as)	**digamos**	**dijéramos** or **dijésemos**
(vosotros/as)	**digáis**	**dijerais** or **dijeseis**
(ellos/ellas/ ustedes)	**digan**	**dijeran** or **dijesen**

IMPERATIVE

di / decid

Use the present subjunctive in all cases other than these **tú** and **vosotros** affirmative forms.

EXAMPLE PHRASES

Pero ¿qué **dices**?
What are you saying?

¿Te **ha dicho** lo de la boda?
Has he told you about the wedding?

Me lo **dijo** ayer.
He told me yesterday.

Siempre nos **decía** que tuviéramos cuidado.
She always used to tell us to be careful.

Yo **diría** que miente.
I'd say he's lying.

Diga lo que **diga**, no le voy a creer.
Whatever he says, I won't believe him.

Si me **dijeras** lo que pasa, a lo mejor podría ayudar.
If you told me what was going on, I could maybe help.

No le **digas** que me has visto.
Don't tell him you've seen me.

Remember that subject pronouns are not used very often in Spanish.

despreocuparse (to stop worrying)

	PRESENT	PRESENT PERFECT
(yo)	**me despreocupo**	**me he despreocupado**
(tú)	**te despreocupas**	**te has despreocupado**
(él/ella/usted)	**se despreocupa**	**se ha despreocupado**
(nosotros/as)	**nos despreocupamos**	**nos hemos despreocupado**
(vosotros/as)	**os despreocupáis**	**os habéis despreocupado**
(ellos/ellas/ustedes)	**se despreocupan**	**se han despreocupado**

	PRETERITE	IMPERFECT
(yo)	**me despreocupé**	**me despreocupaba**
(tú)	**te despreocupaste**	**te despreocupabas**
(él/ella/usted)	**se despreocupó**	**se despreocupaba**
(nosotros/as)	**nos despreocupamos**	**nos despreocupábamos**
(vosotros/as)	**os despreocupasteis**	**os despreocupabais**
(ellos/ellas/ustedes)	**se despreocuparon**	**se despreocupaban**

GERUND	PAST PARTICIPLE
despreocupándose, etc	**despreocupado**

	FUTURE	CONDITIONAL
(yo)	**me despreocuparé**	**me despreocuparía**
(tú)	**te despreocuparás**	**te despreocuparías**
(él/ella/usted)	**se despreocupará**	**se despreocuparía**
(nosotros/as)	**nos despreocuparemos**	**nos despreocuparíamos**
(vosotros/as)	**os despreocuparéis**	**os despreocuparíais**
(ellos/ellas/ustedes)	**se despreocuparán**	**se despreocuparían**

	PRESENT SUBJUNCTIVE	IMPERFECT SUBJUNCTIVE
(yo)	**me despreocupe**	**me despreocupara** or **despreocupase**
(tú)	**te despreocupes**	**te despreocuparas** or **despreocupases**
(él/ella/usted)	**se despreocupe**	**se despreocupara** or **despreocupase**
(nosotros/as)	**nos despreocupemos**	**nos despreocupáramos** or **despreocupásemos**
(vosotros/as)	**os despreocupéis**	**os despreocuparais** or **despreocupaseis**
(ellos/ellas/ustedes)	**se despreocupen**	**se despreocuparan** or **despreocupasen**

IMPERATIVE

despreocúpate / despreocupaos

Use the present subjunctive in all cases other than these **tú** and **vosotros** affirmative forms.

EXAMPLE PHRASES

Deberías **despreocuparte** un poco más de las cosas.
You shouldn't worry so much about things.

Se despreocupa de todo.
He shows no concern for anything.

Se despreocupó del asunto.
He forgot about the matter.

Yo **me despreocuparía** de él.
I wouldn't worry about him.

Despreocúpate porque ya no tiene remedio.
Stop worrying because there's nothing we can do about it now.

Remember that subject pronouns are not used very often in Spanish.

detener (to stop; to arrest)

	PRESENT	PRESENT PERFECT
(yo)	**detengo**	**he detenido**
(tú)	**detienes**	**has detenido**
(él/ella/usted)	**detiene**	**ha detenido**
(nosotros/as)	**detenemos**	**hemos detenido**
(vosotros/as)	**detenéis**	**habéis detenido**
(ellos/ellas/ ustedes)	**detienen**	**han detenido**

	PRETERITE	IMPERFECT
(yo)	**detuve**	**detenía**
(tú)	**detuviste**	**detenías**
(él/ella/usted)	**detuvo**	**detenía**
(nosotros/as)	**detuvimos**	**deteníamos**
(vosotros/as)	**detuvisteis**	**deteníais**
(ellos/ellas/ ustedes)	**detuvieron**	**detenían**

GERUND	PAST PARTICIPLE
deteniendo	**detenido**

	FUTURE	CONDITIONAL
(yo)	**detendré**	**detendría**
(tú)	**detendrás**	**detendrías**
(él/ella/usted)	**detendrá**	**detendría**
(nosotros/as)	**detendremos**	**detendríamos**
(vosotros/as)	**detendréis**	**detendríais**
(ellos/ellas/ ustedes)	**detendrán**	**detendrían**

	PRESENT SUBJUNCTIVE	IMPERFECT SUBJUNCTIVE
(yo)	**detenga**	**detuviera** or **detuviese**
(tú)	**detengas**	**detuvieras** or **detuvieses**
(él/ella/usted)	**detenga**	**detuviera** or **detuviese**
(nosotros/as)	**detengamos**	**detuviéramos** or **detuviésemos**
(vosotros/as)	**detengáis**	**detuvierais** or **detuvieseis**
(ellos/ellas/ ustedes)	**detengan**	**detuvieran** or **detuviesen**

IMPERATIVE

detén / detened

Use the present subjunctive in all cases other than these **tú** and **vosotros** affirmative forms.

EXAMPLE PHRASES

Han detenido a los ladrones.
They've arrested the thieves.

Nos detuvimos en el semáforo.
We stopped at the lights.

¡Queda **detenido**!
You are under arrest!

Nada la **detendrá**.
Nothing will stop her.

Si **te detuvieras** a pensar, nunca harías nada.
If you stopped to think, you'd never do anything.

¡**Deténgase**! Stop!
¡No **te detengas**! Don't stop!

Remember that subject pronouns are not used very often in Spanish.

dirigir (to direct; to run)

	PRESENT	PRESENT PERFECT
(yo)	**dirigo**	**he dirigido**
(tú)	**diriges**	**has dirigido**
(él/ella/usted)	**dirige**	**ha dirigido**
(nosotros/as)	**dirigimos**	**hemos dirigido**
(vosotros/as)	**dirigís**	**habéis dirigido**
(ellos/ellas/ ustedes)	**dirigen**	**han dirigido**

	PRETERITE	IMPERFECT
(yo)	**dirigí**	**dirigía**
(tú)	**dirigiste**	**dirigías**
(él/ella/usted)	**dirigió**	**dirigía**
(nosotros/as)	**dirigimos**	**dirigíamos**
(vosotros/as)	**dirigisteis**	**dirigíais**
(ellos/ellas/ ustedes)	**dirigieron**	**dirigían**

GERUND	PAST PARTICIPLE
dirigiendo	**dirigido**

	FUTURE	CONDITIONAL
(yo)	**dirigiré**	**dirigiría**
(tú)	**dirigirás**	**dirigirías**
(él/ella/usted)	**dirigirá**	**dirigiría**
(nosotros/as)	**dirigiremos**	**dirigiríamos**
(vosotros/as)	**dirigiréis**	**dirigiríais**
(ellos/ellas/ ustedes)	**dirigirán**	**dirigirían**

	PRESENT SUBJUNCTIVE	IMPERFECT SUBJUNCTIVE
(yo)	**dirija**	**dirigiera** or **dirigiese**
(tú)	**dirijas**	**dirigieras** or **dirigieses**
(él/ella/usted)	**dirija**	**dirigiera** or **dirigiese**
(nosotros/as)	**dirijamos**	**dirigiéramos** or **dirigiésemos**
(vosotros/as)	**dirijáis**	**dirigierais** or **dirigieseis**
(ellos/ellas/ ustedes)	**dirijan**	**dirigieran** or **dirigiesen**

IMPERATIVE

dirige / dirigid

Use the present subjunctive in all cases other than these **tú** and **vosotros** affirmative forms.

EXAMPLE PHRASES

Dirijo esta empresa desde hace dos años.
I've been running this company for two years.

Ha dirigido varias películas.
She has directed several films.

No le **dirigió** la palabra.
She didn't say a word to him.

Se dirigía a la parada de autobús.
He was making his way to the bus stop.

Dirigirá la expedición.
He'll be leading the expedition.

Para más información **diríjase** al apartado de correos número 1002.
For further information write to PO Box 1002.

Remember that subject pronouns are not used very often in Spanish.

distinguir (to distinguish)

	PRESENT	PRESENT PERFECT
(yo)	**distingo**	**he distinguido**
(tú)	**distingues**	**has distinguido**
(él/ella/usted)	**distingue**	**ha distinguido**
(nosotros/as)	**distinguimos**	**hemos distinguido**
(vosotros/as)	**distinguís**	**habéis distinguido**
(ellos/ellas/ustedes)	**distinguen**	**han distinguido**

	PRETERITE	IMPERFECT
(yo)	**distinguí**	**distinguía**
(tú)	**distinguiste**	**distinguías**
(él/ella/usted)	**distinguió**	**distinguía**
(nosotros/as)	**distinguimos**	**distinguíamos**
(vosotros/as)	**distinguisteis**	**distinguíais**
(ellos/ellas/ustedes)	**distinguieron**	**distinguían**

GERUND	PAST PARTICIPLE
distinguiendo	**distinguido**

	FUTURE	CONDITIONAL
(yo)	**distinguiré**	**distinguiría**
(tú)	**distinguirás**	**distinguirías**
(él/ella/usted)	**distinguirá**	**distinguiría**
(nosotros/as)	**distinguiremos**	**distinguiríamos**
(vosotros/as)	**distinguiréis**	**distinguiríais**
(ellos/ellas/ustedes)	**distinguirán**	**distinguirían**

	PRESENT SUBJUNCTIVE	IMPERFECT SUBJUNCTIVE
(yo)	**distinga**	**distinguiera** or **distinguiese**
(tú)	**distingas**	**distinguieras** or **distinguieses**
(él/ella/usted)	**distinga**	**distinguiera** or **distinguiese**
(nosotros/as)	**distingamos**	**distinguiéramos** or **distinguiésemos**
(vosotros/as)	**distingáis**	**distinguierais** or **distinguieseis**
(ellos/ellas/ustedes)	**distingan**	**distinguieran** or **distinguiesen**

IMPERATIVE

distingue / distinguid

Use the present subjunctive in all cases other than these **tú** and **vosotros** affirmative forms.

EXAMPLE PHRASES

No lo **distingo** del azul.
I can't tell the difference between it and the blue one.

Nos **ha distinguido** con su presencia.
He has honoured us with his presence.

Se distinguió por su gran valentía.
He distinguished himself by his bravery.

Se distinguía desde lejos.
You could see it from the distance.

Al final **distinguirás** unas notas de otras.
Eventually you'll be able to tell one note from another.

No los **distinguiría**.
I wouldn't be able to tell them apart.

Remember that subject pronouns are not used very often in Spanish.

divertir (to entertain)

	PRESENT	PRESENT PERFECT
(yo)	**divierto**	**he divertido**
(tú)	**diviertes**	**has divertido**
(él/ella/usted)	**divierte**	**ha divertido**
(nosotros/as)	**divertimos**	**hemos divertido**
(vosotros/as)	**divertís**	**habéis divertido**
(ellos/ellas/ ustedes)	**divierten**	**han divertido**

	PRETERITE	IMPERFECT
(yo)	**divertí**	**divertía**
(tú)	**divertiste**	**divertías**
(él/ella/usted)	**divirtió**	**divertía**
(nosotros/as)	**divertimos**	**divertíamos**
(vosotros/as)	**divertisteis**	**divertíais**
(ellos/ellas/ ustedes)	**divirtieron**	**divertían**

GERUND	PAST PARTICIPLE
divirtiendo	**divertido**

	FUTURE	CONDITIONAL
(yo)	**divertiré**	**divertiría**
(tú)	**divertirás**	**divertirías**
(él/ella/usted)	**divertirá**	**divertiría**
(nosotros/as)	**divertiremos**	**divertiríamos**
(vosotros/as)	**divertiréis**	**divertiríais**
(ellos/ellas/ ustedes)	**divertirán**	**divertirían**

	PRESENT SUBJUNCTIVE	IMPERFECT SUBJUNCTIVE
(yo)	**divierta**	**divirtiera** or **divirtiese**
(tú)	**diviertas**	**divirtieras** or **divirtieses**
(él/ella/usted)	**divierta**	**divirtiera** or **divirtiese**
(nosotros/as)	**divirtamos**	**divirtiéramos** or **divirtiésemos**
(vosotros/as)	**divirtáis**	**divirtierais** or **divirtieseis**
(ellos/ellas/ ustedes)	**diviertan**	**divirtieran** or **divirtiesen**

IMPERATIVE

divierte / divertid

Use the present subjunctive in all cases other than these **tú** and **vosotros** affirmative forms.

EXAMPLE PHRASES

Cantamos sólo para **divertirnos**.
We sing just for fun.

Me **divierte** verlos tan serios.
It's amusing to see them looking so serious.

¿**Os habéis divertido** en la fiesta?
Did you enjoy the party?

Nos **divirtió** con sus anécdotas.
He entertained us with his stories.

Nos divertíamos mucho jugando en la playa.
We were having a great time playing on the beach.

Si fueras, **te divertirías** mucho.
If you went you'd have a great time.

Hizo lo posible por que **se divirtieran**.
He did everything he could to make it fun for them.

¡Que **te diviertas**!
Have a good time!

Remember that subject pronouns are not used very often in Spanish.

dormir (to sleep)

	PRESENT	PRESENT PERFECT
(yo)	**duermo**	**he dormido**
(tú)	**duermes**	**has dormido**
(él/ella/usted)	**duerme**	**ha dormido**
(nosotros/as)	**dormimos**	**hemos dormido**
(vosotros/as)	**dormís**	**habéis dormido**
(ellos/ellas/ ustedes)	**duermen**	**han dormido**

	PRETERITE	IMPERFECT
(yo)	**dormí**	**dormía**
(tú)	**dormiste**	**dormías**
(él/ella/usted)	**durmió**	**dormía**
(nosotros/as)	**dormimos**	**dormíamos**
(vosotros/as)	**dormisteis**	**dormíais**
(ellos/ellas/ ustedes)	**durmieron**	**dormían**

	GERUND	PAST PARTICIPLE
	durmiendo	**dormido**

	FUTURE	CONDITIONA
(yo)	**dormiré**	**dormiría**
(tú)	**dormirás**	**dormirías**
(él/ella/usted)	**dormirá**	**dormiría**
(nosotros/as)	**dormiremos**	**dormiríamos**
(vosotros/as)	**dormiréis**	**dormiríais**
(ellos/ellas/ ustedes)	**dormirán**	**dormirían**

	PRESENT SUBJUNCTIVE	IMPERFECT SUBJUNCTIVE
(yo)	**duerma**	**durmiera** or **durmiese**
(tú)	**duermas**	**durmieras** or **durmieses**
(él/ella/usted)	**duerma**	**durmiera** or **durmiese**
(nosotros/as)	**durmamos**	**durmiéramos** or **durmiésemos**
(vosotros/as)	**durmáis**	**durmierais** or **durmieseis**
(ellos/ellas/ ustedes)	**duerman**	**durmieran** or **durmiesen**

IMPERATIVE

duerme / dormid

Use the present subjunctive in all cases other than these **tú** and **vosotros** affirmative forms.

EXAMPLE PHRASES

No **duermo** muy bien.
I don't sleep very well.

Está durmiendo.
She's asleep.

He dormido de un tirón.
I slept like a log.

Se me **durmió** la pierna.
My leg went to sleep.

Se dormía en clase.
She would fall asleep in class.

Si no tomo café, **me dormiré**.
I'll fall asleep if I don't have some coffee.

Yo no **dormiría** en esa casa.
I wouldn't sleep in that house.

Quiero que **duermas** la siesta.
I want you to have a nap.

Si **durmieras** más horas, no estarías tan cansada.
You wouldn't be so tired if you slept for longer.

Remember that subject pronouns are not used very often in Spanish.

elegir (to choose)

	PRESENT	PRESENT PERFECT
(yo)	**elijo**	**he elegido**
(tú)	**eliges**	**has elegido**
(él/ella/usted)	**elige**	**ha elegido**
(nosotros/as)	**elegimos**	**hemos elegido**
(vosotros/as)	**elegís**	**habéis elegido**
(ellos/ellas/ ustedes)	**eligen**	**han elegido**

	PRETERITE	IMPERFECT
(yo)	**elegí**	**elegía**
(tú)	**elegiste**	**elegías**
(él/ella/usted)	**eligió**	**elegía**
(nosotros/as)	**elegimos**	**elegíamos**
(vosotros/as)	**elegisteis**	**elegíais**
(ellos/ellas/ ustedes)	**eligieron**	**elegían**

GERUND	PAST PARTICIPLE
eligiendo	**elegido**

	FUTURE	CONDITIONAL
(yo)	**elegiré**	**elegiría**
(tú)	**elegirás**	**elegirías**
(él/ella/usted)	**elegirá**	**elegiría**
(nosotros/as)	**elegiremos**	**elegiríamos**
(vosotros/as)	**elegiréis**	**elegiríais**
(ellos/ellas/ ustedes)	**elegirán**	**elegirían**

	PRESENT SUBJUNCTIVE	IMPERFECT SUBJUNCTIVE
(yo)	**elija**	**eligiera** or **eligiese**
(tú)	**elijas**	**eligieras** or **eligieses**
(él/ella/usted)	**elija**	**eligiera** or **eligiese**
(nosotros/as)	**elijamos**	**eligiéramos** or **eligiésemos**
(vosotros/as)	**elijáis**	**eligierais** or **eligieseis**
(ellos/ellas/ ustedes)	**elijan**	**eligieran** or **eligiesen**

IMPERATIVE

elige / elegid

Use the present subjunctive in all cases other than these **tú** and **vosotros** affirmative forms.

EXAMPLE PHRASES

Te dan a **elegir** entre dos modelos.
You get a choice of two models.

Nosotros no **elegimos** a nuestros padres, ni ellos nos **eligen** a nosotros.
We don't choose our parents and they don't choose us either.

Creo que **ha elegido** bien.
I think he's made a good choice.

No lo **eligieron** ellos.
It wasn't them who chose it.

Yo **elegiría** el más caro.
I'd choose the most expensive one.

Elija una carta.
Choose a card.

Remember that subject pronouns are not used very often in Spanish.

empezar (to begin)

	PRESENT	PRESENT PERFECT
(yo)	**empiezo**	**he empezado**
(tú)	**empiezas**	**has empezado**
(él/ella/usted)	**empieza**	**ha empezado**
(nosotros/as)	**empezamos**	**hemos empezado**
(vosotros/as)	**empezáis**	**habéis empezado**
(ellos/ellas/ ustedes)	**empiezan**	**han empezado**

	PRETERITE	IMPERFECT
(yo)	**empecé**	**empezaba**
(tú)	**empezaste**	**empezabas**
(él/ella/usted)	**empezó**	**empezaba**
(nosotros/as)	**empezamos**	**empezábamos**
(vosotros/as)	**empezasteis**	**empezabais**
(ellos/ellas/ ustedes)	**empezaron**	**empezaban**

GERUND	PAST PARTICIPLE
empezando	**empezado**

	FUTURE	CONDITIONAL
(yo)	**empezaré**	**empezaría**
(tú)	**empezarás**	**empezarías**
(él/ella/usted)	**empezará**	**empezaría**
(nosotros/as)	**empezaremos**	**empezaríamos**
(vosotros/as)	**empezaréis**	**empezaríais**
(ellos/ellas/ ustedes)	**empezarán**	**empezarían**

	PRESENT SUBJUNCTIVE	IMPERFECT SUBJUNCTIVE
(yo)	**empiece**	**empezara** or **empezase**
(tú)	**empieces**	**empezaras** or **empezases**
(él/ella/usted)	**empiece**	**empezara** or **empezase**
(nosotros/as)	**empecemos**	**empezáramos** or **empezásemos**
(vosotros/as)	**empecéis**	**empezarais** or **empezaseis**
(ellos/ellas/ ustedes)	**empiecen**	**empezaran** or **empezasen**

IMPERATIVE

empieza / empezad

Use the present subjunctive in all cases other than these **tú** and **vosotros** affirmative forms.

EXAMPLE PHRASES

Está a punto de **empezar**.
It's about to start.

¿Cuándo **empiezas** a trabajar en el sitio nuevo?
When do you start work at the new place?

Ha empezado a nevar.
It's started snowing.

Las vacaciones **empezaron** el quince.
The holidays started on the fifteenth.

Empezaba por *p*.
It began with *p*.

La semana que viene **empezaremos** un curso nuevo.
We'll start a new course next week.

Yo **empezaría** desde cero.
I'd start from scratch.

Quiero que **empieces** ya.
I want you to start now.

Si **empezáramos** ahora, acabaríamos a las diez.
If we started now, we'd be finished by ten.

Empieza por aquí.
Start here.

Remember that subject pronouns are not used very often in Spanish.

enfrentarse (a) (to face)

	PRESENT	PRESENT PERFECT
(yo)	**me enfrento**	**me he enfrentado**
(tú)	**te enfrentas**	**te has enfrentado**
(él/ella/usted)	**se enfrenta**	**se ha enfrentado**
(nosotros/as)	**nos enfrentamos**	**nos hemos enfrentado**
(vosotros/as)	**os enfrentáis**	**os habéis enfrentado**
(ellos/ellas/ ustedes)	**se enfrentan**	**se han enfrentado**

	PRETERITE	IMPERFECT
(yo)	**me enfrenté**	**me enfrentaba**
(tú)	**te enfrentaste**	**te enfrentabas**
(él/ella/usted)	**se enfrentó**	**se enfrentaba**
(nosotros/as)	**nos enfrentamos**	**nos enfrentábamos**
(vosotros/as)	**os enfrentasteis**	**os enfrentabais**
(ellos/ellas/ ustedes)	**se enfrentaron**	**se enfrentaban**

GERUND	PAST PARTICIPLE
enfrentándose, etc	**enfrentado**

	FUTURE	CONDITIONAL
(yo)	**me enfrentaré**	**me enfrentaría**
(tú)	**te enfrentarás**	**te enfrentarías**
(él/ella/usted)	**se enfrentará**	**se enfrentaría**
(nosotros/as)	**nos enfrentaremos**	**nos enfrentaríamos**
(vosotros/as)	**os enfrentaréis**	**os enfrentaríais**
(ellos/ellas/ ustedes)	**se enfrentarán**	**se enfrentarían**

	PRESENT SUBJUNCTIVE	IMPERFECT SUBJUNCTIVE
(yo)	**me enfrente**	**me enfrentara** or **enfrentase**
(tú)	**te enfrentes**	**te enfrentaras** or **enfrentases**
(él/ella/usted)	**se enfrente**	**se enfrentara** or **enfrentase**
(nosotros/as)	**nos enfrentemos**	**nos enfrentáramos** or **enfrentásemos**
(vosotros/as)	**os enfrentéis**	**os enfrentarais** or **enfrentaseis**
(ellos/ellas/ ustedes)	**se enfrenten**	**se enfrentaran** or **enfrentasen**

IMPERATIVE

enfréntate / enfrentaos

Use the present subjunctive in all cases other than these **tú** and **vosotros** affirmative forms.

EXAMPLE PHRASES

Tienes que **enfrentarte al** problema.
You have to face up to the problem.

Hoy **se enfrentan** los dos semifinalistas.
The two semifinalists meet today.

Padre e hijo **se han enfrentado** varias veces.
Father and son have had several confrontations.

Se enfrentaban a un futuro incierto.
They faced an uncertain future.

El héroe **se enfrentará** a todo tipo de peligros.
The hero will have to face all kinds of dangers.

No **te enfrentes** con él.
Don't confront him.

Remember that subject pronouns are not used very often in Spanish.

entender (to understand)

	PRESENT	PRESENT PERFECT
(yo)	**entiendo**	**he entendido**
(tú)	**entiendes**	**has entendido**
(él/ella/usted)	**entiende**	**ha entendido**
(nosotros/as)	**entendemos**	**hemos entendido**
(vosotros/as)	**entendéis**	**habéis entendido**
(ellos/ellas/ustedes)	**entienden**	**han entendido**

	PRETERITE	IMPERFECT
(yo)	**entendí**	**entendía**
(tú)	**entendiste**	**entendías**
(él/ella/usted)	**entendió**	**entendía**
(nosotros/as)	**entendimos**	**entendíamos**
(vosotros/as)	**entendisteis**	**entendíais**
(ellos/ellas/ustedes)	**entendieron**	**entendían**

GERUND	PAST PARTICIPLE
entendiendo	**entendido**

	FUTURE	CONDITIONAL
(yo)	**entenderé**	**entendería**
(tú)	**entenderás**	**entenderías**
(él/ella/usted)	**entenderá**	**entendería**
(nosotros/as)	**entenderemos**	**entenderíamos**
(vosotros/as)	**entenderéis**	**entenderíais**
(ellos/ellas/ustedes)	**entenderán**	**entenderían**

	PRESENT SUBJUNCTIVE	IMPERFECT SUBJUNCTIVE
(yo)	**entienda**	**entendiera** or **entendiese**
(tú)	**entiendas**	**entendieras** or **entendieses**
(él/ella/usted)	**entienda**	**entendiera** or **entendiese**
(nosotros/as)	**entendamos**	**entendiéramos** or **entendiésemos**
(vosotros/as)	**entendáis**	**entendierais** or **entendieseis**
(ellos/ellas/ustedes)	**entiendan**	**entendieran** or **entendiesen**

IMPERATIVE

entiende / entended

Use the present subjunctive in all cases other than these **tú** and **vosotros** affirmative forms.

EXAMPLE PHRASES

No lo vas a **entender**.
You won't understand.

No lo **entiendo**.
I don't understand.

Estás entendiéndolo todo al revés.
You're getting the wrong end of the stick.

Creo que lo **he entendido** mal.
I think I've misunderstood.

¿**Entendiste** lo que dijo?
Did you understand what she said?

Mi padre **entendía** mucho de caballos.
My father knew a lot about horses.

Con el tiempo lo **entenderás**.
You'll understand one day.

Yo no lo **entendería** así.
I wouldn't interpret it like that.

Si de verdad me **entendieras**, no habrías dicho eso.
If you really understood me, you would never have said that.

No me **entiendas** mal.
Don't misunderstand me.

Remember that subject pronouns are not used very often in Spanish.

enviar (to send)

	PRESENT	PRESENT PERFECT
(yo)	**envío**	**he enviado**
(tú)	**envías**	**has enviado**
(él/ella/usted)	**envía**	**ha enviado**
(nosotros/as)	**enviamos**	**hemos enviado**
(vosotros/as)	**enviáis**	**habéis enviado**
(ellos/ellas/ ustedes)	**envían**	**han enviado**

	PRETERITE	IMPERFECT
(yo)	**envié**	**enviaba**
(tú)	**enviaste**	**enviabas**
(él/ella/usted)	**envió**	**enviaba**
(nosotros/as)	**enviamos**	**enviábamos**
(vosotros/as)	**enviasteis**	**enviabais**
(ellos/ellas/ ustedes)	**enviaron**	**enviaban**

GERUND	PAST PARTICIPLE
enviando	**enviado**

	FUTURE	CONDITIONAL
(yo)	**enviaré**	**enviaría**
(tú)	**enviarás**	**enviarías**
(él/ella/usted)	**enviará**	**enviaría**
(nosotros/as)	**enviaremos**	**enviaríamos**
(vosotros/as)	**enviaréis**	**enviaríais**
(ellos/ellas/ ustedes)	**enviarán**	**enviarían**

	PRESENT SUBJUNCTIVE	IMPERFECT SUBJUNCTIVE
(yo)	**envíe**	**enviara** or **enviase**
(tú)	**envíes**	**enviaras** or **enviases**
(él/ella/usted)	**envíe**	**enviara** or **enviase**
(nosotros/as)	**enviemos**	**enviáramos** or **enviásemos**
(vosotros/as)	**enviéis**	**enviarais** or **enviaseis**
(ellos/ellas/ ustedes)	**envíen**	**enviaran** or **enviasen**

IMPERATIVE

envía / enviad

Use the present subjunctive in all cases other than these **tú** and **vosotros** affirmative forms.

EXAMPLE PHRASES

¿Cómo lo vas a **enviar**?
How are you going to send it?

Les **envío** el trabajo por correo electrónico.
I send them my work by email.

Ya **está enviando** las invitaciones.
She has already started sending out the invitations.

La **han enviado** a Guatemala.
They've sent her to Guatemala.

Le **envió** el regalo por correo.
He posted her the present.

Me **enviaba** siempre a mí a hacer los recados.
She always sent me to do the errands.

Nos **enviarán** más información.
They'll send us further information.

Yo lo **enviaría** por mensajero.
I'd send it by courier.

Necesitamos que lo **envíes** inmediatamente.
We need you to send it immediately.

Si lo **enviaras** ahora, llegaría el lunes.
If you sent it now it would get there on Monday.

No lo **envíes** sin repasarlo antes.
Don't send it in without checking it first.

Envíe sus datos personales.
Send in your details.

Remember that subject pronouns are not used very often in Spanish.

equivocarse (to make a mistake; to be wrong)

	PRESENT	PRESENT PERFECT
(yo)	**me equivoco**	**me he equivocado**
(tú)	**te equivocas**	**te has equivocado**
(él/ella/usted)	**se equivoca**	**se ha equivocado**
(nosotros/as)	**nos equivocamos**	**nos hemos equivocado**
(vosotros/as)	**os equivocáis**	**os habéis equivocado**
(ellos/ellas/ ustedes)	**se equivocan**	**se han equivocado**

	PRETERITE	IMPERFECT
(yo)	**me equivoqué**	**me equivocaba**
(tú)	**te equivocaste**	**te equivocabas**
(él/ella/usted)	**se equivocó**	**se equivocaba**
(nosotros/as)	**nos equivocamos**	**nos equivocábamos**
(vosotros/as)	**os equivocasteis**	**os equivocabais**
(ellos/ellas/ ustedes)	**se equivocaron**	**se equivocaban**

GERUND	PAST PARTICIPLE
equivocándose, etc	**equivocado**

	FUTURE	CONDITIONAL
(yo)	**me equivocaré**	**me equivocaría**
(tú)	**te equivocarás**	**te equivocarías**
(él/ella/usted)	**se equivocará**	**se equivocaría**
(nosotros/as)	**nos equivocaremos**	**nos equivocaríamos**
(vosotros/as)	**os equivocaréis**	**os equivocaríais**
(ellos/ellas/ ustedes)	**se equivocarán**	**se equivocarían**

	PRESENT SUBJUNCTIVE	IMPERFECT SUBJUNCTIVE
(yo)	**me equivoque**	**me equivocara** or **equivocase**
(tú)	**te equivoques**	**te equivocaras** or **equivocases**
(él/ella/usted)	**se equivoque**	**se equivocara** or **equivocase**
(nosotros/as)	**nos equivoquemos**	**nos equivocáramos** or **equivocásemos**
(vosotros/as)	**os equivoquéis**	**os equivocarais** or **equivocaseis**
(ellos/ellas/ ustedes)	**se equivoquen**	**se equivocaran** or **equivocasen**

IMPERATIVE

equivócate / equivocaos

Use the present subjunctive in all cases other than these **tú** and **vosotros** affirmative forms.

EXAMPLE PHRASES

Si crees que voy a dejarte ir, **te equivocas**.
If you think I'm going to let you go, you're mistaken.

Perdone, **me he equivocado** de número.
Sorry, I've got the wrong number.

Se equivocaron de tren.
They got the wrong train.

Siempre **se equivocaba** de calle.
He always went down the wrong street.

Sobre todo, no **te equivoques** de hora.
Above all, don't get the time wrong.

Si **te equivocaras**, quedarías eliminado del juego.
If you made a mistake, you'd be out of the game.

Remember that subject pronouns are not used very often in Spanish.

erguir (to erect)

	PRESENT	PRESENT PERFECT
(yo)	**yergo**	**he erguido**
(tú)	**yergues**	**has erguido**
(él/ella/usted)	**yergue**	**ha erguido**
(nosotros/as)	**erguimos**	**hemos erguido**
(vosotros/as)	**erguís**	**habéis erguido**
(ellos/ellas/ ustedes)	**yerguen**	**han erguido**

	PRETERITE	IMPERFECT
(yo)	**erguí**	**erguía**
(tú)	**erguiste**	**erguías**
(él/ella/usted)	**irguió**	**erguía**
(nosotros/as)	**erguimos**	**erguíamos**
(vosotros/as)	**erguisteis**	**erguías**
(ellos/ellas/ ustedes)	**irguieron**	**erguían**

GERUND	PAST PARTICIPLE
irguiendo	**erguido**

	FUTURE	CONDITIONAL
(yo)	**erguiré**	**erguiría**
(tú)	**erguirás**	**erguirías**
(él/ella/usted)	**erguirá**	**erguiría**
(nosotros/as)	**erguiremos**	**erguiríamos**
(vosotros/as)	**erguiréis**	**erguiríais**
(ellos/ellas/ ustedes)	**erguirán**	**erguirían**

	PRESENT SUBJUNCTIVE	IMPERFECT SUBJUNCTIVE
(yo)	**yerga**	**irguiera** or **irguiese**
(tú)	**yergas**	**irguieras** or **irguieses**
(él/ella/usted)	**yerga**	**irguiera** or **irguiese**
(nosotros/as)	**irgamos**	**irguiéramos** or **irguiésemos**
(vosotros/as)	**irgáis**	**irguierais** or **irguieseis**
(ellos/ellas/ ustedes)	**yergan**	**irguieran** or **irguiesen**

IMPERATIVE

yergue / erguid

Use the present subjunctive in all cases other than these **tú** and **vosotros** affirmative forms.

EXAMPLE PHRASES

El perro **irguió** las orejas.
The dog pricked up its ears.

La montaña **se erguía** majestuosa sobre el valle.
The mountain rose majestically above the valley.

Tú mantén siempre la cabeza bien **erguida**.
You must always hold your head high.

Remember that subject pronouns are not used very often in Spanish.

errar (to err)

	PRESENT	PRESENT PERFECT
(yo)	**yerro**	**he errado**
(tú)	**yerras**	**has errado**
(él/ella/usted)	**yerra**	**ha errado**
(nosotros/as)	**erramos**	**hemos errado**
(vosotros/as)	**erráis**	**habéis errado**
(ellos/ellas/ ustedes)	**yerran**	**han errado**

	PRETERITE	IMPERFECT
(yo)	**erré**	**erraba**
(tú)	**erraste**	**errabas**
(él/ella/usted)	**erró**	**erraba**
(nosotros/as)	**erramos**	**errábamos**
(vosotros/as)	**errasteis**	**errabais**
(ellos/ellas/ ustedes)	**erraron**	**erraban**

	GERUND	PAST PARTICIPLE
	errando	**errado**

	FUTURE	CONDITIONAL
(yo)	**erraré**	**erraría**
(tú)	**errarás**	**errarías**
(él/ella/usted)	**errará**	**erraría**
(nosotros/as)	**erraremos**	**erraríamos**
(vosotros/as)	**erraréis**	**erraríais**
(ellos/ellas/ ustedes)	**errarán**	**errarían**

	PRESENT SUBJUNCTIVE	IMPERFECT SUBJUNCTIVE
(yo)	**yerre**	**errara** or **errase**
(tú)	**yerres**	**erraras** or **errases**
(él/ella/usted)	**yerre**	**errara** or **errase**
(nosotros/as)	**erremos**	**erráramos** or **errásemos**
(vosotros/as)	**erréis**	**errarais** or **erraseis**
(ellos/ellas/ ustedes)	**yerren**	**erraran** or **errasen**

IMPERATIVE

yerra / errad

Use the present subjunctive in all cases other than these **tú** and **vosotros** affirmative forms.

EXAMPLE PHRASES

Errar es humano.
To err is human.

Ha errado en su decisión.
She has made the wrong decision.

Erró el tiro.
He missed.

Remember that subject pronouns are not used very often in Spanish.

escribir (to write)

	PRESENT	PRESENT PERFECT
(yo)	**escribo**	**he escrito**
(tú)	**escribes**	**has escrito**
(él/ella/usted)	**escribe**	**ha escrito**
(nosotros/as)	**escribimos**	**hemos escrito**
(vosotros/as)	**escribís**	**habéis escrito**
(ellos/ellas/ ustedes)	**escriben**	**han escrito**

	PRETERITE	IMPERFECT
(yo)	**escribí**	**escribía**
(tú)	**escribiste**	**escribías**
(él/ella/usted)	**escribió**	**escribía**
(nosotros/as)	**escribimos**	**escribíamos**
(vosotros/as)	**escribisteis**	**escribíais**
(ellos/ellas/ ustedes)	**escribieron**	**escribían**

GERUND	PAST PARTICIPLE
escribiendo	**escrito**

	FUTURE	CONDITIONAL
(yo)	**escribiré**	**escribiría**
(tú)	**escribirás**	**escribirías**
(él/ella/usted)	**escribirá**	**escribiría**
(nosotros/as)	**escribiremos**	**escribiríamos**
(vosotros/as)	**escribiréis**	**escribiríais**
(ellos/ellas/ ustedes)	**escribirán**	**escribirían**

	PRESENT SUBJUNCTIVE	IMPERFECT SUBJUNCTIVE
(yo)	**escriba**	**escribiera** or **escribiese**
(tú)	**escribas**	**escribieras** or **escribieses**
(él/ella/usted)	**escriba**	**escribiera** or **escribiese**
(nosotros/as)	**escribamos**	**escribiéramos** or **escribiésemos**
(vosotros/as)	**escribáis**	**escribierais** or **escribieseis**
(ellos/ellas/ ustedes)	**escriban**	**escribieran** or **escribiesen**

IMPERATIVE

escribe / escribid

Use the present subjunctive in all cases other than these **tú** and **vosotros** affirmative forms.

EXAMPLE PHRASES

¿Cómo **se escribe** su nombre? How do you spell your name?

¿**Estás escribiendo** la carta? Are you writing the letter?

Eso lo **he escrito** yo.
I wrote that.

Nos escribimos durante un tiempo.
We wrote to each other for a while.

Escribía canciones.
She wrote songs.

¿Me **escribirás**?
Will you write to me?

Yo lo **escribiría** con mayúscula.
I'd write it with a capital letter.

Te he dicho que no **escribas** en la mesa.
I've told you not to write on the table.

Si de verdad **escribiera** bien, ya le habrían publicado algún libro.
If he really was a good writer, he'd have had a book published by now.

Escríbelo en la pizarra.
Write it on the blackboard.

Remember that subject pronouns are not used very often in Spanish.

esforzarse (to make an effort)

	PRESENT	PRESENT PERFECT
(yo)	**me esfuerzo**	**me he esforzado**
(tú)	**te esfuerzas**	**te has esforzado**
(él/ella/usted)	**se esfuerza**	**se ha esforzado**
(nosotros/as)	**nos esforzamos**	**nos hemos esforzado**
(vosotros/as)	**os esforzáis**	**os habéis esforzado**
(ellos/ellas/ ustedes)	**se esfuerzan**	**se han esforzado**

	PRETERITE	IMPERFECT
(yo)	**me esforcé**	**me esforzaba**
(tú)	**te esforzaste**	**te esforzabas**
(él/ella/usted)	**se esforzó**	**se esforzaba**
(nosotros/as)	**nos esforzamos**	**nos esforzábamos**
(vosotros/as)	**os esforzasteis**	**os esforzabais**
(ellos/ellas/ ustedes)	**se esforzaron**	**se esforzaban**

	GERUND	PAST PARTICIPLE
	esforzándose, etc	**esforzado**

	FUTURE	CONDITIONAL
(yo)	**me esforzaré**	**me esforzaría**
(tú)	**te esforzarás**	**te esforzarías**
(él/ella/usted)	**se esforzará**	**se esforzaría**
(nosotros/as)	**nos esforzaremos**	**nos esforzaríamos**
(vosotros/as)	**os esforzaréis**	**os esforzaríais**
(ellos/ellas/ ustedes)	**se esforzarán**	**se esforzarían**

	PRESENT SUBJUNCTIVE	IMPERFECT SUBJUNCTIVE
(yo)	**me esfuerce**	**me esforzara** or **esforzase**
(tú)	**te esfuerces**	**te esforzaras** or **esforzases**
(él/ella/usted)	**se esfuerce**	**se esforzara** or **esforzase**
(nosotros/as)	**nos esforcemos**	**nos esforzáramos** or **esforzásemos**
(vosotros/as)	**os esforcéis**	**os esforzarais** or **esforzaseis**
(ellos/ellas/ ustedes)	**se esfuercen**	**se esforzaran** or **esforzasen**

IMPERATIVE

esfuérzate / esforzaos

Use the present subjunctive in all cases other than these **tú** and **vosotros** affirmative forms.

EXAMPLE PHRASES

Tienes que **esforzarte** si quieres ganar.
You have to make an effort if you want to win.

No **te esfuerzas** lo suficiente.
You don't make enough effort.

Me he esforzado, pero nada.
I've tried my best but haven't got anywhere.

Se esforzó todo lo que pudo por aprobar el examen.
He did his best to pass the exam.

Me esforzaba por entenderla.
I tried hard to understand her.

No **te esfuerces**, no me vas a convencer.
Stop struggling, you're not going to convince me.

Si **te esforzaras** un poco más, lo conseguirías.
You'd manage it if you made a bit more of an effort.

Remember that subject pronouns are not used very often in Spanish.

establecer (to establish)

	PRESENT	PRESENT PERFECT
(yo)	**establezco**	**he establecido**
(tú)	**estableces**	**has establecido**
(él/ella/usted)	**establece**	**ha establecido**
(nosotros/as)	**establecemos**	**hemos establecido**
(vosotros/as)	**establecéis**	**habéis establecido**
(ellos/ellas/ustedes)	**establecen**	**han establecido**

	PRETERITE	IMPERFECT
(yo)	**establecí**	**establecía**
(tú)	**estableciste**	**establecías**
(él/ella/usted)	**estableció**	**establecía**
(nosotros/as)	**establecimos**	**establecíamos**
(vosotros/as)	**establecisteis**	**establecíais**
(ellos/ellas/ustedes)	**establecieron**	**establecían**

GERUND	PAST PARTICIPLE
estableciendo	**establecido**

	FUTURE	CONDITIONAL
(yo)	**estableceré**	**establecería**
(tú)	**establecerás**	**establecerías**
(él/ella/usted)	**establecerá**	**establecería**
(nosotros/as)	**estableceremos**	**estableceríamos**
(vosotros/as)	**estableceréis**	**estableceríais**
(ellos/ellas/ustedes)	**establecerán**	**establecerían**

	PRESENT SUBJUNCTIVE	IMPERFECT SUBJUNCTIVE
(yo)	**establezca**	**estableciera** or **estableciese**
(tú)	**establezcas**	**establecieras** or **establecieses**
(él/ella/usted)	**establezca**	**estableciera** or **estableciese**
(nosotros/as)	**establezcamos**	**estableciéramos** or **estableciésemos**
(vosotros/as)	**establezcáis**	**establecierais** or **establecieseis**
(ellos/ellas/ustedes)	**establezcan**	**establecieran** or **estableciesen**

IMPERATIVE

establece / estableced

Use the present subjunctive in all cases other than these **tú** and **vosotros** affirmative forms.

EXAMPLE PHRASES

Han logrado **establecer** contacto con el barco.
They've managed to make contact with the boat.

La ley **establece** que...
The law states that...

Se ha establecido una buena relación entre los dos países.
A good relationship has been established between the two countries.

En 1945, la familia **se estableció** en Madrid.
In 1945, the family settled in Madrid.

El año que viene **se establecerá** por su cuenta.
Next year she'll set up on her own.

Remember that subject pronouns are not used very often in Spanish.

estar (to be)

	PRESENT	PRESENT PERFECT
(yo)	**estoy**	**he estado**
(tú)	**estás**	**has estado**
(él/ella/usted)	**está**	**ha estado**
(nosotros/as)	**estamos**	**hemos estado**
(vosotros/as)	**estáis**	**habéis estado**
(ellos/ellas/ ustedes)	**están**	**han estado**

	PRETERITE	IMPERFECT
(yo)	**estuve**	**estaba**
(tú)	**estuviste**	**estabas**
(él/ella/usted)	**estuvo**	**estaba**
(nosotros/as)	**estuvimos**	**estábamos**
(vosotros/as)	**estuvisteis**	**estabais**
(ellos/ellas/ ustedes)	**estuvieron**	**estaban**

GERUND	PAST PARTICIPLE
estando	**estado**

	FUTURE	CONDITIONAL
(yo)	**estaré**	**estaría**
(tú)	**estarás**	**estarías**
(él/ella/usted)	**estará**	**estaría**
(nosotros/as)	**estaremos**	**estaríamos**
(vosotros/as)	**estaréis**	**estaríais**
(ellos/ellas/ ustedes)	**estarán**	**estarían**

	PRESENT SUBJUNCTIVE	IMPERFECT SUBJUNCTIVE
(yo)	**esté**	**estuviera** or **estuviese**
(tú)	**estés**	**estuvieras** or **estuvieses**
(él/ella/usted)	**esté**	**estuviera** or **estuviese**
(nosotros/as)	**estemos**	**estuviéramos** or **estuviésemos**
(vosotros/as)	**estéis**	**estuvierais** or **estuvieseis**
(ellos/ellas/ ustedes)	**estén**	**estuvieran** or **estuviesen**

IMPERATIVE

está / estad

Use the present subjunctive in all cases other than these **tú** and **vosotros** affirmative forms.

EXAMPLE PHRASES

Estoy cansado.
I'm tired.

¿Cómo **estás**?
How are you?

¿**Has estado** alguna vez en París?
Have you ever been to Paris?

Estuvimos en casa de mis padres.
We were at my parents'.

¿Dónde **estabas**?
Where were you?

¿A qué hora **estarás** en casa?
What time will you be home?

Dijo que **estaría** aquí a las ocho.
She said she'd be here at eight o'clock.

Avísame cuando **estés** lista.
Let me know when you're ready.

No sabía que **estuviera** tan lejos.
I didn't know it was so far.

¡**Estáte** quieto!
Stay still!

Remember that subject pronouns are not used very often in Spanish.

evacuar (to evacuate)

	PRESENT	PRESENT PERFECT
(yo)	**evacuo**	**he evacuado**
(tú)	**evacuas**	**has evacuado**
(él/ella/usted)	**evacua**	**ha evacuado**
(nosotros/as)	**evacuamos**	**hemos evacuado**
(vosotros/as)	**evacuáis**	**habéis evacuado**
(ellos/ellas/ ustedes)	**evacuan**	**han evacuado**

	PRETERITE	IMPERFECT
(yo)	**evacué**	**evacuaba**
(tú)	**evacuaste**	**evacuabas**
(él/ella/usted)	**evacuó**	**evacuaba**
(nosotros/as)	**evacuamos**	**evacuábamos**
(vosotros/as)	**evacuasteis**	**evacuabais**
(ellos/ellas/ ustedes)	**evacuaron**	**evacuaban**

GERUND	PAST PARTICIPLE
evacuando	**evacuado**

	FUTURE	CONDITIONAL
(yo)	**evacuaré**	**evacuaría**
(tú)	**evacuarás**	**evacuarías**
(él/ella/usted)	**evacuará**	**evacuaría**
(nosotros/as)	**evacuaremos**	**evacuaríamos**
(vosotros/as)	**evacuaréis**	**evacuaríais**
(ellos/ellas/ ustedes)	**evacuarán**	**evacuarían**

	PRESENT SUBJUNCTIVE	IMPERFECT SUBJUNCTIVE
(yo)	**evacue**	**evacuara** or **evacuase**
(tú)	**evacues**	**evacuaras** or **evacuases**
(él/ella/usted)	**evacue**	**evacuara** or **evacuase**
(nosotros/as)	**evacuemos**	**evacuáramos** or **evacuásemos**
(vosotros/as)	**evacuéis**	**evacuarais** or **evacuaseis**
(ellos/ellas/ ustedes)	**evacuen**	**evacuaran** or **evacuasen**

IMPERATIVE

evacua / evacuad

Use the present subjunctive in all cases other than these **tú** and **vosotros** affirmative forms.

EXAMPLE PHRASES

Van a **evacuar** a los heridos.
They're going to evacuate the injured.

Han evacuado la zona.
The area has been evacuated.

Seguirá existiendo peligro mientras no **evacuen** el edificio.
The danger won't be over until the building has been evacuated.

Remember that subject pronouns are not used very often in Spanish.

freír (to fry)

	PRESENT	PRESENT PERFECT
(yo)	**frío**	**he frito**
(tú)	**fríes**	**has frito**
(él/ella/usted)	**fríe**	**ha frito**
(nosotros/as)	**freímos**	**hemos frito**
(vosotros/as)	**freís**	**habéis frito**
(ellos/ellas/ ustedes)	**fríen**	**han frito**

	PRETERITE	IMPERFECT
(yo)	**freí**	**freía**
(tú)	**freíste**	**freías**
(él/ella/usted)	**frio**	**freía**
(nosotros/as)	**freímos**	**freíamos**
(vosotros/as)	**freísteis**	**freíais**
(ellos/ellas/ ustedes)	**frieron**	**freían**

GERUND	PAST PARTICIPLE
friendo	**frito**

	FUTURE	CONDITIONAL
(yo)	**freiré**	**freiría**
(tú)	**freirás**	**freirías**
(él/ella/usted)	**freirá**	**freiría**
(nosotros/as)	**freiremos**	**freiríamos**
(vosotros/as)	**freiréis**	**freiríais**
(ellos/ellas/ ustedes)	**freirán**	**freirían**

	PRESENT SUBJUNCTIVE	IMPERFECT SUBJUNCTIVE
(yo)	**fría**	**friera** or **friese**
(tú)	**frías**	**frieras** or **frieses**
(él/ella/usted)	**fría**	**friera** or **friese**
(nosotros/as)	**friamos**	**friéramos** or **friésemos**
(vosotros/as)	**friais**	**frierais** or **frieseis**
(ellos/ellas/ ustedes)	**frían**	**frieran** or **friesen**

IMPERATIVE

fríe / freíd

Use the present subjunctive in all cases other than these **tú** and **vosotros** affirmative forms.

EXAMPLE PHRASES

No sabe ni **freír** un huevo.
He can't even fry an egg.

He frito el pescado.
I've fried the fish.

Se está friendo demasiado por ese lado.
It's getting overdone on that side.

Lo **frio** en manteca.
She fried it in lard.

Nos **freíamos** de calor.
We were roasting in the heat.

Yo lo **freiría** con menos aceite.
I'd fry it using less oil.

Fríelo en esa sartén.
Fry it in that pan.

Remember that subject pronouns are not used very often in Spanish.

gruñir (to grumble; to growl)

	PRESENT	PRESENT PERFECT
(yo)	**gruño**	**he gruñido**
(tú)	**gruñes**	**has gruñido**
(él/ella/usted)	**gruñe**	**ha gruñido**
(nosotros/as)	**gruñimos**	**hemos gruñido**
(vosotros/as)	**gruñís**	**habéis gruñido**
(ellos/ellas/ ustedes)	**gruñen**	**han gruñido**

	PRETERITE	IMPERFECT
(yo)	**gruñí**	**gruñía**
(tú)	**gruñiste**	**gruñías**
(él/ella/usted)	**gruñó**	**gruñía**
(nosotros/as)	**gruñimos**	**gruñíamos**
(vosotros/as)	**gruñisteis**	**gruñíais**
(ellos/ellas/ ustedes)	**gruñeron**	**gruñían**

GERUND	PAST PARTICIPLE
gruñendo	**gruñido**

	FUTURE	CONDITIONAL
(yo)	**gruñiré**	**gruñiría**
(tú)	**gruñirás**	**gruñirías**
(él/ella/usted)	**gruñirá**	**gruñiría**
(nosotros/as)	**gruñiremos**	**gruñiríamos**
(vosotros/as)	**gruñiréis**	**gruñiríais**
(ellos/ellas/ ustedes)	**gruñirán**	**gruñirían**

	PRESENT SUBJUNCTIVE	IMPERFECT SUBJUNCTIVE
(yo)	**gruña**	**gruñera** or **gruñese**
(tú)	**gruñas**	**gruñeras** or **gruñeses**
(él/ella/usted)	**gruña**	**gruñera** or **gruñese**
(nosotros/as)	**gruñamos**	**gruñéramos** or **gruñésemos**
(vosotros/as)	**gruñáis**	**gruñerais** or **gruñeseis**
(ellos/ellas/ ustedes)	**gruñan**	**gruñeran** or **gruñesen**

IMPERATIVE

gruñe / gruñid

Use the present subjunctive in all cases other than these **tú** and **vosotros** affirmative forms.

EXAMPLE PHRASES

¿A quién **gruñe** el perro?
Who's the dog growling at?

Siempre **está gruñendo**.
He's always grumbling.

El oso nos **gruñía** sin parar.
The bear kept growling at us.

¡No **gruñas** tanto!
Don't grumble so much.

Remember that subject pronouns are not used very often in Spanish.

guiar (to guide)

	PRESENT	PRESENT PERFECT
(yo)	**guío**	**he guiado**
(tú)	**guías**	**has guiado**
(él/ella/usted)	**guía**	**ha guiado**
(nosotros/as)	**guiamos**	**hemos guiado**
(vosotros/as)	**guiais**	**habéis guiado**
(ellos/ellas/ ustedes)	**guían**	**han guiado**

	PRETERITE	IMPERFECT
(yo)	**guie**	**guiaba**
(tú)	**guiaste**	**guiabas**
(él/ella/usted)	**guio**	**guiaba**
(nosotros/as)	**guiamos**	**guiábamos**
(vosotros/as)	**guiasteis**	**guiabais**
(ellos/ellas/ ustedes)	**guiaron**	**guiaban**

GERUND	PAST PARTICIPLE
guiando	**guiado**

	FUTURE	CONDITIONAL
(yo)	**guiaré**	**guiaría**
(tú)	**guiarás**	**guiarías**
(él/ella/usted)	**guiará**	**guiaría**
(nosotros/as)	**guiaremos**	**guiaríamos**
(vosotros/as)	**guiaréis**	**guiaríais**
(ellos/ellas/ ustedes)	**guiarán**	**guiarían**

	PRESENT SUBJUNCTIVE	IMPERFECT SUBJUNCTIVE
(yo)	**guíe**	**guiara** or **guiase**
(tú)	**guíes**	**guiaras** or **guiases**
(él/ella/usted)	**guíe**	**guiara** or **guiase**
(nosotros/as)	**guiemos**	**guiáramos** or **guiásemos**
(vosotros/as)	**guieis**	**guiarais** or **guiaseis**
(ellos/ellas/ ustedes)	**guíen**	**guiaran** or **guiasen**

IMPERATIVE

guía / guiad

Use the present subjunctive in all cases other than these **tú** and **vosotros** affirmative forms.

EXAMPLE PHRASES

Los perros **se guían** por su olfato.
Dogs follow their sense of smell.

Me he guiado por el instinto.
I followed my instinct.

Nos guiamos por un mapa que teníamos.
We found our way using a map we had.

Siempre me protegía y me **guiaba**.
He always protected me and guided me.

Les **guiaré** hasta allí.
I'll take you there.

Guíate por la razón.
Use reason as your guide.

Remember that subject pronouns are not used very often in Spanish.

haber (to have – *auxiliary*)

	PRESENT	PRESENT PERFECT
(yo)	**he**	not used except impersonally
(tú)	**has**	See **hay**
(él/ella/usted)	**ha**	
(nosotros/as)	**hemos**	
(vosotros/as)	**habéis**	
(ellos/ellas/ ustedes)	**han**	

	PRETERITE	IMPERFECT
(yo)	**hube**	**había**
(tú)	**hubiste**	**habías**
(él/ella/usted)	**hubo**	**había**
(nosotros/as)	**hubimos**	**habíamos**
(vosotros/as)	**hubisteis**	**habíais**
(ellos/ellas/ ustedes)	**hubieron**	**habían**

GERUND	PAST PARTICIPLE
habiendo	**habido**

	FUTURE	CONDITIONAL
(yo)	**habré**	**habría**
(tú)	**habrás**	**habrías**
(él/ella/usted)	**habrá**	**habría**
(nosotros/as)	**habremos**	**habríamos**
(vosotros/as)	**habréis**	**habríais**
(ellos/ellas/ ustedes)	**habrán**	**habrían**

	PRESENT SUBJUNCTIVE	IMPERFECT SUBJUNCTIVE
(yo)	**haya**	**hubiera** or **hubiese**
(tú)	**hayas**	**hubieras** or **hubieses**
(él/ella/usted)	**haya**	**hubiera** or **hubiese**
(nosotros/as)	**hayamos**	**hubiéramos** or **hubiésemos**
(vosotros/as)	**hayáis**	**hubierais** or **hubieseis**
(ellos/ellas/ ustedes)	**hayan**	**hubieran** or **hubiesen**

IMPERATIVE

not used

EXAMPLE PHRASES

De **haberlo** sabido, **habría** ido.
If I'd known, I would have gone.

¿**Has** visto eso?
Did you see that?

Eso nunca **había** pasado antes.
That had never happened before.

Habrá que repasarlo.
We'll have to check it.

Habría que limpiarlo.
We should clean it.

Como se **hayan** olvidado los mato.
I'll kill them if they've forgotten.

Si me lo **hubieras** dicho, te lo **habría** traído.
I'd have brought it, if you'd said.

Remember that subject pronouns are not used very often in Spanish.

hablar (to speak; to talk)

	PRESENT	PRESENT PERFECT
(yo)	**hablo**	**he hablado**
(tú)	**hablas**	**has hablado**
(él/ella/usted)	**habla**	**ha hablado**
(nosotros/as)	**hablamos**	**hemos hablado**
(vosotros/as)	**habláis**	**habéis hablado**
(ellos/ellas/ ustedes)	**hablan**	**han hablado**

	PRETERITE	IMPERFECT
(yo)	**hablé**	**hablaba**
(tú)	**hablaste**	**hablabas**
(él/ella/usted)	**habló**	**hablaba**
(nosotros/as)	**hablamos**	**hablábamos**
(vosotros/as)	**hablasteis**	**hablabais**
(ellos/ellas/ ustedes)	**hablaron**	**hablaban**

GERUND	PAST PARTICIPLE
hablando	**hablado**

	FUTURE	CONDITIONAL
(yo)	**hablaré**	**hablaría**
(tú)	**hablarás**	**hablarías**
(él/ella/usted)	**hablará**	**hablaría**
(nosotros/as)	**hablaremos**	**hablaríamos**
(vosotros/as)	**hablaréis**	**hablaríais**
(ellos/ellas/ ustedes)	**hablarán**	**hablarían**

	PRESENT SUBJUNCTIVE	IMPERFECT SUBJUNCTIVE
(yo)	**hable**	**hablara** or **hablase**
(tú)	**hables**	**hablaras** or **hablases**
(él/ella/usted)	**hable**	**hablara** or **hablase**
(nosotros/as)	**hablemos**	**habláramos** or **hablásemos**
(vosotros/as)	**habléis**	**hablarais** or **hablaseis**
(ellos/ellas/ ustedes)	**hablen**	**hablaran** or **hablasen**

IMPERATIVE

habla / hablad

Use the present subjunctive in all cases other than these **tú** and **vosotros** affirmative forms.

EXAMPLE PHRASES

María no **habla** inglés.
María doesn't speak English.

No **nos hablamos** desde hace tiempo.
We haven't spoken to each other for a long time.

Está hablando por teléfono.
He's on the phone.

Hoy **he hablado** con mi hermana.
I've spoken to my sister today.

¿**Has hablado** ya con el profesor?
Have you spoken to the teacher yet?

Luego **hablaremos** de ese tema.
We'll talk about that later.

Recuérdame que **hable** con Daniel.
Remind me to speak to Daniel.

¿Quieres que **hablemos**?
Shall we talk?

Hay que darles una oportunidad para que **hablen**.
We need to give them an opportunity to speak.

Remember that subject pronouns are not used very often in Spanish.

hacer (to do; to make)

	PRESENT	PRESENT PERFECT
(yo)	**hago**	**he hecho**
(tú)	**haces**	**has hecho**
(él/ella/usted)	**hace**	**ha hecho**
(nosotros/as)	**hacemos**	**hemos hecho**
(vosotros/as)	**hacéis**	**habéis hecho**
(ellos/ellas/ ustedes)	**hacen**	**han hecho**

	PRETERITE	IMPERFECT
(yo)	**hice**	**hacía**
(tú)	**hiciste**	**hacías**
(él/ella/usted)	**hizo**	**hacía**
(nosotros/as)	**hicimos**	**hacíamos**
(vosotros/as)	**hicisteis**	**hacíais**
(ellos/ellas/ ustedes)	**hicieron**	**hacían**

GERUND	PAST PARTICIPLE
haciendo	**hecho**

	FUTURE	CONDITIONAL
(yo)	**haré**	**haría**
(tú)	**harás**	**harías**
(él/ella/usted)	**hará**	**haría**
(nosotros/as)	**haremos**	**haríamos**
(vosotros/as)	**haréis**	**haríais**
(ellos/ellas/ ustedes)	**harán**	**harían**

	PRESENT SUBJUNCTIVE	IMPERFECT SUBJUNCTIVE
(yo)	**haga**	**hiciera** or **hiciese**
(tú)	**hagas**	**hicieras** or **hicieses**
(él/ella/usted)	**haga**	**hiciera** or **hiciese**
(nosotros/as)	**hagamos**	**hiciéramos** or **hiciésemos**
(vosotros/as)	**hagáis**	**hicierais** or **hicieseis**
(ellos/ellas/ ustedes)	**hagan**	**hicieran** or **hiciesen**

IMPERATIVE

haz / haced

Use the present subjunctive in all cases other than these **tú** and **vosotros** affirmative forms.

EXAMPLE PHRASES

¿Qué **hace** tu padre?
What does your father do?

Están haciendo mucho ruido.
They're making a lot of noise.

¿Quién **hizo** eso?
Who did that?

Hicieron pintar la fachada del colegio.
They had the front of the school painted.

Lo **hacía** para fastidiarme.
He did it to annoy me.

Lo **haré** yo mismo.
I'll do it myself.

Dijiste que lo **harías.**
You said you'd do it.

¿Quieres que **haga** las camas?
Do you want me to make the beds?

Preferiría que **hiciera** menos calor.
I'd rather it weren't so hot.

Hazlo como te he dicho.
Do it the way I told you.

Remember that subject pronouns are not used very often in Spanish.

hay (there is; there are)

PRESENT
hay

PRESENT PERFECT
ha habido

PRETERITE
hubo

IMPERFECT
había

GERUND
habiendo

PAST PARTICIPLE
habido

FUTURE
habrá

CONDITIONAL
habría

PRESENT SUBJUNCTIVE
haya

IMPERFECT SUBJUNCTIVE
hubiera or **hubiese**

IMPERATIVE
not used

EXAMPLE PHRASES

Esta tarde va a **haber** una manifestación.
There's going to be a demonstration this evening.

Hay una iglesia en la esquina.
There's a church on the corner.

Ha habido una tormenta.
There's been a storm.

Hubo una guerra.
There was a war.

Había mucha gente.
There were a lot of people.

¿**Habrá** suficiente?
Will there be enough?

De este modo **habría** menos accidentes.
That way there would be fewer accidents.

No creo que **haya** mucha gente en el recital.
I don't think there'll be many people at the concert.

Si **hubiera** más espacio, pondría un sofá.
I'd have a sofa if there were more room.

Remember that subject pronouns are not used very often in Spanish.

herir (to injure)

	PRESENT	PRESENT PERFECT
(yo)	**hiero**	**he herido**
(tú)	**hieres**	**has herido**
(él/ella/usted)	**hiere**	**ha herido**
(nosotros/as)	**herimos**	**hemos herido**
(vosotros/as)	**herís**	**habéis herido**
(ellos/ellas/ ustedes)	**hieren**	**han herido**

	PRETERITE	IMPERFECT
(yo)	**herí**	**hería**
(tú)	**heriste**	**herías**
(él/ella/usted)	**hirió**	**hería**
(nosotros/as)	**herimos**	**heríamos**
(vosotros/as)	**heristeis**	**heríais**
(ellos/ellas/ ustedes)	**hirieron**	**herían**

GERUND	PAST PARTICIPLE
hiriendo	**herido**

	FUTURE	CONDITIONAL
(yo)	**heriré**	**heriría**
(tú)	**herirás**	**herirías**
(él/ella/usted)	**herirá**	**heriría**
(nosotros/as)	**heriremos**	**heriríamos**
(vosotros/as)	**heriréis**	**heriríais**
(ellos/ellas/ ustedes)	**herirán**	**herirían**

	PRESENT SUBJUNCTIVE	IMPERFECT SUBJUNCTIVE
(yo)	**hiera**	**hiriera** or **hiriese**
(tú)	**hieras**	**hirieras** or **hirieses**
(él/ella/usted)	**hiera**	**hiriera** or **hiriese**
(nosotros/as)	**hiramos**	**hiriéramos** or **hiriésemos**
(vosotros/as)	**hiráis**	**hirierais** or **hirieseis**
(ellos/ellas/ ustedes)	**hieran**	**hirieran** or **hiriesen**

IMPERATIVE

hiere / herid

Use the present subjunctive in all cases other than these **tú** and **vosotros** affirmative forms.

EXAMPLE PHRASES

Vas a **herir** sus sentimientos.
You're going to hurt her feelings.

Me **hiere** que me digas eso.
I'm hurt that you should say such a thing.

La **han herido** en el brazo.
Her arm's been injured.

Lo **hirieron** en el pecho.
He was wounded in the chest.

La **hería** en lo más hondo.
She was deeply hurt.

Mi madre siempre tenía miedo que nos **hiriéramos**.
My mum was always scared we'd hurt ourselves.

Remember that subject pronouns are not used very often in Spanish.

huir (to escape)

	PRESENT	PRESENT PERFECT
(yo)	**huyo**	**he huido**
(tú)	**huyes**	**has huido**
(él/ella/usted)	**huye**	**ha huido**
(nosotros/as)	**huimos**	**hemos huido**
(vosotros/as)	**huis**	**habéis huido**
(ellos/ellas/ ustedes)	**huyen**	**han huido**

	PRETERITE	IMPERFECT
(yo)	**hui**	**huía**
(tú)	**huiste**	**huías**
(él/ella/usted)	**huyó**	**huía**
(nosotros/as)	**huimos**	**huíamos**
(vosotros/as)	**huisteis**	**huíais**
(ellos/ellas/ ustedes)	**huyeron**	**huían**

GERUND	PAST PARTICIPLE
huyendo	**huido**

	FUTURE	CONDITIONAL
(yo)	**huiré**	**huiría**
(tú)	**huirás**	**huirías**
(él/ella/usted)	**huirá**	**huiría**
(nosotros/as)	**huiremos**	**huiríamos**
(vosotros/as)	**huiréis**	**huiríais**
(ellos/ellas/ ustedes)	**huirán**	**huirían**

	PRESENT SUBJUNCTIVE	IMPERFECT SUBJUNCTIVE
(yo)	**huya**	**huyera** or **huyese**
(tú)	**huyas**	**huyeras** or **huyeses**
(él/ella/usted)	**huya**	**huyera** or **huyese**
(nosotros/as)	**huyamos**	**huyéramos** or **huyésemos**
(vosotros/as)	**huyáis**	**huyerais** or **huyeseis**
(ellos/ellas/ ustedes)	**huyan**	**huyeran** or **huyesen**

IMPERATIVE

huye / huid

Use the present subjunctive in all cases other than these **tú** and **vosotros** affirmative forms.

EXAMPLE PHRASES

No sé por qué me **huye**.
I don't know why he's avoiding me.

Salió **huyendo.**
He ran away.

Ha huido de la cárcel.
He has escaped from prison.

Huyeron del país.
They fled the country.

No quiero que **huyas** como un cobarde.
I dont want you to run away like a coward.

¡Huye! Si te atrapan, te matarán.
Run! If they catch you, they'll kill you.

Remember that subject pronouns are not used very often in Spanish.

imponer (to impose)

	PRESENT	PRESENT PERFECT
(yo)	**impongo**	**he impuesto**
(tú)	**impones**	**has impuesto**
(él/ella/usted)	**impone**	**ha impuesto**
(nosotros/as)	**imponemos**	**hemos impuesto**
(vosotros/as)	**imponéis**	**habéis impuesto**
(ellos/ellas/ ustedes)	**imponen**	**han impuesto**

	PRETERITE	IMPERFECT
(yo)	**impuse**	**imponía**
(tú)	**impusiste**	**imponías**
(él/ella/usted)	**impuso**	**imponía**
(nosotros/as)	**impusimos**	**imponíamos**
(vosotros/as)	**impusisteis**	**imponíais**
(ellos/ellas/ ustedes)	**impusieron**	**imponían**

GERUND	PAST PARTICIPLE
imponiendo	**impuesto**

	FUTURE	CONDITIONAL
(yo)	**impondré**	**impondría**
(tú)	**impondrás**	**impondrías**
(él/ella/usted)	**impondrá**	**impondría**
(nosotros/as)	**impondremos**	**impondríamos**
(vosotros/as)	**impondréis**	**impondríais**
(ellos/ellas/ ustedes)	**impondrán**	**impondrían**

	PRESENT SUBJUNCTIVE	IMPERFECT SUBJUNCTIVE
(yo)	**imponga**	**impusiera** or **impusiese**
(tú)	**impongas**	**impusieras** or **impusieses**
(él/ella/usted)	**imponga**	**impusiera** or **impusiese**
(nosotros/as)	**impongamos**	**impusiéramos** or **impusiésemos**
(vosotros/as)	**impongáis**	**impusierais** or **impusieseis**
(ellos/ellas/ ustedes)	**impongan**	**impusieran** or **impusiesen**

IMPERATIVE

impón / imponed

Use the present subjunctive in all cases other than these **tú** and **vosotros** affirmative forms.

EXAMPLE PHRASES

La vista desde el acantilado **impone** un poco.
The view from the cliff top is quite impressive.

La minifalda **se está imponiendo** de nuevo.
The miniskirt is back in fashion.

Han impuesto la enseñanza religiosa.
They have made religious education compulsory.

El corredor nigeriano **se impuso** en la segunda carrera.
The Nigerian runner triumphed in the second race.

Mi abuelo **imponía** mucho respeto.
My grandfather commanded a lot of respect.

Impondrán multas de hasta 50 euros.
They'll impose fines of up to 50 euros.

Remember that subject pronouns are not used very often in Spanish.

imprimir (to print)

	PRESENT	PRESENT PERFECT
(yo)	**imprimo**	**he imprimido**
(tú)	**imprimes**	**has imprimido**
(él/ella/usted)	**imprime**	**ha imprimido**
(nosotros/as)	**imprimimos**	**hemos imprimido**
(vosotros/as)	**imprimís**	**habéis imprimido**
(ellos/ellas/ ustedes)	**imprimen**	**han imprimido**

	PRETERITE	IMPERFECT
(yo)	**imprimí**	**imprimía**
(tú)	**imprimiste**	**imprimías**
(él/ella/usted)	**imprimió**	**imprimía**
(nosotros/as)	**imprimimos**	**imprimíamos**
(vosotros/as)	**imprimisteis**	**imprimíais**
(ellos/ellas/ ustedes)	**imprimieron**	**imprimían**

GERUND	PAST PARTICIPLE
imprimiendo	**imprimido, impreso**

	FUTURE	CONDITIONAL
(yo)	**imprimiré**	**imprimiría**
(tú)	**imprimirás**	**imprimirías**
(él/ella/usted)	**imprimirá**	**imprimiría**
(nosotros/as)	**imprimiremos**	**imprimiríamos**
(vosotros/as)	**imprimiréis**	**imprimiríais**
(ellos/ellas/ ustedes)	**imprimirán**	**imprimirían**

	PRESENT SUBJUNCTIVE	IMPERFECT SUBJUNCTIVE
(yo)	**imprima**	**imprimiera** or **imprimiese**
(tú)	**imprimas**	**imprimieras** or **imprimieses**
(él/ella/usted)	**imprima**	**imprimiera** or **imprimiese**
(nosotros/as)	**imprimamos**	**imprimiéramos** or **imprimiésemos**
(vosotros/as)	**imprimáis**	**imprimierais** or **imprimieseis**
(ellos/ellas/ ustedes)	**impriman**	**imprimieran** or **imprimiesen**

IMPERATIVE

imprime / imprimid

Use the present subjunctive in all cases other than these **tú** and **vosotros** affirmative forms.

EXAMPLE PHRASES

Una experiencia así **imprime** carácter.
An experience like that is character-building.

¿**Has imprimido** el documento?
Have you printed out the file?

Se imprimieron sólo doce copias del libro.
Only twelve copies of the book were printed.

El sillón **imprimía** un cierto aire de distinción al salón.
The chair gave the living room a certain air of distinction.

Remember that subject pronouns are not used very often in Spanish.

ir (to go)

	PRESENT	PRESENT PERFECT
(yo)	**voy**	**he ido**
(tú)	**vas**	**has ido**
(él/ella/usted)	**va**	**ha ido**
(nosotros/as)	**vamos**	**hemos ido**
(vosotros/as)	**vais**	**habéis ido**
(ellos/ellas/ ustedes)	**van**	**han ido**

	PRETERITE	IMPERFECT
(yo)	**fui**	**iba**
(tú)	**fuiste**	**ibas**
(él/ella/usted)	**fue**	**iba**
(nosotros/as)	**fuimos**	**íbamos**
(vosotros/as)	**fuisteis**	**ibais**
(ellos/ellas/ ustedes)	**fueron**	**iban**

GERUND	PAST PARTICIPLE
yendo	**ido**

	FUTURE	CONDITIONAL
(yo)	**iré**	**iría**
(tú)	**irás**	**irías**
(él/ella/usted)	**irá**	**iría**
(nosotros/as)	**iremos**	**iríamos**
(vosotros/as)	**iréis**	**iríais**
(ellos/ellas/ ustedes)	**irán**	**irían**

	PRESENT SUBJUNCTIVE	IMPERFECT SUBJUNCTIVE
(yo)	**vaya**	**fuera** or **fuese**
(tú)	**vayas**	**fueras** or **fueses**
(él/ella/usted)	**vaya**	**fuera** or **fuese**
(nosotros/as)	**vayamos**	**fuéramos** or **fuésemos**
(vosotros/as)	**vayáis**	**fuerais** or **fueseis**
(ellos/ellas/ ustedes)	**vayan**	**fueran** or **fuesen**

IMPERATIVE

ve / id

Use the present subjunctive in most cases other than these **tú** and **vosotros** affirmative forms.

However, in the 'let's' affirmative form, **vamos** is more common than **vayamos**.

EXAMPLE PHRASES

¿Puedo **ir** contigo?
Can I come with you?

¿**Vamos** a comer al campo?
Shall we have a picnic in the country?

Estoy yendo a clases de natación.
I'm taking swimming lessons.

Ha ido a comprar el pan.
She's gone to buy some bread.

Anoche **fuimos** al cine.
We went to the cinema last night.

El domingo **iré** a Edimburgo.
I'll go to Edinburgh on Sunday.

Dijeron que **irían** andando.
They said they'd walk.

¡Que te **vaya** bien!
Take care of yourself!

Quería pedirte que **fueras** en mi lugar.
I wanted to ask you if you'd go instead of me.

No **te vayas** sin despedirte.
Don't go without saying goodbye.

Vete a hacer los deberes.
Go and do your homework.

Remember that subject pronouns are not used very often in Spanish.

jugar (to play)

	PRESENT	PRESENT PERFECT
(yo)	**juego**	**he jugado**
(tú)	**juegas**	**has jugado**
(él/ella/usted)	**juega**	**ha jugado**
(nosotros/as)	**jugamos**	**hemos jugado**
(vosotros/as)	**jugáis**	**habéis jugado**
(ellos/ellas/ ustedes)	**juegan**	**han jugado**

	PRETERITE	IMPERFECT
(yo)	**jugué**	**jugaba**
(tú)	**jugaste**	**jugabas**
(él/ella/usted)	**jugó**	**jugaba**
(nosotros/as)	**jugamos**	**jugábamos**
(vosotros/as)	**jugasteis**	**jugabais**
(ellos/ellas/ ustedes)	**jugaron**	**jugaban**

GERUND	PAST PARTICIPLE
jugando	**jugado**

	FUTURE	CONDITIONAL
(yo)	**jugaré**	**jugaría**
(tú)	**jugarás**	**jugarías**
(él/ella/usted)	**jugará**	**jugaría**
(nosotros/as)	**jugaremos**	**jugaríamos**
(vosotros/as)	**jugaréis**	**jugaríais**
(ellos/ellas/ ustedes)	**jugarán**	**jugarían**

	PRESENT SUBJUNCTIVE	IMPERFECT SUBJUNCTIVE
(yo)	**juegue**	**jugara** or **jugase**
(tú)	**juegues**	**jugaras** or **jugases**
(él/ella/usted)	**juegue**	**jugara** or **jugase**
(nosotros/as)	**juguemos**	**jugáramos** or **jugásemos**
(vosotros/as)	**juguéis**	**jugarais** or **jugaseis**
(ellos/ellas/ ustedes)	**jueguen**	**jugaran** or **jugasen**

IMPERATIVE

juega / jugad

Use the present subjunctive in all cases other than these **tú** and **vosotros** affirmative forms.

EXAMPLE PHRASES

Juego al fútbol todos los domingos.
I play football every Sunday.

Están jugando en el jardín.
They're playing in the garden.

Le **han jugado** una mala pasada.
They played a dirty trick on him.

Después de cenar **jugamos** a las cartas.
After dinner we played cards.

Se jugaba la vida continuamente.
She was constantly risking her life.

Jugarán contra el Real Madrid.
They'll play Real Madrid.

Jugarías mejor si estuvieras más relajado.
You'd play better if you were more relaxed.

No **juegues** con tu salud.
Don't take risks with your health.

El médico le aconsejó que **jugara** más y leyera menos.
The doctor advised him to play more and read less.

Remember that subject pronouns are not used very often in Spanish.

leer (to read)

	PRESENT	PRESENT PERFECT
(yo)	**leo**	**he leído**
(tú)	**lees**	**has leído**
(él/ella/usted)	**lee**	**ha leído**
(nosotros/as)	**leemos**	**hemos leído**
(vosotros/as)	**leéis**	**habéis leído**
(ellos/ellas/ustedes)	**leen**	**han leído**

	PRETERITE	IMPERFECT
(yo)	**leí**	**leía**
(tú)	**leíste**	**leías**
(él/ella/usted)	**leyó**	**leía**
(nosotros/as)	**leímos**	**leíamos**
(vosotros/as)	**leísteis**	**leíais**
(ellos/ellas/ustedes)	**leyeron**	**leían**

GERUND	PAST PARTICIPLE
leyendo	**leído**

	FUTURE	CONDITIONAL
(yo)	**leeré**	**leería**
(tú)	**leerás**	**leerías**
(él/ella/usted)	**leerá**	**leería**
(nosotros/as)	**leeremos**	**leeríamos**
(vosotros/as)	**leeréis**	**leeríais**
(ellos/ellas/ustedes)	**leerán**	**leerían**

	PRESENT SUBJUNCTIVE	IMPERFECT SUBJUNCTIVE
(yo)	**lea**	**leyera** or **leyese**
(tú)	**leas**	**leyeras** or **leyeses**
(él/ella/usted)	**lea**	**leyera** or **leyese**
(nosotros/as)	**leamos**	**leyéramos** or **leyésemos**
(vosotros/as)	**leáis**	**leyerais** or **leyeseis**
(ellos/ellas/ustedes)	**lean**	**leyeran** or **leyesen**

IMPERATIVE

lee / leed

Use the present subjunctive in all cases other than these **tú** and **vosotros** affirmative forms.

EXAMPLE PHRASES

Hace mucho tiempo que no **leo** nada.
I haven't read anything for ages.

Estoy leyendo un libro muy interesante.
I'm reading a very interesting book.

¿**Has leído** esta novela?
Have you read this novel?

Lo **leí** hace tiempo.
I read it a while ago.

Antes **leía** mucho más.
I used to read a lot more before.

Si os portáis bien, os **leeré** un cuento.
If you behave yourselves, I'll read you a story.

Yo **leería** también la letra pequeña.
I'd read the small print as well.

Quiero que lo **leas** y me digas qué piensas.
I want you to read it and tell me what you think.

No **leas** tan deprisa.
Don't read so fast.

Remember that subject pronouns are not used very often in Spanish.

levantar (to lift)

	PRESENT	PRESENT PERFECT
(yo)	**levanto**	**he levantado**
(tú)	**levantas**	**has levantado**
(él/ella/usted)	**levanta**	**ha levantado**
(nosotros/as)	**levantamos**	**hemos levantado**
(vosotros/as)	**levantáis**	**habéis levantado**
(ellos/ellas/ ustedes)	**levantan**	**han levantado**

	PRETERITE	IMPERFECT
(yo)	**levanté**	**levantaba**
(tú)	**levantaste**	**levantabas**
(él/ella/usted)	**levantó**	**levantaba**
(nosotros/as)	**levantamos**	**levantábamos**
(vosotros/as)	**levantasteis**	**levantabais**
(ellos/ellas/ ustedes)	**levantaron**	**levantaban**

GERUND	PAST PARTICIPLE
levantando	**levantado**

	FUTURE	CONDITIONAL
(yo)	**levantaré**	**levantaría**
(tú)	**levantarás**	**levantarías**
(él/ella/usted)	**levantará**	**levantaría**
(nosotros/as)	**levantaremos**	**levantaríamos**
(vosotros/as)	**levantaréis**	**levantaríais**
(ellos/ellas/ ustedes)	**levantarán**	**levantarían**

	PRESENT SUBJUNCTIVE	IMPERFECT SUBJUNCTIVE
(yo)	**levante**	**levantara** or **levantase**
(tú)	**levantes**	**levantaras** or **levantases**
(él/ella/usted)	**levante**	**levantara** or **levantase**
(nosotros/as)	**levantemos**	**levantáramos** or **levantásemos**
(vosotros/as)	**levantéis**	**levantarais** or **levantaseis**
(ellos/ellas/ ustedes)	**levanten**	**levantaran** or **levantasen**

IMPERATIVE

levanta / levantad

Use the present subjunctive in all cases other than these **tú** and **vosotros** affirmative forms.

EXAMPLE PHRASES

No me importa **levantarme** temprano.
I don't mind getting up early.

Siempre **se levanta** de mal humor.
He's always in a bad mood when he gets up.

Hoy **me he levantado** temprano.
I got up early this morning.

Levantó la maleta como si no pesara nada.
He lifted up the suitcase as if it weighed nothing.

Me levanté y seguí caminando.
I got up and carried on walking.

La noticia le **levantará** el ánimo.
This news will raise her spirits.

Si pudiera **me levantaría** siempre tarde.
I'd sleep in every day, if I could.

No me **levantes** la voz.
Don't raise your voice to me.

Levanta la tapa.
Lift the lid.

Levantad la mano si tenéis alguna duda.
Put up your hands if you are unclear about anything.

Remember that subject pronouns are not used very often in Spanish.

llover (to rain)

PRESENT
llueve

PRESENT PERFECT
ha llovido

PRETERITE
llovió

IMPERFECT
llovía

GERUND
lloviendo

PAST PARTICIPLE
llovido

FUTURE
lloverá

CONDITIONAL
llovería

PRESENT SUBJUNCTIVE
llueva

IMPERFECT SUBJUNCTIVE
lloviera or lloviese

IMPERATIVE
not used

EXAMPLE PHRASES

Hace semanas que no **llueve**.
It hasn't rained for weeks.

Está lloviendo.
It's raining.

Le **han llovido** las ofertas.
He's received lots of offers.

Llovió sin parar.
It rained non-stop.

Llovía a cántaros.
It was pouring down.

Sabía que le **lloverían** las críticas.
She knew she would be much criticized.

Espero que no **llueva** este fin de semana.
I hope it won't rain this weekend.

Si no **lloviera** podríamos salir a dar una vuelta.
We could go for a walk if it wasn't raining.

Remember that subject pronouns are not used very often in Spanish.

lucir (to shine)

	PRESENT	PRESENT PERFECT
(yo)	**luzco**	**he lucido**
(tú)	**luces**	**has lucido**
(él/ella/usted)	**luce**	**ha lucido**
(nosotros/as)	**lucimos**	**hemos lucido**
(vosotros/as)	**lucís**	**habéis lucido**
(ellos/ellas/ ustedes)	**lucen**	**han lucido**

	PRETERITE	IMPERFECT
(yo)	**lucí**	**lucía**
(tú)	**luciste**	**lucías**
(él/ella/usted)	**lució**	**lucía**
(nosotros/as)	**lucimos**	**lucíamos**
(vosotros/as)	**lucisteis**	**lucíais**
(ellos/ellas/ ustedes)	**lucieron**	**lucían**

GERUND	PAST PARTICIPLE
luciendo	**lucido**

	FUTURE	CONDITIONAL
(yo)	**luciré**	**luciría**
(tú)	**lucirás**	**lucirías**
(él/ella/usted)	**lucirá**	**luciría**
(nosotros/as)	**luciremos**	**luciríamos**
(vosotros/as)	**luciréis**	**luciríais**
(ellos/ellas/ ustedes)	**lucirán**	**lucirían**

	PRESENT SUBJUNCTIVE	IMPERFECT SUBJUNCTIVE
(yo)	**luzca**	**luciera** or **luciese**
(tú)	**luzcas**	**lucieras** or **lucieses**
(él/ella/usted)	**luzca**	**luciera** or **luciese**
(nosotros/as)	**luzcamos**	**luciéramos** or **luciésemos**
(vosotros/as)	**luzcáis**	**lucierais** or **lucieseis**
(ellos/ellas/ ustedes)	**luzcan**	**lucieran** or **luciesen**

IMPERATIVE

luce / lucid

Use the present subjunctive in all cases other than these **tú** and **vosotros** affirmative forms.

EXAMPLE PHRASES

Ahí no **luce** nada.
It doesn't look very good there.

¡Anda, que **te has lucido**!
Well, you've excelled yourself!

Lucían las estrellas.
The stars were shining.

Lucirá un traje muy elegante.
She will be wearing a very smart outfit.

Luciría más con otros zapatos.
It would look much better with a different pair of shoes.

Quiero que esta noche **luzcas** tú el collar.
I want you to wear the necklace tonight.

Remember that subject pronouns are not used very often in Spanish.

morir (to die)

	PRESENT	PRESENT PERFECT
(yo)	**muero**	**he muerto**
(tú)	**mueres**	**has muerto**
(él/ella/usted)	**muere**	**ha muerto**
(nosotros/as)	**morimos**	**hemos muerto**
(vosotros/as)	**morís**	**habéis muerto**
(ellos/ellas/ ustedes)	**mueren**	**han muerto**

	PRETERITE	IMPERFECT
(yo)	**morí**	**moría**
(tú)	**moriste**	**morías**
(él/ella/usted)	**murió**	**moría**
(nosotros/as)	**morimos**	**moríamos**
(vosotros/as)	**moristeis**	**moríais**
(ellos/ellas/ ustedes)	**murieron**	**morían**

GERUND	PAST PARTICIPLE
muriendo	**muerto**

	FUTURE	CONDITIONAL
(yo)	**moriré**	**moriría**
(tú)	**morirás**	**morirías**
(él/ella/usted)	**morirá**	**moriría**
(nosotros/as)	**moriremos**	**moriríamos**
(vosotros/as)	**moriréis**	**moriríais**
(ellos/ellas/ ustedes)	**morirán**	**morirían**

	PRESENT SUBJUNCTIVE	IMPERFECT SUBJUNCTIVE
(yo)	**muera**	**muriera** or **muriese**
(tú)	**mueras**	**murieras** or **murieses**
(él/ella/usted)	**muera**	**muriera** or **muriese**
(nosotros/as)	**muramos**	**muriéramos** or **muriésemos**
(vosotros/as)	**muráis**	**murierais** or **murieseis**
(ellos/ellas/ ustedes)	**mueran**	**murieran** or **muriesen**

IMPERATIVE

muere / morid

Use the present subjunctive in all cases other than these **tú** and **vosotros** affirmative forms.

EXAMPLE PHRASES

¡**Me muero** de hambre!
I'm starving!

Se está muriendo.
She's dying.

Se le **ha muerto** el gato.
His cat has died.

Se murió el mes pasado.
He died last month.

Me moría de ganas de contárselo.
I was dying to tell her.

Cuando te lo cuente **te morirás** de risa.
You'll kill yourself laughing when I tell you.

Yo **me moriría** de vergüenza.
I'd die of shame.

Cuando **me muera**...
When I die...

¡Por favor, no **te mueras**!
Please don't die!

Estoy muerto de miedo.
I'm scared stiff.

Remember that subject pronouns are not used very often in Spanish.

mover (to move)

	PRESENT	PRESENT PERFECT
(yo)	**muevo**	**he movido**
(tú)	**mueves**	**has movido**
(él/ella/usted)	**mueve**	**ha movido**
(nosotros/as)	**movemos**	**hemos movido**
(vosotros/as)	**movéis**	**habéis movido**
(ellos/ellas/ ustedes)	**mueven**	**han movido**

	PRETERITE	IMPERFECT
(yo)	**moví**	**movía**
(tú)	**moviste**	**movías**
(él/ella/usted)	**movió**	**movía**
(nosotros/as)	**movimos**	**movíamos**
(vosotros/as)	**movisteis**	**movíais**
(ellos/ellas/ ustedes)	**movieron**	**movían**

GERUND	PAST PARTICIPLE
moviendo	**movido**

	FUTURE	CONDITIONAL
(yo)	**moveré**	**movería**
(tú)	**moverás**	**moverías**
(él/ella/usted)	**moverá**	**movería**
(nosotros/as)	**moveremos**	**moveríamos**
(vosotros/as)	**moveréis**	**moveríais**
(ellos/ellas/ ustedes)	**moverán**	**moverían**

	PRESENT SUBJUNCTIVE	IMPERFECT SUBJUNCTIVE
(yo)	**mueva**	**moviera** or **moviese**
(tú)	**muevas**	**movieras** or **movieses**
(él/ella/usted)	**mueva**	**moviera** or **moviese**
(nosotros/as)	**movamos**	**moviéramos** or **moviésemos**
(vosotros/as)	**mováis**	**movierais** or **movieseis**
(ellos/ellas/ ustedes)	**muevan**	**movieran** or **moviesen**

IMPERATIVE

mueve / moved

Use the present subjunctive in all cases other than these **tú** and **vosotros** affirmative forms.

EXAMPLE PHRASES

El perro no dejaba de **mover** la cola.
The dog kept wagging its tail.

Se está moviendo.
It's moving.

¿**Has movido** ese mueble de sitio?
Have you moved that piece of furniture?

No **se movieron** de casa.
They didn't leave the house.

Antes **se movía** en esos ambientes.
He used to move in those circles.

Prométeme que no **te moverás** de aquí.
Promise me you won't move from here.

No **te muevas**.
Don't move.

Mueve un poco las cajas para que podamos pasar.
Move the boxes a bit so that we can get past.

Remember that subject pronouns are not used very often in Spanish.

nacer (to be born)

	PRESENT	PRESENT PERFECT
(yo)	**nazco**	**he nacido**
(tú)	**naces**	**has nacido**
(él/ella/usted)	**nace**	**ha nacido**
(nosotros/as)	**nacemos**	**hemos nacido**
(vosotros/as)	**nacéis**	**habéis nacido**
(ellos/ellas/ ustedes)	**nacen**	**han nacido**

	PRETERITE	IMPERFECT
(yo)	**nací**	**nacía**
(tú)	**naciste**	**nacías**
(él/ella/usted)	**nació**	**nacía**
(nosotros/as)	**nacimos**	**nacíamos**
(vosotros/as)	**nacisteis**	**nacíais**
(ellos/ellas/ ustedes)	**nacieron**	**nacían**

GERUND	PAST PARTICIPLE
naciendo	**nacido**

	FUTURE	CONDITIONAL
(yo)	**naceré**	**nacería**
(tú)	**nacerás**	**nacerías**
(él/ella/usted)	**nacerá**	**nacería**
(nosotros/as)	**naceremos**	**naceríamos**
(vosotros/as)	**naceréis**	**naceríais**
(ellos/ellas/ ustedes)	**nacerán**	**nacerían**

	PRESENT SUBJUNCTIVE	IMPERFECT SUBJUNCTIVE
(yo)	**nazca**	**naciera** or **naciese**
(tú)	**nazcas**	**nacieras** or **nacieses**
(él/ella/usted)	**nazca**	**naciera** or **naciese**
(nosotros/as)	**nazcamos**	**naciéramos** or **naciésemos**
(vosotros/as)	**nazcáis**	**nacierais** or **nacieseis**
(ellos/ellas/ ustedes)	**nazcan**	**nacieran** or **naciesen**

IMPERATIVE

nace / naced

Use the present subjunctive in all cases other than these **tú** and **vosotros** affirmative forms.

EXAMPLE PHRASES

Nacen cuatro niños por minuto.
Four children are born every minute.

Ha nacido antes de tiempo.
It was premature.

Nació en 1980.
He was born in 1980.

¿Cuándo **naciste**?
When were you born?

En aquella época había muchos más niños que **nacían** en casa.
Many more babies were born at home in those days.

Nacerá el año que viene.
It will be born next year.

Queremos que **nazca** en España.
We want it to be born in Spain.

Si **naciera** hoy, sería tauro.
He'd be a Taurus if he were born today.

Remember that subject pronouns are not used very often in Spanish.

negar (to deny; to refuse)

	PRESENT	PRESENT PERFECT
(yo)	**niego**	**he negado**
(tú)	**niegas**	**has negado**
(él/ella/usted)	**niega**	**ha negado**
(nosotros/as)	**negamos**	**hemos negado**
(vosotros/as)	**negáis**	**habéis negado**
(ellos/ellas/ustedes)	**niegan**	**han negado**

	PRETERITE	IMPERFECT
(yo)	**negué**	**negaba**
(tú)	**negaste**	**negabas**
(él/ella/usted)	**negó**	**negaba**
(nosotros/as)	**negamos**	**negábamos**
(vosotros/as)	**negasteis**	**negabais**
(ellos/ellas/ustedes)	**negaron**	**negaban**

GERUND	PAST PARTICIPLE
negando	**negado**

	FUTURE	CONDITIONAL
(yo)	**negaré**	**negaría**
(tú)	**negarás**	**negarías**
(él/ella/usted)	**negará**	**negaría**
(nosotros/as)	**negaremos**	**negaríamos**
(vosotros/as)	**negaréis**	**negaríais**
(ellos/ellas/ustedes)	**negarán**	**negarían**

	PRESENT SUBJUNCTIVE	IMPERFECT SUBJUNCTIVE
(yo)	**niegue**	**negara** or **negase**
(tú)	**niegues**	**negaras** or **negases**
(él/ella/usted)	**niegue**	**negara** or **negase**
(nosotros/as)	**neguemos**	**negáramos** or **negásemos**
(vosotros/as)	**neguéis**	**negarais** or **negaseis**
(ellos/ellas/ustedes)	**nieguen**	**negaran** or **negasen**

IMPERATIVE

niega / negad

Use the present subjunctive in all cases other than these **tú** and **vosotros** affirmative forms.

EXAMPLE PHRASES

No lo puedes **negar**.
You can't deny it.

Me niego a creerlo.
I refuse to believe it.

Me **ha negado** el favor.
He wouldn't do me this favour.

Se negó a venir con nosotros.
She refused to come with us.

Decían que era el ladrón, pero él lo **negaba**.
They said that he was the thief, but he denied it.

No me **negarás** que es barato.
You can't say it's not cheap.

Si lo **negaras**, nadie te creería.
If you denied it, nobody would believe you.

No lo **niegues**.
Don't deny it.

Remember that subject pronouns are not used very often in Spanish.

oír (to hear)

	PRESENT	PRESENT PERFECT
(yo)	**oigo**	**he oído**
(tú)	**oyes**	**has oído**
(él/ella/usted)	**oye**	**ha oído**
(nosotros/as)	**oímos**	**hemos oído**
(vosotros/as)	**oís**	**habéis oído**
(ellos/ellas/ ustedes)	**oyen**	**han oído**

	PRETERITE	IMPERFECT
(yo)	**oí**	**oía**
(tú)	**oíste**	**oías**
(él/ella/usted)	**oyó**	**oía**
(nosotros/as)	**oímos**	**oíamos**
(vosotros/as)	**oísteis**	**oíais**
(ellos/ellas/ ustedes)	**oyeron**	**oían**

GERUND	PAST PARTICIPLE
oyendo	**oído**

	FUTURE	CONDITIONAL
(yo)	**oiré**	**oiría**
(tú)	**oirás**	**oirías**
(él/ella/usted)	**oirá**	**oiría**
(nosotros/as)	**oiremos**	**oiríamos**
(vosotros/as)	**oiréis**	**oiríais**
(ellos/ellas/ ustedes)	**oirán**	**oirían**

	PRESENT SUBJUNCTIVE	IMPERFECT SUBJUNCTIVE
(yo)	**oiga**	**oyera** or **oyese**
(tú)	**oigas**	**oyeras** or **oyeses**
(él/ella/usted)	**oiga**	**oyera** or **oyese**
(nosotros/as)	**oigamos**	**oyéramos** or **oyésemos**
(vosotros/as)	**oigáis**	**oyerais** or **oyeseis**
(ellos/ellas/ ustedes)	**oigan**	**oyeran** or **oyesen**

IMPERATIVE

oye / oíd

Use the present subjunctive in all cases other than these **tú** and **vosotros** affirmative forms.

EXAMPLE PHRASES

No **oigo** nada.
I can't hear anything.

Hemos estado oyendo las noticias.
We've been listening to the news.

¿**Has oído** eso?
Did you hear that?

Lo **oí** por casualidad.
I heard it by chance.

No **oía** muy bien.
He couldn't hear very well.

Oirías mal.
You must have misunderstood.

¡**Oiga!** ¡A ver si mira por dónde va!
Excuse me! Why don't you look where you're going?

Óyeme bien, no vuelvas a hacer eso.
Now listen carefully; don't do that again.

Remember that subject pronouns are not used very often in Spanish.

oler (to smell)

	PRESENT	PRESENT PERFECT
(yo)	**huelo**	**he olido**
(tú)	**hueles**	**has olido**
(él/ella/usted)	**huele**	**ha olido**
(nosotros/as)	**olemos**	**hemos olido**
(vosotros/as)	**oléis**	**habéis olido**
(ellos/ellas/ ustedes)	**huelen**	**han olido**

	PRETERITE	IMPERFECT
(yo)	**olí**	**olía**
(tú)	**oliste**	**olías**
(él/ella/usted)	**olió**	**olía**
(nosotros/as)	**olimos**	**olíamos**
(vosotros/as)	**olisteis**	**olíais**
(ellos/ellas/ ustedes)	**olieron**	**olían**

GERUND	PAST PARTICIPLE
oliendo	**olido**

	FUTURE	CONDITIONAL
(yo)	**oleré**	**olería**
(tú)	**olerás**	**olerías**
(él/ella/usted)	**olerá**	**olería**
(nosotros/as)	**oleremos**	**oleríamos**
(vosotros/as)	**oleréis**	**oleríais**
(ellos/ellas/ ustedes)	**olerán**	**olerían**

	PRESENT SUBJUNCTIVE	IMPERFECT SUBJUNCTIVE
(yo)	**huela**	**oliera** or **oliese**
(tú)	**huelas**	**olieras** or **olieses**
(él/ella/usted)	**huela**	**oliera** or **oliese**
(nosotros/as)	**olamos**	**oliéramos** or **oliésemos**
(vosotros/as)	**oláis**	**olierais** or **olieseis**
(ellos/ellas/ ustedes)	**huelan**	**olieran** or **oliesen**

IMPERATIVE

huele / oled

Use the present subjunctive in all cases other than these **tú** and **vosotros** affirmative forms.

EXAMPLE PHRASES

Huele a pescado.
It smells of fish.

El perro **estaba oliendo** la basura.
The dog was sniffing the rubbish.

Se ha olido algo.
He's started to suspect.

A mí el asunto me **olió** mal.
I thought there was something fishy about it.

Olía muy bien.
It smelled really nice.

Con esto ya no **olerá**.
This will take the smell away.

Si te **oliera** a quemado, apágalo.
If you smell it burning, turn it off.

Remember that subject pronouns are not used very often in Spanish.

pagar (to pay; to pay for)

	PRESENT	PRESENT PERFECT
(yo)	**pago**	**he pagado**
(tú)	**pagas**	**has pagado**
(él/ella/usted)	**paga**	**ha pagado**
(nosotros/as)	**pagamos**	**hemos pagado**
(vosotros/as)	**pagáis**	**habéis pagado**
(ellos/ellas/ustedes)	**pagan**	**han pagado**

	PRETERITE	IMPERFECT
(yo)	**pagué**	**pagaba**
(tú)	**pagaste**	**pagabas**
(él/ella/usted)	**pagó**	**pagaba**
(nosotros/as)	**pagamos**	**pagábamos**
(vosotros/as)	**pagasteis**	**pagabais**
(ellos/ellas/ustedes)	**pagaron**	**pagaban**

GERUND	PAST PARTICIPLE
pagando	**pagado**

	FUTURE	CONDITIONAL
(yo)	**pagaré**	**pagaría**
(tú)	**pagarás**	**pagarías**
(él/ella/usted)	**pagará**	**pagaría**
(nosotros/as)	**pagaremos**	**pagaríamos**
(vosotros/as)	**pagaréis**	**pagaríais**
(ellos/ellas/ustedes)	**pagarán**	**pagarían**

	PRESENT SUBJUNCTIVE	IMPERFECT SUBJUNCTIVE
(yo)	**pague**	**pagara** or **pagase**
(tú)	**pagues**	**pagaras** or **pagases**
(él/ella/usted)	**pague**	**pagara** or **pagase**
(nosotros/as)	**paguemos**	**pagáramos** or **pagásemos**
(vosotros/as)	**paguéis**	**pagarais** or **pagaseis**
(ellos/ellas/ustedes)	**paguen**	**pagaran** or **pagasen**

IMPERATIVE

paga / pagad

Use the present subjunctive in all cases other than these **tú** and **vosotros** affirmative forms.

EXAMPLE PHRASES

Se puede **pagar** con tarjeta de crédito.
You can pay by credit card.

¿Cuánto te **pagan** al mes?
How much do they pay you a month?

No **han pagado** el alquiler.
They haven't paid the rent.

Lo **pagué** en efectivo.
I paid for it in cash.

Me **pagaban** muy poco.
I got paid very little.

Yo te **pagaré** la entrada.
I'll pay for your ticket.

¡Quiero que **pague** por lo que me ha hecho!
I want him to pay for what he's done to me!

Si **pagase** sus deudas, se quedaría sin nada.
He'd be left with nothing if he paid his debts.

No les **pagues** hasta que lo hayan hecho.
Don't pay them until they've done it.

Págame lo que me debes.
Pay me what you owe me.

Remember that subject pronouns are not used very often in Spanish.

partir (to cut; to leave)

	PRESENT	PRESENT PERFECT
(yo)	**parto**	**he partido**
(tú)	**partes**	**has partido**
(él/ella/usted)	**parte**	**ha partido**
(nosotros/as)	**partimos**	**hemos partido**
(vosotros/as)	**partís**	**habéis partido**
(ellos/ellas/ustedes)	**parten**	**han partido**

	PRETERITE	IMPERFECT
(yo)	**partí**	**partía**
(tú)	**partiste**	**partías**
(él/ella/usted)	**partió**	**partía**
(nosotros/as)	**partimos**	**partíamos**
(vosotros/as)	**partisteis**	**partíais**
(ellos/ellas/ustedes)	**partieron**	**partían**

GERUND	PAST PARTICIPLE
partiendo	**partido**

	FUTURE	CONDITIONAL
(yo)	**partiré**	**partiría**
(tú)	**partirás**	**partirías**
(él/ella/usted)	**partirá**	**partiría**
(nosotros/as)	**partiremos**	**partiríamos**
(vosotros/as)	**partiréis**	**partiríais**
(ellos/ellas/ustedes)	**partirán**	**partirían**

	PRESENT SUBJUNCTIVE	IMPERFECT SUBJUNCTIVE
(yo)	**parta**	**partiera** or **partiese**
(tú)	**partas**	**partieras** or **partieses**
(él/ella/usted)	**parta**	**partiera** or **partiese**
(nosotros/as)	**partamos**	**partiéramos** or **partiésemos**
(vosotros/as)	**partáis**	**partierais** or **partieseis**
(ellos/ellas/ustedes)	**partan**	**partieran** or **partiesen**

IMPERATIVE

parte / partid

Use the present subjunctive in all cases other than these **tú** and **vosotros** affirmative forms.

EXAMPLE PHRASES

¿Te **parto** un trozo de queso?
Shall I cut you a piece of cheese?

Partiendo de la base de que...
Assuming that...

El remo **se partió** en dos.
The oar broke in two.

Se partían de risa.
They were splitting their sides laughing.

La expedición **partirá** mañana de París.
The expedition will set off from Paris tomorrow.

Eso le **partiría** el corazón.
That would break his heart.

No **partas** todavía el pan.
Don't slice the bread yet.

Pártelo por la mitad.
Cut it in half.

Remember that subject pronouns are not used very often in Spanish.

pedir (to ask for; to ask)

	PRESENT	PRESENT PERFECT
(yo)	**pido**	**he pedido**
(tú)	**pides**	**has pedido**
(él/ella/usted)	**pide**	**ha pedido**
(nosotros/as)	**pedimos**	**hemos pedido**
(vosotros/as)	**pedís**	**habéis pedido**
(ellos/ellas/ ustedes)	**piden**	**han pedido**

	PRETERITE	IMPERFECT
(yo)	**pedí**	**pedía**
(tú)	**pediste**	**pedías**
(él/ella/usted)	**pidió**	**pedía**
(nosotros/as)	**pedimos**	**pedíamos**
(vosotros/as)	**pedisteis**	**pedíais**
(ellos/ellas/ ustedes)	**pidieron**	**pedían**

GERUND	PAST PARTICIPLE
pidiendo	**pedido**

	FUTURE	CONDITIONAL
(yo)	**pediré**	**pediría**
(tú)	**pedirás**	**pedirías**
(él/ella/usted)	**pedirá**	**pediría**
(nosotros/as)	**pediremos**	**pediríamos**
(vosotros/as)	**pediréis**	**pediríais**
(ellos/ellas/ ustedes)	**pedirán**	**pedirían**

	PRESENT SUBJUNCTIVE	IMPERFECT SUBJUNCTIVE
(yo)	**pida**	**pidiera** or **pidiese**
(tú)	**pidas**	**pidieras** or **pidieses**
(él/ella/usted)	**pida**	**pidiera** or **pidiese**
(nosotros/as)	**pidamos**	**pidiéramos** or **pidiésemos**
(vosotros/as)	**pidáis**	**pidierais** or **pidieseis**
(ellos/ellas/ ustedes)	**pidan**	**pidieran** or **pidiesen**

IMPERATIVE

pide / pedid

Use the present subjunctive in all cases other than these **tú** and **vosotros** affirmative forms.

EXAMPLE PHRASES

¿Cuánto **pide** por el coche?
How much is he asking for the car?

La casa **está pidiendo** a gritos una mano de pintura.
The house is crying out to be painted.

Hemos pedido dos cervezas.
We've ordered two beers.

No nos **pidieron** el pasaporte.
They didn't ask us for our passports.

Pedían dos millones de rescate.
They were demanding a two-million ransom.

Si se entera, te **pedirá** explicaciones.
If he finds out, he'll ask you for an explanation.

Nunca te **pediría** que hicieras una cosa así.
I'd never ask you to do anything like that.

Y que sea lo último que me **pidas**.
And don't ask me for anything else.

Pídele el teléfono.
Ask her for her telephone number.

Remember that subject pronouns are not used very often in Spanish.

pensar (to think)

	PRESENT	PRESENT PERFECT
(yo)	**pienso**	**he pensado**
(tú)	**piensas**	**has pensado**
(él/ella/usted)	**piensa**	**ha pensado**
(nosotros/as)	**pensamos**	**hemos pensado**
(vosotros/as)	**pensáis**	**habéis pensado**
(ellos/ellas/ ustedes)	**piensan**	**han pensado**

	PRETERITE	IMPERFECT
(yo)	**pensé**	**pensaba**
(tú)	**pensaste**	**pensabas**
(él/ella/usted)	**pensó**	**pensaba**
(nosotros/as)	**pensamos**	**pensábamos**
(vosotros/as)	**pensasteis**	**pensabais**
(ellos/ellas/ ustedes)	**pensaron**	**pensaban**

GERUND	PAST PARTICIPLE
pensando	**pensado**

	FUTURE	CONDITIONAL
(yo)	**pensaré**	**pensaría**
(tú)	**pensarás**	**pensarías**
(él/ella/usted)	**pensará**	**pensaría**
(nosotros/as)	**pensaremos**	**pensaríamos**
(vosotros/as)	**pensaréis**	**pensaríais**
(ellos/ellas/ ustedes)	**pensarán**	**pensarían**

	PRESENT SUBJUNCTIVE	IMPERFECT SUBJUNCTIVE
(yo)	**piense**	**pensara** or **pensase**
(tú)	**pienses**	**pensaras** or **pensases**
(él/ella/usted)	**piense**	**pensara** or **pensase**
(nosotros/as)	**pensemos**	**pensáramos** or **pensásemos**
(vosotros/as)	**penséis**	**pensarais** or **pensaseis**
(ellos/ellas/ ustedes)	**piensen**	**pensaran** or **pensasen**

IMPERATIVE

piensa / pensad

Use the present subjunctive in all cases other than these **tú** and **vosotros** affirmative forms.

EXAMPLE PHRASES

¿**Piensas** que vale la pena?
Do you think it's worth it?

¿Qué **piensas** del aborto?
What do you think about abortion?

Está pensando en comprarse un piso.
He's thinking about buying a flat.

¿Lo **has pensado** bien?
Have you thought about it carefully?

Pensaba que vendrías.
I thought you'd come.

Yo no me lo **pensaría** dos veces.
I wouldn't think about it twice.

Me da igual lo que **piensen**.
I don't care what they think.

Si **pensara** eso, te lo diría.
If I thought that, I'd tell you.

No **pienses** que no quiero ir.
Don't think that I don't want to go.

No lo **pienses** más.
Don't give it another thought.

Remember that subject pronouns are not used very often in Spanish.

perder (to lose)

	PRESENT	PRESENT PERFECT
(yo)	**pierdo**	**he perdido**
(tú)	**pierdes**	**has perdido**
(él/ella/usted)	**pierde**	**ha perdido**
(nosotros/as)	**perdemos**	**hemos perdido**
(vosotros/as)	**perdéis**	**habéis perdido**
(ellos/ellas/ ustedes)	**pierden**	**han perdido**

	PRETERITE	IMPERFECT
(yo)	**perdí**	**perdía**
(tú)	**perdiste**	**perdías**
(él/ella/usted)	**perdió**	**perdía**
(nosotros/as)	**perdimos**	**perdíamos**
(vosotros/as)	**perdisteis**	**perdíais**
(ellos/ellas/ ustedes)	**perdieron**	**perdían**

GERUND	PAST PARTICIPLE
perdiendo	**perdido**

	FUTURE	CONDITIONAL
(yo)	**perderé**	**perdería**
(tú)	**perderás**	**perderías**
(él/ella/usted)	**perderá**	**perdería**
(nosotros/as)	**perderemos**	**perderíamos**
(vosotros/as)	**perderéis**	**perderíais**
(ellos/ellas/ ustedes)	**perderán**	**perderían**

	PRESENT SUBJUNCTIVE	IMPERFECT SUBJUNCTIVE
(yo)	**pierda**	**perdiera** or **perdiese**
(tú)	**pierdas**	**perdieras** or **perdieses**
(él/ella/usted)	**pierda**	**perdiera** or **perdiese**
(nosotros/as)	**perdamos**	**perdiéramos** or **perdiésemos**
(vosotros/as)	**perdáis**	**perdierais** or **perdieseis**
(ellos/ellas/ ustedes)	**pierdan**	**perdieran** or **perdiesen**

IMPERATIVE

pierde / perded

Use the present subjunctive in all cases other than these **tú** and **vosotros** affirmative forms.

EXAMPLE PHRASES

Siempre **pierde** las llaves.
He's always losing his keys.

Ana es la que saldrá **perdiendo**.
Ana is the one who will lose out.

He perdido dos kilos.
I've lost two kilos.

Perdimos dos a cero.
We lost two nil.

Perdían siempre.
They always used to lose.

Date prisa o **perderás** el tren.
Hurry up or you'll miss the train.

¡No **te** lo **pierdas**!
Don't miss it!

No **pierdas** esta oportunidad.
Don't miss this opportunity.

Remember that subject pronouns are not used very often in Spanish.

poder (to be able to)

	PRESENT	PRESENT PERFECT
(yo)	**puedo**	**he podido**
(tú)	**puedes**	**has podido**
(él/ella/usted)	**puede**	**ha podido**
(nosotros/as)	**podemos**	**hemos podido**
(vosotros/as)	**podéis**	**habéis podido**
(ellos/ellas/ ustedes)	**pueden**	**han podido**

	PRETERITE	IMPERFECT
(yo)	**pude**	**podía**
(tú)	**pudiste**	**podías**
(él/ella/usted)	**pudo**	**podía**
(nosotros/as)	**pudimos**	**podíamos**
(vosotros/as)	**pudisteis**	**podíais**
(ellos/ellas/ ustedes)	**pudieron**	**podían**

GERUND	PAST PARTICIPLE
pudiendo	**podido**

	FUTURE	CONDITIONAL
(yo)	**podré**	**podría**
(tú)	**podrás**	**podrías**
(él/ella/usted)	**podrá**	**podría**
(nosotros/as)	**podremos**	**podríamos**
(vosotros/as)	**podréis**	**podríais**
(ellos/ellas/ ustedes)	**podrán**	**podrían**

	PRESENT SUBJUNCTIVE	IMPERFECT SUBJUNCTIVE
(yo)	**pueda**	**pudiera** or **pudiese**
(tú)	**puedas**	**pudieras** or **pudieses**
(él/ella/usted)	**pueda**	**pudiera** or **pudiese**
(nosotros/as)	**podamos**	**pudiéramos** or **pudiésemos**
(vosotros/as)	**podáis**	**pudierais** or **pudieseis**
(ellos/ellas/ ustedes)	**puedan**	**pudieran** or **pudiesen**

IMPERATIVE

puede / poded

Use the present subjunctive in all cases other than these **tú** and **vosotros** affirmative forms.

EXAMPLE PHRASES

¿**Puedo** entrar?
Can I come in?

Puede que llegue mañana.
He may arrive tomorrow.

No **he podido** venir antes.
I couldn't come before.

Pudiste haberte hecho daño.
You could have hurt yourself.

¡Me lo **podías** haber dicho!
You could have told me!

Estoy segura de que **podrá** conseguirlo.
I'm sure he'll succeed.

¿**Podrías** ayudarme?
Could you help me?

Ven en cuanto **puedas**.
Come as soon as you can.

Si no **pudiera** encontrar la casa, te llamaría al móvil.
If I weren't able to find the house, I'd call you on your mobile.

Remember that subject pronouns are not used very often in Spanish.

poner (to put)

	PRESENT	PRESENT PERFECT
(yo)	**pongo**	**he puesto**
(tú)	**pones**	**has puesto**
(él/ella/usted)	**pone**	**ha puesto**
(nosotros/as)	**ponemos**	**hemos puesto**
(vosotros/as)	**ponéis**	**habéis puesto**
(ellos/ellas/ustedes)	**ponen**	**han puesto**

	PRETERITE	IMPERFECT
(yo)	**puse**	**ponía**
(tú)	**pusiste**	**ponías**
(él/ella/usted)	**puso**	**ponía**
(nosotros/as)	**pusimos**	**poníamos**
(vosotros/as)	**pusisteis**	**poníais**
(ellos/ellas/ustedes)	**pusieron**	**ponían**

GERUND	PAST PARTICIPLE
poniendo	**puesto**

	FUTURE	CONDITIONAL
(yo)	**pondré**	**pondría**
(tú)	**pondrás**	**pondrías**
(él/ella/usted)	**pondrá**	**pondría**
(nosotros/as)	**pondremos**	**pondríamos**
(vosotros/as)	**pondréis**	**pondríais**
(ellos/ellas/ustedes)	**pondrán**	**pondrían**

	PRESENT SUBJUNCTIVE	IMPERFECT SUBJUNCTIVE
(yo)	**ponga**	**pusiera** or **pusiese**
(tú)	**pongas**	**pusieras** or **pusieses**
(él/ella/usted)	**ponga**	**pusiera** or **pusiese**
(nosotros/as)	**pongamos**	**pusiéramos** or **pusiésemos**
(vosotros/as)	**pongáis**	**pusierais** or **pusieseis**
(ellos/ellas/ustedes)	**pongan**	**pusieran** or **pusiesen**

IMPERATIVE

pon / poned

Use the present subjunctive in all cases other than these **tú** and **vosotros** affirmative forms.

EXAMPLE PHRASES

¿Dónde **pongo** mis cosas?
Where shall I put my things?

¿Qué **pone** en la carta?
What does the letter say?

¿Le **has puesto** azúcar a mi café?
Have you put any sugar in my coffee?

Todos **nos pusimos** de acuerdo.
We all agreed.

Lo **pondré** aquí.
I'll put it here.

¿Le **pondrías** más sal?
Would you add more salt?

Ponlo ahí encima.
Put it on there.

Remember that subject pronouns are not used very often in Spanish.

prohibir (to ban; to prohibit)

	PRESENT	PRESENT PERFECT
(yo)	**prohíbo**	**he prohibido**
(tú)	**prohíbes**	**has prohibido**
(él/ella/usted)	**prohíbe**	**ha prohibido**
(nosotros/as)	**prohibimos**	**hemos prohibido**
(vosotros/as)	**prohibís**	**habéis prohibido**
(ellos/ellas/ustedes)	**prohíben**	**han prohibido**

	PRETERITE	IMPERFECT
(yo)	**prohibí**	**prohibía**
(tú)	**prohibiste**	**prohibías**
(él/ella/usted)	**prohibió**	**prohibía**
(nosotros/as)	**prohibimos**	**prohibíamos**
(vosotros/as)	**prohibisteis**	**prohibíais**
(ellos/ellas/ustedes)	**prohibieron**	**prohibían**

GERUND	PAST PARTICIPLE
prohibiendo	**prohibido**

	FUTURE	CONDITIONAL
(yo)	**prohibiré**	**prohibiría**
(tú)	**prohibirás**	**prohibirías**
(él/ella/usted)	**prohibirá**	**prohibiría**
(nosotros/as)	**prohibiremos**	**prohibiríamos**
(vosotros/as)	**prohibiréis**	**prohibiríais**
(ellos/ellas/ustedes)	**prohibirán**	**prohibirían**

	PRESENT SUBJUNCTIVE	IMPERFECT SUBJUNCTIVE
(yo)	**prohíba**	**prohibiera** or **prohibiese**
(tú)	**prohíbas**	**prohibieras** or **prohibieses**
(él/ella/usted)	**prohíba**	**prohibiera** or **prohibiese**
(nosotros/as)	**prohibamos**	**prohibiéramos** or **prohibiésemos**
(vosotros/as)	**prohibáis**	**prohibierais** or **prohibieseis**
(ellos/ellas/ustedes)	**prohíban**	**prohibieran** or **prohibiesen**

IMPERATIVE

prohíbe / prohibid

Use the present subjunctive in all cases other than these **tú** and **vosotros** affirmative forms.

EXAMPLE PHRASES

Deberían **prohibirlo**.
It should be banned.

Te **prohíbo** que me hables así.
I won't have you talking to me like that!

Han prohibido el acceso a la prensa.
The press have been banned.

Le **prohibieron** la entrada en el bingo.
She was not allowed into the bingo hall.

El tratado **prohibía** el uso de armas químicas.
The treaty prohibited the use of chemical weapons.

Lo **prohibirán** más tarde o más temprano.
Sooner or later they'll ban it.

Yo esa música la **prohibiría**.
If it were up to me, that music would be banned.

"**prohibido** fumar"
"no smoking"

Remember that subject pronouns are not used very often in Spanish.

querer (to want; to love)

	PRESENT	PRESENT PERFECT
(yo)	**quiero**	**he querido**
(tú)	**quieres**	**has querido**
(él/ella/usted)	**quiere**	**ha querido**
(nosotros/as)	**queremos**	**hemos querido**
(vosotros/as)	**queréis**	**habéis querido**
(ellos/ellas/ ustedes)	**quieren**	**han querido**

	PRETERITE	IMPERFECT
(yo)	**quise**	**quería**
(tú)	**quisiste**	**querías**
(él/ella/usted)	**quiso**	**quería**
(nosotros/as)	**quisimos**	**queríamos**
(vosotros/as)	**quisisteis**	**queríais**
(ellos/ellas/ ustedes)	**quisieron**	**querían**

GERUND	PAST PARTICIPLE
queriendo	**querido**

	FUTURE	CONDITIONAL
(yo)	**querré**	**querría**
(tú)	**querrás**	**querrías**
(él/ella/usted)	**querrá**	**querría**
(nosotros/as)	**querremos**	**querríamos**
(vosotros/as)	**querréis**	**querríais**
(ellos/ellas/ ustedes)	**querrán**	**querrían**

	PRESENT SUBJUNCTIVE	IMPERFECT SUBJUNCTIVE
(yo)	**quiera**	**quisiera** or **quisiese**
(tú)	**quieras**	**quisieras** or **quisieses**
(él/ella/usted)	**quiera**	**quisiera** or **quisiese**
(nosotros/as)	**queramos**	**quisiéramos** or **quisiésemos**
(vosotros/as)	**queráis**	**quisierais** or **quisieseis**
(ellos/ellas/ ustedes)	**quieran**	**quisieran** or **quisiesen**

IMPERATIVE

quiere / quered

Use the present subjunctive in all cases other than these **tú** and **vosotros** affirmative forms.

EXAMPLE PHRASES

Lo hice sin **querer.**
I didn't mean to do it.

Te **quiero**.
I love you.

Quiero que vayas.
I want you to go.

Tú lo **has querido**.
You were asking for it.

No **quería** decírmelo.
She didn't want to tell me.

¿**Querrá** firmarme un autógrafo?
Will you give me your autograph?

Querría que no hubiera pasado nunca.
I wish it had never happened.

¡Por lo que más **quieras**! ¡Cállate!
For goodness' sake, shut up!

Quisiera preguntar una cosa.
I'd like to ask something.

Remember that subject pronouns are not used very often in Spanish.

reducir (to reduce)

	PRESENT	PRESENT PERFECT
(yo)	**reduzco**	**he reducido**
(tú)	**reduces**	**has reducido**
(él/ella/usted)	**reduce**	**ha reducido**
(nosotros/as)	**reducimos**	**hemos reducido**
(vosotros/as)	**reducís**	**habéis reducido**
(ellos/ellas/ ustedes)	**reducen**	**han reducido**

	PRETERITE	IMPERFECT
(yo)	**reduje**	**reducía**
(tú)	**redujiste**	**reducías**
(él/ella/usted)	**redujo**	**reducía**
(nosotros/as)	**redujimos**	**reducíamos**
(vosotros/as)	**redujisteis**	**reducíais**
(ellos/ellas/ ustedes)	**redujeron**	**reducían**

GERUND	PAST PARTICIPLE
reduciendo	**reducido**

	FUTURE	CONDITIONAL
(yo)	**reduciré**	**reduciría**
(tú)	**reducirás**	**reducirías**
(él/ella/usted)	**reducirá**	**reduciría**
(nosotros/as)	**reduciremos**	**reduciríamos**
(vosotros/as)	**reduciréis**	**reduciríais**
(ellos/ellas/ ustedes)	**reducirán**	**reducirían**

	PRESENT SUBJUNCTIVE	IMPERFECT SUBJUNCTIVE
(yo)	**reduzca**	**redujera** or **redujese**
(tú)	**reduzcas**	**redujeras** or **redujeses**
(él/ella/usted)	**reduzca**	**redujera** or **redujese**
(nosotros/as)	**reduzcamos**	**redujéramos** or **redujésemos**
(vosotros/as)	**reduzcáis**	**redujerais** or **redujeseis**
(ellos/ellas/ ustedes)	**reduzcan**	**redujeran** or **redujesen**

IMPERATIVE

reduce / reducid

Use the present subjunctive in all cases other than these **tú** and **vosotros** affirmative forms.

EXAMPLE PHRASES

Al final todo **se reduce** a eso.
In the end it all comes down to that.

Le **han reducido** la pena a dos meses.
His sentence has been reduced to two months.

Se ha reducido la tasa de natalidad.
The birth rate has fallen.

Sus gastos **se redujeron** a la mitad.
Their expenses were cut by half.

Reducirán la producción en un 20%.
They'll cut production by 20%.

Reduzca la velocidad.
Reduce speed.

Remember that subject pronouns are not used very often in Spanish.

rehusar (to refuse)

	PRESENT	PRESENT PERFECT
(yo)	**rehúso**	**he rehusado**
(tú)	**rehúsas**	**has rehusado**
(él/ella/usted)	**rehúsa**	**ha rehusado**
(nosotros/as)	**rehusamos**	**hemos rehusado**
(vosotros/as)	**rehusáis**	**habéis rehusado**
(ellos/ellas/ ustedes)	**rehúsan**	**han rehusado**

	PRETERITE	IMPERFECT
(yo)	**rehusé**	**rehusaba**
(tú)	**rehusaste**	**rehusabas**
(él/ella/usted)	**rehusó**	**rehusaba**
(nosotros/as)	**rehusamos**	**rehusábamos**
(vosotros/as)	**rehusasteis**	**rehusabais**
(ellos/ellas/ ustedes)	**rehusaron**	**rehusaban**

	GERUND	PAST PARTICIPLE
	rehusando	**rehusado**

	FUTURE	CONDITIONAL
(yo)	**rehusaré**	**rehusaría**
(tú)	**rehusarás**	**rehusarías**
(él/ella/usted)	**rehusará**	**rehusaría**
(nosotros/as)	**rehusaremos**	**rehusaríamos**
(vosotros/as)	**rehusaréis**	**rehusaríais**
(ellos/ellas/ ustedes)	**rehusarán**	**rehusarían**

	PRESENT SUBJUNCTIVE	IMPERFECT SUBJUNCTIVE
(yo)	**rehúse**	**rehusara** or **rehusase**
(tú)	**rehúses**	**rehusaras** or **rehusases**
(él/ella/usted)	**rehúse**	**rehusara** or **rehusase**
(nosotros/as)	**rehusemos**	**rehusáramos** or **rehusásemos**
(vosotros/as)	**rehuséis**	**rehusarais** or **rehusaseis**
(ellos/ellas/ ustedes)	**rehúsen**	**rehusaran** or **rehusasen**

IMPERATIVE

rehúsa / rehusad

Use the present subjunctive in all cases other than these **tú** and **vosotros** affirmative forms.

EXAMPLE PHRASES

Rehúso tomar parte en esto.
I refuse to take part in this.

Ha rehusado la oferta de trabajo.
He declined the job offer.

Su familia **rehusó** hacer declaraciones.
His family refused to comment.

Remember that subject pronouns are not used very often in Spanish.

reír (to laugh)

	PRESENT	PRESENT PERFECT
(yo)	**río**	**he reído**
(tú)	**ríes**	**has reído**
(él/ella/usted)	**ríe**	**ha reído**
(nosotros/as)	**reímos**	**hemos reído**
(vosotros/as)	**reís**	**habéis reído**
(ellos/ellas/ustedes)	**ríen**	**han reído**

	PRETERITE	IMPERFECT
(yo)	**reí**	**reía**
(tú)	**reíste**	**reías**
(él/ella/usted)	**rio**	**reía**
(nosotros/as)	**reímos**	**reíamos**
(vosotros/as)	**reísteis**	**reíais**
(ellos/ellas/ustedes)	**rieron**	**reían**

GERUND	PAST PARTICIPLE
riendo	**reído**

	FUTURE	CONDITIONAL
(yo)	**reiré**	**reiría**
(tú)	**reirás**	**reirías**
(él/ella/usted)	**reirá**	**reiría**
(nosotros/as)	**reiremos**	**reiríamos**
(vosotros/as)	**reiréis**	**reiríais**
(ellos/ellas/ustedes)	**reirán**	**reirían**

	PRESENT SUBJUNCTIVE	IMPERFECT SUBJUNCTIVE
(yo)	**ría**	**riera** or **riese**
(tú)	**rías**	**rieras** or **rieses**
(él/ella/usted)	**ría**	**riera** or **riese**
(nosotros/as)	**riamos**	**riéramos** or **riésemos**
(vosotros/as)	**riais**	**rierais** or **rieseis**
(ellos/ellas/ustedes)	**rían**	**rieran** or **riesen**

IMPERATIVE

ríe / reíd

Use the present subjunctive in all cases other than these **tú** and **vosotros** affirmative forms.

EXAMPLE PHRASES

Se echó a **reír**.
She burst out laughing.

Se ríe de todo.
She doesn't take anything seriously.

¿De qué **te ríes**?
What are you laughing at?

Siempre **están riéndose** en clase.
They're always laughing in class.

Me reía mucho con él.
I always had a good laugh with him.

Te reirás cuando te lo cuente.
You'll have a laugh when I tell you about it.

Que **se rían** lo que quieran.
Let them laugh as much as they want.

No **te rías** de mí.
Don't laugh at me.

¡Tú **ríete**, pero he pasado muchísimo miedo!
You may laugh, but I was really frightened.

Remember that subject pronouns are not used very often in Spanish.

reñir (to scold; to quarrel)

	PRESENT	PRESENT PERFECT
(yo)	**riño**	**he reñido**
(tú)	**riñes**	**has reñido**
(él/ella/usted)	**riñe**	**ha reñido**
(nosotros/as)	**reñimos**	**hemos reñido**
(vosotros/as)	**reñís**	**habéis reñido**
(ellos/ellas/ ustedes)	**riñen**	**han reñido**

	PRETERITE	IMPERFECT
(yo)	**reñí**	**reñía**
(tú)	**reñiste**	**reñías**
(él/ella/usted)	**riñó**	**reñía**
(nosotros/as)	**reñimos**	**reñíamos**
(vosotros/as)	**reñisteis**	**reñíais**
(ellos/ellas/ ustedes)	**riñeron**	**reñían**

GERUND	PAST PARTICIPLE
riñendo	**reñido**

	FUTURE	CONDITIONAL
(yo)	**reñiré**	**reñiría**
(tú)	**reñirás**	**reñirías**
(él/ella/usted)	**reñirá**	**reñiría**
(nosotros/as)	**reñiremos**	**reñiríamos**
(vosotros/as)	**reñiréis**	**reñiríais**
(ellos/ellas/ ustedes)	**reñirán**	**reñirían**

	PRESENT SUBJUNCTIVE	IMPERFECT SUBJUNCTIVE
(yo)	**riña**	**riñera** or **riñese**
(tú)	**riñas**	**riñeras** or **riñeses**
(él/ella/usted)	**riña**	**riñera** or **riñese**
(nosotros/as)	**riñamos**	**riñéramos** or **riñésemos**
(vosotros/as)	**riñáis**	**riñerais** or **riñeseis**
(ellos/ellas/ ustedes)	**riñan**	**riñeran** or **riñesen**

IMPERATIVE

riñe / reñid

Use the present subjunctive in all cases other than these **tú** and **vosotros** affirmative forms.

EXAMPLE PHRASES

Se pasan el día entero **riñendo**.
They spend the whole day quarrelling.

Ha reñido con su novio.
She has fallen out with her boyfriend.

Les **riñó** por llegar tarde a casa.
She told them off for getting home late.

Nos **reñía** sin motivo.
She used to tell us off for no reason.

Si se entera, te **reñirá**.
He'll tell you off if he finds out.

No la **riñas**, no es culpa suya.
Don't tell her off, it's not her fault.

¡Niños, no **riñáis**!
Children, don't quarrel!

Remember that subject pronouns are not used very often in Spanish.

repetir (to repeat)

	PRESENT	PRESENT PERFECT
(yo)	**repito**	**he repetido**
(tú)	**repites**	**has repetido**
(él/ella/usted)	**repite**	**ha repetido**
(nosotros/as)	**repetimos**	**hemos repetido**
(vosotros/as)	**repetís**	**habéis repetido**
(ellos/ellas/ ustedes)	**repiten**	**han repetido**

	PRETERITE	IMPERFECT
(yo)	**repetí**	**repetía**
(tú)	**repetiste**	**repetías**
(él/ella/usted)	**repitió**	**repetía**
(nosotros/as)	**repetimos**	**repetíamos**
(vosotros/as)	**repetisteis**	**repetíais**
(ellos/ellas/ ustedes)	**repitieron**	**repetían**

GERUND	PAST PARTICIPLE
repitiendo	**repetido**

	FUTURE	CONDITIONAL
(yo)	**repetiré**	**repetiría**
(tú)	**repetirás**	**repetirías**
(él/ella/usted)	**repetirá**	**repetiría**
(nosotros/as)	**repetiremos**	**repetiríamos**
(vosotros/as)	**repetiréis**	**repetiríais**
(ellos/ellas/ ustedes)	**repetirán**	**repetirían**

	PRESENT SUBJUNCTIVE	IMPERFECT SUBJUNCTIVE
(yo)	**repita**	**repitiera** or **repitiese**
(tú)	**repitas**	**repitieras** or **repitieses**
(él/ella/usted)	**repita**	**repitiera** or **repitiese**
(nosotros/as)	**repitamos**	**repitiéramos** or **repitiésemos**
(vosotros/as)	**repitáis**	**repitierais** or **repitieseis**
(ellos/ellas/ ustedes)	**repitan**	**repitieran** or **repitiesen**

IMPERATIVE

repite / repetid

Use the present subjunctive in all cases other than these **tú** and **vosotros** affirmative forms.

EXAMPLE PHRASES

¿Podría **repetirlo**, por favor?
Could you repeat that, please?

Le **repito** que es imposible.
I'm telling you again that it is impossible.

Se lo **he repetido** mil veces, pero no escucha.
I've told him hundreds of times but he won't listen.

Repetía una y otra vez que era inocente.
He kept repeating that he was innocent.

Si sigue así, **repetirá** curso.
If she goes on like this, she'll end up having to repeat the year.

Espero que no **se repita**.
I hope this won't happen again.

Repetid detrás de mí...
Repeat after me...

Remember that subject pronouns are not used very often in Spanish.

resolver (to solve)

	PRESENT	PRESENT PERFECT
(yo)	**resuelvo**	**he resuelto**
(tú)	**resuelves**	**has resuelto**
(él/ella/usted)	**resuelve**	**ha resuelto**
(nosotros/as)	**resolvemos**	**hemos resuelto**
(vosotros/as)	**resolvéis**	**habéis resuelto**
(ellos/ellas/ ustedes)	**resuelven**	**han resuelto**

	PRETERITE	IMPERFECT
(yo)	**resolví**	**resolvía**
(tú)	**resolviste**	**resolvías**
(él/ella/usted)	**resolvió**	**resolvía**
(nosotros/as)	**resolvimos**	**resolvíamos**
(vosotros/as)	**resolvisteis**	**resolvíais**
(ellos/ellas/ ustedes)	**resolvieron**	**resolvían**

GERUND	PAST PARTICIPLE
resolviendo	**resuelto**

	FUTURE	CONDITIONAL
(yo)	**resolveré**	**resolvería**
(tú)	**resolverás**	**resolverías**
(él/ella/usted)	**resolverá**	**resolvería**
(nosotros/as)	**resolveremos**	**resolveríamos**
(vosotros/as)	**resolveréis**	**resolveríais**
(ellos/ellas/ ustedes)	**resolverán**	**resolverían**

	PRESENT SUBJUNCTIVE	IMPERFECT SUBJUNCTIVE
(yo)	**resuelva**	**resolviera** or **resolviese**
(tú)	**resuelvas**	**resolvieras** or **resolvieses**
(él/ella/usted)	**resuelva**	**resolviera** or **resolviese**
(nosotros/as)	**resolvamos**	**resolviéramos** or **resolviésemos**
(vosotros/as)	**resolváis**	**resolvierais** or **resolvieseis**
(ellos/ellas/ ustedes)	**resuelvan**	**resolvieran** or **resolviesen**

IMPERATIVE

resuelve / resolved

Use the present subjunctive in all cases other than these **tú** and **vosotros** affirmative forms.

EXAMPLE PHRASES

Trataré de **resolver** tus dudas.
I'll try to answer your questions.

Enfadarse no **resuelve** nada.
Getting angry doesn't help at all.

No **hemos resuelto** los problemas.
We haven't solved the problems.

Resolvimos el problema entre todos.
We solved the problem together.

No te preocupes, ya lo **resolveremos**.
Don't worry, we'll get it sorted.

Yo lo **resolvería** de otra forma.
I'd sort it out another way.

Hasta que no lo **resuelva** no descansaré.
I won't rest until I've sorted it out.

Remember that subject pronouns are not used very often in Spanish.

reunir (to put together; to gather)

	PRESENT	PRESENT PERFECT
(yo)	**reúno**	**he reunido**
(tú)	**reúnes**	**has reunido**
(él/ella/usted)	**reúne**	**ha reunido**
(nosotros/as)	**reunimos**	**hemos reunido**
(vosotros/as)	**reunís**	**habéis reunido**
(ellos/ellas/ustedes)	**reúnen**	**han reunido**

	PRETERITE	IMPERFECT
(yo)	**reuní**	**reunía**
(tú)	**reuniste**	**reunías**
(él/ella/usted)	**reunió**	**reunía**
(nosotros/as)	**reunimos**	**reuníamos**
(vosotros/as)	**reunisteis**	**reuníais**
(ellos/ellas/ustedes)	**reunieron**	**reunían**

GERUND	PAST PARTICIPLE
reuniendo	**reunido**

	FUTURE	CONDITIONAL
(yo)	**reuniré**	**reuniría**
(tú)	**reunirás**	**reunirías**
(él/ella/usted)	**reunirá**	**reuniría**
(nosotros/as)	**reuniremos**	**reuniríamos**
(vosotros/as)	**reuniréis**	**reuniríais**
(ellos/ellas/ustedes)	**reunirán**	**reunirían**

	PRESENT SUBJUNCTIVE	IMPERFECT SUBJUNCTIVE
(yo)	**reúna**	**reuniera** or **reuniese**
(tú)	**reúnas**	**reunieras** or **reunieses**
(él/ella/usted)	**reúna**	**reuniera** or **reuniese**
(nosotros/as)	**reunamos**	**reuniéramos** or **reuniésemos**
(vosotros/as)	**reunáis**	**reunierais** or **reunieseis**
(ellos/ellas/ustedes)	**reúnan**	**reunieran** or **reuniesen**

IMPERATIVE

reúne / reunid

Use the present subjunctive in all cases other than these **tú** and **vosotros** affirmative forms.

EXAMPLE PHRASES

Hemos conseguido **reunir** suficiente dinero.
We've managed to raise enough money.

Hace tiempo que no **me reúno** con ellos.
I haven't seen them for ages.

Reunió a todos para comunicarles la noticia.
He called them all together to tell them the news.

No **reunía** los requisitos.
She didn't satisfy the requirements.

Se reunirán el viernes.
They'll meet on Friday.

Necesito encontrar un local que **reúna** las condiciones.
I need to find premises that will meet the requirements.

Consiguió que su familia **se reuniera** tras una larga separación.
She managed to get her family back together again after a long separation.

Antes de acusarle, **reúne** las pruebas suficientes.
Get enough evidence together before accusing him.

Remember that subject pronouns are not used very often in Spanish.

rogar (to beg; to pray)

	PRESENT	PRESENT PERFECT
(yo)	**ruego**	**he rogado**
(tú)	**ruegas**	**has rogado**
(él/ella/usted)	**ruega**	**ha rogado**
(nosotros/as)	**rogamos**	**hemos rogado**
(vosotros/as)	**rogáis**	**habéis rogado**
(ellos/ellas/ ustedes)	**ruegan**	**han rogado**

	PRETERITE	IMPERFECT
(yo)	**rogué**	**rogaba**
(tú)	**rogaste**	**rogabas**
(él/ella/usted)	**rogó**	**rogaba**
(nosotros/as)	**rogamos**	**rogábamos**
(vosotros/as)	**rogasteis**	**rogabais**
(ellos/ellas/ ustedes)	**rogaron**	**rogaban**

GERUND	PAST PARTICIPLE
rogando	**rogado**

	FUTURE	CONDITIONAL
(yo)	**rogaré**	**rogaría**
(tú)	**rogarás**	**rogarías**
(él/ella/usted)	**rogará**	**rogaría**
(nosotros/as)	**rogaremos**	**rogaríamos**
(vosotros/as)	**rogaréis**	**rogaríais**
(ellos/ellas/ ustedes)	**rogarán**	**rogarían**

	PRESENT SUBJUNCTIVE	IMPERFECT SUBJUNCTIVE
(yo)	**ruegue**	**rogara** or **rogase**
(tú)	**ruegues**	**rogaras** or **rogases**
(él/ella/usted)	**ruegue**	**rogara** or **rogase**
(nosotros/as)	**roguemos**	**rogáramos** or **rogásemos**
(vosotros/as)	**roguéis**	**rogarais** or **rogaseis**
(ellos/ellas/ ustedes)	**rueguen**	**rogaran** or **rogasen**

IMPERATIVE

ruega / rogad

Use the present subjunctive in all cases other than these **tú** and **vosotros** affirmative forms.

EXAMPLE PHRASES

Les **rogamos** acepten nuestras disculpas.
Please accept our apologies.

Te **ruego** que me lo devuelvas.
Please give it back to me.

"**Se ruega** no fumar"
"Please do not smoke"

Me **rogó** que le perdonara.
He begged me to forgive him.

Le **rogaba** a Dios que se curara.
I prayed to God to make him better.

Ruega por mí.
Pray for me.

Remember that subject pronouns are not used very often in Spanish.

romper (to break)

	PRESENT	PRESENT PERFECT
(yo)	**rompo**	**he roto**
(tú)	**rompes**	**has roto**
(él/ella/usted)	**rompe**	**ha roto**
(nosotros/as)	**rompemos**	**hemos roto**
(vosotros/as)	**rompéis**	**habéis roto**
(ellos/ellas/ ustedes)	**rompen**	**han roto**

	PRETERITE	IMPERFECT
(yo)	**rompí**	**rompía**
(tú)	**rompiste**	**rompías**
(él/ella/usted)	**rompió**	**rompía**
(nosotros/as)	**rompimos**	**rompíamos**
(vosotros/as)	**rompisteis**	**rompíais**
(ellos/ellas/ ustedes)	**rompieron**	**rompían**

GERUND	PAST PARTICIPLE
rompiendo	**roto**

	FUTURE	CONDITIONAL
(yo)	**romperé**	**rompería**
(tú)	**romperás**	**romperías**
(él/ella/usted)	**romperá**	**rompería**
(nosotros/as)	**romperemos**	**romperíamos**
(vosotros/as)	**romperéis**	**romperíais**
(ellos/ellas/ ustedes)	**romperán**	**romperían**

	PRESENT SUBJUNCTIVE	IMPERFECT SUBJUNCTIVE
(yo)	**rompa**	**rompiera** or **rompiese**
(tú)	**rompas**	**rompieras** or **rompieses**
(él/ella/usted)	**rompa**	**rompiera** or **rompiese**
(nosotros/as)	**rompamos**	**rompiéramos** or **rompiésemos**
(vosotros/as)	**rompáis**	**rompierais** or **rompieseis**
(ellos/ellas/ ustedes)	**rompan**	**rompieran** or **rompiesen**

IMPERATIVE

rompe / romped

Use the present subjunctive in all cases other than these **tú** and **vosotros** affirmative forms.

EXAMPLE PHRASES

La cuerda **se** va a **romper**.
The rope is going to snap.

Siempre **están rompiendo** cosas.
They're always breaking things.

Se ha roto una taza.
A cup's broken.

Se rompió el jarrón.
The vase broke.

Yo nunca **rompería** una promesa.
I'd never break a promise.

Si lo **rompiera**, tendría que pagarlo.
If you broke it, you'd have to pay for it.

Rompe con él, si ya no le quieres.
If you don't love him any more, finish with him.

Cuidado, no lo **rompas**.
Careful you don't break it.

Remember that subject pronouns are not used very often in Spanish.

saber (to know)

	PRESENT	PRESENT PERFECT
(yo)	**sé**	**he sabido**
(tú)	**sabes**	**has sabido**
(él/ella/usted)	**sabe**	**ha sabido**
(nosotros/as)	**sabemos**	**hemos sabido**
(vosotros/as)	**sabéis**	**habéis sabido**
(ellos/ellas/ ustedes)	**saben**	**han sabido**

	PRETERITE	IMPERFECT
(yo)	**supe**	**sabía**
(tú)	**supiste**	**sabías**
(él/ella/usted)	**supo**	**sabía**
(nosotros/as)	**supimos**	**sabíamos**
(vosotros/as)	**supisteis**	**sabíais**
(ellos/ellas/ ustedes)	**supieron**	**sabían**

	GERUND	PAST PARTICIPLE
	sabiendo	**sabido**

	FUTURE	CONDITIONAL
(yo)	**sabré**	**sabría**
(tú)	**sabrás**	**sabrías**
(él/ella/usted)	**sabrá**	**sabría**
(nosotros/as)	**sabremos**	**sabríamos**
(vosotros/as)	**sabréis**	**sabríais**
(ellos/ellas/ ustedes)	**sabrán**	**sabrían**

	PRESENT SUBJUNCTIVE	IMPERFECT SUBJUNCTIVE
(yo)	**sepa**	**supiera** or **supiese**
(tú)	**sepas**	**supieras** or **supieses**
(él/ella/usted)	**sepa**	**supiera** or **supiese**
(nosotros/as)	**sepamos**	**supiéramos** or **supiésemos**
(vosotros/as)	**sepáis**	**supierais** or **supieseis**
(ellos/ellas/ ustedes)	**sepan**	**supieran** or **supiesen**

IMPERATIVE

sabe / sabed

Use the present subjunctive in all cases other than these **tú** and **vosotros** affirmative forms.

EXAMPLE PHRASES

No lo **sé**.
I don't know.

¿**Sabes** una cosa?
Do you know what?

¿Cuándo lo **has sabido**?
When did you find out?

No **supe** qué responder.
I didn't know what to answer.

Pensaba que lo **sabías**.
I thought you knew.

Nunca se **sabrá** quién la mató.
We'll never know who killed her.

Si no le tuvieras tanto miedo al agua, ya **sabrías** nadar.
If you weren't so afraid of water, you'd already be able to swim.

Que yo **sepa**, vive en París.
As far as I know, she lives in Paris.

¡Si **supiéramos** al menos dónde está!
If only we knew where he was!

Remember that subject pronouns are not used very often in Spanish.

sacar (to take out)

	PRESENT	PRESENT PERFECT
(yo)	**saco**	**he sacado**
(tú)	**sacas**	**has sacado**
(él/ella/usted)	**saca**	**ha sacado**
(nosotros/as)	**sacamos**	**hemos sacado**
(vosotros/as)	**sacáis**	**habéis sacado**
(ellos/ellas/ ustedes)	**sacan**	**han sacado**

	PRETERITE	IMPERFECT
(yo)	**saqué**	**sacaba**
(tú)	**sacaste**	**sacabas**
(él/ella/usted)	**sacó**	**sacaba**
(nosotros/as)	**sacamos**	**sacábamos**
(vosotros/as)	**sacasteis**	**sacabais**
(ellos/ellas/ ustedes)	**sacaron**	**sacaban**

GERUND	PAST PARTICIPLE
sacando	**sacado**

	FUTURE	CONDITIONAL
(yo)	**sacaré**	**sacaría**
(tú)	**sacarás**	**sacarías**
(él/ella/usted)	**sacará**	**sacaría**
(nosotros/as)	**sacaremos**	**sacaríamos**
(vosotros/as)	**sacaréis**	**sacaríais**
(ellos/ellas/ ustedes)	**sacarán**	**sacarían**

	PRESENT SUBJUNCTIVE	IMPERFECT SUBJUNCTIVE
(yo)	**saque**	**sacara** or **sacase**
(tú)	**saques**	**sacaras** or **sacases**
(él/ella/usted)	**saque**	**sacara** or **sacase**
(nosotros/as)	**saquemos**	**sacáramos** or **sacásemos**
(vosotros/as)	**saquéis**	**sacarais** or **sacaseis**
(ellos/ellas/ ustedes)	**saquen**	**sacaran** or **sacasen**

IMPERATIVE

saca / sacad

Use the present subjunctive in all cases other than these **tú** and **vosotros** affirmative forms.

EXAMPLE PHRASES

¿**Me sacas** una foto?
Will you take a photo of me?

Estás sacando las cosas de quicio.
You're blowing things out of all proportion.

Ya **he sacado** las entradas.
I've already bought the tickets.

Saqué un 7 en el examen.
I got a 7 in the exam.

¿De dónde **sacaba** tanto dinero?
Where did he get so much money from?

Yo no **sacaría** todavía ninguna conclusión.
I wouldn't draw any conclusions yet.

Quiero que **saques** inmediatamente esa bicicleta de casa.
I want you to get that bike out of the house immediately.

Si te **sacaras** el carnet de conducir, serías mucho más independiente.
You'd be much more independent if you got your driving licence.

No **saques** la cabeza por la ventanilla.
Don't lean out of the window.

Remember that subject pronouns are not used very often in Spanish.

salir (to go out)

	PRESENT	PRESENT PERFECT
(yo)	**salgo**	**he salido**
(tú)	**sales**	**has salido**
(él/ella/usted)	**sale**	**ha salido**
(nosotros/as)	**salimos**	**hemos salido**
(vosotros/as)	**salís**	**habéis salido**
(ellos/ellas/ ustedes)	**salen**	**han salido**

	PRETERITE	IMPERFECT
(yo)	**salí**	**salía**
(tú)	**saliste**	**salías**
(él/ella/usted)	**salió**	**salía**
(nosotros/as)	**salimos**	**salíamos**
(vosotros/as)	**salisteis**	**salíais**
(ellos/ellas/ ustedes)	**salieron**	**salían**

	GERUND	PAST PARTICIPLE
	saliendo	**salido**

	FUTURE	CONDITIONAL
(yo)	**saldré**	**saldría**
(tú)	**saldrás**	**saldrías**
(él/ella/usted)	**saldrá**	**saldría**
(nosotros/as)	**saldremos**	**saldríamos**
(vosotros/as)	**saldréis**	**saldríais**
(ellos/ellas/ ustedes)	**saldrán**	**saldrían**

	PRESENT SUBJUNCTIVE	IMPERFECT SUBJUNCTIVE
(yo)	**salga**	**saliera** or **saliese**
(tú)	**salgas**	**salieras** or **salieses**
(él/ella/usted)	**salga**	**saliera** or **saliese**
(nosotros/as)	**salgamos**	**saliéramos** or **saliésemos**
(vosotros/as)	**salgáis**	**salierais** or **salieseis**
(ellos/ellas/ ustedes)	**salgan**	**salieran** or **saliesen**

IMPERATIVE

sal / salid

Use the present subjunctive in all cases other than these **tú** and **vosotros** affirmative forms.

EXAMPLE PHRASES

Hace tiempo que no **salimos**.
We haven't been out for a while.

Está saliendo con un compañero de trabajo.
She's going out with a colleague from work.

Ha salido.
She's gone out.

Su foto **salió** en todos los periódicos.
Her picture appeared in all the newspapers.

Salía muy tarde de trabajar.
He used to finish work very late.

Te dije que **saldría** muy caro.
I told you it would work out very expensive.

Espero que todo **salga** bien.
I hope everything works out all right.

Si **saliera** elegido...
If I were elected...

Por favor, **salgan** por la puerta de atrás.
Please leave via the back door.

Remember that subject pronouns are not used very often in Spanish.

satisfacer (to satisfy)

	PRESENT	PRESENT PERFECT
(yo)	**satisfago**	**he satisfecho**
(tú)	**satisfaces**	**has satisfecho**
(él/ella/usted)	**satisface**	**ha satisfecho**
(nosotros/as)	**satisfacemos**	**hemos satisfecho**
(vosotros/as)	**satisfacéis**	**habéis satisfecho**
(ellos/ellas/ustedes)	**satisfacen**	**han satisfecho**

	PRETERITE	IMPERFECT
(yo)	**satisfice**	**satisfacía**
(tú)	**satisficiste**	**satisfacías**
(él/ella/usted)	**satisfizo**	**satisfacía**
(nosotros/as)	**satisficimos**	**satisfacíamos**
(vosotros/as)	**satisficisteis**	**satisfacíais**
(ellos/ellas/ustedes)	**satisficieron**	**satisfacían**

GERUND	PAST PARTICIPLE
satisfaciendo	**satisfecho**

	FUTURE	CONDITIONAL
(yo)	**satisfaré**	**satisfaría**
(tú)	**satisfarás**	**satisfarías**
(él/ella/usted)	**satisfará**	**satisfaría**
(nosotros/as)	**satisfaremos**	**satisfaríamos**
(vosotros/as)	**satisfaréis**	**satisfaríais**
(ellos/ellas/ustedes)	**satisfarán**	**satisfarían**

	PRESENT SUBJUNCTIVE	IMPERFECT SUBJUNCTIVE
(yo)	**satisfaga**	**satisficiera** or **satisficiese**
(tú)	**satisfagas**	**satisficieras** or **satisficieses**
(él/ella/usted)	**satisfaga**	**satisficiera** or **satisficiese**
(nosotros/as)	**satisfagamos**	**satisficiéramos** or **satisficiésemos**
(vosotros/as)	**satisfagáis**	**satisficierais** or **satisficieseis**
(ellos/ellas/ustedes)	**satisfagan**	**satisficieran** or **satisficiesen**

IMPERATIVE

satisfaz or **satisface / satisfaced**

Use the present subjunctive in all cases other than these **tú** and **vosotros** affirmative forms.

EXAMPLE PHRASES

No me **satisface** nada el resultado.
I'm not at all satisfied with the result.

Ha satisfecho mis expectativas.
It came up to my expectations.

Eso **satisfizo** mi curiosidad.
That satisfied my curiosity.

Aquella vida **satisfacía** todas mis necesidades.
That lifestyle satisfied all my needs.

Le **satisfará** saber que hemos cumplido nuestros objetivos.
You'll be happy to know that we have achieved our objectives.

Me **satisfaría** mucho más que estudiaras una carrera.
I'd be far happier if you went to university.

Remember that subject pronouns are not used very often in Spanish.

seguir (to follow)

	PRESENT	PRESENT PERFECT
(yo)	**sigo**	**he seguido**
(tú)	**sigues**	**has seguido**
(él/ella/usted)	**sigue**	**ha seguido**
(nosotros/as)	**seguimos**	**hemos seguido**
(vosotros/as)	**seguís**	**habéis seguido**
(ellos/ellas/ ustedes)	**siguen**	**han seguido**

	PRETERITE	IMPERFECT
(yo)	**seguí**	**seguía**
(tú)	**seguiste**	**seguías**
(él/ella/usted)	**siguió**	**seguía**
(nosotros/as)	**seguimos**	**seguíamos**
(vosotros/as)	**seguisteis**	**seguíais**
(ellos/ellas/ ustedes)	**siguieron**	**seguían**

GERUND	PAST PARTICIPLE
siguiendo	**seguido**

	FUTURE	CONDITIONAL
(yo)	**seguiré**	**seguiría**
(tú)	**seguirás**	**seguirías**
(él/ella/usted)	**seguirá**	**seguiría**
(nosotros/as)	**seguiremos**	**seguiríamos**
(vosotros/as)	**seguiréis**	**seguiríais**
(ellos/ellas/ ustedes)	**seguirán**	**seguirían**

	PRESENT SUBJUNCTIVE	IMPERFECT SUBJUNCTIVE
(yo)	**siga**	**siguiera** or **siguiese**
(tú)	**sigas**	**siguieras** or **siguieses**
(él/ella/usted)	**siga**	**siguiera** or **siguiese**
(nosotros/as)	**sigamos**	**siguiéramos** or **siguiésemos**
(vosotros/as)	**sigáis**	**siguierais** or **siguieseis**
(ellos/ellas/ ustedes)	**sigan**	**siguieran** or **siguiesen**

IMPERATIVE

sigue / seguid

Use the present subjunctive in all cases other than these **tú** and **vosotros** affirmative forms.

EXAMPLE PHRASES

Si **sigues** así, acabarás mal.
If you go on like this you'll end up badly.

¿Te **han seguido**?
Have you been followed?

Siguió cantando como si nada.
He went on singing as if nothing was the matter.

El ordenador **seguía** funcionando a pesar del apagón.
The computer went on working in spite of the power cut.

Les **estuvimos siguiendo** mucho rato.
We followed them for a long time.

Nos seguiremos viendo.
We will go on seeing each other.

Quiero que **sigas** estudiando.
I want you to go on with your studies.

Si **siguieras** mis consejos, te iría muchísimo mejor.
You'd be much better off if you followed my advice.

Siga por esta calle hasta el final.
Go on till you get to the end of the street.

Remember that subject pronouns are not used very often in Spanish.

sentir (to feel; to be sorry)

	PRESENT	PRESENT PERFECT
(yo)	**siento**	**he sentido**
(tú)	**sientes**	**has sentido**
(él/ella/usted)	**siente**	**ha sentido**
(nosotros/as)	**sentimos**	**hemos sentido**
(vosotros/as)	**sentís**	**habéis sentido**
(ellos/ellas/ ustedes)	**sienten**	**han sentido**

	PRETERITE	IMPERFECT
(yo)	**sentí**	**sentía**
(tú)	**sentiste**	**sentías**
(él/ella/usted)	**sintió**	**sentía**
(nosotros/as)	**sentimos**	**sentíamos**
(vosotros/as)	**sentisteis**	**sentíais**
(ellos/ellas/ ustedes)	**sintieron**	**sentían**

GERUND	PAST PARTICIPLE
sintiendo	**sentido**

	FUTURE	CONDITIONAL
(yo)	**sentiré**	**sentiría**
(tú)	**sentirás**	**sentirías**
(él/ella/usted)	**sentirá**	**sentiría**
(nosotros/as)	**sentiremos**	**sentiríamos**
(vosotros/as)	**sentiréis**	**sentiríais**
(ellos/ellas/ ustedes)	**sentirán**	**sentirían**

	PRESENT SUBJUNCTIVE	IMPERFECT SUBJUNCTIVE
(yo)	**sienta**	**sintiera** or **sintiese**
(tú)	**sientas**	**sintieras** or **sintieses**
(él/ella/usted)	**sienta**	**sintiera** or **sintiese**
(nosotros/as)	**sintamos**	**sintiéramos** or **sintiésemos**
(vosotros/as)	**sintáis**	**sintierais** or **sintieseis**
(ellos/ellas/ ustedes)	**sientan**	**sintieran** or **sintiesen**

IMPERATIVE

siente / sentid

Use the present subjunctive in all cases other than these **tú** and **vosotros** affirmative forms.

EXAMPLE PHRASES

Te vas a **sentir** sola.
You'll feel lonely.

Siento mucho lo que pasó.
I'm really sorry about what happened.

Ha sentido mucho la muerte de su padre.
He has been greatly affected by his father's death.

Sentí un pinchazo en la pierna.
I felt a sharp pain in my leg.

Me sentía muy mal.
I didn't feel well at all.

Al principio **te sentirás** un poco raro.
You'll feel a bit strange at first.

Yo **sentiría** mucho que se fuera de la empresa.
I'd be really sorry if you left the firm.

No creo que lo **sienta**.
I don't think she's sorry.

Sería mucho más preocupante si no **sintiera** la pierna.
It would be much more worrying if he couldn't feel his leg.

Remember that subject pronouns are not used very often in Spanish.

ser (to be)

	PRESENT	PRESENT PERFECT
(yo)	**soy**	**he sido**
(tú)	**eres**	**has sido**
(él/ella/usted)	**es**	**ha sido**
(nosotros/as)	**somos**	**hemos sido**
(vosotros/as)	**sois**	**habéis sido**
(ellos/ellas/ustedes)	**son**	**han sido**

	PRETERITE	IMPERFECT
(yo)	**fui**	**era**
(tú)	**fuiste**	**eras**
(él/ella/usted)	**fue**	**era**
(nosotros/as)	**fuimos**	**éramos**
(vosotros/as)	**fuisteis**	**erais**
(ellos/ellas/ustedes)	**fueron**	**eran**

GERUND	PAST PARTICIPLE
siendo	**sido**

	FUTURE	CONDITIONAL
(yo)	**seré**	**sería**
(tú)	**serás**	**serías**
(él/ella/usted)	**será**	**sería**
(nosotros/as)	**seremos**	**seríamos**
(vosotros/as)	**seréis**	**seríais**
(ellos/ellas/ustedes)	**serán**	**serían**

	PRESENT SUBJUNCTIVE	IMPERFECT SUBJUNCTIVE
(yo)	**sea**	**fuera** or **fuese**
(tú)	**seas**	**fueras** or **fueses**
(él/ella/usted)	**sea**	**fuera** or **fuese**
(nosotros/as)	**seamos**	**fuéramos** or **fuésemos**
(vosotros/as)	**seáis**	**fuerais** or **fueseis**
(ellos/ellas/ustedes)	**sean**	**fueran** or **fuesen**

IMPERATIVE

sé / sed

Use the present subjunctive in all cases other than these **tú** and **vosotros** affirmative forms.

EXAMPLE PHRASES

Soy español.
I'm Spanish.

Estás siendo muy paciente con él.
You're being very patient with him.

Ha sido un duro golpe.
It was a major blow.

¿**Fuiste** tú el que llamó?
Was it you who phoned?

Era de noche.
It was dark.

Será de Joaquín.
It must be Joaquin's.

Eso **sería** estupendo.
That would be great.

O **sea**, que no vienes.
So you're not coming.

No **seas** tan perfeccionista.
Don't be such a perfectionist.

¡**Sed** buenos!
Behave yourselves!

Remember that subject pronouns are not used very often in Spanish.

soler (to be in the habit of; to be accustomed to)

	PRESENT	PRESENT PERFECT
(yo)	**suelo**	not used
(tú)	**sueles**	
(él/ella/usted)	**suele**	
(nosotros/as)	**solemos**	
(vosotros/as)	**soléis**	
(ellos/ellas/ ustedes)	**suelen**	

	PRETERITE	IMPERFECT
(yo)	not used	**solía**
(tú)		**solías**
(él/ella/usted)		**solía**
(nosotros/as)		**solíamos**
(vosotros/as)		**solíais**
(ellos/ellas/ ustedes)		**solían**

GERUND	PAST PARTICIPLE
soliendo	not used

	FUTURE	CONDITIONAL
(yo)	not used	not used
(tú)		
(él/ella/usted)		
(nosotros/as)		
(vosotros/as)		
(ellos/ellas/ ustedes)		

	PRESENT SUBJUNCTIVE	IMPERFECT SUBJUNCTIVE
(yo)	**suela**	**soliera** or **soliese**
(tú)	**suelas**	**solieras** or **solieses**
(él/ella/usted)	**suela**	**soliera** or **soliese**
(nosotros/as)	**solamos**	**soliéramos** or **soliésemos**
(vosotros/as)	**soláis**	**solierais** or **solieseis**
(ellos/ellas/ ustedes)	**suelan**	**solieran** or **soliesen**

IMPERATIVE

not used

EXAMPLE PHRASES

Suele salir a las ocho.
He usually goes out at eight.

Solíamos ir todos los años a la playa.
We used to go to the beach every year.

Remember that subject pronouns are not used very often in Spanish.

soltar (to let go of; to release)

	PRESENT	PRESENT PERFECT
(yo)	**suelto**	**he soltado**
(tú)	**sueltas**	**has soltado**
(él/ella/usted)	**suelta**	**ha soltado**
(nosotros/as)	**soltamos**	**hemos soltado**
(vosotros/as)	**soltáis**	**habéis soltado**
(ellos/ellas/ ustedes)	**sueltan**	**han soltado**

	PRETERITE	IMPERFECT
(yo)	**solté**	**soltaba**
(tú)	**soltaste**	**soltabas**
(él/ella/usted)	**soltó**	**soltaba**
(nosotros/as)	**soltamos**	**soltábamos**
(vosotros/as)	**soltasteis**	**soltabais**
(ellos/ellas/ ustedes)	**soltaron**	**soltaban**

GERUND	PAST PARTICIPLE
soltando	**soltado**

	FUTURE	CONDITIONAL
(yo)	**soltaré**	**soltaría**
(tú)	**soltarás**	**soltarías**
(él/ella/usted)	**soltará**	**soltaría**
(nosotros/as)	**soltaremos**	**soltaríamos**
(vosotros/as)	**soltaréis**	**soltaríais**
(ellos/ellas/ ustedes)	**soltarán**	**soltarían**

	PRESENT SUBJUNCTIVE	IMPERFECT SUBJUNCTIVE
(yo)	**suelte**	**soltara** or **soltase**
(tú)	**sueltes**	**soltaras** or **soltases**
(él/ella/usted)	**suelte**	**soltara** or **soltase**
(nosotros/as)	**soltemos**	**soltáramos** or **soltásemos**
(vosotros/as)	**soltéis**	**soltarais** or **soltaseis**
(ellos/ellas/ ustedes)	**suelten**	**soltaran** or **soltasen**

IMPERATIVE
suelta / soltad

Use the present subjunctive in all cases other than these **tú** and **vosotros** affirmative forms.

EXAMPLE PHRASES

Al final logró **soltarse**.
Eventually she managed to break free.

No para de **soltar** tacos.
He swears all the time.

¿Por qué no **te sueltas** el pelo?
Why don't you have your hair loose?

Han soltado a los rehenes.
They've released the hostages.

Soltó una carcajada.
He burst out laughing.

Te **soltaré** el brazo si me dices dónde está.
I'll let go of your arm if you tell me where he is.

Te dije que lo **soltaras**.
I told you to let it go.

No **sueltes** la cuerda.
Don't let go of the rope.

¡**Suéltame**!
Let me go!

Remember that subject pronouns are not used very often in Spanish.

sonar (to sound; to ring)

	PRESENT	PRESENT PERFECT
(yo)	**sueno**	**he sonado**
(tú)	**suenas**	**has sonado**
(él/ella/usted)	**suena**	**ha sonado**
(nosotros/as)	**sonamos**	**hemos sonado**
(vosotros/as)	**sonáis**	**habéis sonado**
(ellos/ellas/ ustedes)	**suenan**	**han sonado**

	PRETERITE	IMPERFECT
(yo)	**soné**	**sonaba**
(tú)	**sonaste**	**sonabas**
(él/ella/usted)	**sonó**	**sonaba**
(nosotros/as)	**sonamos**	**sonábamos**
(vosotros/as)	**sonasteis**	**sonabais**
(ellos/ellas/ ustedes)	**sonaron**	**sonaban**

GERUND	PAST PARTICIPLE
sonando	**sonado**

	FUTURE	CONDITIONAL
(yo)	**sonaré**	**sonaría**
(tú)	**sonarás**	**sonarías**
(él/ella/usted)	**sonará**	**sonaría**
(nosotros/as)	**sonaremos**	**sonaríamos**
(vosotros/as)	**sonaréis**	**sonaríais**
(ellos/ellas/ ustedes)	**sonarán**	**sonarían**

	PRESENT SUBJUNCTIVE	IMPERFECT SUBJUNCTIVE
(yo)	**suene**	**sonara** or **sonase**
(tú)	**suenes**	**sonaras** or **sonases**
(él/ella/usted)	**suene**	**sonara** or **sonase**
(nosotros/as)	**sonemos**	**sonáramos** or **sonásemos**
(vosotros/as)	**sonéis**	**sonarais** or **sonaseis**
(ellos/ellas/ ustedes)	**suenen**	**sonaran** or **sonasen**

IMPERATIVE

suena / sonad

Use the present subjunctive in all cases other than these **tú** and **vosotros** affirmative forms.

EXAMPLE PHRASES

¿**Te suena** su nombre?
Does her name sound familiar?

Ha sonado tu móvil.
Your mobile rang.

Justo en ese momento **sonó** el timbre.
Just then the bell rang.

Sonabas un poco triste por teléfono.
You sounded a bit sad on the phone.

Estaba sonando el teléfono.
The phone was ringing.

Hay que esperar a que **suene** un pitido.
We have to wait until we hear a beep.

¡**Suénate** la nariz!
Blow your nose!

Remember that subject pronouns are not used very often in Spanish.

temer (to be afraid)

	PRESENT	PRESENT PERFECT
(yo)	**temo**	**he temido**
(tú)	**temes**	**has temido**
(él/ella/usted)	**teme**	**ha temido**
(nosotros/as)	**tememos**	**hemos temido**
(vosotros/as)	**teméis**	**habéis temido**
(ellos/ellas/ ustedes)	**temen**	**han temido**

	PRETERITE	IMPERFECT
(yo)	**temí**	**temía**
(tú)	**temiste**	**temías**
(él/ella/usted)	**temió**	**temía**
(nosotros/as)	**temimos**	**temíamos**
(vosotros/as)	**temisteis**	**temíais**
(ellos/ellas/ ustedes)	**temieron**	**temían**

GERUND	PAST PARTICIPLE
temiendo	**temido**

	FUTURE	CONDITIONAL
(yo)	**temeré**	**temería**
(tú)	**temerás**	**temerías**
(él/ella/usted)	**temerá**	**temería**
(nosotros/as)	**temeremos**	**temeríamos**
(vosotros/as)	**temeréis**	**temeríais**
(ellos/ellas/ ustedes)	**temerán**	**temerían**

	PRESENT SUBJUNCTIVE	IMPERFECT SUBJUNCTIVE
(yo)	**tema**	**temiera** or **temiese**
(tú)	**temas**	**temieras** or **temieses**
(él/ella/usted)	**tema**	**temiera** or **temiese**
(nosotros/as)	**temamos**	**temiéramos** or **temiésemos**
(vosotros/as)	**temáis**	**temierais** or **temieseis**
(ellos/ellas/ ustedes)	**teman**	**temieran** or **temiesen**

IMPERATIVE

teme / temed

Use the present subjunctive in all cases other than these **tú** and **vosotros** affirmative forms.

EXAMPLE PHRASES

Me temo que no.
I'm afraid not.

Se temen lo peor.
They fear the worst.

–Ha empezado a llover. –**Me** lo **temía**.
"It's started raining." – "I was afraid it would."

Temí ofenderles.
I was afraid of offending them.

Temían por su seguridad.
They feared for their security.

No **temas.**
Don't be afraid.

Remember that subject pronouns are not used very often in Spanish.

tener (to have)

	PRESENT	PRESENT PERFECT
(yo)	**tengo**	**he tenido**
(tú)	**tienes**	**has tenido**
(él/ella/usted)	**tiene**	**ha tenido**
(nosotros/as)	**tenemos**	**hemos tenido**
(vosotros/as)	**tenéis**	**habéis tenido**
(ellos/ellas/ ustedes)	**tienen**	**ha tenido**

	PRETERITE	IMPERFECT
(yo)	**tuve**	**tenía**
(tú)	**tuviste**	**tenías**
(él/ella/usted)	**tuvo**	**tenía**
(nosotros/as)	**tuvimos**	**teníamos**
(vosotros/as)	**tuvisteis**	**teníais**
(ellos/ellas/ ustedes)	**tuvieron**	**tenían**

GERUND	PAST PARTICIPLE
teniendo	**tenido**

	FUTURE	CONDITIONAL
(yo)	**tendré**	**tendría**
(tú)	**tendrás**	**tendrías**
(él/ella/usted)	**tendrá**	**tendría**
(nosotros/as)	**tendremos**	**tendríamos**
(vosotros/as)	**tendréis**	**tendríais**
(ellos/ellas/ ustedes)	**tendrán**	**tendrían**

	PRESENT SUBJUNCTIVE	IMPERFECT SUBJUNCTIVE
(yo)	**tenga**	**tuviera** or **tuviese**
(tú)	**tengas**	**tuvieras** or **tuvieses**
(él/ella/usted)	**tenga**	**tuviera** or **tuviese**
(nosotros/as)	**tengamos**	**tuviéramos** or **tuviésemos**
(vosotros/as)	**tengáis**	**tuvierais** or **tuvieseis**
(ellos/ellas/ ustedes)	**tengan**	**tuvieran** or **tuviesen**

IMPERATIVE
ten / tened

Use the present subjunctive in all cases other than these **tú** and **vosotros** affirmative forms.

EXAMPLE PHRASES

Tengo sed.
I'm thirsty.

Están teniendo muchos problemas con el coche.
They're having a lot of trouble with the car.

Ha tenido una gripe muy fuerte.
She's had very bad flu.

Tuvimos que irnos.
We had to leave.

No **tenía** suficiente dinero.
She didn't have enough money.

Tendrás que pagarlo tú.
You'll have to pay for it yourself.

Tendrías que comer más.
You should eat more.

No creo que **tenga** suficiente dinero.
I don't think I've got enough money.

Si **tuviera** tiempo, haría un curso de catalán.
If I had time, I'd do a Catalan course.

Ten cuidado.
Be careful.

No **tengas** miedo.
Don't be afraid.

Remember that subject pronouns are not used very often in Spanish.

tocar (to touch; to play)

	PRESENT	PRESENT PERFECT
(yo)	**toco**	**he tocado**
(tú)	**tocas**	**has tocado**
(él/ella/usted)	**toca**	**ha tocado**
(nosotros/as)	**tocamos**	**hemos tocado**
(vosotros/as)	**tocáis**	**habéis tocado**
(ellos/ellas/ ustedes)	**tocan**	**ha tocado**

	PRETERITE	IMPERFECT
(yo)	**toqué**	**tocaba**
(tú)	**tocaste**	**tocabas**
(él/ella/usted)	**tocó**	**tocaba**
(nosotros/as)	**tocamos**	**tocábamos**
(vosotros/as)	**tocasteis**	**tocabais**
(ellos/ellas/ ustedes)	**tocaron**	**tocaban**

	GERUND	PAST PARTICIPLE
	tocando	**tocado**

	FUTURE	CONDITIONAL
(yo)	**tocaré**	**tocaría**
(tú)	**tocarás**	**tocarías**
(él/ella/usted)	**tocará**	**tocaría**
(nosotros/as)	**tocaremos**	**tocaríamos**
(vosotros/as)	**tocaréis**	**tocaríais**
(ellos/ellas/ ustedes)	**tocarán**	**tocarían**

	PRESENT SUBJUNCTIVE	IMPERFECT SUBJUNCTIVE
(yo)	**toque**	**tocara** or **tocase**
(tú)	**toques**	**tocaras** or **tocases**
(él/ella/usted)	**toque**	**tocara** or **tocase**
(nosotros/as)	**toquemos**	**tocáramos** or **tocásemos**
(vosotros/as)	**toquéis**	**tocarais** or **tocaseis**
(ellos/ellas/ ustedes)	**toquen**	**tocaran** or **tocasen**

IMPERATIVE

toca / tocad

Use the present subjunctive in all cases other than these **tú** and **vosotros** affirmative forms.

EXAMPLE PHRASES

Toca el violín.
He plays the violin.

Te **toca** fregar los platos.
It's your turn to do the dishes.

Me **ha tocado** el peor asiento.
I've ended up with the worst seat.

Le **tocó** la lotería.
He won the lottery.

Me **tocaba** tirar a mí.
It was my turn.

Sabía que me **tocaría** ir a mí.
I knew I'd be the one to have to go.

No lo **toques**.
Don't touch it.

Tócalo, verás que suave.
Touch it and see how soft it is.

Remember that subject pronouns are not used very often in Spanish.

torcer (to twist)

	PRESENT	PRESENT PERFECT
(yo)	**tuerzo**	**he torcido**
(tú)	**tuerces**	**has torcido**
(él/ella/usted)	**tuerce**	**ha torcido**
(nosotros/as)	**torcemos**	**hemos torcido**
(vosotros/as)	**torcéis**	**habéis torcido**
(ellos/ellas/ ustedes)	**tuercen**	**han torcido**

	PRETERITE	IMPERFECT
(yo)	**torcí**	**torcía**
(tú)	**torciste**	**torcías**
(él/ella/usted)	**torció**	**torcía**
(nosotros/as)	**torcimos**	**torcíamos**
(vosotros/as)	**torcisteis**	**torcíais**
(ellos/ellas/ ustedes)	**torcieron**	**torcían**

GERUND	PAST PARTICIPLE
torciendo	**torcido**

	FUTURE	CONDITIONAL
(yo)	**torceré**	**torcería**
(tú)	**torcerás**	**torcerías**
(él/ella/usted)	**torcerá**	**torcería**
(nosotros/as)	**torceremos**	**torceríamos**
(vosotros/as)	**torceréis**	**torceríais**
(ellos/ellas/ ustedes)	**torcerán**	**torcerían**

	PRESENT SUBJUNCTIVE	IMPERFECT SUBJUNCTIVE
(yo)	**tuerza**	**torciera** or **torciese**
(tú)	**tuerzas**	**torcieras** or **torcieses**
(él/ella/usted)	**tuerza**	**torciera** or **torciese**
(nosotros/as)	**torzamos**	**torciéramos** or **torciésemos**
(vosotros/as)	**torzáis**	**torcierais** or **torcieseis**
(ellos/ellas/ ustedes)	**tuerzan**	**torcieran** or **torciesen**

IMPERATIVE

tuerce / torced

Use the present subjunctive in all cases other than these **tú** and **vosotros** affirmative forms.

EXAMPLE PHRASES

Acaba de **torcer** la esquina.
She has just turned the corner.

El sendero **tuerce** luego a la derecha.
Later on the path bends round to the right.

Se le **ha torcido** la muñeca.
She's sprained her wrist.

Se me **torció** el tobillo.
I twisted my ankle.

Tuerza a la izquierda.
Turn left.

Tuércelo un poco más.
Twist it a little more.

Remember that subject pronouns are not used very often in Spanish.

traer (to bring)

	PRESENT	PRESENT PERFECT
(yo)	**traigo**	**he traído**
(tú)	**traes**	**has traído**
(él/ella/usted)	**trae**	**ha traído**
(nosotros/as)	**traemos**	**hemos traído**
(vosotros/as)	**traéis**	**habéis traído**
(ellos/ellas/ustedes)	**traen**	**han traído**

	PRETERITE	IMPERFECT
(yo)	**traje**	**traía**
(tú)	**trajiste**	**traías**
(él/ella/usted)	**trajo**	**traía**
(nosotros/as)	**trajimos**	**traíamos**
(vosotros/as)	**trajisteis**	**traíais**
(ellos/ellas/ustedes)	**trajeron**	**traían**

GERUND	PAST PARTICIPLE
trayendo	**traído**

	FUTURE	CONDITIONAL
(yo)	**traeré**	**traería**
(tú)	**traerás**	**traerías**
(él/ella/usted)	**traerá**	**traería**
(nosotros/as)	**traeremos**	**traeríamos**
(vosotros/as)	**traeréis**	**traeríais**
(ellos/ellas/ustedes)	**traerán**	**traerían**

	PRESENT SUBJUNCTIVE	IMPERFECT SUBJUNCTIVE
(yo)	**traiga**	**trajera** or **trajese**
(tú)	**traigas**	**trajeras** or **trajeses**
(él/ella/usted)	**traiga**	**trajera** or **trajese**
(nosotros/as)	**traigamos**	**trajéramos** or **trajésemos**
(vosotros/as)	**traigáis**	**trajerais** or **trajeseis**
(ellos/ellas/ustedes)	**traigan**	**trajeran** or **trajesen**

IMPERATIVE

trae / traed

Use the present subjunctive in all cases other than these **tú** and **vosotros** affirmative forms.

EXAMPLE PHRASES

¿Me puedes **traer** una toalla?
Can you bring me a towel?

Nos **está trayendo** muchos problemas.
It's causing us a lot of trouble.

¿**Has traído** lo que te pedí?
Have you brought what I asked for?

Traía un vestido nuevo.
She was wearing a new dress.

No **trajo** el dinero.
He didn't bring the money.

Me pregunto qué **se traerán** entre manos.
I wonder what they're up to.

Se lo **traería** de África.
He must have brought it over from Africa.

Dile que **traiga** a algún amigo.
Tell him to bring a friend with him.

Trae eso.
Give that here.

Remember that subject pronouns are not used very often in Spanish.

valer (to be worth)

	PRESENT	PRESENT PERFECT
(yo)	**valgo**	**he valido**
(tú)	**vales**	**has valido**
(él/ella/usted)	**vale**	**ha valido**
(nosotros/as)	**valemos**	**hemos valido**
(vosotros/as)	**valéis**	**habéis valido**
(ellos/ellas/ ustedes)	**valen**	**han valido**

	PRETERITE	IMPERFECT
(yo)	**valí**	**valía**
(tú)	**valiste**	**valías**
(él/ella/usted)	**valió**	**valía**
(nosotros/as)	**valimos**	**valíamos**
(vosotros/as)	**valisteis**	**valíais**
(ellos/ellas/ ustedes)	**valieron**	**valían**

GERUND	PAST PARTICIPLE
valiendo	**valido**

	FUTURE	CONDITIONAL
(yo)	**valdré**	**valdría**
(tú)	**valdrás**	**valdrías**
(él/ella/usted)	**valdrá**	**valdría**
(nosotros/as)	**valdremos**	**valdríamos**
(vosotros/as)	**valdréis**	**valdríais**
(ellos/ellas/ ustedes)	**valdrán**	**valdrían**

	PRESENT SUBJUNCTIVE	IMPERFECT SUBJUNCTIVE
(yo)	**valga**	**valiera** or **valiese**
(tú)	**valgas**	**valieras** or **valieses**
(él/ella/usted)	**valga**	**valiera** or **valiese**
(nosotros/as)	**valgamos**	**valiéramos** or **valiésemos**
(vosotros/as)	**valgáis**	**valierais** or **valieseis**
(ellos/ellas/ ustedes)	**valgan**	**valieran** or **valiesen**

IMPERATIVE

vale / valed

Use the present subjunctive in all cases other than these **tú** and **vosotros** affirmative forms.

EXAMPLE PHRASES

No puede **valerse** por sí mismo.
He can't look after himself.

¿Cuánto **vale** eso?
How much is that?

¿Vale?
OK?

No le **valió** de nada suplicar.
Begging got her nowhere.

No **valía** la pena.
It wasn't worth it.

Valdrá unos 500 euros.
It must cost around 500 euros.

Yo no **valdría** para enfermera.
I'd make a hopeless nurse.

Valga lo que **valga**, lo compro.
I'll buy it, no matter how much it costs.

Remember that subject pronouns are not used very often in Spanish.

vencer (to win; to beat)

	PRESENT	PRESENT PERFECT
(yo)	**venzo**	**he vencido**
(tú)	**vences**	**has vencido**
(él/ella/usted)	**vence**	**ha vencido**
(nosotros/as)	**vencemos**	**hemos vencido**
(vosotros/as)	**vencéis**	**habéis vencido**
(ellos/ellas/ ustedes)	**vencen**	**han vencido**

	PRETERITE	IMPERFECT
(yo)	**vencí**	**vencía**
(tú)	**venciste**	**vencías**
(él/ella/usted)	**venció**	**vencía**
(nosotros/as)	**vencimos**	**vencíamos**
(vosotros/as)	**vencisteis**	**vencíais**
(ellos/ellas/ ustedes)	**vencieron**	**vencían**

GERUND	PAST PARTICIPLE
venciendo	**vencido**

	FUTURE	CONDITIONAL
(yo)	**venceré**	**vencería**
(tú)	**vencerás**	**vencerías**
(él/ella/usted)	**vencerá**	**vencería**
(nosotros/as)	**venceremos**	**venceríamos**
(vosotros/as)	**venceréis**	**venceríais**
(ellos/ellas/ ustedes)	**vencerán**	**vencerían**

	PRESENT SUBJUNCTIVE	IMPERFECT SUBJUNCTIVE
(yo)	**venza**	**venciera** or **venciese**
(tú)	**venzas**	**vencieras** or **vencieses**
(él/ella/usted)	**venza**	**venciera** or **venciese**
(nosotros/as)	**venzamos**	**venciéramos** or **venciésemos**
(vosotros/as)	**venzáis**	**vencierais** or **vencieseis**
(ellos/ellas/ ustedes)	**venzan**	**vencieran** or **venciesen**

IMPERATIVE

vence / venced

Use the present subjunctive in all cases other than these **tú** and **vosotros** affirmative forms.

EXAMPLE PHRASES

Tienes que **vencer** el miedo.
You must overcome your fear.

El plazo de matrícula **vence** mañana.
Tomorrow is the last day for registration.

Finalmente le **ha vencido** el sueño.
At last, he was overcome by sleep.

Vencimos por dos a uno.
We won two-one.

Le **vencía** la curiosidad.
His curiosity got the better of him.

Nuestro ejército **vencerá**.
Our army will be victorious.

No dejes que te **venza** la impaciencia.
Don't let your impatience get the better of you.

Remember that subject pronouns are not used very often in Spanish.

venir (to come)

	PRESENT	PRESENT PERFECT
(yo)	**vengo**	**he venido**
(tú)	**vienes**	**has venido**
(él/ella/usted)	**viene**	**ha venido**
(nosotros/as)	**venimos**	**hemos venido**
(vosotros/as)	**venís**	**habéis venido**
(ellos/ellas/ ustedes)	**vienen**	**han venido**

	PRETERITE	IMPERFECT
(yo)	**vine**	**venía**
(tú)	**viniste**	**venías**
(él/ella/usted)	**vino**	**venía**
(nosotros/as)	**vinimos**	**veníamos**
(vosotros/as)	**vinisteis**	**veníais**
(ellos/ellas/ ustedes)	**vinieron**	**venían**

GERUND	PAST PARTICIPLE
viniendo	**venido**

	FUTURE	CONDITIONAL
(yo)	**vendré**	**vendría**
(tú)	**vendrás**	**vendrías**
(él/ella/usted)	**vendrá**	**vendría**
(nosotros/as)	**vendremos**	**vendríamos**
(vosotros/as)	**vendréis**	**vendríais**
(ellos/ellas/ ustedes)	**vendrán**	**vendrían**

	PRESENT SUBJUNCTIVE	IMPERFECT SUBJUNCTIVE
(yo)	**venga**	**viniera** or **viniese**
(tú)	**vengas**	**vinieras** or **vinieses**
(él/ella/usted)	**venga**	**viniera** or **viniese**
(nosotros/as)	**vengamos**	**viniéramos** or **viniésemos**
(vosotros/as)	**vengáis**	**vinierais** or **vinieseis**
(ellos/ellas/ ustedes)	**vengan**	**vinieran** or **viniesen**

IMPERATIVE
ven / venid

Use the present subjunctive in all cases other than these **tú** and **vosotros** affirmative forms.

EXAMPLE PHRASES

Vengo andando desde la playa.
I've walked all the way from the beach.

La casa **se está viniendo** abajo.
The house is falling apart.

Ha venido en taxi.
He came by taxi.

Vinieron a verme al hospital.
They came to see me in hospital.

La noticia **venía** en el periódico.
The news was in the paper.

¿**Vendrás** conmigo al cine?
Will you come to the cinema with me?

A mí me **vendría** mejor el sábado.
Saturday would be better for me.

¡**Venga**, vámonos!
Come on, let's go!

No **vengas** si no quieres.
Don't come if you don't want to.

¡**Ven** aquí!
Come here!

Remember that subject pronouns are not used very often in Spanish.

ver (to see)

	PRESENT	PRESENT PERFECT
(yo)	**veo**	**he visto**
(tú)	**ves**	**has visto**
(él/ella/usted)	**ve**	**ha visto**
(nosotros/as)	**vemos**	**hemos visto**
(vosotros/as)	**veis**	**habéis visto**
(ellos/ellas/ ustedes)	**ven**	**han visto**

	PRETERITE	IMPERFECT
(yo)	**vi**	**veía**
(tú)	**viste**	**veías**
(él/ella/usted)	**vio**	**veía**
(nosotros/as)	**vimos**	**veíamos**
(vosotros/as)	**visteis**	**veíais**
(ellos/ellas/ ustedes)	**vieron**	**veían**

	GERUND	PAST PARTICIPLE
	viendo	**visto**

	FUTURE	CONDITIONAL
(yo)	**veré**	**vería**
(tú)	**verás**	**verías**
(él/ella/usted)	**verá**	**vería**
(nosotros/as)	**veremos**	**veríamos**
(vosotros/as)	**veréis**	**veríais**
(ellos/ellas/ ustedes)	**verán**	**verían**

	PRESENT SUBJUNCTIVE	IMPERFECT SUBJUNCTIVE
(yo)	**vea**	**viera** or **viese**
(tú)	**veas**	**vieras** or **vieses**
(él/ella/usted)	**vea**	**viera** or **viese**
(nosotros/as)	**veamos**	**viéramos** or **viésemos**
(vosotros/as)	**veáis**	**vierais** or **vieseis**
(ellos/ellas/ ustedes)	**vean**	**vieran** or **viesen**

IMPERATIVE

ve / ved

Use the present subjunctive in all cases other than these **tú** and **vosotros** affirmative forms.

EXAMPLE PHRASES

No **veo** muy bien.
I can't see very well.

Están viendo la televisión.
They're watching television.

No **he visto** esa película.
I haven't seen that film.

¿**Viste** lo que pasó?
Did you see what happened?

Los **veía** a todos desde la ventana.
I could see them all from the window.

Eso ya se **verá**.
We'll see.

No **veas** cómo se puso.
He got incredibly worked up.

¡Si **vieras** cómo ha cambiado todo aquello!
If you could see how everything has changed.

Veamos, ¿qué le pasa?
Let's see now, what's the matter?

Remember that subject pronouns are not used very often in Spanish.

verter (to pour)

	PRESENT	PRESENT PERFECT
(yo)	**vierto**	**he vertido**
(tú)	**viertes**	**has vertido**
(él/ella/usted)	**vierte**	**ha vertido**
(nosotros/as)	**vertemos**	**hemos vertido**
(vosotros/as)	**vertéis**	**habéis vertido**
(ellos/ellas/ustedes)	**vierten**	**han vertido**

	PRETERITE	IMPERFECT
(yo)	**vertí**	**vertía**
(tú)	**vertiste**	**vertías**
(él/ella/usted)	**vertió**	**vertía**
(nosotros/as)	**vertimos**	**vertíamos**
(vosotros/as)	**vertisteis**	**vertíais**
(ellos/ellas/ustedes)	**vertieron**	**vertían**

GERUND	PAST PARTICIPLE
vertiendo	**vertido**

	FUTURE	CONDITIONAL
(yo)	**verteré**	**vertería**
(tú)	**verterás**	**verterías**
(él/ella/usted)	**verterá**	**vertería**
(nosotros/as)	**verteremos**	**verteríamos**
(vosotros/as)	**verteréis**	**verteríais**
(ellos/ellas/ustedes)	**verterán**	**verterían**

	PRESENT SUBJUNCTIVE	IMPERFECT SUBJUNCTIVE
(yo)	**vierta**	**vertiera** or **vertiese**
(tú)	**viertas**	**vertieras** or **vertieses**
(él/ella/usted)	**vierta**	**vertiera** or **vertiese**
(nosotros/as)	**vertamos**	**vertiéramos** or **vertiésemos**
(vosotros/as)	**vertáis**	**vertierais** or **vertieseis**
(ellos/ellas/ustedes)	**viertan**	**vertieran** or **vertiesen**

IMPERATIVE

vierte / verted

Use the present subjunctive in all cases other than these **tú** and **vosotros** affirmative forms.

EXAMPLE PHRASES

Primero **viertes** el contenido del sobre en un recipiente.
First you empty out the contents of the packet into a container.

Me **has vertido** agua encima.
You've spilt water on me.

Vertió un poco de leche en el cazo.
He poured some milk into the saucepan.

Se vertían muchos residuos radioactivos en el mar.
A lot of nuclear waste was dumped in the sea.

Se verterán muchas lágrimas por esto.
A lot of tears will be shed over this.

Ten cuidado no **viertas** el café.
Be careful you don't knock over the coffee.

Por favor, **vierta** el contenido del bolso sobre la mesa.
Please empty out your bag on the table.

Remember that subject pronouns are not used very often in Spanish.

vestir (to dress)

	PRESENT	PRESENT PERFECT
(yo)	**visto**	**he vestido**
(tú)	**vistes**	**has vestido**
(él/ella/usted)	**viste**	**ha vestido**
(nosotros/as)	**vestimos**	**hemos vestido**
(vosotros/as)	**vestís**	**habéis vestido**
(ellos/ellas/ ustedes)	**visten**	**han vestido**

	PRETERITE	IMPERFECT
(yo)	**vestí**	**vestía**
(tú)	**vestiste**	**vestías**
(él/ella/usted)	**vistió**	**vestía**
(nosotros/as)	**vestimos**	**vestíamos**
(vosotros/as)	**vestisteis**	**vestíais**
(ellos/ellas/ ustedes)	**vistieron**	**vestían**

GERUND	PAST PARTICIPLE
vistiendo	**vestido**

	FUTURE	CONDITIONAL
(yo)	**vestiré**	**vestiría**
(tú)	**vestirás**	**vestirías**
(él/ella/usted)	**vestirá**	**vestiría**
(nosotros/as)	**vestiremos**	**vestiríamos**
(vosotros/as)	**vestiréis**	**vestiríais**
(ellos/ellas/ ustedes)	**vestirán**	**vestirían**

	PRESENT SUBJUNCTIVE	IMPERFECT SUBJUNCTIVE
(yo)	**vista**	**vistiera** or **vistiese**
(tú)	**vistas**	**vistieras** or **vistieses**
(él/ella/usted)	**vista**	**vistiera** or **vistiese**
(nosotros/as)	**vistamos**	**vistiéramos** or **vistiésemos**
(vosotros/as)	**vistáis**	**vistierais** or **vistieseis**
(ellos/ellas/ ustedes)	**vistan**	**vistieran** or **vistiesen**

IMPERATIVE

viste / vestid

Use the present subjunctive in all cases other than these **tú** and **vosotros** affirmative forms.

EXAMPLE PHRASES

Tengo una familia que **vestir** y que alimentar.
I have a family to feed and clothe.

Viste bien.
She's a smart dresser.

Estaba vistiendo a los niños.
I was dressing the children.

Me he vestido en cinco minutos.
It took me five minutes to get dressed.

Se vistió de princesa.
She dressed up as a princess.

Vestía pantalones vaqueros y una camiseta.
He was wearing jeans and a T-shirt.

Su padre **vestirá** de uniforme.
Her father will wear a uniform.

¡**Vístete** de una vez!
For the last time, go and get dressed!

Remember that subject pronouns are not used very often in Spanish.

vivir (to live)

	PRESENT	PRESENT PERFECT
(yo)	**vivo**	**he vivido**
(tú)	**vives**	**has vivido**
(él/ella/usted)	**vive**	**ha vivido**
(nosotros/as)	**vivimos**	**hemos vivido**
(vosotros/as)	**vivís**	**habéis vivido**
(ellos/ellas/ ustedes)	**viven**	**han vivido**

	PRETERITE	IMPERFECT
(yo)	**viví**	**vivía**
(tú)	**viviste**	**vivías**
(él/ella/usted)	**vivió**	**vivía**
(nosotros/as)	**vivimos**	**vivíamos**
(vosotros/as)	**vivisteis**	**vivíais**
(ellos/ellas/ ustedes)	**vivieron**	**vivían**

GERUND	PAST PARTICIPLE
viviendo	**vivido**

	FUTURE	CONDITIONAL
(yo)	**viviré**	**viviría**
(tú)	**vivirás**	**vivirías**
(él/ella/usted)	**vivirá**	**viviría**
(nosotros/as)	**viviremos**	**viviríamos**
(vosotros/as)	**viviréis**	**viviríais**
(ellos/ellas/ ustedes)	**vivirán**	**vivirían**

	PRESENT SUBJUNCTIVE	IMPERFECT SUBJUNCTIVE
(yo)	**viva**	**viviera** or **viviese**
(tú)	**vivas**	**vivieras** or **vivieses**
(él/ella/usted)	**viva**	**viviera** or **viviese**
(nosotros/as)	**vivamos**	**viviéramos** or **viviésemos**
(vosotros/as)	**viváis**	**vivierais** or **vivieseis**
(ellos/ellas/ ustedes)	**vivan**	**vivieran** or **viviesen**

IMPERATIVE

vive / vivid

Use the present subjunctive in all cases other than these **tú** and **vosotros** affirmative forms.

EXAMPLE PHRASES

Me gusta **vivir** sola.
I like living on my own.

¿Dónde **vives**?
Where do you live?

Siempre **han vivido** muy bien.
They've always had a very comfortable life.

Vivían de su pensión.
They lived on his pension.

Viviremos en el centro de la ciudad.
We'll live in the city centre.

Si pudiéramos, **viviríamos** en el campo.
We'd live in the country if we could.

Si **vivierais** más cerca, nos veríamos más a menudo.
We'd see each other more often if you lived nearer.

¡Viva!
Hurray!

Remember that subject pronouns are not used very often in Spanish.

volcar (to overturn)

	PRESENT	PRESENT PERFECT
(yo)	**vuelco**	**he volcado**
(tú)	**vuelcas**	**has volcado**
(él/ella/usted)	**vuelca**	**ha volcado**
(nosotros/as)	**volcamos**	**hemos volcado**
(vosotros/as)	**volcáis**	**habéis volcado**
(ellos/ellas/ustedes)	**vuelcan**	**han volcado**

	PRETERITE	IMPERFECT
(yo)	**volqué**	**volcaba**
(tú)	**volcaste**	**volcabas**
(él/ella/usted)	**volcó**	**volcaba**
(nosotros/as)	**volcamos**	**volcábamos**
(vosotros/as)	**volcasteis**	**volcabais**
(ellos/ellas/ustedes)	**volcaron**	**volcaban**

GERUND	PAST PARTICIPLE
volcando	**volcado**

	FUTURE	CONDITIONAL
(yo)	**volcaré**	**volcaría**
(tú)	**volcarás**	**volcarías**
(él/ella/usted)	**volcará**	**volcaría**
(nosotros/as)	**volcaremos**	**volcaríamos**
(vosotros/as)	**volcaréis**	**volcaríais**
(ellos/ellas/ustedes)	**volcarán**	**volcarían**

	PRESENT SUBJUNCTIVE	IMPERFECT SUBJUNCTIVE
(yo)	**vuelque**	**volcara** or **volcase**
(tú)	**vuelques**	**volcaras** or **volcases**
(él/ella/usted)	**vuelque**	**volcara** or **volcase**
(nosotros/as)	**volquemos**	**volcáramos** or **volcásemos**
(vosotros/as)	**volquéis**	**volcarais** or **volcaseis**
(ellos/ellas/ustedes)	**vuelquen**	**volcaran** or **volcasen**

IMPERATIVE

vuelca / volcad

Use the present subjunctive in all cases other than these **tú** and **vosotros** affirmative forms.

EXAMPLE PHRASES

Se vuelca en su trabajo.
She throws herself into her work.

Se han volcado con nosotros.
They've been very kind to us.

El camión **volcó**.
The lorry overturned.

Si sigues moviéndote, harás que **vuelque** el bote.
If you keep on moving like that, you'll make the boat capsize.

Ten cuidado, no **vuelques** el vaso.
Be careful not to knock over the glass.

Vuelca el contenido sobre la cama.
Empty the contents onto the bed.

Remember that subject pronouns are not used very often in Spanish.

volver (to return)

	PRESENT	PRESENT PERFECT
(yo)	**vuelvo**	**he vuelto**
(tú)	**vuelves**	**has vuelto**
(él/ella/usted)	**vuelve**	**ha vuelto**
(nosotros/as)	**volvemos**	**hemos vuelto**
(vosotros/as)	**volvéis**	**habéis vuelto**
(ellos/ellas/ustedes)	**vuelven**	**han vuelto**

	PRETERITE	IMPERFECT
(yo)	**volví**	**volvía**
(tú)	**volviste**	**volvías**
(él/ella/usted)	**volvió**	**volvía**
(nosotros/as)	**volvimos**	**volvíamos**
(vosotros/as)	**volvisteis**	**volvíais**
(ellos/ellas/ustedes)	**volvieron**	**volvían**

GERUND	PAST PARTICIPLE
volviendo	**vuelto**

	FUTURE	CONDITIONAL
(yo)	**volveré**	**volvería**
(tú)	**volverás**	**volverías**
(él/ella/usted)	**volverá**	**volvería**
(nosotros/as)	**volveremos**	**volveríamos**
(vosotros/as)	**volveréis**	**volveríais**
(ellos/ellas/ustedes)	**volverán**	**volverían**

	PRESENT SUBJUNCTIVE	IMPERFECT SUBJUNCTIVE
(yo)	**vuelva**	**volviera** or **volviese**
(tú)	**vuelvas**	**volvieras** or **volvieses**
(él/ella/usted)	**vuelva**	**volviera** or **volviese**
(nosotros/as)	**volvamos**	**volviéramos** or **volviésemos**
(vosotros/as)	**volváis**	**volvierais** or **volvieseis**
(ellos/ellas/ustedes)	**vuelvan**	**volvieran** or **volviesen**

IMPERATIVE

vuelve / volved

Use the present subjunctive in all cases other than these **tú** and **vosotros** affirmative forms.

EXAMPLE PHRASES

Mi padre **vuelve** mañana.
My father's coming back tomorrow.

Se **está volviendo** muy pesado.
He's becoming a real pain in the neck.

Ha vuelto a casa.
He's gone back home.

Me volví para ver quién era.
I turned round to see who it was.

Volvía agotado de trabajar.
I used to come back exhausted from work.

Todo **volverá** a la normalidad.
Everything will go back to normal.

Yo **volvería** a intentarlo.
I'd try again.

No quiero que **vuelvas** a las andadas.
I don't want you to go back to your old ways.

No **vuelvas** por aquí.
Don't come back here.

¡**Vuelve** a la cama!
Go back to bed!

Remember that subject pronouns are not used very often in Spanish.

zurcir (to darn)

	PRESENT	PRESENT PERFECT
(yo)	**zurzo**	**he zurcido**
(tú)	**zurces**	**has zurcido**
(él/ella/usted)	**zurce**	**ha zurcido**
(nosotros/as)	**zurcimos**	**hemos zurcido**
(vosotros/as)	**zurcís**	**habéis zurcido**
(ellos/ellas/ustedes)	**zurcen**	**han zurcido**

	PRETERITE	IMPERFECT
(yo)	**zurcí**	**zurcía**
(tú)	**zurciste**	**zurcías**
(él/ella/usted)	**zurció**	**zurcía**
(nosotros/as)	**zurcimos**	**zurcíamos**
(vosotros/as)	**zurcisteis**	**zurcíais**
(ellos/ellas/ustedes)	**zurcieron**	**zurcían**

	GERUND	PAST PARTICIPLE
	zurciendo	**zurcido**

	FUTURE	CONDITIONAL
(yo)	**zurciré**	**zurciría**
(tú)	**zurcirás**	**zurcirías**
(él/ella/usted)	**zurcirá**	**zurciría**
(nosotros/as)	**zurciremos**	**zurciríamos**
(vosotros/as)	**zurciréis**	**zurciríais**
(ellos/ellas/ustedes)	**zurcirán**	**zurcirían**

	PRESENT SUBJUNCTIVE	IMPERFECT SUBJUNCTIVE
(yo)	**zurza**	**zurciera** or **zurciese**
(tú)	**zurzas**	**zurcieras** or **zurcieses**
(él/ella/usted)	**zurza**	**zurciera** or **zurciese**
(nosotros/as)	**zurzamos**	**zurciéramos** or **zurciésemos**
(vosotros/as)	**zurzáis**	**zurcierais** or **zurcieseis**
(ellos/ellas/ustedes)	**zurzan**	**zurcieran** or **zurciesen**

IMPERATIVE

zurce / zurcid

Use the present subjunctive in all cases other than these **tú** and **vosotros** affirmative forms.

EXAMPLE PHRASES

¿Quién le **zurce** las camisas?
Who darns his shirts?

Se pasa el día **zurciéndole** la ropa.
She spends the whole day darning his clothes.

¡Que te **zurzan**!
Get lost!

Remember that subject pronouns are not used very often in Spanish.

How to use the Verb Index

The verbs in bold are the model verbs which you will find in the Verb Tables. All the other verbs follow one of these patterns, so the number next to each verb indicates which pattern fits this particular verb. For example, **acampar** (to camp) follows the same pattern as **hablar** (number 118 in the Verb Tables). All the verbs are in alphabetical order. Superior numbers ([1] etc) refer you to notes on page 127. These notes explain any differences between verbs and their model.

INDEX INDEX INDEX INDEX INDEX

Notes

[1] The verbs **anochecer**, **atardecer**, **granizar**, **helar**, **llover**, **nevar**, **nublarse** and **tronar** are used almost exclusively in the infinitive and third person singular forms.

[2] The **past participle** of the verb **pudrir** is **podrido**.